ISBN 978-1-330-69217-2
PIBN 10093022

For support please visit www.forgottenbooks.com

1 MONTH OF
FREE
READING

at

www.ForgottenBooks.com

By purchasing this book you are
eligible for one month membership to
ForgottenBooks.com, giving you
unlimited access to our entire
collection of over 700,000 titles via
our web site and mobile apps.

To claim your free month visit:

www.forgottenbooks.com/free93022

English
Français
Deutsche
Italiano
Español
Português

www.forgottenbooks.com

Mythology Photography **Fiction**
Fishing Christianity **Art** Cooking
Essays Buddhism Freemasonry
Medicine **Biology** Music **Ancient
Egypt** Evolution Carpentry Physics
Dance Geology **Mathematics** Fitness
Shakespeare **Folklore** Yoga Marketing
Confidence Immortality Biographies
Poetry **Psychology** Witchcraft
Electronics Chemistry History **Law**
Accounting **Philosophy** Anthropology
Alchemy Drama Quantum Mechanics
Atheism Sexual Health **Ancient History**
Entrepreneurship Languages Sport
Paleontology Needlework Islam
Metaphysics Investment Archaeology
Parenting Statistics Criminology
Motivational

American Teachers Series

The Teaching of Biology in the Secondary School

BY

FRANCIS E. LLOYD, A.M.

AND

MAURICE A. BIGELOW, Ph.D.

PROFESSORS IN TEACHERS COLLEGE, COLUMBIA UNIVERSITY

LONGMANS, GREEN, AND CO.
91 AND 93 FIFTH AVENUE, NEW YORK
LONDON AND BOMBAY
1904

L6

UNIVERSITY PRESS · JOHN WILSON
AND SON · CAMBRIDGE, U.S.A.

Contents

THE TEACHING OF BOTANY AND OF NATURE STUDY

THE TEACHING OF ZOÖLOGY, INCLUDING HUMAN PHYSIOLOGY

CHAPTER IV

CHAPTER V

CHAPTER VI

CHAPTER VII

CHAPTER VIII

CHAPTER IX

THE TEACHING OF BOTANY AND OF NATURE STUDY

"... respecting the true measure of value [of education] there can be no dispute. Every one in contending for the worth of any particular order of information does so by showing its bearing upon some part of life. . . . How to live? — that is the essential question for us. Not how to live in a mere material sense only, but in the widest sense. . . . To prepare us for complete living is the function which education has to discharge."

—SPENCER, H. *Education: Intellectual, Moral, and Physical.*

AMERICAN TEACHERS SERIES

EDITED BY

JAMES E. RUSSELL, Ph.D.

DEAN OF TEACHERS COLLEGE, COLUMBIA UNIVERSITY

THE TEACHING OF BIOLOGY IN THE SECONDARY SCHOOL

BY

FRANCIS E. LLOYD, A.M.

AND

MAURICE A. BIGELOW, Ph.D.

PROFESSORS IN TEACHERS COLLEGE, COLUMBIA UNIVERSITY

Prefatory Note

THE advances which botany has made in America during the last twenty-five years have been not alone in the science itself and in its economic phases, but also in the field of education. From being an occasional study, it has become in our best schools a constant element in the curriculum. Instead of the superficial examination of the external structures of flowers — a study supposed to be rather of the nature of an accomplishment than a means for wholesome discipline — the good course in botany of the present time presents the important ideas of all the phases of the science, and is based upon the observation and experimentation of living plants.

These changes have made necessary the employment of teachers with a special mental equipment for their peculiar task. From being taught incidentally, botany has become the chief concern of a large body of men and women who have received the best training our schools have afforded. The most important criticism which may be made at the present time is that those who enter the profession of teaching in the field of botany, and its allied subject, zoölogy, do so generally without any special consideration of the problems which they are called upon to face in their work.

It is to bring the student face to face with these problems, and to prepare him for their intelligent consideration, that this book has been written. Whether the solutions offered for such problems as have been discussed merit acceptance is of secondary moment, if in the use of these pages the student is stimulated to study carefully the subject of botany, not alone from the point of view of the scientist, but also from that of the educator. If the essay excites " to self-activity, which is the best effect of any book," its chief use will be accomplished.

With this thought in mind, I have not hesitated to champion my own views on the kind of a course which should be given in the high school. To this end, though not to this end alone, I have presented in so much detail as the space at my disposal would permit, an outline for such a course. Its usefulness will lie in indicating the more important bearings and correlations of the various topics taken up and the most useful materials for laboratory work.

With regard to the value of nature study there may be remarked a considerable difference of opinion among educators. Many persons are fully persuaded that it constitutes a most important element of the elementary curriculum, and would make it the " centre " of the child's study. Others, on the contrary, basing their judgments upon the more or less satisfactory results which have thus far accrued, look with disfavor upon the whole movement towards the introduction of nature-study into education.

Believing that nature study has both a content and a function of real merit which justify it in the school, we must still admit that they are at present rather ill-defined. And admitting that the results have been in a measure disappointing, we cannot but believe that this is due to causes which are normally to be expected, and which will at length be removed. It has been my object in the early chapters to defend the cause of nature study as a factor in early education, and to discover to the student certain fundamental guiding principles, the failure to fully recognize which has, in my belief, been a chief cause of the failure of the subject.

In the preparation of this work I have had the help and

criticism of my teacher, Professor George Macloskie of Princeton University, and of Professor Herbert Maule Richards of Barnard College, both of whom have read and criticised the whole of the manuscript. Professor Richards has, in addition, made valuable suggestions in regard to the choice and use of cryptogamic materials, and has read the proof sheets. It is a great pleasure to express here my cordial appreciation of their very great kindness.

F. E. Ll.

TEACHERS COLLEGE,
    March, 1904.

The

Teaching of Botany and of Nature Study

CHAPTER I

THE VALUE OF SCIENCE, AND PARTICULARLY OF BIOLOGY, IN EDUCATION

BIBLIOGRAPHY

Bessey, C. E.   Science and Culture. Proc. N. E. A., p. 939.   1896.

Butler, N. M.   What Knowledge is of Most Worth ?   EDUCATIONAL REVIEW, 10: 105.   September, 1895.

Butler, N. M.   The Scope and Functions of Secondary Education. EDUCATIONAL REVIEW, 16: 15–27.   1898.

Carhart, H. S.   The Humanistic Element in Science.   Proc. N. E. A., p. 943.   1896.

Coulter, J. M.   The Mission of Science in Education.   SCIENCE, II. 12: 281–293.   24 August, 1900.

Fitch, J. G.   Lectures on Teaching, Chapter XIV.   New York.   1901.

Goebel, K.   Organography of Plants.   (Translation by Balfour.) Oxford.   1900.

Henfrey, Arthur.   On the Educational Claims of Modern Science: Lecture delivered before the London Society of Arts.   Pp. 89–116 of volume entitled The Culture demanded by Modern Life.   New York, '. Appleton & Co.   1887.

Huxley, T. H.   Science and Education.   Collected Essays, Vol. II.   D. Appleton & Co.   1898.

James, W.   Talks to Teachers on Psychology, and to Students on some of Life's Ideals.   New York, H. Holt & Co.   1900.

Jordan, D. S.   Nature Study and Moral Culture.   Proc. N. E. A.,). 130.   1896.

Norton, W. H.   The Social Service of Science.   SCIENCE, II., 13: 644. 26 April, 1901.

Pearson, Karl.   Grammar of Science.   London, A. & C. Black. 1900.

Sedgwick, Wm. T.   Educational Value of the Method of Science. EDUCATIONAL REVIEW, 5: 243.   March, 1893.

Spencer, H. Education: Intellectual, Moral, and Physical. London, Williams & Norgate. New York, D. Appleton & Co. 1860.
Spencer, H. Principles of Biology. New York, D. Appleton & Co. 1900.
Whitney, Miss M. W. Scientific Study and Work for Women. EDUCATION, 3: 58. September, 1882.

THAT biology is of value in formal education may be defended upon general and upon special grounds. Both botany and zoölogy, as co-ordinate divisions of biology, have educational values which may be similarly defended. It will then be seen that a general argument for science in education will include biology, but we may not therefore conclude, without further investigation into the special merits of the latter, that it must have a place in a scheme of education. Nor, similarly, may a general argument for biology be regarded as applying equally to botany and to zoölogy. These, in turn, must be justified by their own peculiar merits and advantages.

We may for practical considerations hold to the statement that, in order to get along in this world, we must be able and willing to do things. For people who work life is made up, for the most part, of effort added to effort in the attempt to get something and to get somewhere, which, as property and as ideals, are worth while. To be sure we may have various conceptions of what is worth our effort. With both the direction of impulse and of effort, and with the bettering of ideals, the process called education has to do.

The young of animals spend all their waking moments doing something, and are thus prepared for adult life. But we are all sufficiently aware of the fact that these **General Aim of Conscious Work.** actions are by no means under any great degree of direction, and they are, therefore, more or less haphazard. The better directed these efforts, however, the more definite and beneficial the results. This is true of human kind, both of the mind and of the body. Conscious efforts slowly but in the long run unfailingly react upon the mind to make it a more efficient tool. Gradually these efforts come more and more under control. On the whole, with increasing maturity a better judgment is developed as to what is worth while to do, and a better directed effort is maintained toward getting in the way of doing it.

✔ If this conception of the aim of formal education be correct we must conclude that science, and biology as a part of science, to be of any value as an educational factor, must accomplish two things. It must supply standards of thought and action, and it must help men and women to prompt and successful endeavor. **The Task of Science in Education.**

The desired results may be expected if it can be shown that science has something in common with ordinary life; and its value will be proportional to the extent to which this is true.

Now it has been clearly shown by others that science, in a narrow sense, has nothing which it can claim as peculiar to itself except the materials with which it deals. The mental processes by which the generalizations of science have been attained are, however, the normal operations of the human mind, refined and applied with accuracy. Indeed, an important lesson which we learn from science is the great value of these mental operations when so controlled.[1]

It must be conceded, therefore, that all the sciences, indeed all studies which use the scientific method of thought, have, by virtue of this fact, certain values in education.

To accept this statement, however, without further thought is to rob unjustly all subjects of their special value. No one would for a moment assert that arithmetic and history, chemistry and literature, have the same educational value. Although the method of thought may be common to them all, certainly each one of these fields of thought has its own peculiar value in education, since each subject has a content, derived from experience, which is of a different sort and which touches life in a different way from the others.[2]

If, then, we conclude that all sciences have a like general value in education, based upon their common use of similar

---

[1] See Pearson, Karl, *Grammar of Science*, p. 12; Carhart, '96.
[2] Butler, N. M., '95.

mental operations, and if we further conclude that the special values of each of these may be different, we must set to ourselves the task of examining each branch of science in order to determine what its special value is, if it have any. For the present the subject of biology must be thus examined.

I must furthermore take occasion to indicate the importance of science in education by pointing out that it differs **Value of the** from other studies in that it has to do with objec-**Study of** tive realities and our intellectual interpretations **Objective** **Realities.** based upon them. Now in life we are constantly dealing with two classes of realities, *feelings* [1] and *things*. I use feelings to include the whole emotional life, — our loves and hates, ideals and ambitions. We all know from every-day experience that these are often at variance with our judgments, and our selfish motives are often opposed to both our best individual and social interests.[2] It is evident that education has to do with the improvement of this condition, which is due to ignorance and to lack of strength to bring our emotions into correspondence with the world about us. We need to know, and we must raise our ideals to the level of our knowledge. We seek an uncompromising recognition of the truth and an unwavering determination not to be led astray by sophistries. The study of objective things by means of t scientific method will, we believe, do this, because it not o1 trains the intellect but enforces the acceptance of ideals, a1 thus tends to improve human conduct.[3]

We have indicated that science, in so far as its method thought has a common quality with that of every-day life, is 1 value in education ; and further, that as science deals directl with objective realities, it constitutes the foundation of know' edge, without, however, failing to instil high ideals of though and action.

---

[1] Huxley, T. H., Science and Education, *Collected Essays*, Vol. III. New York, 1898.

[2] Pearson, Karl, *Grammar of Science*, p. 3.

[3] Butler, N. M., '95; Jordan, D. S., '96.

It is now our purpose to examine the field of biological thought, in order thereby to get some appreciation of its relation to human life, and at the same time of **The Special** its educational value. [For the present we shall **Value of Bi-** discuss three aspects of this relation which indicate **ology in** the general values of biology in education.] **Education.**

We may rightly examine /first] of all the pleasure value of biology. It is very generally true that we are led into a study because we take æsthetic pleasure in the things **Pleasure** with which it deals, and it is the pleasure that we **Value of** continually experience, as well as the other good **Biology.** effects which accrue, which keeps us at it, unless, indeed, it becomes for some reason a perfunctory task.

In holding a broad view of education, therefore, we may justly claim that it should be made responsible, not only for the preparation of the man to think and to do those things well which duty and necessity put upon him, but also for the culti- vation of that type of mind which is able so to interpret duty and necessity that work shall have a pleasurable quality to it. This quality is characteristic of the resourceful, many- sided mind, one which does not remain unexpanded, but which, by virtue of a considerable degree of familiarity with different sources of pleasurable thought, grows in richness and interest and in power of reflection. Such is the man whose interest may amount even to a hobby, who is constantly and pleasantly occupied, and upon whose hands time does not hang heavily. Not only this. It makes one valuable and interest- ing to his fellow-men. "A man riding his hobby is not the most undesirable member of society. It is rather the indif- ferent member, who has not vigor enough to find a hobby."[1] The value of an avocation lies not alone in the immediate pleasure it brings: it reflects upon the whole life in a health- ful way; it is the play of the mind which refreshingly prepares it for its work.

In contrast that person's condition is pitiable whose atti-

---

[1]. Whitney, M. W., '82·

tude toward pleasure is passive; who, insufficient in himself, has to depend upon pastimes. It is upon such that pleasure, degraded to amusement, soon palls, and it is then that he finds himself open to an attack of what Red Saunders, in a delightful story by Henry Wallace Phillips, picturesquely calls " measles of the mind," because he has " nothing to do." This fur- nishes the clue to our thought, namely, that during school days, when the mind is plastic and impressionable, there shall be a very earnest endeavor to offer opportunities for children to become acquainted with plants and animals. Later on in life this knowledge may serve the useful turn of leading its possessors to engage their spare time in enjoyable pursuits, in the direction of study and observation, which, like that of music, entail no bad effect.

It is peculiarly true of biology that its relations to human life are so numerous and intimate that almost all people, young and old, readily find pleasure in pursuit of it, and that as knowledge and experience are extended the opportunities and capacities for enjoyment are multiplied.

This matter, in its effect upon human life, particularly in certain directions, is far more important than on the surface it may appear. We refer to the problem of the betterment of the rural population. The recognition of this need is seen in many directions, as for example, educationally in the cen- tralization of the schools, the special education of the farmer, and otherwise in the improved postal service, the movement for good roads, tree planting, and like things of educational as well as of economic value. But in the direction of the de- velopment of the æsthetic side of their natures the people of the country have almost wholly been neglected. This is, of course, inevitable in a new country, though it is regretfully true in the majority of older ones. But the conditions under which this can longer continue to be true are now no more. As a class, American farmers are more restive under their conditions than in any other country, and one evidence of this is seen in the flow of population from the country into the city. While this is desirable and necessary up to a certain limit, it is nevertheless true that there are many who are driven from the country rather than attracted to the city. One cure for the undesirableness and unattractiveness of country life may be found in the broadening of the interest of the people by the development of their æsthetic pleasures, especially those connected with the study of animate nature, as well as by increasing their intellectual grasp of their work. Some work in the right direction has already been done in certain quarters, and the effort cannot be too much commended. This has been done by the circulation of suggestions and information, through the medium of Nature Study Leaflets, for the planting of trees, the beautifying of school grounds, and the arrangement of gardens. Nothing, perhaps, in the country looks so desolate as the average schoolhouse, which with a little well-directed effort could be made attractive. At the same time the work may be done so as to institute a part of education ; in fact, it must be done in this way if it is to bear permanent results in the lives of the pupils. It is eminently proper also that a very considerable stress should be laid upon the artistic side of garden making, for here in the garden are opportunities in abundance for the normal expression of æsthetic feelings. We believe, therefore, that in elementary education the work in nature study should be directed toward elementary agriculture and horticulture, and that these should be managed so as to cultivate a desire for the beautiful, and also good taste and intelligence in its gratification.

All this is true also for the townspeople, but in a special way. The opportunities in cities are far more restricted, and it becomes a much more serious task to provide for the great numbers of children. The most important step toward meeting this need lies in the effort to give to the young mind an intelligent and appreciative attitude toward nature, and this may be done by the worthy teacher through nature study and biology for the child and youth.

In the second place, we propose to show that biology has a

special value in education because of the discipline which it gives to the mind engaged in its study. We have already drawn attention to the fact that in biological science we are concerned, not with a different method of thought, but with different materials from those of the other sciences. It follows, therefore, that whatever differences in educational value the various sciences possess these must be due chiefly to the nature of the things with which they deal. And the likeness of value by the same token must be referred to the common factor of method. In the paragraphs which now follow we are to ask ourselves in what ways biology is peculiar as to materials, and what these indicate as to its distinctive values in education.

Biology as Discipline in Method of Thought.

As compared with other natural sciences, the materials with which the biologist has to concern himself are more complex. This is, of course, connected with the fact that the phenomena of life are as much more complex and diverse than inorganic phenomena as the "physical basis of life" is more complex structurally than other non-living substances. The structure of the parts of a living body cannot be understood except in the light of the functions which they perform or the work which they do; and the reverse is equally true, that in order to comprehend the behavior of an organ or body as a whole, attention must be given to its structure.

The truth of this is more apparent when we realize that such distinctions as for the sake of convenience we draw between physiology and morphology are, to adopt the language of Goebel, artificial and imperfect, and they may be maintained only so long as they do good service. "As a matter of fact, it [*i. e.* the study of morphology alone] has finally led to one-sidedness, and its outcome has not infrequently been empty theorizing. In nature the form and function of an organ stand in the most intimate relation to each other; one is caused by the other."[1] Herbert Spencer[2] has

[1] Goebel, K., *Organography of Plants*, p. 4.
[2] *Principles of Biology*, Vol. II., p. 4.

also emphasized the point. "Science can give no true interpretation of Nature without keeping the co-operation of structure and function constantly in view."

It is inevitable that bodies of which it is true that there is a constant adjustment between each of their parts and the rest, and between each part, together with the whole, and the environment, involving constant change of form and function, should offer difficult and complex materials for study.

Again, the difficulty of study of biological materials is not at all decreased by the conditions of our advancing knowledge. We know so little and so many things remain to be searched out that we constantly have to stop and proclaim our ignorance. The teacher cannot, therefore, bring to the student a finished product. Many explanations must be made tentatively but not gratuitously, and the appeal to experiment and logical tests must be constant. Many apparently sound interpretations, even though they appear in books, must be frankly cast aside. Many teachers feel that it is an unsatisfactory task when "I don't know" must be the more frequent answer. There is, however, no real reason for this feeling. It is precisely in this that biology finds its power as training. It makes us question everything for which we do not find evidence, and in leading us to confess our ignorance makes for intellectual honesty.

Not only, then, are the materials themselves, if objectively considered, difficult of observation, but the reasoning based upon these observations is correspondingly complex and elusive, and the ratio of probability to the number of observations less than in other natural sciences. We shall recur to these points in another part of this work, where we shall, in more detail, show their practical bearings on teaching. For the present we may say that these features of biological study may readily be thought on first consideration to be serious disadvantages to its use in education, and of course they certainly increase the difficulty of the pedagogics concerned. What, however, educationally considered, seem to be disadvantages, are really advantages when we consider the end of education, which in a broad sense is to prepare for living. In life we are called upon to make an immense number of inferences and judgments, upon the correctness of which our well-being and happiness rest. The more complex the circumstances requiring judgment, the more delicate and cautious must the latter be, and the more profoundly are our lives affected by the results contingent upon it.

Indeed, the practical affairs of life are of such complexity as to call for a delicate, complex, and cautious judgment, and any study which beyond others will develop to any degree whatever such a judgment will have an educational value correlated with the delicacy of reasoning demanded by its materials. In other words, if we regard the study of human affairs as sociology — a very complex study, involving the understanding of the workings of the body and of the mind of the individual taken alone and in segregate — that study which most nearly approaches in complexity that of sociology, and is at the same time of practical use in elementary education, must have the definite value above indicated.

We may by way of summary present the case in somewhat different form. Life for each individual is a series of sociological problems of a very practical nature. Each of these has to be examined to determine the facts involved, and some conclusion must be drawn as to the course of action to be pursued. The conclusions arrived at are then examined in the light of former experience. These operations are not always consciously gone through with; on the contrary, they are in the very great proportion of cases quite rapid and unconscious, and in the young and the unthinking, for whom the problems are comparatively simple, entirely so. Nevertheless, this process, which is induction first of all, then deduction, is the logic of real life, with which we are busied from infancy to old age.

But, like the action of the untutored body, the greatest effectiveness of thought comes with its voluntary and intelligent control, when the case demands it, aside from habitual thought and action. In addition to the fact that biology, or some phase of it, as a subject of study is especially pleasing to some people, — a matter which in its relation to education we have above discussed,— its value as discipline may be estimated in part by its parallelism in detail to the method of thought in real life; and we have already shown that this method of thought is rendered like that of real life by virtue of the complexity of materials making for caution.[1] And this is our contention as to the training obtainable in the special field of biology, in the general methods of thought in life.

In the third place there attaches to biological study a peculiar humanistic value, as measured by its usefulness in the amelioration of human conditions. To recount even the achievements of biology alone, aside from science as a whole, would take us too far from the main line of the present discussion. We shall, however, point out somewhat definitely the more important sociological factors which the biologist has influenced. We may mention first the matter of disease and its control. The mere determination of one fact, namely, the causal relation between certain organisms and disease, lies at the foundation of a vast and efficient method of preventive hygiene so far reaching in its results that among enlightened peoples many diseases which once were the scourge of whole continents are now no longer feared because we know how to control the conditions under which these diseases spread. What we now fear is ignorance which begets negligence and indifference to sanitary conditions.

The results of efforts in these directions as they become known through the public prints[2] constitute in the shape of information a means of public education; and while people in general are far from realizing anything like a satisfactory conception of social and individual cleanliness, to say nothing of

Humanistic Value in Relation to Health.

---

[1] Henfrey, '87, p. 99.
[2] One of the triumphs of modern science is seen in the wonderful record made in the control of yellow fever in the city of Havana after American occupancy.

practice, nevertheless a new meaning attaches to the word, which will sooner or later be realized in the practical hygiene of daily life. But while the spread of information concerning the results of scientific inquiry and the application of methods of hygiene through the medium of the press, and by the work of boards of health and other forms of public service, is a means of great value in the education of the public at large, we are convinced that the only certain way of doing the same thing with results of permanent value is through the education of the youth, not only by the dissemination of information, but also by training in the method of thought by which progress in knowledge of this kind is made. For, we repeat, it is training in exact methods of scientific thought which alone makes constant improvement possible. Upon the ability to appreciate the value of and to use the scientific method rests the faith that the results which accrue to science may and must be received and applied to human life.

Again, we may notice the great debt which agriculture owes to biological science. At the present time the agricultural **To Food Production.** class is the largest, and it is and will remain the chief of economic forces. The efficiency of the labor of this class depends upon the intelligent use of the soil, which is depleted by the growth of crops. How to get the best results in food value from these crops, and at the same time to maintain the quality of the soil, are questions, therefore, worthy of the most earnest efforts of the human mind. The justification of this statement may be found in the splendid discoveries concerning the relation of living organisms to the nitrogen content of the soil. In these discoveries is contained the solution of the problem of the renewal of the soil, and to them will be due the preservation of the quality of the soil in spite of the constant seaward drain of the nitrogen compounds from the land by the sewage systems of centres of population. The practical application of our knowledge is as yet not completely worked out, but this is only the matter of a short time and of effort. Even at this moment, however, it may be recorded as one of the great achievements of modern biological science.[1]

The investigation of soils is but one line of work. Many other problems of this and of kindred nature are constantly occupying the attention of naturalists. We may cite at random the conservation of our forests, the selection of better races of stock and of food plants, the diagnosis and control of plant and animal diseases, the discovery, and the exact study of the characters and properties of medicinal plants, the proper manipulation of food products and of raw materials for manufactures, in which the action of bacteria plays so large a rôle, and other kinds of investigation of far-reaching results in its effect upon the welfare of man.[2] Upon such work the government of America spends at present the large but still very inadequate sum of approximately $5,013,960 (1903), and no moneys are put to better use.

It would appear that the youth of the country should not be ignorant of the function of the State in these matters ; of the nature of the work which is carried on by the public service in the persons of biologists who are devoting their lives to it ; of the chief results which have accrued ; or of their own responsibilities as citizens with intelligent interest in the welfare of their country and of the human family. There is, indeed, no greater nor less reason for this than for the study of the history of their country. As the integrity of our own form of government rests ultimately upon the intelligent exercise of the powers of citizenship, so the work of the government in the conservation of our natural resources may be carried forward to a legitimate and successful issue only with the acquiescence and intelligent support of the population.

---

[1] Since writing this, the problem above indicated has been worked out in its practical bearings in a remarkable way by Dr. G. T. Moore, of the United States Department of Agriculture. For an account by him see Bacteria and the Nitrogen Problem, *Yearbook of the United States Department of Agriculture*, p. 333. 1902.

[2] For a good discussion of the present topic, see Norton, W. H., The Social Service of Science. *Science*, II., 13: 644. 26 April, 1901.

To this end the people must be educated in the subject-matter and method of biological thought, and this must be done in such a way as to disseminate the most useful and important information concerning the relation of biology to human progress; and we assert that to give the study of biology this useful trend is not in the least to lower the educational and culture value, but the rather to render more people intelligent and cultured in a broad and true sense.

Perhaps one of the greatest services to humanity which has ever been rendered by science is that seen in the effect which it has had upon the nature of labor, and the esteem **To Labor.** in which the laborer is held.[1] This is, of course, due to no one cause, and is, indeed, a phenomenon too complex for a mere tyro in economics to attempt to analyze. But certainly one of the factors among many others is found in the development of skilled labor, and this is due to the application of science to agriculture and the industries, and in the recognition of the needs of the people in the building up of technical and scientific schools. By virtue of these things the dignity of the laborer is in the measure of the intelligence which he brings to his labor. Recurring to the farmer, we know that a few years ago his work was a mere drudgery to which was brought no scientific thought or skill. The idea of equipping special institutions for the education of the rural youth in the best and most scientific methods of farming was not dreamed of.[2] Nowadays the farmer ought to be and often is an active scientific observer, working in co-operation with the State in the solution of vast and important problems. Technical education itself,

---

[1] See also Fitch, J. G., *Lectures on Teaching*, Chapter XIV.

[2] There has been a growing criticism of late years that institutions whose aim has been to educate the agricultural classes in their calling have failed to do this. This defect, so far as it is true, is, however, not due to education, but to imperfect education and wrong ideals. It may readily be admitted that some young men have become puffed up with the pride of imperfect knowledge, but this is an argument for making education more efficient in this direction.

so closely connected with labor as it is, owes to the sciences its recognition as part of a training in real culture. " . . . The laboratory sciences . . . have justified the educational value of the methods of the gymnasium and the workshop." They, "by analogy as well as by physiology, have shown the educational merits of physical culture, manual training, and general handicraft; . . . have demonstrated for all time that there are efficient instruments in the educational workshop other than the printed page and the voice of the teacher, other convenient and important avenues to the brain than the optic and auditory nerves, along which the teacher may work."[1] Biological science, as evidenced by our illustration, is to a great extent responsible for this change.

The time when the sniff of superiority of the city-bred person at the mention of the " hayseed " will be replaced by a look of thoughtful appreciation of the dignity of the farmer's work will come when biological science, as given to the public schools, will have its proper informational content, and is taught so as to impress the mind with a due appreciation of the real and fundamental character of the intellectual task before the farmer.[2]

Lastly, we find that biology has before it a great part in the solution of the most profound problems concerning the moral and physical well-being of the race — that involved in the relation of the sexes. This problem, it has **Sex.** well been said, taxes all the wisdom of the preacher, jurist, and physician, and we may venture to assert that none of these can compass the ends in view without the help of the well-trained and high-souled teacher of biology. It is quite unnecessary to recount in this connection the evils which every intelligent man and woman knows to arise from the moral distortion incident to the warping of the sexual 'nature by artificial and immoral conditions.

---

[1] Sedgwick, '93, p. 245.
[2] See *Annual Report*, United States Department Agriculture. 1901.

It is patent to the thinking mind that every stratum of society is affected by these evils, and it is keeping very far within the limits of truth to say that not only the physical and moral welfare of the individual but the very foundations of society and the integrity of nations may be destroyed by a moral pestilence of this kind.

If we grant this to be true — as those cognizant of the facts will readily do — what is more evident than that the way to cure the evil is by the demolition of ignorance and by putting truth in its place? In this matter as in others formal education must be made to supplement home training, and when such is absent — and perhaps far more frequently than not it is — to take its place.

We must not be understood to advocate a sort of preaching or moralizing method in which the chief method of promulgating the good is by the description of evil. Education should by this time have seen the futility of attempting to increase morality in this way. Positive ethics have little enough effect on morals ; nothing good can be said of negative ethics. But we do mean to assert unequivocally that the unhealthful conditions above referred to can be removed by the bringing to the young mind clean, accurate knowledge of the essential facts of physiology and of reproduction, through the agency of a skilful teacher of biology. Thus right habits of thought will be started at the time when this is easiest, and at least the youth will have begun to tread the right path which leads to purity of life. James's remarks concerning habits are just as pertinent here as elsewhere — " Education is for behavior, and habits are the stuff of which behavior consists." [1]

This knowledge to be the most useful must come in its natural place in a course in biology, and every appearance of unusual effort to come at or to avoid the subject must be avoided.

We desire to lay stress on this point, for if a teacher be sus-

---

[1] James, W., *Talks to Teachers*, p. 66.

pected of unnaturalness, or of any but the most transparently honest of motives, his work is undone. The information received must be in such form and proportion that it may appear to be what it really is — a part of biological knowledge to be treated as openly as any other part, without offence to good judgment.

We shall attempt further on to show that an introduction to an essential knowledge of generative processes may most appropriately and effectively be made in a course in botany.

Biology, then, has a special humanistic value, by virtue of its content of information, which is necessary to an intelligent, well-balanced, and clean man, capable of appreciating the work of the race and the mutual debt of man to man, and capable also of high moral living. This is the stuff of which good citizenship is made.

In the foregoing paragraphs we have endeavored to present in a general form an argument for the use of biology in education. The points are summarized as **Summary.** follows:

In life we are constantly engaged in making efforts to accomplish ends. These efforts may be undirected and unintelligent, or they may be under direction; and intelligent formal education has for its purpose the control and the direction of effort toward ideals which experience has taught us to be worth our effort. With better control of effort comes better judgment, and this reacts on the individual, rendering subsequent action still more direct and efficacious. Our task is to point out that biology may contribute to these ends in education. It is pointed out that the method of thought is common to all science; therefore, that the special value of biology in education must be indicated chiefly by the nature of the material with which it deals.

The subjects of education are concerned with two classes of realities, — feelings and things, — and use respectively symbols and objects. The study of biology, because it is a study with objective realities, tends to develop the disinterested judgment, to teach the individual how to adjust himself to his surroundings, and to raise the ideals of life.

Biology has certain special values in education. First, it has been argued that biology has a special value in its usefulness in multiplying the interests of the mind, thus furnishing sources of pleasure which are deep and lasting and which produce no bad effects. They are such as are within the reach of all. We have especially emphasized the importance of the development of the æsthetic side of life as making for contentment and pleasure.

Secondly, we have shown that biology has a special value as discipline. It is a complex and therefore a difficult study, and calls for a large degree of caution in its method of thought. In this it resembles real life more nearly than the other natural sciences, and has an educational value indicated by its similarity thereto.

Thirdly, it has a humanistic value, measured by the amount and value of the information it brings. This information concerns various phases of human life as they have been affected by the application of biological science. We have cited the knowledge of the nature of many diseases, the field of agriculture and of labor, and the profoundly important matter of the relation of the sexes as being matters concerning which biology brings most valuable information, and so makes for a saner and more normal view of life.

CHAPTER II

NATURE STUDY

BIBLIOGRAPHY

Bailey, L. H. Botany: an Elementary Text-Book. Paragraphs for the Teacher. New York, The MacMillan Co. 1900.

Bailey, L. H. The Nature Study Idea. New York, Doubleday, Page & Co. 1903.

Harris, W. T. The Study of Natural Science: its Uses and Dangers. EDUCATION, 10: 277. January, 1890.

Harris, W. T. Horace Mann. EDUCATIONAL REVIEW, 12: 104. September, 1896.

Henkle, W. D. Proc. N. E. A., p. 59. 1870.

Hinsdale, B. A. Horace Mann and the Common School Revival in the United States. New York, Charles Scribner's Sons. 1898.

Hodge, C. F. Nature Study and Life. Boston, Ginn & Co. 1902.

Huxley, T. H. Science and Education. Collected Essays. Vol. III. New York, D. Appleton & Co. 1898.

Huxley, L. Life and Letters of Thomas Henry Huxley. New York, D. Appleton & Co. 1901.

Huxley, T. H. Method and Results. Collected Essays. Vol. I.

Hyslop, J. H. Elements of Logic: Theoretical and Practical. New York, Charles Scribners' Sons. 1892.

James, W. Talks to Teachers on Psychology, and to Students on Some of Life's Ideals. New York, H. Holt & Co. 1900.

Jordan, D. S. Nature Study and Moral Culture. Proc. N. E. A., p. 130. 1896.

Lathrop, Delia A. Object Lessons: their Value and Place in Education. Proc. N. E. A., p. 49. 1870.

Lloyd, F. E. Aims of Nature Study. TEACHERS COLLEGE RECORD, 1: No. 2. March, 1900.

Lloyd, F. E. Plant Ecology for the Elementary School. NEW YORK TEACHERS' MONOGRAPHS, 4: 81-89. March, 1902.

Pearson, Karl. Grammar of Science. London, A. & C. Black. 1900.

Sedgwick, Wm. T. Educational Value of the Method of Science. EDUCATIONAL REVIEW, 5: 243. March, 1893.

Soule, C. G. Nature Study in the Schools. OUTLOOK, p. 224. 27 January, 1900.

de Vries, Hugo. The Origin of Species by Mutation. SCIENCE, II.,
15: 721. 9 May 1902.
    Weismann, August. On Germinal Selection (1895). Chicago.
The Open Court Publishing Co. 1896.
    Woodward, C. M. The Change of Front in Education. SCIENCE,
II., 14: 474. 27 September, 1901.
    Article, Nature Study. NEW INTERNATIONAL ENCYCLOPÆDIA.
    What is Nature Study? SCIENCE, II., 16: 910. 5 December, 1902.

WE have in the foregoing chapter endeavored to show what
we hold to be the general value of science and what the special
value of biology in education. It has been necessary in so
doing to confine discussion to broad considerations, and we
have reserved a more special treatment of certain points for the
present chapter and for those dealing with botany and zoölogy
in the secondary schools. We have now before us the task
of presenting to the student the problem involved in the relation of science to elementary education, commonly considered
under the title of nature study. This is deemed necessary, because, since the advent of nature study into the elementary curriculum, the amount and kind of work done in the high school
has come to depend in an intimate way upon the quality of the
elementary teaching. And the same ideals apply to both schools,
— poor work in one makes difficult the attainment of proper
standards in the other. The principles, therefore, set forth in
the present chapter, while directed especially toward the elementary school, are to be recognized as a part of our general
plea for the acceptance of biology in education.
    It will, I believe, be unnecessary to my purpose to attempt
a formal definition of what is meant, or is supposed to be
meant, by the name nature study. This has been discussed
by a number of able students,[1] with a more or less satisfactory
result. Nor is it worth while for us to object to the name,
which undoubtedly, in some minds, connotes a great deal that

---

[1] Bailey, L. H., *The Nature Study Idea*. What is meant by Nature
Study? *Science*, II., 16 : 910. 5 December, 1902. Soule, C. G., Nature
Study in the Schools.

savors of the superficial and sentimental, and not without reason. Indeed, we have heard it on good authority that in some quarters, while the value of elementary science is not brought into question, the name "nature study" has been avoided, evidence enough, it would seem, that the failures, of which not a little has been said, are due, not to the matter itself, but to the fad-like whimsicalities of very enthusiastic persons. Enthusiasm is a good thing; but if we have to reckon with such economic forces as schoolboards and taxpayers, whose conservatism is extreme, we must be sure that it does not overreach our knowledge and efficiency as teachers. Nevertheless, nature study as a name, as surely as what it stands for, or ought to, has come to stay with us, and it embodies a group of ideas which as a whole are distinctly modern.

Nor shall we avoid the issue arising from the fact that the subject has fallen into a certain amount of disrepute among educators. That imperfection and some degree of failure should attend the attempt to place a subject so complex in its materials and bearings in a school system so large and various in its development as that of America, is inevitable and to be expected. And that some educators should, through ignorance, or through conservatism or impatience, be unwilling to give the matter a fair trial is also to be expected.

It will serve a good purpose if we point out that the failures are palpably due, not to the inutility of the subject, but to the inferior ability of teachers — who in the majority of cases may be otherwise efficient — to handle a subject which calls for unusual preparation and insight. What has been expected is that teachers who are not only ignorant of nature, but to whom the materials are, for lack of training and of the proper spirit, unwelcome and often obnoxious, should, provided with a meagre outline and a poor text, give a successful course in nature study. The wonder is, not that some have failed, but that any have succeeded. To pass judgment, therefore, upon the results of science in education when it is taught by untrained persons as a temporary expedient or as an experiment, is obviously unjust, as Huxley in defence of elementary scientific education years ago pointed out.[1]

In view of this explanation of the partial failure of nature study to meet the expectations of some educators, we are led to present in what follows a discussion of the values of science, especially of the study of organic nature, in elementary education, believing that a clear understanding of these will lead to an increased demand for and the better preparation of competent teachers in this important field of work.

That this task is not amiss I hold because I believe that it is educationally a great wrong to fail to supply children during their formal education with opportunities for preserving in themselves their love of nature and their natural desires and powers of observation, and to neglect to train their reasoning faculties. It is of great interest to us that Horace Mann experienced such a deprivation, shared by many others, and that he has recorded his complaint. He tells us " that, as a child, he had never enjoyed the free intercourse with nature that his ardent mind craved. Speaking of himself and of the children with whom he mingled, he says that, although their faculties were growing and receptive, they were taught very little ; on the other hand, much obstruction was thrown between them and nature's teachings. Their eyes were never trained to distinguish forms and colors." [2]

One of Horace Mann's most pertinent criticisms of the school methods of his time is that " the memory was the only mental faculty especially appealed to ; the most comprehensive generalizations were given to the children, instead of the facts upon which they were based ; all ideas that did not come from the book were contraband." [3] And it is instructive to note in connection with these criticisms of school methods that Mann

---

[1] *Science and Education*, p. 167.

[2] Hinsdale, B. A., *Horace Mann and the Common School Revival in the United States*, p. 80.

[3] Hinsdale, *loc. cit.*, p. 78.

emphatically and continually upheld the doctrine that the most important idea for students to get is that of the causal relation. This was a constant educational idea of his, and it shows that he had a clear insight into the scientific method and its value for education. Perhaps the most important of his educational documents in its spirit and appreciation of the importance of this method in elementary education is the Ninth Report of the Commissioner of Education,[1] published in 1845, in which he commends the system of instruction by induction instead of deduction and the importance of substituting investigation for memorizing.

The first attempt to remedy the condition of public education criticised by Horace Mann was seen in the " object lesson " movement, a geographical extension in practice of **The Object** the method of instruction by observation [2] of that **Lesson.** German school of education of which Comenius was the founder and Pestalozzi the later world-renowned interpreter and spokesman. It is beyond my intention to attempt a detailed historical review of the educational reform movement, but it will serve a useful purpose to examine the " object lesson " as a means of education, since it will help us the better to estimate the importance of the more modern development of nature study.

What the object lesson was and what educational value it was claimed to possess have been well summarized by Miss Lathrop.[3]

An object lesson, according to Miss Lathrop, is not something which is read or recited by the teacher to her pupils, nor is it a lecture by her. Further, it is not something which is identical with the " objective " or illustrative teaching which was at that time (1870) under discussion nor with oral instruction. The positive contention is made that, in such a

---

[1] Harris, W. T., *Educational Review*, S. '96·

[2] *Anschauungsunterricht.*

[3] Lathrop, Delia A., Object Lessons : Their Value and Place in Education. Proc. N. E. A., 1870, p. 49.

lesson an object to be studied must be present, and that it demands the use of the child's senses, and the exercise must be conversational and under the guidance of the teacher. Concerning the value of the work the claims which were put forth are these: (1) That it is a means for the development of the powers of observation and judgment, and leads the mind of the children into new fields of inquiry and so discovers new aptitudes; it affords an opportunity for the unification of the child's knowledge; (2) it prepares for and supplements books; (3) it cultivates ease and exactness of expression, and (4) it affords variety and so brings rest.

Perhaps as much interest attaches to Miss Lathrop's statement of the objections which were directed against the object lesson at the time when she wrote the paper from which I quote, since they have been many times repeated. It was urged by the critics of the object lesson: (1) that there was not time enough in the curriculum for its reception; (2) that it made too much hard work for the teachers; (3) that the lessons became mechanical; (4) that the bright scholars were led out while the duller ones were constantly left farther and farther behind; (5) that the instruction was not systematic, and (6) that teachers were incompetent. It is obvious that no one of these objections is directed against the value of the work itself, and the tacit admission that it has a definite value reduces the objections to criticisms which are to be removed by a study of relative values of various subjects as compared with science, and by planning the curriculum and the mechanism of the school in accordance; as for the incompetency of teachers, all that may be said is, that if the only way is to have the subject taught by them, the standard of preparation should be raised and incompetency removed.

From this brief statement concerning the value of the object lesson we may gather the following conclusions. While the object lesson was very imperfect, both in its method and results, it must be admitted that it contained the central principle of the method of nature study in that it recognized the value of the study of objective realities by the use of the senses. It recognized also the importance of the training obtained thereby in observation, and to some degree at least the ethical value of such study. The imperfection of its method, on the other hand, which stood in the way of any great or permanent degree of usefulness, lay chiefly in the incompetency of the teacher and his failure to grasp the scientific method, in the consequent indifference to the conditions of true study on the part of the child in that the provision of materials was scanty, and these were heterogeneous and unrelated, thus throwing object study into striking contrast to the nature study of to-day, which includes in addition to the elements of the biological and physical sciences a practical training in the elements of agriculture and horticulture. These, it is reassuring to know, can be made, in spite of their practical worth, the basis for sound elementary scientific education.

We may now pass on to consider somewhat fully the aims and values of nature study. I may well take my point of departure in a spirited statement of Huxley, since it **The Aim of** contains, I believe, in a nutshell the whole and true **Education.** conception of the end of education. "I take it that the whole object of education is, in the first place, to train the faculties of the young in such a manner as to give their possessors the best chance of being happy and useful in their generation; and, in the second place, to furnish them with the most important portions of that immense capitalized experience of the human race which we call knowledge of various kinds. I am using the term knowledge in its widest possible sense; and the question is, what subjects to select by training and discipline in which the object I have just defined may be best attained."[1]

Let us now examine the field of nature study to see in detail in what way we may expect that it will con- **Nature Study** tribute toward the end of making people "happy **in Education.** and useful." In doing this, however, the discussion is of ne-

[1] Huxley, T. H., *Science and Education.*

cessity confined to biological nature study, but in so doing
we shall assume that what is said may be applied, with due
modification, to the other natural sciences.

The study of nature appeals very strongly to great numbers
of people through their normal interests, and its value in this
regard is unquestioned.   It gives them something
**Popular In-
terest in
Nature.** to think about and to do, and is in itself so varied
a resource of observation and pleasure that in many
cases it serves as an outlet for interest and energy remaining
from the toil of life.   How widespread such interest is may be
judged from the numbers of clubs, societies, and the like, among
people with mutual interests in nature, and the same thing is
shown by the great demand for books about nature which
the market does not fail to supply.   To be sure, the interest of
which we speak is in many instances trivial, and may be in
itself little better than the collection of some useless stuff like
tobacco tags, but we should go far astray if we supposed that
the value of it was indicated by this alone.   The important fact
is that interest in natural objects takes people away from the
artificial and brings them into contact with the great out-of-
doors.   We quote a passage concerning this interest from
Hodge's " Nature Study and Life " which well expresses the
value of such interest.   Speaking of the selection of topics for a
nature-study course, he says : " Will it form or help to form an
important, lifelong interest, — an interest not tech-
Its Value. nical or superficial, touching life only on the surface
here and there, and at long intervals, but one that lies close to
the heart, to the home, and to all that makes life worth living?
The value of such an interest is inestimable.   It may add a
sparkle to the eye, elasticity to the step, and a glow to every
heart-beat, and be the most efficient safeguard against idleness
and waste of time, evil and temptation of every sort." — " To
find such an interest in some worthy nature-love is to discover
the fountain of youth." [1]

---

[1] Hodge, C. F., *Nature Study and Life*, p. 24.

It thus appeals to that subtle bond of sympathy existing between man and nature; one, however, which may not be reasoned about, but which we know tends to lead us into pleasant paths of thought and action.[1]

If we might claim for nature study only this, we should have argument enough for its introduction into the curriculum, for this interest has been observed repeatedly to react upon the whole activity of the child by supplying concrete, observable things to look at, to handle, and to experiment with. It gives the occasion for the use of all the senses and of the reason as well; it has led to the institution of outdoor work in garden making, the collecting of various objects, and similar pursuits. This has, in a very peculiar sense, appealed to the whole of the child's activity, besides reacting on the school life in a healthful way hygienically.

We should, before leaving this matter, lay stress on the generalized, innate character of this interest in nature. It makes little odds to us how we get it, so that we recognize its existence in children, and make proper use of it in their education. We know it is a good thing **And its Generalized Character.** to have, and we know that many people lose it simply because of disuse, because the school did not give them a fair opportunity. Time and again, it is the burden of the complaint of many people that their youthful interest in nature did not receive nurture at the proper time. Similarly, a normal child's body is a veritable whirlwind of activity, not alone in the use of senses and muscles, but in intellectual inquiry about the things about them which they appreciate directly by means of their senses.[2] And it is, moreover, a distinct edu- **None too Young.** cational advantage that this bodily and mental activity begins so early that even in the first grade, scientific work, accurate so far as it goes, may be done, and done in

---

[1] For a most valuable discussion of the point here alluded to, see James's *Essay*, p. 229. 1900.

[2] ". . . there is no limit to the intellectual craving of a young child." Huxley, T. H., *Collected Essays*. Vol. III., p. 123.

such fashion that every bit of it is full of real interest to the children.

These two groups of activities — bodily and mental — of the child are in the schoolroom apparently at war with each other, **Using the Bodily Activity of the Child.** and around the idea that this antagonism is necessary much folderol pedantry has grown up. The advent of hygienic conceptions and the introduction of physical exercise is in recognition of the evil and an attempt to educate properly both sides of the child. Nature study makes this possible, because it uses both mental and bodily activities. It not only makes necessary the use of the senses in observation and of the reason, with all that word implies, but in its method it can be used for the exercise of the muscles in an unconscious way, which is the more productive of good because used in connection with the play of mental interests. Nature study, therefore, comes as a subject for the school with this special advantage, shared in part by manual training, and its effect for good upon education is not easily overestimated.

We have spoken above of the value of nature study as fostering an interest in and sympathy with nature which we regard as **Natural Interest the Point of Departure.** innate ; and we have regarded an interest which appears trifling when superficially considered to be better than none. But it is the special function of education to use such interest as a point of departure, and to build it up into a more thoughtful, living interest, which will lead the individual to a fuller emotional and rational life. We place the word " emotional " first for a reason which we believe sound, namely, because the emotions or feelings are springs of conduct, and determine in a large measure our attitude toward and our action in the world about us. Even the attitude **Emotions and the Reason.** toward the use of the reason which is properly regarded as the characteristic of a scientific thinker (by which we mean not alone those dealing with the sciences proper, but all who can and do use the scientific method of thought) is the outcome of an emotional conception of the value of reason. We believe that to think properly is good, to think slovenly is bad. The former will lead us aright, the latter will not. There are records of heroism facing failure upon failure, to emerge at last victorious from a fight in which reason was the only weapon and faith the sustaining power, impalpable but real.

A phase of this interest in nature to which it is related in a very subtle and complex way is the interpretation of natural objects as beautiful. This in many cases furnishes the primary motive, and it should not be disregarded in education. Extension of knowledge which is **Interpretation of Nature as Beautiful.** thus had will supply a wider and more varied field for the play of the æsthetic sensibilities, and as its result the person should have a keener and fuller appreciation of nature. More knowledge and a stronger creative imagination should go hand in hand; and we must look, at no very distant date it is to be hoped, for a more truly spiritual and at the same time a more virile conception of the meaning of beauty and truth, which shall bring each into harmony with the other.[1] I once had an experience which illustrates my meaning. A lady who was wearing a pin in which the stone was a piece of polished "satin spar" from Niagara was under the impression that it was "petrified foam." Upon being told the real nature of the stone, she declared that the object had lost its value and beauty for her, and that she wished she had not been told![2]

To teach a better interpretation of nature, for which education as a whole is striving, is one aim of nature study, for it is to science that we look for the training which shall attain this result. "The scientific interpretation of phenomena, the scientific account of the universe, is, therefore, the only one which can permanently satisfy the æsthetic judgment, for it is the only one which can never be entirely contradicted by our observation and experience. It is necessary to strongly emphasize this

---

[1] Pearson, Karl, *The Grammar of Science*, p. 35. The writings of such authors as Thoreau, White, and Bolles, exemplify a legitimate æsthetic interpretation of nature.

[2] Read in Huxley's *Life and Letters*, Vol. II., pp. 143, 144.

side of science, for we are frequently told that the growth of science is destroying the beauty and poetry of life. It is undoubtedly rendering many of the old interpretations of life meaningless, because it demonstrates that they are false to the facts which they profess to describe. It does not follow from this, however, that the æsthetic and scientific judgments are opposed; the fact is, that with the growth of our scientific knowledge the basis of the æsthetic judgment is changing and must change. There is more real beauty in what science has to tell us of the chemistry of a distant star, or in the life history of a protozoön, than in any cosmogony produced by the creative imagination of a pre-scientific age. By 'more real beauty' we are to understand that the æsthetic judgment will find more satisfaction, more permanent delight, in the former than in the latter. It is this continual gratification of the æsthetic judgment which is one of the chief delights of the pursuit of pure science."[1]

To illustrate this contention we may point out that scientific knowledge does not of necessity trammel the æsthetic judgment, for a well-balanced mind certainly can and does actually divest itself during the enjoyment of æsthetic sensations of the consideration of the machinery which produces them. At the same time I am aware of exceptions in the persons of highly gifted scientific men who have lost their power of enjoying nature, but I believe that these do not indicate any general tendency. On the other hand, I have received testimony to the effect that the enjoyment of nature is not experienced until something of its working is understood, a condition which I believe is far more usual and normal.

In the immediately foregoing paragraphs I have taken the ground that the increase of real knowledge must result in a refinement of the emotional life, and I have spoken of the relation of the emotions to the reason, and in the interpretation of nature as beautiful. There is still another phase of the emo-

---

[1] Pearson, K., *Grammar of Science*, p. 35.

tional attitude which remains to be especially mentioned, in the cultivation of which we may look for the development of the spiritual aspect of life which expresses itself in morality.

I attempt to use the word "spiritual" advisedly, but the word means such different things, frequently unessential, to different people that I shall endeavor to make Science and clear my meaning. It is often said that education Character. aims at the formation of character and any system of education, nay, any factor in education which does not have this for its purpose is to that degree useless. The character, then, is that imponderable but real sum total of ideal and action which makes a man recognizable as good or bad, and therefore as a desirable or undesirable member of society. Inasmuch, however, as the ideal or our emotional attitude determines largely the nature of our conscious actions, and, indeed, our unconscious actions also, to the extent that the latter grow by habit into the former, it follows that the emotional life, in order that it be for our good, must become more and more refined, and this refinement of emotional life is spiritualization. The ideal then becomes the spiritual when it is good and tends to produce good actions or moral living. Any process in education which, by supplying good ideals of any kind, be it of reason, or beauty, or of ethics, will help to spiritualize.

I take issue with Mr. Harris when he says, " While, therefore, we must acknowledge the importance of science study in the elementary schools, we must not ignore its non-spiritualizing tendency due to exaggerating the importance of inventorying external facts. Its enthusiasm for things and events in time and space makes it undervalue facts of introspection which are more fundamental than facts of external observation."[1] According to Mr. Harris, scientific instruction is justified by its significance as a factor in civilization ; but the methods of science study do not have a spiritualizing tendency.

If by the "spiritual " Mr. Harris means that realm of the

---

[1] Harris, W. T., 1890, p. 287.

ideal and mystical which most persons accept as a norm of living without so much as a doubt or question, then, to be sure, we must admit the truth of his statement. Science *does* lead to doubt and to questioning ; this we at once and gladly admit. But we declare, also, that introspective processes unless carried on in scientific fashion are no more suited to determining what the truth is than the examination of objective things. Science does not recognize the spiritual which either does not or is reluctant to examine for fear of uncomfortable disclosures. The truly spiritual is that man who, knowing, so far as in him lies, the true and the false, sticks to the course ordered by the former, with the sublime faith that right cannot beget wrong, and who can say with the master of Balliol that the great soul of the world is just.

A part of this spiritualization is due to the cultivation of intellectual honesty, of which we shall try to get a clear conception. **Intellectual Honesty.** We cannot wholly separate it from what for the sake of contrast we may call common honesty, but it sets off against the latter by its quality of extension to the subjective which makes it, par excellence, an honesty for the sake of the right rather than for policy's sake. We should be far from asserting that common honesty is merely a matter of policy, and that its sin is in being found out. What we do say is that a common phenomenon is the mind which, while strictly honest in the practical transactions of life, is distinctly inhonest (to avoid the implication of the ordinary form, dishonest) in intellectual affairs. This is the style of mind which, rather than looking at evidence squarely in the face, and with the will to act in consonance with knowledge, is ready to follow the leadings of authority without examination of its basis ; which, instead of looking for real content of truth, is easily cheated by " luxuriance of fiction " or, what is still worse, the willingness to indulge in it. There are timid minds who will see a fearsome teaching of doubt in these lines, but we shall have to pass such by with the comment that the fear which prevents people from using their mental powers is a subjective business which is as much of a bugaboo as a ghost with a turnip lantern for a head. The fear may be real enough, but its cause needs only to be examined honestly to discover its real character.

Since our purpose is to point out the fact of intellectual honesty, and to urge it as an ideal rather than to analyze it, we cannot do better than to present to the reader some powerful passages which, in exposing the attitude of master minds to view, serve as inspiriting examples of heroism in the realm of thought. It is to be earnestly recommended to those who are preparing for the profession of teaching that they read and reflect upon the works of the authors who are quoted.

Concerning Descartes, Huxley [1] says: "There is a path that leads to truth so surely that any one who will follow it must needs reach the goal, whether his capacity be great or small. And there is one guiding rule by which a man may always find this path, and keep himself from straying when he has found it. This golden rule is — give unqualified assent to no propositions but those the truth of which is so clear and distinct that they cannot be doubted." "Descartes" obeyed "this command deliberately; and, as a matter of religious duty, stripped off all his beliefs and reduced himself to a state of intellectual nakedness, until such time as he could satisfy himself which were fit to be worn. He thought a bare skin healthier than the most respectable and well-cut clothing of what might, possibly, be mere shoddy." [2] He "prepared to go on living while he doubted," "he would not lie to himself — would under no penalties say 'I am sure' of that of which he was not sure." [3]

Huxley, in that remarkable letter addressed to Kingsley, further says, "Sit down before fact as a little child, be prepared to give up every preconceived notion, follow humbly wherever and to whatever abysses nature leads, or you shall learn noth-

---

[1] On Descartes's Discourse Touching the Method of Using One's Reason Rightly, and of Seeking Scientific Truth (1870). *Coll. Essays.* Vol. I.

[2] *Loc. cit.*   [3] *Loc. cit.*

ing. I have only begun to learn content and peace of mind since I have resolved at all risks to do this."[1]

" But for this to be clear we must bear in mind what almost all forget, that the rewards of life are contingent upon obedience to the whole law — physical as well as moral — and that moral obedience will not atone for physical sin, or *vice versa*."[2]

Intellectual honesty, therefore, which is an outgrowth of experience with facts, begets faith in the order of nature and in the workings of its laws and the will to order one's life in accord with them. It is in this that we see the relation of the study of nature to the spiritual development of the man.

Another side of the character which can, by the proper means in nature study, be reached effectively, is that which **Respect for Others.** concerns itself with the welfare of others, and is to be found in respect for the rights and properties of others, and in the willing observance of laws which are made for the protection of public and private health, property, and pleasure. Such laws, while in a measure in themselves educative, as has on a previous page been pointed out, depend for their efficacy upon general recognition of their need and value. By bringing the individual to a knowledge of the facts and relations upon which such laws are based, and by training in the method by which they are obtained, is the only sure way to get the necessary recognition.

We may look for real progress in public cleanliness, and the consequent reduction of zymotic disease, when the knowledge of its nature is common knowledge ; for without such knowledge, precept and law are of little avail. The same is true of regulations applying to insect pests, noxious weeds, and every kind of troublesome thing inimical to health and comfort. Some real knowledge of the amount of care, time, patience, and money, and of the chance for success or failure of raising a shrub or tree will do more in getting a boy to voluntarily respect public

---

[1] Huxley, Leonard, *Life and Letters of Thomas Henry Huxley.* Vol. I., p. 231.

[2] *Loc. cit.*, p. 236.

parks than all the police which a city can afford to place in watch over it; for the small boy knows no authority but his own pleasure, and respect must be voluntary. If the boys of a neighborhood make the raising of peaches and grapes impossible, a better remedy than the jail would be to start them raising peaches and grapes of their own.[1] A study of the detailed laws for the amelioration of the conditions of the region in which a child lives is just as pertinent to his efficient education as that of the principles upon which his government is based.

In the preceding discussion we have frequently made use of such expressions as "real knowledge," "method of thought," "making knowledge a real experience," and the like, and it shall be our aim now to make clear what is meant.

Any science as an educational factor has two parts, information and method; or we may put it: (1) facts and relations determined with more or less probability to be true; (2) **Method of** the processes of acquisition which will enable us to **Study and** discover, arrange, and reason about new facts. It is **Content.** obviously the business of a teacher of any subject, such as nature study, to determine what there is in the way of ascertained knowledge content which students ought to know about; and it is equally the teacher's business to understand the method of its acquisition, and also how these methods have been and are now used.

But the teacher has a further task, which is more difficult and also more important. It is to learn how to impart information in such a manner that it shall not take the form of a **How to im-** mere multiplication table; for it is quite certain **part Informa-** that when nature study, for example, becomes on **tion.** its informational side a memory exercise, it will defeat its own ends. It will become slavish, a dry task which will repel the pupil. This is a danger which is attendant upon the use of books, in addition to the tendency which is always present to

---

[1] Hodge, C. F., *Nature Study and Life*, p. 29.

cloud the vision with an unhealthful atmosphere of authority. If, then, we regard our inherited information as so much knowledge, the teacher's problem is to make it real to each individual, and this may be done only by giving it a suitable association in the mind. Such associations must originally be pleasurable ; there must be the feeling of doing something and getting something worth while. A simple illustration is this. If it is desired that children should learn that some plant embryos have two seed leaves, this may be done by the copy-book method. The teacher might write down on the blackboard, " Plants are divided into two groups," etc., and the poor little folks commanded to write it out ten times. They would then probably have it " graven on the tablets of their memory." Or the children might be asked to collect some flower and vegetable seeds, and an excursion might be planned with this in view. The seeds might then be planted and watched, and the behavior of the seedlings noted. This method would consume more time and energy, but the reader will not have to waste much time in deciding which method of gaining knowledge will make it real to the child. No matter how great our enthusiasm may be, we suppose that even the latter method may fail in some cases, and that some children, especially those who are so unfortunate as to be too much the prisoners of city

Dependence on the Emotions. streets, may be too blasé to feel that anything of the kind is worth while. But in education as in everything else we must place our reliance upon those principles which have the greatest degree of probability for good results.

But another alternative might be introduced into our illustrations. The teacher might supply a specimen of each kind of plant, as to the number of seed leaves, and the children be set to making drawings, and in short doing what is generally called laboratory work. This method would have the advantage of allowing the children actually to see the objects; they would really observe and record. The criticism which may be made is that the method is good with students old enough to acquire in a short time a good number of facts which may be related in the mind; and with students old enough so that they do not unwillingly compose themselves to the mental effort necessary to see the relations of things. For young folks, whose efforts often lack direction, a single lesson is too likely to lack mental association and will entirely fail of the pleasurable associations that are derived by doing something in the way of planting or of watching for something to happen. There must be "joyous activity" (James). The laboratory method must therefore be understood in a broad light as meaning all kinds of effort to find out about nature; otherwise it will be too strait for children in the lower grades.

One difficulty which will be seen in the suggestion above given, and which to some minds constitutes a serious objection to an apparently slow and inefficient method of presenting information, namely, that there is not A Slow Method. time enough in the curriculum to carry it out, even admitting its desirability. And indeed it does look like a big task to take all the intellectual inheritance of even a single subject and transmit it to the children of the elementary schools. But in the first place the term "intellectual inheritance," while useful in expressing what we mean, looks as a matter of fact rather imposing. The amount of actual information necessary to be given is small. This is due to the fact that the method of using types enables the student to get a generalized view of a large field of knowledge; and by a careful use of the methods of acquiring knowledge, he gets a real notion of its validity, because he knows how. it has been acquired, and because he knows also that the criteria of knowledge which he is taught to apply have been used.

Again, by the method which we would advocate, and as illustrated by the second alternative of our illustration, although the aim of a given piece of work as stated may be quite restricted, it is found true that many opportunities are constantly presenting themselves incidentally for observation, and the student is naturally led into new fields of thought. This discovery of ever-widening channels for investigation is one of the features of the study of nature which makes it an especially invigorating exercise, which is at once as much so to young minds as to old, since problems adaptable to either are abundant. It is, then, but a step for a pupil from ignorance to independent thought under the skilful guidance of a good teacher; and any fact gleaned in such an operation, no matter how imperfect, is usually firmly held in the mind.

It appears from the immediately foregoing discussion that, while we admit and urge the claim that in nature study certain information should be given, it will be evident to the student that what we have said concerning the method of doing this is closely connected with the method of acquisition of knowledge, which we shall now pass on to inquire into.

We have endeavored to make clear in the first chapter that the scientific method of thought is common to all the sciences Scientific proper, but is not peculiar to them, beyond that to Method of them must be referred the lesson of the real impor-Thought in Nature Study. tance and nature of this method of thought. It is therefore clear that although nature study is no one science, yet having for its materials those of nature, and for its aim in part the understanding of natural phenomena, its method of thought is the scientific. It will then be to our purpose to get a clear idea of what that method is, and to this end we shall analyze it, and discuss separately the distinct operations involved. It must, however, constantly be remembered that when the mind is in play the operations are interwoven, so that it is only by reflection that the various operations may be recognized.

The conclusions arrived at by reasoning may be vitiated either by the falsity of the methods of the latter, or by failure to base it upon facts. If the reasoning is right and the facts wrong, the process may be instructive as an example of logic, but the inferences drawn may not be relied upon; and logic for the scientist is a means to an end. It becomes, therefore, of first importance that the determination of the facts be exact; and this may be easy or difficult according to the nature of the materials with which one is concerned, calling for ordinary or for special powers of perception. The operation is usually spoken of as observation ; and it has been repeated over so many times *ad nauseam* by every writer upon the subject that nature study cultivates the powers of observation, that there appears to be no special reason why we should do more than mention the fact. There are, however, one or two matters of which we must speak. First, the matter of observation, when regarded as the foundation of all reasoning which gives conclusions which are true,[1] is seen in a light which displays the true dignity of the operation. Upon it depends the validity of all human knowledge and therefore all human welfare. Those who determine facts lay the foundations for the superstructure of human thought. " It is better to know a little than to know so many things that are not so," is an aphorism with a pertinent lesson in it. Sound education cannot be had, therefore, when insufficient attention is given to the training of the child in habits of strict observation and of demanding facts of others when they are necessary. The latter, which is the habit of asking first for the facts in a problem, is a generalized habit which grows out of the former. It will be patent, therefore, that the work of the teacher is to aim at establishing *an attitude of mind* and not simply at developing keenness of sight or of touch or hearing.[2]

Observation.

----

[1] We shall not attempt to qualify our statements with reference to the doctrine of probability. The student will realize that, in dealing with human knowledge, we are dealing with degrees of probability of truth. See Pearson, K., *Grammar of Science*, Chapter IV.

[2] Henkle, W. D. (Proc. N. E. A., 59, 1870), in criticising the claim that object lessons taught observation, said that " study in one direction does not necessarily fit one for study in another." This is in part true and in part false. For example, one may be keen in the observation of flowers and not see the birds around him or hear them. But the point to be taken account of in education is that, first, the observing power of a child is normally keen enough. What he has to learn is to direct it, — that is, to confine the attention to a particular field and observe to some purpose. The second is to realize the necessity and value of observation, and to keep up the habit.

It is to the point also to remark that there is no reason why we should distinguish invidiously between one sense and With all the another.   One may be more useful than another Senses.   is in a particular field.   It is the conviction of the truth of this that is in part responsible for the development of manual training.[1]   The more senses there may be employed in any particular exercise of observation, the greater the impression on the mind and the more healthful and invigorating the process. The botanist or zoölogist who is engaged in studying an object is not content with seeing ;   he draws, colors, models, does everything and uses every means of observation to reassure himself ; and there is a mental exhilaration in finding that one operation verifies another.   There is also the effect of creating more far-reaching and useful mental associations, and a cultivation of the visual memory and constructive imagination, the exercise of which is of unquestionable use to the active brain. The school has far too long been engaged in training one kind of memory, the extreme result of which is seen in the Chinese system of education and its products.   The same tendency is seen in England where the examination system prevails.

Again, exercises in observation, to be effective in the cultivation of a proper attitude of mind, must be of the kind known At First   as " first hand."   The material to be observed Hand.   must be available for the child, and he must be judiciously led to observe by the means which an intelligent teacher will be able to use, with a minimum of suggestion of the facts to be observed.   Comenius and his followers laid stress upon independent observation ;   and in the failure to realize this lies the educational weakness of the " verification " method of the earlier laboratory manuals.   This method, while of undoubted use when one wishes to accumulate a large fund of information for particular purposes, as when in preparation for a calling, such as medicine, is certainly not useful as training in good, probing observation.   The whole value of

---

[1] Sedgwick, '93.

nature study is the creation of "large interests" with lasting quality; and the best way to defeat this end is to use persistently the "verification method" with young children. To attain the end, therefore, for which we are seeking, the child must have abundance of material, the value of which he must appreciate, which he must study for himself, and not be told about or read of. He must value the material, that is, he must know by his own experience what it costs to get it. He will then be inclined to make the best use of it. And in this is a strong argument for the use of the school garden where pupils can raise their own materials for adornment and use, and for properly conducted field work beyond the precincts of the school.

Thirdly, there is, in relation with the operations which we are discussing, an important principle to be kept in mind, the neglect of which has led to a very large amount of fallacious teaching and pedantry. It is that a thing and its name are two different matters with an arbitrary albeit useful relation, and that this relation may be useful to some and not to others. It may be well for a zoölogist to be able to call an article of a beetle's leg the tarsus, but the same may not be true of a little fellow seven years old. By analogy it may be seen that the same seven-year-old subject may have no particular use for the information that a beetle has six legs; but at any rate, if he is looking after a crop of potatoes he will in all probability acquire that fact, and this in connection with some useful operation, such as finding out that a pest to him must be a pest to humanity in general.

A name helps us to talk about a thing; and when pupil and teacher fully understand this they will both be better off. The study of simple facts in relation to other simple facts will be a cure for this form of pedantry of which we speak, by supplanting it. When the necessity for a name arises, its *raison d'être* is appreciated, and then any name mutually and generally understood will do. The observation of things is not learning the name of things, and it is the mark of an ignorant mind that it can be cheated with a name provided only that it is big enough.

Lastly, it is true that although the observation of facts is the first step in the building up of a body of knowledge, it is not necessarily the easiest.   On the contrary, it is in many cases the most laborious part of it and calls for the most patient and painstaking care on the part of the observer.   But the investigator, that is, any one who is at work upon a problem, sees what he is after; he has, so to speak, a vision of the future and knows what he is driving at.   A child, on the other hand, knows in a vivid way the present only, and to that extent observation is meaningless.   There follows from this two important principles, namely, that relatively simple problems shall be taken for the simple mind;[1] and secondly, observation must be made upon materials, the fate of which is a matter of the child's interest.   The habit of looking to the future intelligently and planning for it is a habit which is developed most highly in civilized man, and it cannot be started at too early an age. The best sort of lessons in this direction are learned by the experience gained by growing crops, on a suitable scale, to be sure, and by finding out the cost of production.   In this we have another pertinent argument for the institution of the school garden, in adding to the pupil's work the element of futurity, and in giving him a real opportunity to appreciate the value of human effort.

There are some subsidiary processes of observation of which we may briefly speak.   These are analysis and discrimination.

Analysis.   When we desire to know anything about an object which comes under our notice, the first thing we do is to examine its parts, and in proportion to our desire to comprehend the object do we carry out our analysis in an orderly and exhaustive way.

The general destructiveness of children is prompted by a

---

[1] This appears axiomatic, but we state it rather to emphasize the importance of grading observation work carefully by the suitable choice of problems.

desire to see the works, and is not a vicious propensity. Their destructiveness is a crude method of analysis. True, it may become vicious if left unguided, but like curiosity in general it is useful in leading to investigation. It is therefore quite proper to introduce at suitable times, especially in the later years of the elementary schools, work which enters somewhat more deeply into the structure of plants and animals, at least enough observation of internal parts as will serve for a basis for experimental work in ecology and physiology, the introduction of which, however, we justify also upon other considerations.

In the examination of more or less similar objects we find it necessary to distinguish between them, to see their likenesses and differences. In this way as children we exer- **Discrimina-** cise the power of discrimination and that which is **tion.** contingent on it, the ability to classify, in making collections of objects, and, in a more or less crude way, in arrangement of like with like. It is clear that the ability to recognize things as similar and dissimilar is, in reality, the beginning of generalization; and careful study when young of groups of objects and the construction of definitions which shall be exact, is training in the power of generalization which deserves a place in the elementary curriculum. This could be done, for example, if in a school garden the different varieties of beans, of tomatoes, and so on, were raised by different children; each pupil might then study the materials of others, and get at ideas by comparison, which at once would lead to classification on the one hand and immediately useful information about varieties of vegetables on the other.

Discrimination is not at all easy if the objects are at all complex or if the differences are slight; and there is considerable danger that teachers give work to young children which is not only useless but quite beyond their reach. To know the commoner kinds of trees is generally regarded as useful and enjoyable, but to expect children in the lower grades to know different oaks or willows or maples is unreasonable, while they may, however, be able to distinguish the oak from the maple, the ash from the elm. To study classification of animals or plants is for the most part, we believe, entirely beyond the realm of nature study and should be left to the high school.

In what has just been said in the two preceding paragraphs we have anticipated ourselves somewhat. The third step in the process which we are examining is that of combining in the mind a group of like concepts, and forming what is known as an induction. By this means we are able to put into brief form, by a sort of " mental shorthand," a large number of observations. In this manner the orderly mind may be regarded as "a set of pigeon holes " appropriately labelled, into which our observational experiences are placed on file. The more orderly the brain, *ceteris paribus*, the greater the number of facts which may be disposed of in an orderly manner and which may be used.

It is, however, to be noted that although we may assert some quality of a large number of objects, that is, we may group a large number of facts together in one group and then into an inclusive statement, thus forming an induction, we do not extend, by this, our actual knowledge.[1] The ability, however, to subsume under a short formula a large number of observations is an indication of the mind's grasp. " . . . The power of sifting and arranging perceptions, the power of rapidly passing from sense impression to fitting exertion, is seen to be a factor of paramount importance to man in the battle of life." [2]

Reflection will show, however, that the mind does not rest content with such definitions, but seeks rather to extend its sway over the field of the unobserved. It is obviously

Inference.

impossible for an individual, or for all individuals, to observe all the facts subsumed under one generalization. The passage from the observed to the unobserved is by a logical

---

[1] The student should consult Hyslop's *Elements of Logic: Theoretical and Practical*, for a lucid discussion of induction and deduction.

[2] Pearson, K., *Grammar of Science*, p. 103.

leap known as inference, the probability of the truth of which is affected by the number of observations upon which it rests. If upon the study of a number of plants it is found hat some have two seed leaves and some one, the induction may be drawn that these plants may be arranged into two groups, each characterized by the number of seed leaves. If, further, it is concluded that all plants may be so grouped, we make an inference which will as a matter of fact be incorrect, but illustrates well its relation to the number of observations. And this error is one which might actually be made in the schoolroom or garden by children. It is worth while to say here that many teachers would miss a good opportunity for scientific training by saying outright that the inference is wrong. It would pedagogically be much better to get the children to see exactly what they had done, and to get them to put a question mark after their conclusion. They should then be led to see that it is necessary to seek for more facts. Their own work and thought may thus be used as a *stimulus to further investigation*. Instead of thinking a mental task done, therefore, they will see that they will be cultivating that inquiring attitude of mind which is characterized by the ability and willingness to suspend judgment. This cannot be the case unless the student learns to apprehend the doctrine of probability and the value of submitting his conclusions to the test. The importance of this is well attested by an actual instance of the acceptance of a sweeping generalization based upon one observation. In 1891 it was discovered that in the plant *Casuarina* the pollen tube had the following peculiar behavior. Instead of passing through the micropyle of the ovule, as is true in very many cases, and at that time supposed to be in all except *Casuarina*, it penetrated through the tissues of the style and placenta, through the funicle, chalaza, and nucellus, following in its course the supernumerary embryo sacs, and so reaching the egg. Inasmuch as *Casuarina*, for other reasons, is regarded as approaching the primitive dicotyledons, the investigator was led to propose a taxonomic arrangement of these plants into two groups, the Porogams and Chalazogams, and this generalization was adopted in Engler and Prantl's Natuerlichen Pflanzenfamilien   A short time later it was found that other plants showed similar characters, and that in some families both modes of behavior of the pollen tube occurred. Thus a broad inference based on one physiological fact collapsed, as might have been expected. It is clear from the simple character of the illustration given above, that the habit of avoiding such fallacious ways of thought is well within the reach of children in the elementary school, and that, even if older minds do fall into error, such a habit is well worth cultivating in the young.

We have said that a student should be led to see the necessity of testing his conclusions by reference to more observations. **Deduction.** This brings us to the last point in this discussion concerning the reasoning process, that of deduction. The inability, for practical reasons, to observe all the facts makes it necessary to use possibly incomplete formulæ in our thinking, and to attempt to explain by these the phenomena which come under our notice. This is a part of the scientific method of thought. The unscientific mind differs from the scientific mind in the ease with which it falls into the belief that a generalization once made, especially if it gets into a book, is of necessity true. The consequent unreadiness to throw aside an hypothesis which is insufficient to cover the case, and with which the facts subsequently observed are out of harmony, is a mental paralysis which ends in complete stagnation of thought. " For the person who is convinced that he has found the right explanation is not going to seek for it."[1] That this tendency is found in trained minds and has to be guarded against is apparent to any one who is acquainted with the trend of the post-Darwinian discussions on the origin of species.[2]

The habit of testing our knowledge as we go along, and of

[1] Weismann, August, *On Germinal Selection* (1895). Chicago, 1896. P. 17.
[2] For a general and pertinent criticism, see Hugo de Vries, *The Origin of Species by Mutation.*

laying aside preconceived or incomplete ideas, is, then, of paramount importance, and we believe we are in no wise justified in allowing the cultivation of such a habit to be left for the years beyond those of the grammar school. And let it be said that these steps in thought are no artificial matters which are to be arbitrarily introduced into the curriculum. Children actually use them properly or improperly, and it becomes of the highest importance to see to it that the former obtains. It is not necessary that children should study logic ; they *use* logic and the teacher who is not keen in scenting logical fallacies, and who is not skilful in leading the young thinker aright, is incompetent. The problem for the teacher is chiefly to keep alive the attitude of inquiry which children have, and to teach them to acquire and to keep to right habits of thinking. The chief criticism in this regard against education is that this ability of children to think clearly is blunted ; for they are naturally keen, as every one who has had to face their questioning knows. It is not necessary, furthermore, to suppose that these methods of thought are merely schoolroom exercises, for they are called for in all intelligent work, and the garden offers just as good an opportunity for their cultivation as anywhere.

Inasmuch as for practical reasons the end of education is informational as well as disciplinary, it may easily be apprehended that it is impossible for a student to work to a very great extent inductively. There is a limit **Students' Work mainly Deductive.** in the inductive method which is very soon reached. The "method of discovery" which has been overworked by very many teachers has been condemned justifiably because it laid stress on induction to the sacrifice of information. Its advocates do not seem to have comprehended the wide field of deduction. We have in practice to use the observations of others as well as our own, depending upon the uniformity of mental processes in normal minds and the validity of their observations. By the choice of materials also, we as teachers are habitually making it unnecessary for a student to multiply his observations by long research and thus allow him to draw inferences which would, but for the selection of proper materials, probably be invalid. That is, we select types for study, and not a heterogeneous multitude of animals or plants, and we enable a student to get at his intellectual inheritance quickly. It would be quite impossible for a child ten years of age to collate the facts upon which is based our knowledge of nitrogenous bacteria, even by the verification method, to say nothing of the method of discovery ; but we ask him to verify some portions of our well-attested knowledge by the examination of certain easily observable facts concerning root tubercles and the relation of these to the growth of leguminous plants. Such knowledge may become a part of one's self by *using it* and seeing that it is true because consonant with further experience. Such work is deductive, and most experimental work is of this kind. We do not set up a lot of indiscriminate experiments ; but relying upon some guiding supposition, we do a definite experiment to see if the result accords with the hypothesis. But no one for this reason decries the use of experiments. The main consideration for the teacher is to see to it that an experiment when performed shall be "logically conclusive." The results shall be stated in

Value of Experiment. such wise that only that which is actually taught by an experiment shall be included, and then what principle it is used to illustrate. As a result of failure to follow these rules, many errors creep in, thus completely defeating the value of experimental work. One of the most common is found in connection with plant physiology. When an experiment is performed with a tap root showing that it responds to the stimulus of gravitation, a pupil is frequently allowed to state, as his conclusion, that roots grow downward, — a conclusion not only illogical but false. The recognition of such fallacies, and the strict adherence to what is learned and what is not learned by an experiment, is as good training in the scientific method as any other, since it makes for the critical attitude of mind. The discussion of the value of experiment would be incomplete if its importance in helping the teacher and student to steer clear of certain prevalent fallacies of thought were overlooked. We have in mind those which are made in the attempt by the teacher to discover to the child the adaptation of organic forms to their environment. Because we believe organisms to be essentially adaptive, we are easily led to suppose that every organ, whatever it may be and however insignificant, must be explained to have some use, or the teacher's duty is not done, and in this lies the danger to which we refer. And we must blame, not so much the teacher of perhaps somewhat limited opportunities for mental training, as the many clever writers who have written so many fairy tales about plants and animals, without paying any attention to the rigid examination of the facts. The fallacy lies in the gratuitous explanation of the functions of organs, without submitting the matter to experimental proof, or at least a test of some kind. To be sure, the uses of many organs are obvious at a glance. We can have no doubt of the usual **Adaptation** use of a horse's leg, though we may discover further **and Experi-** uses by injudicious experiment. But this is not **mental Proof.** always the case, especially if the use is passive, or if it does not involve a readily observed mechanical relation ; such, for illustration, as the use of the wings of seeds or fruits. We have, of course, read accounts of these structures, and we have been too readily persuaded that their use, as organs for dissemination, is perfect, and without any doubt determined. Now, as a matter of fact, there is some doubt of this, in the case of some plants at least, and at any rate the subject is still open to experiment. Moreover, because some wings do serve this function with some degree of efficiency, it by no means follows that all wings on seeds and fruits have a like function. There are some dehiscent fruits which are supplied with very definite wings ; in which case it is obvious that they must serve some other function. While it may not be possible always for the teacher or pupil to undertake the complete solution of such a problem, so much as is done on the subject may be done with the exercise of some degree of critical judgment. This may be done by the application of experimental methods, by which means may be determined, not only the use of an organ, but also its actual value or degree of efficiency. This tends to eliminate the hazy and inexact and untrue, and to cultivate accuracy of thought and statement. The position which Jackman has taken in regard to quantitative work is therefore a good one.

The gratuitous manner of treating the subject of adaptation in organisms is perhaps the greatest objection which may be advanced against the use of ecology in elementary education, for the reason that ecology is that part of the science of botany, or of zoölogy, which concerns itself especially with the fact and method of adjustment of the organism to its environment. The subject is as old as the study of natural history; but the word ecology, which is of recent coinage, stands for the most modern development of the study which nowadays has for its aim the exact and so far as possible *experimental* determination of the relation of organism and environment. It is obvious, therefore, that no searching work may be done without the synthesis of all

Ecology in Nature Study. kinds of knowledge of the organism, — structural, morphological, and physiological. Nevertheless, we desire to bring to the notice of children the great principle of adaptation, and it would be a singular sort of nature study which did not. The thing for every teacher to keep in mind is that, *so far as possible, everything shall be subjected to some sort of experimental test*, remembering that it is better for a pupil to deal with a few well-determined facts in illustration of a principle than it is to get an inexact and poetic view of a subject, based upon hearsay and the opinion of the incompetent. The method of teaching ecology as much as any other part of a science "shall be unfailingly rational; that facts, though essential, shall be rated as less important than the principles which underlie them." [1]

In speaking of experiment we are led to show its importance

Cause and Purpose. in its bearing on another form of logical error which teachers who deal with living organisms are very likely to fall into, and which tends to take all the vitality out of

---

[1] Woodward, C. M., *The Change of Front in Education.*

the study of living things. It is the improper use of the teleo-logical interpretation of nature and its confusion with the causal relation.[1] Technically it is called the fallacy of *post hoc ergo propter hoc.* The difficulty is a very subtle one, for the reason that the use of words in speaking of these matters is often misleading. The prevalence of a confusion of language and of ideas in elementary books on botany and zoölogy, and in nature study "readers," have lent a weight of authority to the kind of reasoning to which we refer, so that teachers again and again fall into the error of indulging in guesswork in total ignorance of the underlying fallacy. An illustration will make my meaning clearer.

The embryo of the squash, during its sprouting, develops a protuberance ("peg," "heel") on the side of its stem which, in conjunction with the hypocotyl and cotyledons, effectually opens the seed-coat, and thus the cotyledons are early set free when otherwise they would be kept for some time pinched together by the seed-coat, as indeed sometimes happens. Now, it has been shown [2] that the production of the "peg" in the cucurbits is a geotropic response, and takes place on one side of the stem or the other, according to the position of the embryo with reference to the horizontal. It had been claimed previously to Noll's work that the seed-coats acted as a stimulus, but that this is not true is shown by the fact that the peg may be produced after the seed-coats are removed.

Now in speaking about this very interesting organ in the squash seedling, one very easily falls into logical and verbal error. "Why does the squash seedling have a peg," is usually

---

[1] In this connection the student should read the discussion of Cause and Effect. Pearson's *Grammar of Science.* See also Lloyd, F. E., Plant Ecology for the Elementary School. *New York Teachers' Monographs*, 4: pp. 81–89. March, 1902.

[2] Noll, F. Zur Keimungs-Physiologie der Cucurbitaceen. *Landwirtsch. Jahrb.* 1901. *Ergänzungsband* I. In addition to gravitation, the production of the peg is conditioned by the bending of the axis. See a summary in English by Lloyd, F. E. The "Peg," or "Heel," in Seedlings of the Cucurbitaceæ. *Torreya*, 1: 120. October, 1901.

answered by saying, " In order to open the seed-coat " ; or it may be said that the squash has a peg " because it needs it to open the seed-coat." That is, the action of the peg is placed in the position of cause, whereas it is an effect, and the efficient cause for the production of the peg must be sought for in the sum total of activities set free by the stimulus of gravitation. It is reasonable enough to ask what the peg is good for — to inquire into the behavior or purpose of the mechanism ; and the answer should be sought by the experimental method, the method which is used to determine the cause of its production. These are really two different questions often by confusion lumped into one.

Again, it is known that when a tap root bends, the secondary roots which are produced in the region of the bending grow on the convex side of the tap root and not on the concave side. It can be shown that the purpose [1] of this is a more effective distribution of roots in the soil. If we now ask why secondary roots are produced in this manner we should properly look

---

[1] Concerning the use of the word "purpose," I quote the following:

" By the expression, This or that mechanism has a Purpose in an organism, one understands really nothing more than that this contributes to the ability of the organism to exist. . . . 'To the purpose' means, therefore, in general, the same as 'capable of existence' and it would be foolishness to waste even a word as to whether one may use the term in *this* sense or not. This implies, however, that there is absolutely no scientific merit in maintaining of any organic mechanism whatever that it is in general to the purpose, or contributes to the capability of existence, since that is self-evident. On the other hand, it is in certain circumstances very important and profitable *to demonstrate how far and under what conditions* a given mechanism in the organism is of purpose; in what way this contributes, in combination with other mechanisms, to the capability of existence of a given organism; and strictly speaking, the whole of physiology is essentially occupied with such demonstrations." (Sachs' *Physiology of Plants*, English translation, p. 10.)

" It must, however, never be forgotten that the purpose of any given phenomenon can only be determined by an external observer on the basis of the facts which come under his notice. Ideas of purpose being mental are not and can never be the direct causes of anything that takes place in the plant. It is therefore always the object of Physiology to investigate the ways and means by which, under certain external conditions, and with varying internal dispositions, some particular final result is produced, and to trace *the chain of causes which lead to this result*." (Pfeffer, Physiology of Plants, English translation, Vol. I., p. 9.) (All italics mine.)

to the structural and physiological conditions within the tap root which cause the one-sided production of secondary roots. If we mean by the question to ask what advantage or disadvantage to the plant there is in the arrangement, we can better state the inquiry in this or some corresponding form.

Each of these questions is legitimate, but each is distinct, and to avoid error should be kept so. The teleology which rests upon efficient evidence, experimental or otherwise, is scientific and is an aim of physiology. So also is the explanation in terms of causality. To fail to distinguish these brings minds, old and young alike, into a state of confusion not easily rectified.

This is educationally wrong, for one of the things which we desire above all to have the human being learn, and learn well, is the significance of the causal relation. " In the struggle for existence man has won his dictatorship over other forms of life by his power of foreseeing the effects which flow from antecedent causes." [1]

What, then, shall a teacher do to avoid the error? We answer, first, by understanding the fallacy himself; and secondly, by using language which is not so likely to be capable of a double interpretation. Thus we may say, " What is the cause? " instead of " Why? " when the causal relation is to be understood ; and " What is the use of? " or " What is the function of? " when the teleological aspect is examined into. This is not merely a quibble over the use of words ; for if words are to be used to express ideas, and the person has clear and good ideas, it is worth while to acquire the habit of finding and sticking to the correct forms of speech. Looseness of diction is just as vicious in expressing scientific ideas as any other. The candidate for the teaching profession should reflect on this point and decide for himself on the validity of the argument advanced.

In this chapter I have endeavored to set forth the reason why nature study should form a part of elementary education.

---

[1] Pearson, K., *Grammar of Science*, p. 137.

Apparent failure of nature study in some quarters is to be referred to inefficient teachers. It is claimed that to rob children of opportunities to study natural objects by the inductive method is wrong.

A criticism of the object lesson shows that its chief weakness lies in the fact that in practice it failed to lay enough emphasis upon the strict application of the scientific method of thought and of proper educational methods derived therefrom. Its failure is therefore chiefly connected with the teacher's lack of scientific training. Nature study lays emphasis constantly upon work by the pupils carried on by the method of science.

Nature study helps to make people "happy and useful." Commencing with an innate generalized interest in nature, it preserves and refines this. It is especially valuable in formal education because it is in every way adapted to the healthful development of mind and body in the young. It helps to lead them to a more rational kind of living, because, while it gives training in ability to use the processes of reasoning, it does not neglect æsthetic considerations, but leads to a better interpretation of nature as beautiful. Furthermore, nature study by teaching a stricter adherence to facts makes for that intellectual honesty which produces true character; it supplies ideals and thus in the educational sense contributes to the spiritualization of man. It teaches respect for others.

Nature study is of value because of the information it gives, and because by inculcating right habits of thought it tends to produce a scientific attitude of mind.

Information must be imparted in such wise as not to raise authority above independence of thought. Only such information may be imparted which is associated with the mental activity of the pupil.

The scientific method of thought is analyzed and shown to be simple and to be the natural method in children. The severity of problems given, which depends upon the nature of the materials, must be suited to their mental capacity, and the materials of nature study offer all possible shades of difficulty.

The value of experiment is pointed out, and the importance of strict adherence to the teachings of an experiment as part of the scientific method is emphasized.

The fallacies which creep into teaching, such as the confusion of the teleological and causal interpretations applied to organic nature, are pointed out, together with the errors in language which accompanies them.

CHAPTER III

THE VALUE OF BOTANY IN SECONDARY EDUCATION

BIBLIOGRAPHY

Andrews, E. A. False and True Criticism of the Public School. EDUCATIONAL REVIEW, **21** : 258. 1901.

Galloway, B. T. Applied Botany, Retrospective and Prospective. SCIENCE, II., **16** : 49–59. 11 July, 1902.

Ganong, W. F. The Teaching Botanist. New York, The Macmillan Co. 1899.

Ganong, W. F. The Cardinal Principles of Morphology. BOTANICAL GAZETTE, **31** : 426–434. June, 1901.

Goebel, K. Organography (translation by Balfour). Oxford, Clarendon Press.

Huxley, T. H. On the Educational Value of the Natural History Sciences (1854). Essay II. Science and Education. New York, D. Appleton & Co. 1898.

Macbride, T. H. Botany: How Much, and When. Iowa Teachers' Association. December 28, 1898.

von Sachs, J. History of Botany. Oxford, Clarendon Press. 1890.

Spencer, H. Principles of Biology. New York, D. Appleton & Co. 1900.

Spencer, H. Education : Intellectual, Moral, and Physical. New York, D. Appleton & Co. 1860.

Thorndike, E. L. Sentimentality in Science Teaching. EDUCATIONAL REVIEW, **17** : 57. January, 1899.

Tolman, A. H. Natural Science in a Literary Education. POPULAR SCIENCE MONTHLY, **49** : 98. September, 1896.

Wilson, E. B. Presidential Address before the American Society of Naturalists. SCIENCE, II., **13** : 14–23. 4 January, 1901.

In the first and second chapters we have entered into a somewhat detailed account of what is conceived to be the value of science in general and of biology in particular in education. What has thus been said in a general way, we may assume to be true in regard to botany. It therefore remains to discuss such peculiar features of botany as are of importance to the educator in determining its place in education, and especially those aspects of the subject which are of importance in the education of the youth of high-school age. It is therefore an elementary course in botany with which we are concerned ; one which is planned to meet the needs of the average person, who will not in all probability be a botanist, and whose only chance to get that which botany offers as a guide to " complete living " will be limited, likely enough, to a half-year of opportunity in the high school. We as teachers believe that education in science and in its methods contributes definitely toward the making of better workers, better parents, better members of society, and better citizens. We believe, also, that botany has its full share of adaptability and value in these regards. It is, however, no less important to know what specifically is the part it may and should play in education, than to know in a general way that what may be predicted in regard to science as a whole is true also of its several parts.

The Duty of the Teacher in Botany.

It is true, of course, that just as all departments of science merge into each other, and are by no means sharply demarked the one from the other, we cannot attribute to botany, or to any other one of these departments, a value which is more than a relative one. But this relative value, greater or less than that of the other subjects, it has, and it is the business of the

To determine its Relative Value in Education.

educator in this subject to know as exactly as possible what this value is.

Nor may the fact that botany, together with the other sciences, has received so much recognition as to give it, without much doubt, a place more or less settled in the curriculum, beguile us into the belief that this is no more a duty upon us. Curricula, as Herbert Spencer [1] has shown in his treatise on education, have been and indeed are still, in some countries more so than in others, the expression of custom. Since the

---

[1] *Education: Intellectual, Moral, and Physical.* " Men dress their children's minds as they do their bodies, in the prevailing fashion."

date when this classic of Spencer's was written there has been a
constantly increasing change in public opinion among the progressive western nations; and the time will come when the
sciences will be the generally accepted style. Then,
**When
Science in
Education
shall be the
Custom.** what has been true of the "humanities," so-called,
will probably also be true of the sciences. And if
that time comes when conservatism shall put the
muzzle on the inquiring mouth, when "everybody studies science
nowadays," will be made to do service for a real reason, then,
without the peradventure of a doubt, will the teaching of the
subject become formal and lifeless. The hope that the inquiring attitude of the scientific mind will be so common a possession of the people that the bonds of custom will be loosed
so as to make this condition impossible is a vain one. When
we contemplate the widespread ignorance of the common
**Then is it in
Greatest Dan-
ger of Deca-
dence.** knowledge of living which exists at the present day
in spite of modern education; when we realize the
lesson of history that all reformation of lasting
quality is slow, and when we face the fact that, even for those
best informed and best trained in the scientific method, it is
still very hard to set and still more so to live up to a standard of
rational living, — it is at once evident to the reflective mind that
the warning here given is no idle one. Especially is this true
of botany. The necessity of rescuing this subject from the
girls' school, where it has become one of the "accomplish-
**Special Dan-
ger for
Botany.** ments," has been for some years upon us; nor is
the rescue yet complete. It is still thought of as a
girl's study — save the name — and the impression
that of necessity it cannot be anything else is so widespread as
to offer a distinct barrier to the successful teaching of boys of
super-virile age. This statement has received the testimony of
many teachers; and while the attitude is not an insuperable
obstacle, and is one which by the power of a good teacher may
be overcome, it is one of the real difficulties of education which
has grown out of misconceptions. We turn our attention, therefore, in this chapter to the consideration of those aspects of

botany which justify its presentation to persons of high-school age.

Concerning the pleasure value of botany but little needs to be said. That the objects which form the materials of botany appeal to the mind as having beauty of form, order, and color; that the growth and behavior of plants excite and hold the interest of many with the power of fascination; that their care is a source of comfort and solace to some or of vigorous and intelligent enjoyment to others; that all these and many other aspects of man's attitude to the vegetable world are real and full of meaning to us; yet we must take the position that it is not in any sense the primary and only in a limited sense the secondary object of the teacher of botany to concern himself with these things. The teacher of botany is not concerned with æsthetics. This ground we take unequivocally, but in giving reasons why botany shall constitute a part of education we may not neglect to show that one of these is to be found in the attitude which the human mind takes toward plants, either consciously or unconsciously. If this relation is one which in its more imperfect and unconscious realization results in pleasure; if the contemplation of the myriad varieties of form and activity in a relatively superficial way leads the mind into pleasant avenues of thought; and if the imperfect acquaintance with the habits and beauties of plants stimulates the imagination of the poet and his reader, we must believe that **Wider Knowledge brings greater Pleasure.** the more perfect and conscious realization of the relations of man to the vegetable world will beget greater pleasure; that a more searching examination and better understanding of the significance of plants and their business will lead to richer fields of intellectual and emotional delights; and that a fuller knowledge of these organisms and their ways will furnish vastly more material for the play of the æsthetic imagination. If this be true, that the greater our knowledge and information the wider and deeper our pleasure and the truer the æsthetic feeling, then we may properly urge this as a reason why the great mass of the people who live more "by sentiment than by riches"[1] should have an opportunity to get a knowledge of plants and of human thought concerning them.

Further, the argument is strengthened by the realization of the fact that for many persons a keen interest in some field of thought stands as a powerful incentive to activity. This proposition has been fully presented by E. B. Wilson, in his Presidential address before the American Society of Naturalists,[2] in its application to the specialist in the study of natural history.

"I have said that the keynote of Agassiz's life and work was his love of nature ; and in this respect I believe that he was typical of the great naturalists of every age. It has of late become the fashion in some quarters to look with a certain condescension on what is styled the "sentimental side" of natural history ; on that keen primary interest in biological phenomena for their own sake, apart from their scientific analysis, that was characteristic of so many of the earlier naturalists. I can but believe that such an attitude shows a lack of insight into the real motives and sources of inspiration of all great observers and discoverers. Every critical analysis of the progress of science leads to a recognition of the vital importance of the imaginative faculty in all research of a high order ; and in this regard great masters of creative science, such as Faraday or Darwin, have rightly been placed beside the great masters of creative art. . . . We must recognize that there is no more potent spring of scientific research than a lively interest in the facts — in other words, the æsthetic satisfaction that lies in the mere observation of natural phenomena. Read the intimate records of the lives of great discoverers in every field of science, and you cannot fail to be struck with this. From this source flows the impulse to analyze by experiment, to correlate by comparison, and thus to discover law. The primary impulse of the naturalist is thus given by the love of nature ; and I believe that the

---

[1] *Outlook*, November 11, 1902.
[2] *Science*, II. Vol. XIII., 14–23. January 4, 1901.

scientific naturalist should welcome every movement towards the cultivation of general interest in natural history. We may therefore regard it as a happy omen for the future of our science that in every direction we see the signs of increasing interest in field work, in nature study, and in the teaching of natural history in our schools."

In this paragraph which we have quoted we find that the belief is expressed that a " general interest in natural history " is to be regarded as a " happy omen for the future " of the science. But it is more than this. It is an equally happy omen for the future of the people.[1] Pleasure and interest in the facts of natural history are as real and potent for the amelioration of the life of the amateur as of the naturalist. To be sure, of those who study botany only a small proportion will become amateur botanists. The number of those whose outlook will be widened and whose pleasure will be heightened as a result of this study is, however, greater ; and few will altogether escape its influence if we assume the right kind of a teacher. Nevertheless, it would not be an improper ambition for the teacher of botany so to present the subject as to prepare his students in the best manner possible for good amateur work in this field. To do this is no mean task and requires the best kind of teaching, and we may safely say that were this done the work which would thus result would accomplish all the other ends of the course.

We are now in a position to see that, although a direct consideration of the æsthetic aspect of plants is not contemplated as a part of the teacher's work, the fact of the emotional attitude towards these organisms and their relations to their environment, including man, is of the highest importance, and its recognition is of no mean importance in deciding upon the

Real Interest and Enjoyment the Mainspring of Activity.

---

[1] For a discussion of the value of science to specialists in other lines of work, literature especially, see Tolman, A. H., Natural Science in a Literary Education. *Popular Science Monthly*, **49**: 98. September, 1896.

value of a course in botany, and upon the reason for its introduction into the course of study in the secondary schools.

Before leaving this part of our argument we must remove any
doubt as to our meaning. Much has been said, and properly,
" Sentimen-   against the tendency in science teaching which has
talism."   been described as sentimentalism. A strong case
against this error has been made by Thorndike,[1] the gist of
whose arraignment is found in the condemnation of the teaching of that indiscriminate love of animals and plants which leads
to grave misconception of the relative values of life. Science
teaches us that we should value human life, health, and comfort,
and human progress, both material and intellectual, more highly
than the life of any animal or plant. The sentimentalism, therefore, which refuses to take the life of a frog or of a plant, in
order that a child may get a saner conception of life, is false.
But it must also be evident that an absence of reverence, a
true and useful sentiment, which leads a teacher to be indifferent to the feelings of others, is to be deplored ; and when the
obligation of the teacher to overcome prejudices in students by
thoughtful and tactful means is overlooked, this is equally to
be inveighed against. The teacher of botany is both at an advantage and a disadvantage, as compared with the teacher of
zoölogy, in this case. The materials of botany naturally call
forth expressions of the æsthetic emotions, and the danger of
falling into meaningless talk is consequently greater ; while
on the other hand, since plants are living things, the evident
absence of sentience — so far as we understand it — in them
offers an opportunity to study living things without keen distress
for the loss of life. At the same time, the latter fact offers no
excuse for a reckless waste of plant life ; and the teacher will do
well not to ignore the element of sacrifice and so increase the
attitude of reverence toward living things, a quality which is entirely lacking in many people of coarse sentiment.

---

[1] Thorndike, E. L., Sentimentality in Science Teaching. *Educational Review*, 17 : 57. January, 1899.

But in spite of the danger here recognized we must state unequivocally that botany must have its part in that education of
the future which " will focus on the feelings, sentiments, emotions, and try to do something for the heart, out of which are
the issues of life." [1]

We may also find an argument for the use of a subject in
general education in the nature and extent of its informational
content. The usefulness, therefore, in a narrower
sense, of its materials, the dependence of man   Informational
                                               Content of
upon them, and the ways and extent to which they   Botany.
touch upon human welfare, are the indices of its educational
force in this regard.[2] The question to be asked then, is, to
what degree and in what way do plants relate themselves to the
human family and its welfare, and in the answer to this we may
find the argument which we seek.

The fundamental necessity of the human race is that of food.
Whether we regard the occupations of primitive man or those
of the highest type of civilization, the one constant, imperative
demand is for food. The earlier methods of food production
were solely empirical, a relatively scant population and simple
demands necessitating only crude methods. Increase in population and division of labor have made necessary
more and more efficient methods of food produc-   The Impor-
                                           tance of Pho-
tion so as to get the greatest quantity and best   tosynthesis.
quality. It has become, therefore, an increasingly severe intellectual task to determine what these methods are, and this determination depends upon the knowledge of plant physiology
and of the relation of plants to the soil. A most fundamental
fact of plant physiology which stands in relation to the knowledge of food production is the process of photosynthesis, the
process by which plants, by means of their green coloring matter,
or chlorophyll, are able, in the presence of sunlight, to manufac-
ture food, from which energy may be obtained for the remaining

---

[1] Stanley Hall, quoted by Andrews, E. A., False and True Criticism
of the Public School. *Educational Review*, **22** : 258. 1901.
[2] See a very valuable paper by Galloway, B. T. 1902.

physiological necessities.   Setting aside the possible behavior of certain of the bacteria, the physiology of which is at present but little understood, we may state that at the present time all the energy expended by plants and animals, including man, in the physiological processes of their bodies, comes in the first instance from the sunlight, and is stored up by the help of chlorophyll in the final product of photosynthesis — starch.   To have established this fact is an achievement of very great and fundamental importance, both in the realm of pure science and in its relations to the practical questions depending in any way upon the growth of plants.   It becomes, therefore, the duty and privilege of the botanical teacher to bring the pupil into the possession of such knowledge.

A second discovery of botanical science of scarcely less weight is that it is possible, by the manipulation of bacterial organisms, **The Source of** to maintain, or indeed increase the store of nitrogen **Nitrogen.** of the soil.   It has for many years been realized, and that long before the remedy was worked out, that the repeated growth of food plants so depletes the nitrogen content of the soil that it becomes in a few years impossible to raise a profitable crop.   The difficulty has been partially met in an empirical way by methods of crop rotation, clover, or some other suitable leguminous plant, playing the rôle of a constant factor in the rotation series, and also by adding to the soil fertilizers containing nitrogen in some form.   The former method was carried on wherever possible for years in ignorance of the exact conditions, and is of course impossible where, as in some soils of wide extent, the suitable legumes will not grow.   The latter method has its limitations in the supply of artificial fertilizers, since the sources of these cease sooner or later to be productive.   The complete understanding, both theoretical and practical, of the behavior of nitrogenous bacteria offers the only solution of the problem thus presented, and when the time comes, as it will in the near future, that this knowledge is complete, as far as practical demands are concerned, the capacity of the soil for the production of crops may be in-

creased beyond our present dreams.[1]   Furthermore, this is but
one puzzle of a large group concerning the relations of plants to
the soil, all of which are before the student of plant physiology
for solution, and upon which the welfare of man depends.

Again, and closely connected with the general problem of
food supply is that of the improvement of crops by hybridization and selection.   Here, too, we find that at an
early date efforts were made to better the products   **Selection and
Hybridiza-**
of plants, at first unconsciously and later empirically.   **tion.**
Since the fuller understanding of the facts of evolution, our
knowledge has been increased and clarified ; and within the last
five years the activity of students in this direction has increased
in a manner unparalleled in the history of botany.   Some are
going in for the more theoretical sides of the question and some
for the practical sides, and it is remarkable that both classes of
workers are gradually coming together on common ground.

But the problem of crop improvement is not only a general
one, but one requiring a special solution in each locality and
for each kind of crop.   It is not the question of raising the
best wheat, but the best wheat in Minnesota or Dakota.   The
botanist in one locality cannot necessarily answer the question
for one of another, although common knowledge and mutual
experiences contribute to the general end.   For all these
different workers, however, the facts of evolution, and of selection, and of the possible improvements of plant races by
hybridization — fundamental knowledge however imperfect, —
are the basis for study and experiment, and such knowledge is
the common inheritance, to be in ignorance of which is a misfortune individually and socially considered.

It will be observed, however, that the work of the plant
improver rests upon exact knowledge of the form   **Knowledge of**
and relationships of plants.   Indeed, a knowledge   **Plant Forms.**
of classification is fundamental to any broad understanding of

---

[1] See Moore, G. T., Bacteria and the Nitrogen Problem.   *Yearbook
United States Department of Agriculture*, pp. 333–342.   1902.

plant problems and their solution. For a student, therefore, to have any fair conception of these matters, it is not enough to know something of their physiology, but also of their external appearances and relationships, — in short, of the basis of their classification. Such information is not alone useful in the direction above indicated, but also in many other practical matters.

For example, there is no question as to the value of a public park in a crowded city, or indeed in a city of any kind. But suppose, in the planting of a large area of valuable park land that in the absence of a large proportion of exact information concerning plant forms the planting was carried out by guesswork. What would be the result in the waste of time and money and in the inferiority of ultimate results is only partially evident, but it would be too great to justify such a course to any but a very slight extent. But such a problem is the same as that which confronts every one who has even so little as a window garden to plan for; for this much is a considerable task for most people.[1] It is not too much, therefore, to say that the value of the information in the direction of knowing what plants to grow and how to care for them justifies in part the use of botany in education. Of course we must believe that much of such information may well have been obtained in the elementary school. When this is not the case, it should not be neglected in the high school; and in any case the work here should amplify the knowledge gained earlier by the application of broad principles.

Not only is some knowledge of plant relationship valuable and necessary to the understanding to some degree of the importance and significance of the science of botany as related to man, but it is of itself a large and ennobling idea. It is knowledge of the highest type, and the kind which helps the mind to conceptions of nature which are impossible without it. To have information of this kind, coupled with the knowledge

---

[1] Harshberger, J. W., Home and School Window Gardens. *Education*, 18 : 555. May, 1898.

of the method of thought involved, gives us intellectual enjoyment, and in this the informational and æsthetic values of the study overlap.

But plants, while all-important in their relation to food supply, and while the understanding of their structure and physiology is the only sure basis for the development of ability to **Plants are** increase their value to us, are vastly important in **Sources for other Materi-** other directions. In them are the sources of hun- **als than Food.** dreds of materials for the manufactures and for the healing of bodily ills. Among the plants, too, are those by whose agency many of the arts are made possible, such as the preparation of cheese, hemp, and a long list of others; and among the plants, again, are found the organisms which stand in causal relation to many plant and animal diseases. May we not in all truth say that for a boy or girl to pass out of the high school into life, where the real struggle begins, without a fair appreciation of these matters is unfortunate; and may we not believe that such appreciation means the broadening of the outlook and strengthening of the moral and intellectual fibre?

Without unduly prolonging the presentation of these and similar claims, we may point out that the science of botany is in its informational content, both in extent and kind, second to no other science. It touches upon human interests fundamentally at every point, and these are of such a kind that to be ignorant of their relations to botany is to be robbed of that knowledge which throws light upon literature, the arts and the manufactures, and upon the conditions under which alone the human race may prosper. The citizen who is without a fair degree of such knowledge is unable to act intelligently in his relation to public affairs, and the efforts of the more enlightened classes toward the amelioration of the conditions of life can find but scanty support in the citizen of this type. A plan of general education, therefore, which neglects botany neglects one of the subjects which Herbert Spencer describes as having "transcendent value."[1]

---

[1] *Education: Intellectual, Moral, and Physical*, p. 95.

We have adduced two arguments for the introduction of botany into the high-school course, the one from the æsthetic, the second from the informational aspects of bot-

Disciplinary Value of Botany. any. We will now consider a third argument to the same end, — that, namely, which is based upon its disciplinary value. This may be sought in those peculiarities of botanical science as such which differentiate it from other sciences, and in those characteristics of the subject which render it of special service in the presentation of particular topics, what in other words we may call its pedagogical advantages.

It has been shown in the first chapter that those characters of educational import which distinguish a particular branch of science are due to its content of materials, and not to its method of thought, since the latter is common to all sciences and to every-day life.[1] To attempt, therefore, to distinguish between zoölogy and botany in regard to their general values as discipline is unnecessary to our purpose.

But it is, however, also true that a given science may, because of peculiarities inherent in the materials, be more useful than others in illustrating particular phases of the scientific method. It may for the same reason be of special use for the study of certain parts of our knowledge, and therefore for making this knowledge real to the student.

With regard to the first of these considerations it may fairly be claimed that botany lends itself to an especial degree to the

Botany Especially Useful for Experimentation. teacher and student for the study of physiology by the experimental method. The materials are on the whole easier to obtain and to keep in good condition, and illustrate most of the physiological processes of animals and plants equally well. Plants are more easily controlled than animals, and experimentation with them does not offend the sensibilities so easily. Furthermore, the photosynthetic activity of green plants offers a subject for beautifully simple and conclusive experiments which are capable of

---

[1] Huxley, T. H., *Science and Education*, p. 45.

thorough logical control. To be sure the reactions of plants are not usually sudden, and certain phases of the natural history of animals appear to have advantages in this; for without doubt the quick responses of animals relieve the pupil of the exercise of patience, which in plant study is rather more necessary, while on the other hand the slowness of plant reactions undoubtedly gives more opportunity for reflection. The work with animals is, however, on the whole of a less fundamental character, while their richness of variety of mechanisms constitutes a mass of materials which render them in this respect more attractive for study. This is illustrated in the matter of respiration. The mechanical side of the operation in plants is reduced to the simplest conditions, while in animals the mechanics are so varied and complex that to the student's vision the real nature of the operation may frequently become clouded, interesting as the mechanisms are. In plants, however, the anatomical aspect is so simple that the student is thereby brought more directly into contact with the physiological operation. These features of the study of botany are worth mention, not so much to show any absolute advantage over zoölogy, but rather to emphasize the importance of making the most of those parts of the subject which have special advantages.

Again, germinating seeds and young seedlings are most excellently adapted for illustrating various physiological processes by experimentation. Materials are so cheap that the cost is a negligible factor. Fundamental facts about irritability, adaptation, expenditure of energy, need and use of food, and respiration, are susceptible of conclusive proof with the minimum of apparatus and most simple conditions. Some teachers of botany have felt, with a degree of justification, that work with seeds appears to students of the high-school age as rather beneath their dignity. And so, in truth, it is in the hands of a teacher that does not know how to get the most out of experimentation, by enforcing a rigid application of methods of thought as applied thereto. We are inclined to think that when a subject does not compel the respect

Usefulness of Seedlings for Experiment.

of the student it is so because of the teacher's lack of comprehension rather than the fault of the materials. A bit of bark covered with *Pleurococcus* in the hands of such a teacher would probably be as meaningless.

The relation of plants to water is another topic for simple experimentation which offers a splendid field for developing

Relation of Plants to Water. thought power, and further is capable of experiments which may be graded from the very simple to the very difficult, with or without the use of the microscope. This subject has attracted a good deal of attention of late because of the prominent place it has been given in leading text-books, and some very simple and beautiful experiments have been devised. We shall discuss these more in detail farther on ; our object here is again to emphasize the great importance and ease of this phase of botany and its correlated educational advantages.

Another subject, as yet generally neglected but full of meaning, is that of digestion. It is possible with appropriate plant

Digestion. materials to demonstrate clearly with little cost of time and trouble all the essential features of a process, the understanding of which illuminates the knowledge of the analogous process in the human body in a remarkable way.

Not only do plants serve a very useful turn in making simple experiments in fundamental physiology easily possible, but they

Advantages for Morphological Study. offer materials which for the study of homology is unsurpassed, if equalled, by zoölogical materials. It is true enough that plant morphology has become formal and comparatively meaningless. But in recent years the study has become revivified by the emphasis which has been laid on the study of living plants, and by the removal of subjective notions which have been allowed to grow up. Instead of accepting the dictum that plants have a definite number of elemental organs, of which all others are modifications, a formal view handed down from Goethe,[1] we have come

---

[1] The teacher should acquaint himself with modern morphological ideas by reading Goebel's *Organography*, the translation of which is

to understand that these organs are not always present, nor are they the only categories of organs which a plant may have. The distinctions between the older and newer morphology are not, however, absolute, but they certainly stand in contrast when examined,[1] and the most striking feature of the contrast is to be found in the more vital, dynamic conception of plants characteristic of the newer morphology. The advantages offered by plants in the study of morphology are to be found in the ease with which an experimental study of the uses and activities of homologous parts may be made. From such work it is learned that the physiological values of corresponding parts may vary and that corresponding structural differences exist. These facts serve to illustrate the fundamental biological principle that changes of the functions of organs are accompanied by corresponding changes in their form, a conception of the greatest worth in attempting to explain the morphology of organisms.

For the purpose of such experimentation no materials are better adapted than, for example, developing seedlings, in which the homologies are few and apparent, and in which it is easy to find wide variations of habit and function with all possible intermediate conditions. Simple problems of this kind may be followed by others of gradually increasing difficulty, in the solution of which not only are the powers of observation and experiment exercised, but the immediate use of observation in thought is made possible.

In the opening chapter occasion was taken to point out that perhaps the most subtle sociological problem which we have to face is that which, complex and elusive as it is, rests in the first instance upon the simple fact of repro- **Social Prob-** duction. The problem is, what may formal educa- **lem Relating** tion do toward the raising of the moral tone of the community. **to Sex.** It is lamentably true that the matters which concern life in the

---

nearing completion (Oxford University Press), and Spencer's *Principles of Biology.*

[1] See Ganong, W. F., The Cardinal Principles of Morphology. *Botanical Gazette,* 31 : 426–434. June, 1901.

most intimate way, which when understood aright may make for human progress and happiness, may and do make for degradation and misery incalculable and unthinkable. This is not the place for a disquisition upon the social good and evil related to sex, but it is the place to point out that, although the problem is ethical, psychological, and sociological, and therefore does not fall wholly within the province of biology, it nevertheless has its biological aspect, and that this in practice is mainly educational. The word reform is in no great favor with the biologist, and he looks askance at heal-alls, for experience teaches him that betterment is a very slow process ; and the more complex and hidden the evil the slower its eradication. But he and the educator are one in the opinion that there is no safeguard of the mind and body more potent than knowledge. And while this is contested by many who mistake ignorance for innocence, it is not our province here to disabuse them. The educator must, however, reckon with the facts of prejudice and of the force of custom ; and, doing so, he must determine what course of action to take.

In this as in other matters concerning human welfare, we are forced to an issue on the question whether we shall let children grow up in ignorance of certain facts and relations, and, relying upon the chances that things will take care of themselves largely, depend upon general precept and more or less exemplary examples ; or whether we shall make the knowledge which every one should have the common property of youth, placing our faith in the exact and predetermined method of teaching, rather than shirk this responsibility.   It is not for a moment to be doubted that in every so-called practical concern of life the second of these alternatives would be adopted. When we prepare a child for business we give him knowledge of the principles and practices of commerce ; if we wish him to be a good lawyer or physician or a skilful artisan we open to him all the knowledge upon which his success depends. What the State needs, however, above all things is good citizenship, good fatherhood and motherhood, good men and women, but do we in preparation for these give them even the fundamental facts of needful knowledge?

What, then, may botany do to meet this demand? It is plainly the business of biology to teach the fundamentals of the whole scope of the study. On the physiological side, the knowledge of reproduction is fundamental and may not be ignored. Yet to do this without offence to prejudice and good feeling is not so easy as to see the duty of doing it. It becomes necessary to bring the essential facts of reproduction to the attention and understanding of high-school pupils so that they shall view them as a normal part of knowledge. Assuming the personal factor in the teacher to be all that is desired, the materials found among plants are especially well adapted to this end. This can be done in a mixed class with full propriety, and with so much the more normal a result, by approaching the problem through the facts of vegetative reproduction, followed by the sexual method as seen in such a form as *Spirogyra* in which the gametes are practically equivalent. The next step is to the condition of heterogamy, and the more fundamental of secondary sexual characters are then noted. The absence of highly specialized secondary sexual characters makes it easy to avoid any pointed or suggestive discussion, while the main facts are sufficiently obvious.

Botany especially adapted to give Knowledge of Reproduction.

Let it be understood that it is the biological aspect of the matter alone with which the teacher has to do. His duty may be said to be done when he has made this phase of physiology as clear as he is expected to make other facts. For the rest we place our trust in the belief that right and pure ideas will assert themselves, and that the mind of the pupil will be the more frank and open to the exercise of moral living.

We have attempted to show that the value of botany in education is threefold, corresponding to the æsthetic, informational, and disciplinary aspects of the subject.

Summary.

People are more or less interested in plants and their behavior, and get pleasure from their contemplation. But wider knowledge brings more materials for the mind to work with, and a heightened pleasure. As 'pure interest and enjoyment are the mainspring of ·human activity in general, as they are of the naturalist in particular, to increase the interest of the people in botany makes for more pleasurable and better living. The danger of " sentimentalism " is pointed out, as well as the demand that botany shall do its part in the amelioration of human life in the higher sense.

It is further shown that the extent to which the welfare of man is dependent upon the activities of plants is the measure of the informational value of botany. Some of the more important relations are pointed out, among which are the dependence of man ·upon the photosynthetic activity of plants, and upon certain plants which become agents for making available the nitrogen of the air.

Moreover, in the study of botany there are certain disciplinary values, which are peculiar to it in the extent of their practical application. It is especially valuable for the study of fundamental physiology by virtue of the nature of its materials, and lends itself peculiarly well to experimentation. It has certain advantages, due to the nature of its materials, in the study of simple morphology from a physiological aspect. Especially emphasized is its usefulness in discovering to the young student the fundamental facts of reproduction in a clear, unhampered way ; as is also the duty of the teacher in doing this.

For these three general reasons, it is argued that the value of botany is of definite and peculiar value in education, in addition to the general value which it possesses in common with zoölogy and other sciences.

CHAPTER IV

PRINCIPLES DETERMINING THE CONTENT OF A BOTANICAL COURSE

BIBLIOGRAPHY

Bessey, C. E. Discussion reported in Proc. N. E. A., p. 953. 1895.

Bergen, J. Y. Botany as an Alternative in College Admission Re-[quirements. EDUCATIONAL REVIEW, 11: 452. 1896.

Campbell, D. H. Elementary Botany in the High School and College. SCHOOL AND COLLEGE, 1: 211. 1892.

Cook, O. F. On Biological Text-Books and Teachers. SCIENCE, II., 9: 541–545. April, 1899.

Ganong, W. F. Advances in Science Teaching. SCIENCE, II., 9: 96–100. 20 January, 1899.

Ganong, W. F. Suggestions for an Attempt to Secure a Standard College Entrance Option in Botany. SCIENCE, II., 13: 611–616. 19 April, 1901.

Ganong, W. F. The Teaching Botanist. New York. The Macmillan Co. 1899.

Ganong, W. F., and Lloyd, F. E. Third Report of a Committee appointed by the Society for Plant Morphology and Physiology at Baltimore, December 28, 1900, to consider the Formulation of a Standard College Entrance Option in Botany. SCHOOL SCIENCE. May, 1902.

Macbride, T. H. Botany: How Much and When. Read before the Iowa State Teachers' Association. December 28, 1898.

Macmillan, C. Current Methods in Botanical Instruction. EDUCATION, 12: 460. April, 1892.

von Sachs, Julius. History of Botany. Oxford, 1890.

Underwood, L. M. The Study of Botany in High Schools. JOURNAL OF PEDAGOGY, 9: No. 2. April, 1898. (Contr. Dept. Bot. Col. Univ. 144.)

Wager, H. The Teaching of Botany in Schools. SCHOOL WORLD, 3: 422. 1901.

Botany for Schools. AMERICAN JOURNAL OF EDUCATION, 4: 168–175. 1829.

IN the foregoing chapter we have sought for botany a place in secondary education for the broad reasons of its æsthetic, informational, and disciplinary values. It becomes our duty, assuming that botany shall have such a place, to determine the principles underlying the selection of the content of the course. That this content shall be, in detail, the same for all high schools we would hardly claim, although we give adherence to the view that a generally accepted objective standard is desirable for several reasons.

Botany must establish its right to a part in secondary education equally with other branches of study. Those studies **Value of an** which are best established have generally accepted **Objective** standards of the quality and quantity of work to be **Standard.** expected. Although the mere acceptance of such a uniform standard does not establish the educational value and position of a study, at least no study which claims for itself such a place can be independent of the necessity of establishing a standard. The value of a uniform standard, then, in this regard is to be found in the general agreement thereby established as to what botany has in it of general educational value. A uniform standard is, in essence, a statement of what general knowledge botany contains which may be regarded as the **A Statement** best intellectual inheritance within its limits, and **of Intellectual** what therefore is best for general knowledge and **Inheritance.** culture. If any subject has a content of this nature it ought to be possible to determine what it is, although it is not necessarily an easy task, since the relative newness of a subject and consequent unformed general opinion are obstacles, in some degree, to the solution of the question. Nevertheless, botanists on the one hand and educators in general on the other hand have cause for congratulation that this task has been partially done, and the results have been embodied in a report, now accessible to all interested, upon a college entrance option which represents an aggregate of opinion derived from many and wide sources.[1] The contents of this report will receive consideration later.

That this result is, in a peculiar sense, of very great value to botany as a science on the one hand and to education in gen-

---

[1] Ganong, W. F., and Lloyd, F. E. Third Report of a Committee, etc.

eral on the other is evident from the fact that botany has had a very significant history in the annals of education.[1] Its history is unique in the circumstance that of all the phases of botanical study which are necessary and useful in education, but one has received any great amount of attention, to the practical exclusion of the rest without making good the usurpation by the use of the right scientific methods. We refer to the fact that classi- **Great Need in Botany of such a Uniform Agreement.** fication of the higher plants has been until recently the be-all and end-all of botanical study. What the position and value of this part of botany is in education we shall discuss beyond. Here it is sufficient to point out the result for which this singular state of affairs is in large part responsible. This is, that botany is usually thought to be a mere æsthetic exercise, suitable only for girls. This idea we can trace back in Amer- ican education as far as 1829, when a contributor to a lead- ing journal of education[2] wrote that botany is peculiarly fitted for girls' schools, and is admirably adapted to the tastes, feelings, and capacities of females, " as is demonstrated by the fact that the majority of our botanists are females." Ludicrous as this idea seems to those whose experience has taught them that as for difficulty there is nothing to choose between botany and zoölogy, it is nevertheless a real and not imaginary state of affairs that botany to-day is reaping a harvest from the dissemi- nation of this impression. Both such misconception and con- sequent one-sided and perfunctory teaching, if it can be called teaching, have been the cause for the widespread notion that botany is a sort of play, with a quasi-scientific aspect, reserved for those intellectually incompetent persons who with idle time on their hands have nothing better to do than to acquire the simulacra of knowledge. It is this sort of thing that has won the undisguised contempt of people with wits, and we would beseech those who have the issues of sound education at heart to continue the lashings which from time to time they

---

[1] Macmillan, C., '92.
[2] *American Journal of Education*, 4: 168-175. 1829.

have bestowed upon those who take such a superficial view of botanical education.[1]

It is frequently acknowledged by disinterested persons that they hold this unfortunate opinion about botany, and it is clear that they got it in their early education when the extent of their efforts at intellectual work based upon plants consisted in picking a few flowers to pieces and groping about for suitable names to attach to them.

In view, therefore, of such facts, and facts they are, it is plainly the duty of those who are responsible for the credit of botanical teaching that an end shall be put to this anomalous condition of things. This can be done by insistence upon proper training of teachers, and by presenting to school authorities and to the public at large, a carefully considered, generally accepted formulation of what they believe to be the true content of botany for secondary education. The full understanding and recognition of such a formula is the great desideratum of botany at present, but one which, the facts warrant us to believe, will be satisfied in the near future. It will then remain for the teachers throughout the country to live up to the standard.

Furthermore, a third reason for the formulation of a standard in botany is seen in the necessity of arranging a graded series of studies in science from the kindergarten to the college.[2]

The sciences in elementary schools take the form of nature study, and as such should contribute an adequate preparation for the work of the high schools. There should, **Need of Graded Work in Science.** therefore, be no profitless duplication of studies, either in materials or in the nature of their study. If, then, a definite standard of what shall be the botany of the secondary school is generally accepted, and if such a standard gives detailed information as to the scope and nature of the work, the remaining problem is to do those things in elemen-

---

[1] An excellent editorial touching this and similar conceptions appears in the *New York Times'* Saturday Review of Art and Literature for May 31, 1902.

[2] Ganong, W. F., Advances in Science Teaching.

tary education which shall serve at once its aims, and as preparation for the more definite study of the separate sciences in the high school. Thus may the demand for a uniform, graded course of instruction be satisfied, and the practical equivalence of botany and of science with other fields of study be brought up to the now generally acknowledged theoretical equivalence.

Another value of formulating a standard of this kind is the means it affords for the mutual information of botanists and teachers as to each other's views. In this way the differences of opinion are argued about, experiences compared and all possible facts bearing upon the subject are brought out. Some differences of opinion are thus removed, while others are justified and remain as a goad to further research into the reasons for them. There is necessarily some compromise, but concessions should not be made for the sake of peace. Differences should be looked at honestly and removed only upon a clear understanding of the problems they represent, and upon the mutual agreement that the problems are fairly solved. Such a standard serves also to hold before intending teachers an index of the amount and quality of their teaching. It will forbid one-sidedness both in method and materials, and what is still more important, it will demand adequate preparation for teaching, without which all attempt at a betterment of botany in secondary education will be of little avail. This sort of service has been done from time to time by thoroughly good text-books for secondary schools. The authors of these books have been men of reputation and authority and with genuine interest in elementary education in botany. Concerning such works we shall have more to say.

But such standards as are generally accepted are, because of their formulated character, not without their drawbacks, due largely, however, to a misconception of their uses. There is the tendency toward the making of text-books which contain just what the standard calls for, and with it the tendency to use these books in cramming

Value of a Standard in Unifying Views.

Aid in Education of Teachers.

Dangers of Accepted Standards.

for examinations. The work then becomes mechanical. Things are remembered, but no point of view or method of thought is gained. These bad results have been evident for a long time in England, where the examination system has attained a high degree of false importance. The danger in America is not, however, very great, since the standard as such need not be known except to teachers, and since the numbers of those who qualify for entrance to college, while constantly on the increase, will never constitute a very large proportion of those who have to remain content with high-school work. The danger may be further offset by a thoroughgoing effort to shape the questions of examinations in such a way as to make the candidate use his knowledge in answering them, rather than to call for a categorical answer of a number of facts held in the memory. Such boards of examiners as the College Examination Board of the Middle States and Maryland have it in their prerogative and power to do a great deal toward enforcing the right kind of instruction by insisting upon the careful formulation of questions to the end of calling forth the best thought-effort of the student. This is true also of the work of the teacher. It is of the utmost importance that he shall be skilled in questioning, in doing which he should always keep in mind the principle that, at every turn, the pupil shall be compelled so to arrange his facts that they shall stand in clear logical relation to his generalizations and inferences. This applies to the conducting of laboratory work as well as to the quiz. We shall return again to the form and uses of questions in botanical work.

Importance of Proper Questions.

For such a large country as America, again, it is not possible, and if it were, it would be unprofitable to expect the acceptance of a detailed standard, for the reason that the conditions here and there are widely different. And obviously a great hindrance is to be found in the wide difference of floras. The teacher should, however, know the flora of his own region, and should use the materials available for study, rather than attempt to use those

Possible Suppression of Individuality.

forms which may be mentioned in the books. Again, in attempting to live closely to standard there would inevitably be some impatience at an artificial hard-and-fast criterion. So long as teachers, too, are scientists, as it is to be hoped they always will be, so long will there be a large amount of individuality in their teaching. Too many detailed instructions and demands tend to curtail the teacher's freedom of action, and individuality is likely to be lost, a condition which is earnestly to be avoided.

While not closing our eyes to the possible disadvantage of such an arrangement, we see in a general standard very definite values which more than compensate for the dangers. These are (1) in the interest of the science itself which "as a study has become low in public opinion, good public opinion,"[1] by making it plain to all who have interest in the matter that a good course in botany is possible and what the content of such a course should be. (2) As a means of unifying opinion, and of bringing that degree of uniformity which must obtain in a course from the kindergarten to the college before any study can rightly claim a permanent place in a system of education. Thus, in fact, may botany be shown to be on a par with other studies, behind which it must not fall as a means of training and culture in the widest sense. A standard is necessary, also, in bringing the colleges into closer touch with the high school, and so contributing to the uniformity of education in general. (3) A generally accepted standard is also of great value in educating teachers, and it tends, through them, to bring teaching to a uniformly high standard of excellence in quality and quantity.

The formulation of an optimum standard is, however, one thing, and its general acceptance in the fullest sense another. No one having the real interests of education at heart will either attempt to force the adoption or will himself adopt a standard without seeking for its rationale. We have held, moreover, that it is only

General Principles underlying Course in Botany necessary.

---

[1] Ganong, W. F., Advances in Science Teaching.

in a large way that such may be received in a big country with wide differences in available materials and in the individuality of teachers. What, therefore, is of more fundamental importance is to reach a general agreement upon principles which shall be kept in mind in planning and carrying out a course in botany. If such principles can be formulated and are generally accepted, general agreement on the content of the course will follow naturally. What, then, are these principles? We shall state what appears to be the answer to this question as a series of propositions which in order to clearness and mutual understanding are separated from each other.

The first of these is based upon the fact that in a very wide and real sense the high school is the college of the people. Only a very small proportion will ever find further **Botany in the High School must be Botany for the Masses.** opportunities for study than it supplies; and of those who do enjoy further opportunity for education, few will continue to pursue the study of botany. It follows, then, that whatever is done in botany in the high school must be planned and carried out first of all and principally for the high-school pupil, and only secondarily for the candidate for the college. In the course in botany, therefore, the pupil must find those elements of the study which will fit him better for his struggle with circumstances than he would be fitted without it. Such a course must, therefore, be regarded not as training in order to make botanists, or to pass an examination, but it must have as its aim the opening of the mind to the realm of botanical fact and thought, so as to equip the average person with those qualities and abilities which will buttress his character and make him a more intelligent and thoughtful citizen. This is to be compassed by adherence to other principles to be mentioned, of which one is, that the **Present and Permanent Interest.** choice of topics and materials shall include those which will contribute to the present and permanent interest of the student. No good can be accomplished by a study in which there is not some real, live interest on the part of the pupil, and this is especially true of those

studies which do not have the inertia derived from long acceptance and from obvious usefulness. Children may not like to
study arithmetic, but they know that it must be studied and
they do not question very much why. But botany is in a different situation. It depends for its success as a factor in education very largely on its appeal to the emotions and reason.
How this appeal may be made effective is not subject to direction, such as we may put down in print. It depends upon the
skill of the instructor, and upon his own attitude in large part.
Some things, however, may be said concerning the matter.
Botany must illuminate every-day life, and must therefore deal
with familiar things [1] in a way which will raise them above the
common level. People should see in a common plant those
things which call out pleasurable intellectual association ; it must
be full of meaning and not an excuse for a terminology or
nomenclature. By inference, that botanical teaching
which does not give to the student a point of view **Importance of a Point of View.**
must within a large measure fail. Facts fade from
the memory, especially facts which have been gained without a
point of view which correlates them ; but a viewpoint holds its
place. It is in its own essence a very part of mental life, and
once established will remain for all time. No real, profitable,
permanent interest may be had otherwise. If the exercise of
botany which happens to concern itself with leaves, takes up, for
example, the shapes of leaves, and the student is expected to
interest himself in fitting the various forms to a terminology, he
may actually be coaxed into a sort of interest in some cases.
Even assuming that he does, it is quite evident that the terminology of leaf shapes is not going to be of any permanent interest but to a trifling few, because it is of little use except in
technical descriptive botany. It is a good thing to know the
names of a few elementary shapes, such as square, round, oval,
and the like, because we use them often in daily life. But
hastate, spatulate, repand, etc., are of too limited service.

---

[1] Cook, O. F., On Biological Text-Books and Teachers.

The reasoning which would persuade us that the application of exact terms to the corresponding objects justifies the use of botany of this kind is just as applicable to the exact description by terminology of any objects whatever.[1] A small amount of terminology is useful, but there are so many other things that are more so that we cannot justify the amount formerly supposed to be of value. If, however, a leaf is viewed as a living, working organ of a living, active plant; if it is shown by experiment that in order to do this work certain conditions are necessary or else the work is not performed; if it can be demonstrated that in the absence of leaves other organs may become adapted to do the work of leaves, or again that the peculiar power of the leaf is lost altogether in a parasitic plant, — then the form of a leaf is seen to mean something, and the manner of its workings to throw light upon its structure. If it is at all possible for a person to get a point of view, this is a way to do it, and a very good way, as many teachers will attest. If the mind works in any degree after such experiences, it will tend to ask similar questions about other leaves; and the effort, if any is made, on seeing a new and differently shaped leaf, will not be to get a name for its shape, but an interpretation in dynamic terms of its work and usefulness to the plant. The mental operation would tend toward the demand for an experiment, to test the validity of the thought. The person would get just as much — or rather more — pleasure out of mental operations of this kind than out of the other kind, and the information gained would react on the mind to stimulate it to more difficult tasks· On the one hand, there would be the constant and increasingly difficult task of getting names; on the other, there would be new problems to solve and greater power to solve them. The choice is evident, if our premises are correct. The course which is not arranged and carried out so as to give a point of view is insufficient; and the truth of this is quite independent of any topics or phase of the study whatsoever.

---

[1] See also Campbell, D. H., *Elementary Botany in High School and College.*

" Pupils must be interested in the plant as a *living thing*, pushing its way amidst fierce competition in a more or less hostile environment," [1] and it is this thought which has justified the success which has attended the teaching of such men as Spalding, Ganong, Atkinson, and Bergen, and which underlies the oft-repeated claim that botany, as well as the other sciences, should develop the spirit of inquiry. [2] But a spirit of inquiry cannot be identified with a desire for descriptive names, be they applied to things or processes ; it is entirely dependent upon a point of view. If the teacher, therefore, find that he cannot illuminate a particular part of the work with a point of view, let him drop it and take hold of something else which he can. And then he would better spend his spare moments, if he has any, in finding out what may be the matter with his knowledge on this particular subject.

We pass on to consider another principle, namely, that which holds that of the content of a subject the very best shall constitute the basis of the course. The educator is always confronted with the practical problem of making the best use of a small amount of time.

The Best of its Content in a Botany Course

He frequently finds himself compelled to discriminate between the more and the less important, and to lay aside relatively meaningless detail. It is his duty to work over the subject, and select those phases of it which shall best represent to the student the whole science. The student on his side may justly claim to be made aware of his birthright; to know what the great students of botany have determined and made sure for the future. " Every science should give its students a general view of its subject-matter." [3] Certain implications follow this principle, adherence to which forbids the use of one part of botany to the exclusion of the rest ; it forbids, too, that the

---

[1] Bergen, J. Y., Botany as an Alternative in College Admission Requirements.

[2] Wager, H., The Teaching of Botany in Schools. *School World*, 3 : 422. 1901

[3] Cook, O. F., On Biological Text-Books and Teachers.

teacher should, because of his own learning and interests, ignore
the necessity of weighing carefully the importance of the different parts of the subject.   He must, if he have an honest attitude
toward the needs of the student, examine the claims of all our
knowledge, and determine what are those matters which may be
used in secondary education which will give the right conception of what botany deals with.   It is evident from the history
of the teaching of botany that this has not always been done.
At one time taxonomy, or rather flower analysis, occupies the
field to the exclusion of everything else ; and when a reform
sweeps over us this in turn is excluded and comparative
morphology claims attention.   The pendulum which has done
figurative duty for so long swings to extremes, and teachers run
after new if not false gods in the guise of fads.   When a science
such as botany is new in the educational field, this is not an
unqualified evil.   It educates the teacher, and he needs it.   He
who follows a fad for a time, and who thereby learns, may get
new ideas and different points of view.   He is therefore better
off than the teacher who is so much in a rut that he is unwilling
to arouse himself to get out of it.

But while we may determine and agree upon what for education are the best parts of botany, we may, nevertheless, not
thereby be able to settle their relative importance.
in a Well-
Proportioned   To the scientific botanist each part may be equally
View,
important with the others, while to the average
person one part may be of much greater importance, either
from the viewpoint of what is good for him or of what he himself wants.   It is clearly true, however, that as educators we
must endeavor to see what of discipline, what of information,
and what of culture value each part may have ; and the student,
on the other hand, must be allowed to see, not alone what the
parts of botanical study are, but how they are related to each
other.[1]   What is needed, therefore, is a course in botany of
which all its parts are represented in proportion to their signifi-

[1] Bessey, C. E.   Proc. N. E. A., p. 953.   1895.   Ganong, *The Teaching Botanist*, p. 3.

cance as knowledge and as discipline, and that these shall be so presented as to appear to the student to be what they really are, namely, the interrelated parts of a whole. To present the physiology of plants with- *and as Properly Related in the Whole,* out showing its importance in the interpretation of form; to introduce classification without showing the bearing of morphology and geographical distribution upon our understanding of it and without presenting therewith the idea of evolution, — to do thus is to make it impossible for a student to get a fair understanding of what botanical study is or the real significance of any of its parts. " If this be admitted, it follows that the optimum course in botany must treat the science, not by divisions, but synthetically, must include training in the elements of anatomy, morphology, physiology, ecology, and classification, and cannot be limited to any one or two of them."[1] This principle, which has been accepted notably by Spalding, Bergen, and Ganong, has been ably defended by Ganong, and has attained a considerable recognition in the actions of the Society for Plant Morphology and Physiology,[2] The New York State Science Teachers' Association,[3] The College Entrance Examination Board of the Association of Colleges and Preparatory Schools of the Middle States and Maryland,[4] and by many botanists. What of the content of the divisions of botany, and in what way they may be co-ordinated in such a course, described by Ganong as synthetic, will occupy our attention beyond.

We are led by the logic which has guided us thus far to another step in the argument, in holding that, just *and the* as the parts of the subject must be presented in *Whole in Relation to other* their interrelation, so also should the teacher *Knowledge.* show that botany as a whole does not stand alone, com-

[1] Ganong, *The Teaching Botanist*, p. 3.
[2] The Report which was adopted by this Society was first printed in 1901, and a third revised edition appeared in *School Science* in May, 1902.
[3] See the Proceedings for December, 1901. *Univ. State New York Bulletin* 269, October, 1902, p. 736.
[4] College Entrance Examination Board, etc. Document 8.

pletely separated from other knowledge and from human experience.[1] While botany is indebted to other sciences for much which has enabled us to understand plants, it is nevertheless true also that the sciences owe much to botany. Pfeffer's record of an error, in connection with other things, led van t' Hoff to his splendid discovery that the three fundamental laws for gas pressure are applicable to the osmotic pressure of solutions. This is but one instance of many which might be mentioned in illustration did space permit.

The relations of botany to zoölogy are too obvious to need discussion, and the value of certain phases of botany in helping the pupil to understand animal physiology has already been alluded to and needs no further amplification. Its relations to human welfare in the practical application of botanical principles to arts and manufactures have, too, been discussed; and the importance of all these relations, which show that botany does not stand alone, but occupies an equally dignified and important position co-ordinate with and related to other knowledge, should not be overlooked in education, but from time to time should be pointed out in a clear way by the teacher.

The principles which have first been presented above, although not without their bearing upon the method of presentation of the subject, have their chief function in guiding the teacher in the selection of topics constituting the course. We shall now present three other guiding principles, having to do chiefly with method. It will be seen that these are not co-ordinate with those principles already advanced, or exclusive of them, but are in fact implied; yet it serves a useful purpose to treat them separately, by way of emphasizing what has been said in the earlier part of the present chapter.

The first of these is that the dignity of the subject must be made evident, and this to boys as well as to girls. There is a feeling among some eminent teachers that certain prevalent

---

[1] ". . . The division of science into separate subjects is due merely to a convenient mental abstraction. . . ." Pfeffer, W., *Physiology of Plants*, p. 6.

methods of approach and presentation of botany do not command the respect of high-school students, especially boys, and strenuous objections have been raised to such **The Dignity of the Subject must be Apparent.** methods on these grounds. It is therefore really pertinent to our ends to give attention to this very matter, the failure to do which has brought botany into disrepute. This condition, while in part due to the exceedingly one-sided choice of subject-matter, is in no small measure to be charged up to the inability of teachers to bring out the powerful aspects of botany. What, then, may be done to avoid the imputation in the minds of pupils that botany is beneath their serious consideration ? Certainly this : the work must make strenuous demands on them. The study must be difficult enough so that pupils may not get the impression that they can easily do it all. In academic parlance it must not be a ' snap.' If it is regarded as such it is certainly no fault of the subject. We would even maintain that, granting the hindrance of prejudice on the part of pupils, it makes little difference where you begin and what you deal with, their respect may be commanded if the teacher has knowledge enough and knows how to handle it. What is more, it should be the aim of the teacher to make the study of such a subject as botany or zoölogy do duty, in some part at least, for plain, old-fashioned discipline. One great practical value of the laboratory teaching in education lies in the possibility of doing this, because of the responsibility it places on the student to do things for himself. He must be in a measure his own monitor. He must realize that if he would do something he must do it independently and not under compunction.

Independently ordered good behavior is therefore a great end to be sought after for the student. But how can this be attained unless botany commends itself to the respect of the student as worthy of his serious thought? We hold that unless this condition is secured the botany is, as the student comes under such circumstances to believe, not worth while, and no motive is then present for earnest endeavor on his part.

But simply to make it difficult it is patent is not enough. It must have the right content. What this is, we have already **Historical** endeavored to show, may be determined by other **Allusion.** principles. Again, it serves the same useful purpose to give the student some idea of the character of the men whose lives have been spent in the pursuit of botany, of the extent and nature of their studies, of the difficulties which they overcame, and the effect of their studies upon modern thought. This gives a human touch which brings it home to a thoughtful student, and may reach, if anything may, the sympathy and respect of a careless or indifferent one. The teacher should do this in an effective way, in connection with the appropriate topics, and to this end a study of von Sachs' *History of Botany* will be good preparation. By means of historical allusion the subject is viewed with a perspective which heightens its force and interest, and commands deeper respect. And it may further be said in support of the value of this method that the culture viewpoint demands that people should not be ignorant of the chief facts about the great leaders of thought in botany any more than elsewhere. Such men are Sprengel, Leeuwenhoek, Linnæus, Robert Brown, Hofmeister, Sachs, Pasteur, Darwin, and Asa Gray. If example has any force, if ideals as exemplified in the work of such men have any meaning for us, surely it is not amiss to give students some idea of the value of their lives and thought.

And this leads us to the second principle which shall guide us in the selection of method. It is this. The study of botany **Respect for** has a direct bearing upon human life and welfare, **Human Life.** and it should be made to heighten their significance to the average mind. An imperfect understanding of these matters is far too widespread. Ill-mannered people who ignore the rights of others mingle with the well-intentioned to form a throng of those vicious and prejudiced and ignorant who stand in the way of human progress and comfort. It is the business of formal education to combat these by the enlightenment of their minds and those of their children. In this botany can and must play its part. The teacher, therefore, must set before himself the task of arranging his knowledge so that his methods of teaching will set these matters in their true light. One part of plant study is especially important in this regard, namely, that dealing with bacteria, for it is in connection with the knowledge of these forms that the mutual obligations of people may be peculiarly emphasized. It is this lesson, therefore, rather than the morphological aspect of bacteria, which is of so great moment in elementary work.

Finally, the method of the teacher in presenting a course in botany shall be such as to exemplify, at all points, the method of thought by which the knowledge of botany has been gained. "Every science should give its stu-

Method of Teaching shall exemplify Method of Thought.

dents an introductory acquaintance with its methods of investigation."[1] We have sufficiently for our purpose already examined the nature of this method, which has been described by Huxley as "*trained and organized common sense.*"[2] Cook (*loc. cit.*) has held that to this end "it is desirable to make a careful dissection and thorough microscopic examination of at least one animal or plant"; but, while this may be justified on other grounds, we maintain that it is not what is studied but rather how the course as a whole is carried out that gains the end desired. One exercise or one dissection is not enough to enforce the whole lesson of method of thought. Granting that a complete and thorough dissection of a plant is to be desired, yet a teacher who failed to see the importance of exemplifying the method of thought at all times would easily undo the good effects of a few days' work. The task, therefore, is to bring each part of the work into its relations with all the rest. An "inexorable logic" should bind it all together and make it a unified whole, and this should depend chiefly upon that which the student has himself been able to observe. This is no easy task, and calls for earnest devotion to a high ideal of teaching.

---

[1] Cook, O. F., On Biological Text-Books and Teachers.
[2] *Science and Education*, p. 45.

In the present chapter, the values of an objective standard for a course in botany have been discussed and its dangers pointed out. The formulation of a course in botany, and therefore of such a standard, must be based upon broad and accepted principles. These are as follows.

The botany of the high school must be botany for the masses. It must therefore make not only for their immediate but for their permanent interest. To this end a point of view is necessary rather than the learning of facts, an "intelligent appreciation of a few truths rather than an ill-digested mass of facts." A course in botany must offer the best of its content, arranged quantitatively so as to give to the student a well-proportioned view. The facts must therefore be given in their proper relation to each other and to the whole, and the whole in its relation to other knowledge.

Certain important principles which it is conceived should influence the teacher's method have also received attention. These are: (1) That the dignity of the subject must be made apparent to the pupil, and the means to this end have been presented; (2) the course shall be carried out also to the result that people shall have an increased respect for human life and welfare. Finally, the method of the teacher shall be such as to exemplify at every point the intellectual processes used in acquiring a knowledge of the science.

CHAPTER V

THE VARIOUS TYPES OF BOTANICAL COURSES

BIBLIOGRAPHY

Atkinson, G. F.   Methods of Teaching Botany in the Secondary Schools.   Univ. State of New York.   REGENT'S BULLETIN.   No. 42. August, 1897.

Atkinson, G. F.   Method of Teaching Botany in the Secondary Schools.   ASA GRAY BULLETIN, 6: 102–105.   December, 1898.

Barnes, C. R.   The Progress and Problems of Plant Physiology. Presidential Address, Section G. Proc. A. A. A. S. 1899.   SCIENCE, II., 10: 316.   1899.

Barnes, C. R.   Plant Physiology in the High School.   SCHOOL SCIENCE, 2: 320–324.   December, 1902.

Beal, W. J.   How Shall a Young Person Study Botany?   Proc. 5th Annual Conf., New York State Science Teachers Association.   December, 28–29, 1900.

Brendel, F.   Historical Sketch of the Science of Botany in North America from 1635–1840.   AMERICAN NATURALIST, 13: 754–771.   December, 1897.

Campbell, D. H.   Elementary Botany in High School and College. SCHOOL AND COLLEGE, 1: 211.   April, 1892.

Coulter, J. M.   The Future of Systematic Botany.   Proc. A. A. A. S.   SCIENCE, 18: 127.   4 Sept., 1891.

Everman, B. E.   The Teaching of Biology in the Public School. PLANT WORLD, 1: 119.   1897–1898.

Farlow, W. G.   Biological Teaching in Colleges.   POPULAR SCIENCE MONTHLY, 28: 581.   March, 1886.

Galloway, B. T.   Applied Botany: Retrospective and Prospective. SCIENCE, II., 16: 49–59.   11 July, 1902.

Ganong, W. F.   The Teaching Botanist.   New York.   The Macmillan Co.   1899.

Ganong, W. F.   Cardinal Principles of Morphology.   BOTANICAL GAZETTE, 31: 426–434.   June, 1901.

Goebel, K.   Organography.   Oxford.   Clarendon Press.   1900.

Lloyd, F. E.   The Course in Botany in the Horace Mann School. TEACHERS' COLLEGE RECORD, 2: No. 1.   January, 1901.

Macmillan, C.   Current Methods in Botanical Instruction.   EDUCATION, 12: 460.   April, 1892.

Robinson, B. L.   The Problems and Possibilities of Systematic Botany.   SCIENCE, II., 14: 465.   1901.

Thiselton-Dyer, W. T.   Address before the Biological Section, British Association for the Advancement of Science. September, 1888.

. **Underwood, L. M.**   The Study of Botany in High Schools. JOURNAL OF PEDAGOGY, 11 : No. 2. April, 1898.

Underwood, L. M. The Last Quarter. A Reminiscence and an Outlook. Address of the Retiring President, Botanical Society of America, June, 1900. SCIENCE, II. 12 : 161–170. 3 August, 1900.

The various Text-Books, the titles of which appear in Chapter X.

HAVING previously explained to the student the value of botany for education as regards its æsthetic, informational, and disciplinary phases, and having enlarged upon some general principles for which, underlying as they do the determination of the content of the course, we seek general acceptance, we now take up for special consideration the different types of courses in botany. These will be examined in their historical sequences, and an effort will be made to place a just estimate upon their relative values in elementary education.

The phase of botany which has for the longest period been dominant both in secondary education and in the college is

Descriptive Botany. Flower Analysis.   descriptive botany, especially that part of it dealing with the flowering plants. It is the merit or rather the lack of merit of this, taken alone for the purposes of education, that has formed for the most part the issue of the discussions in recent years on botanical teaching. The course in botany of the kind to which we refer consisted, in its better aspect, of a preliminary study of the more obvious morphological features of the flowering plants, with especial stress laid upon those structures which serve best in following up diagnostic descriptions of plants which were to be collected, "analyzed," pressed, and mounted. Sometimes the student was required to make a floral diagram ; more often to fill in ruled sheets calling for the insertion of technical terms descrip-

Content of this Kind of Course.   tive of the various parts of the plant. The number of plants to be collected and named, this representing a criterion of success or failure, was usually fifty. In some cases something was said about the functions of the parts, by way of information, but nothing of this kind was ever subjected to the test of experimentation. Little or nothing was said about the cryptogams, a few ferns excepted; and when perchance one or more of these intruders appeared in the herbarium, the ruled blank accompanying it seemed to lack adaptability, with the results that a name was obtained by hook or by crook and attached to it, but no notion of the real nature of the plant was gained. It was an unfortunate outcast from good society. This, briefly stated, was the content of such a course. Whether, as education, it was relatively good or bad was a fortuitous circumstance, and dependent upon the chance that the teacher really knew some botany — the rare exception.

In defence of this kind of work it is claimed that it brings the pupil into acquaintance with plants about him, or, as one has put it, "to know plants." What is generally meant To Know is that, when one walks through the fields or woods Plants. he is able to remark "Here is *Ranunculus bulbosus*," or "There is *Sanguinaria canadensis*," to which may be added some observations about the charm or beauty of the flowers, or about the possession of an herbarium specimen. We take purposely the worst meaning, because it embodies more exactly the issue, and because this kind of thing actually meets the conception in the minds of many of "knowing a plant." Laying aside the æsthetic factor as being of no more or less importance than a like interest in any other object, and regarding the herbarium possession as having no significance except as possibly having involved some training in neatness and orderliness — which is not peculiar to botany — what does the ability to reel off the names of a few plants signify? To be sure it has a fictitious value in that it looks learned, and may impress the hearer who is cheated by high-sounding names. Further than this, it implies nothing of related knowledge. The person may have made once a formal description in arbitrary terminology of the various organs of a score of plants, but the facts gleaned stand alone and unrelated to any others. Nothing is known about the relation of one plant to another or to other organisms, or its devel-

opment, or the conditions of its existence. In short, the whole
thing is an act of memory without the use of the reason, and
has the same false value that remembering what "the fabled
labors of a fabled demi-god" has. It is not even an orna-
ment to a cultured person.

This ability to recall names and terms means that the place
of the real has been usurped by the unreal; names have been
made to replace related facts. The value of nomenclature has been misconceived. As Farlow has
put it, pupils "think they have comprehended the
thing when they christen it a high-sounding name."[1]   One
cannot therefore be said to " know a plant " when one knows its
name, any more than he can be said to know a man when he
knows no more about him than this.   And that people generally regard with open-eyed admiration a person who can dis-
play a memory for names — especially " Latin names " — is a
proof of the necessity that education should be rid of those
methods which tend to preserve the integrity of that portion of
the people which can be fooled all the time.

**Names in-
stead of
Things.**

But because it has happened that the teaching of botany
which has lacked educational merit has been confined chiefly to
descriptive botany, it does not follow that this part of the subject has in itself no value in a course.   Any portion of a science
may be poorly taught and thereby condemnation may be
brought upon it.   It will therefore be pertinent to look carefully
into the objections which may be urged against the way in which
descriptive botany has been handled.   Thus may we profit by
the defects of the past and learn how to improve the teaching
of the future.

The essence of the biological method is comparison.   To
get ideas of morphology we must compare plants and their
organs.   To get ideas of relationship we must compare.   To
arrive at the general idea of physiology we must compare the
behavior of organisms.   But what has the descriptive botany
of elementary education been?   It has been an examination

---

[1] *Popular Science Monthly*, **28** : 581.   1885.

and collection of a mass of facts without organizing these by a method of thought. If comparison was indulged in at all it was comparison of a plant with its de- Lack of Comparison.
scription in a book.[1] If the plant did not fit the book it was forced to do so, and if the "student" failed in this, so much the worse for the plant. As a result this study of botany — as we call it by courtesy — has magnified symbols rather than the things symbolized, and has helped to strengthen the reverence for books and authority already too strong. The fifty more or fewer plants examined in this way have been " so many isolated objects that practically have nothing to do with each other, and are simply to be labeled and filed away." [2] Hunting for a name by means of a key is sometimes hard business. The plant, after all, will not be forced into a really satisfactory and orderly set of pigeon holes, so that the most strenuous part of the process — keying — has usually been commenced in the index, thanks to the happy circumstance of knowing the common name. Evasion of work has been the aim of the pupil, and what little good might have come from honest effort has been avoided. False notions of what botany is and is good for have followed in the wake of this march in the dark, and the earnest teacher has to face the remarks of good students to the effect that they would rather get their botany from zoölogists than from botanists! If this really indicates the true condition of botanical teaching in our best schools to-day — which it does only in part — then it is a very dullard who does not see his duty.

Again the examination of a few plants in the once prevalent fashion of carefully avoiding the hard and small ones, means a bit of detailed information of a few plants instead of a knowledge of principles. One of the big ideas which a student should get from the study of plant forms is Knowledge of a few Plants.
that of evolution. He should have an opportunity of looking

---

[1] Campbell, D. H., *Elementary Botany in High School and College*, p. 212.

[2] Campbell, D. H., *loc. cit.*

into the kind of evidence which underlies this idea. The study of classification must be so ordered that it shall not be thought of as an end in itself, — a cataloguing system for the disposal of objects, — but as an expression of our ideas of plant relationships as a body of evidence for the acceptance of a general formula. Of greater value than a prejudiced notion that a plant must fit a description is the notion that plants are organisms which do not stand still. If the student does not get some such notions as these he has not been done justice and the science is improperly represented. The principles of biological education set forth in a previous chapter are pretty much all violated. The kind of thing which has passed for education in botany has not contributed as it should have to broad training and therefore to good citizenship, and has probably deterred many a person from choosing botany as a profession. "While the high school is not for the training of specialists, it certainly is not to kill them off." [1]

Another great defect of this obsolescent method of presenting botany, expressed in part in the preceding paragraph, is **Static Point of View.** the utterly false conception which grows up in the mind as to the nature of the plant. It is the conception that plants are formal, changeless objects made up of a definite number of morphological elements which, as modified organs, appear somewhat differently in different plants. Thus, according to this idea, the flowering plants have the morphological elements of root, stem, leaf, and hair, and whatever else a plant may appear to have, or whatever of these it does not have, it is necessarily made up of these elements and these **Rather than the Dynamic.** alone.[2] The idea that some plants possess none of these organs, and that all of these organs must have, at some time and in some way, *arisen anew* is totally foreign to this static conception of plants. The ideas that

---

[1] Everman, B. E., The Teaching of Biology in the Public Schools.

[2] For a good discussion of the contrast between the older and newer morphology, see Ganong, W. F., Cardinal Principles of Morphology. See also Essay VIII. in his *Teaching Botanist*.

an organism is a centre of activities, physical and chemical, that it is the scene of struggle and response to the factors of its environment, internal and external, and that its form and structure are nothing more or less than a record of these motions and changes, and a measure of their forces and directions, — these are left totally in abeyance. To be sure, these ideas are themselves comparatively new,[1] so that the teacher of fifty years ago is not to be censured for not seeking the dynamic rather than the static point of view; but that there has been a change in botany in the direction of this better and fuller appreciation of the plant, and that many teachers are not only backward in adopting it but are entirely ignorant of it, are reasons enough for showing the defects of botanical education in the lack of its adoption. In this newer conception we should find the source of an inspiration to teaching, and the teacher to whom botany is the lifeless thing depicted by Macmillan by a pathetic schoolroom selection [2] would do well to make a struggle after it.

We have shown, then, that the part of botanical science just discussed, as employed in education, has not done, on the whole, what it should. It has led to a deficient understanding of the object and scope of botany; it has lacked a vitalizing point of view; it has brought the subject into much discussed and much to be deplored disrepute. What is, then, our conclusion? That it is the deficiency of this part of the subject for education, and that therefore it must be thrown out? Not at all. The case is perfectly clear. A true classification of plants is an expression of our knowledge of the affinities of plants based upon the sum total of our knowledge of behavior and structure internal and external.[8] Not only this. Systematic botany has in the past played a very important part in exploring the range of plant

Conclusion as to Descriptive Botany.

---

[1] See Goebel's *Organography*, Chapter I.

[2] *Education*, **12** : 460. April, 1892.

[8] Thiselton-Dyer, W. T., Address before the Biological Section of the British Association, September, 1888. Coulter, J. M., The Future of Systematic Botany. Robinson, B. L., Problems and Possibilities of Systematic Botany.

materials, and thus giving a stimulus for research in physiological, morphological, and economic directions.[1]   It is the oldest
part of botany, and from it, as the branches from the main
trunk, have sprung the other departments of botanical knowledge which therefore are not separate and distinct, but the
interdependent and interrelated parts of a whole. Many botanists, moreover, can trace their permanent, intelligent interest in
plants to an early interest in collection and classification, and it
may therefore not be said that such interest is always barren of
Something of results.   To neglect this field in elementary educa-
Classification
must be
taught.   tion would, I conclude, be doing as much injustice
to student and subject as to neglect other parts.
The complaint made is directed, then, not at classification
properly apprehended, but against the teachers who have failed
in this apprehension; who have themselves been blind to the
realities of the subject and who therefore have been "blind
leaders of the blind."   The remedy for this pathological
condition is in the proper preparation of the teacher, and in
some inquiry into the relative status of descriptive botany and
classification to other parts of botany, into its educational
content and adaptability to the student, and into the means of
vitalizing it with a point of view which makes for a conception which shall accord with the rest of botanical knowledge.
How these things are to be done will be treated in a following
chapter.

During recent years the teaching of botany in the high
school has, in some restricted quarters, taken a sudden and
Advent of   remarkable turn in the nature of a reaction against
Type Course
into the High the herbalist regime.   This has been due to the
School.   better preparation of high-school teachers by university methods, which preparation, however, has been con-

---

[1] Galloway, B. T., Applied Botany: Retrospective and Prospective.
[2] The student, in order to gain an historical review, should read
von Sachs' *History of Botany*, Brendel's Historical Sketch of the
Science of Botany in North America from 1635–1840, and Underwood,
L. M., The Last Quarter — a Reminiscence and an Outlook.

fined entirely to training in the subject, while a study of school conditions, and the needs of pupils of high-school age was entirely overlooked. The result of this one-sided preparation of teachers, which, however, was better by far than the iusufficient preparation previously obtained, has been the infiltration of college and university courses into the high school. It is easy to see how this has happened. A person studying biology by the method inaugurated chiefly by Huxley, first in England and afterwards by him and his personal representative Martin, in America, was placed in possession of an array of chiefly morphological facts about a series of animals and plants, which, put together, were intended to illustrate the hypothetical progressive steps by which organisms have passed through in time in producing the highly complex types of the present day. To substantiate the fact of evolution was the chief aim of such a course. The method of study was ordinarily that of verification, while the development of individual initiative in thought and act was largely ignored. There have been notable exceptions to the general rule, it is true, the most notable of which was the method of Agassiz, which has been recently described by Beal.[1] Agassiz's method consisted in stripping a man of pride and support by bringing him into direct contact with some form, such as a starfish, and leaving him **Method of** to find out things for himself without aid of any **Agassiz.** kind. This was heroic treatment, and the product was commensurate with his method. It is obvious, however, that such tactics have restricted application and cannot be employed generally.

For the most part, however, the method of verification, with the explicit directions for observation and, when necessary, dissection, found in a laboratory manual, was that employed. The student examined a series of "types," from which circumstance such a course has come to be called a "type course." The comparison of the form studied, the significance of the similarities and differences as a basis for phylogenetic arrange-

---

[1] How Shall a Young Person Study Botany ?

ments of organisms, — in brief, the thinking part of the work, was usually done by the instructor and discovered to the student through the medium of the lecture, so that, with ordinary intelligence, the large ideas involved were obtained and, to a degree, appreciated without the acquisition by the student of the independence of effort and judgment which should characterize the work of an efficient teacher. In the minds of such, the type course became a sort of alpha and omega of biological training in high school as well as college, while it is in the latter alone that such work, properly managed, belongs. As a consequence, when the newly fledged Bachelor or Master, or much less frequently, Doctor, passed into his life work as a teacher — in the event that teaching did not happen to be a convenient stepping-stone to "something better" — he, without a thought as to the fitness of things, offered the same course which to him, it is only justice to say, appeared to be rich in thought and significance. He gave a type course in the high school. He assumed that what appealed to his maturer mind would appeal with equal force to the mind of a young pupil. He saw no reason why the difficult microscopic work necessitated at the very outset and continually throughout the course was not equally adaptable to the work of the high school, unless perchance the absence of microscopes offered an unanswerable one. The absence of physiological treatment, and of the point of view, so necessary to the conception of the evolution of living organisms, was not appreciated. The course became in his hands one in comparative minute anatomy, more or less beyond the comprehension of his students. Laboratory manual and text-books adapted to the college were used, and the whole resembled a badly fitting suit of clothes; for though it lacked the necessary features of adaptation, it answered the immediate purpose. It did at least some things which are definitely good to do. In using types of both plants and animals, it pointed out that these are to be compared in order to a fair understanding of natural history; it has thus helped to raise the study of plants from effeminacy to a place of some dignity in education. It showed to those ignorant of it that plants and animals are on a parity in the organic creation, and that both must be understood comparatively before the whole truth is to be had. It has showed, moreover, that there is some other way of studying plants than by examining the outsides of some of them guided by an analytical key. And it was not long till some of the botanists who were awake to the circumstances took the hint and prepared manuals for the laboratory study of plants alone after the method of Huxley and Martin.

Good Results
of Type
Course.

We may now examine the type course with reference to its efficiency in the secondary school, and to this end we must point out that there have been two methods of presenting it, according to the way in which it was approached. One of these is the so-called "logical method"—the method which takes it for granted that the arrangement of ideas parallel to the progression of evolution, as illustrated by various forms from simple to complex, is the only really logical method. The advocates of this view appear to have forgotten, or possibly have never appreciated, the fact that this arrangement is one which expresses a subjective idea which was gained by naturalists who themselves did not approach the subject in this way. By this method, the study of types was begun by the examination of the simple forms, and because they are simple structurally, the student was misled into believing, on *a priori* grounds, that their physiology is as simple. As the study advanced the physiological questions were gradually lost sight of and the structural ones usurped its place.

Two Subsidi-
ary Methods
of presenting
the Type
Course.

Simple to
Complex.

By the second method, which was later adopted by Huxley,[1] the examination of types was approached from the other end of the series, and the complex forms were studied first. Aside from the fact that the physiology of the simple forms is really very complex and difficult to understand,

Complex to
Simple.

---

[1] See preface by Huxley, T. H., to Huxley and Martin's *Practical Biology*. London and New York. The Macmillan Co., 1892.

a further reason especially pertinent to the high-school problem, is, that the distress and floundering which is unavoidable
when a young student is put to work on a completely strange
set of objects, the seeing of which even involves the use of
an instrument which makes them still more strange, to say
nothing of the technical difficulties to be overcome, are in
this way obviated.   The student begins with the relatively
known and proceeds to investigate the unknown by natural
psychological steps.   On the assumption that the type course is
the only one which is properly adapted to the high school, the
second of these subsidiary methods is undoubtedly the better,
and this we shall have to keep in mind when we consider below
the advantages offered by a different arrangement of the study.

The good points of the type course, laying aside the distinction of methods of approach, are somewhat as follows.   I
do not attempt to make any distinction between
Good Features of Type Course. the type course as embracing plants and animals,
or as confined to plants, although we are concerned
here especially with the latter.   The study was directed, not
only at external features, but at internal structures as well.   The
examination of characters was not carried on with the object of
determining a name by a comparison with a descriptive diagnosis.
Indeed the name was given at once, and no reference to classification in a narrow sense was made.   The study was, therefore,
compared with the older method of descriptive botany, more
intensive and thorough.   Fewer types were studied and these ,
more deeply.   The comparative method of study, so far as it was
carried out, involved, as it should, the comparison of structural
features of the organisms themselves, each with the other.
The study was on the whole a study of related things and not
of isolated objects.   Again, the facts observed by this method of
comparison, — albeit the comparisons were by the instructor
rather than the student, were subjected to interpretation in
terms of the theory of descent, and a large idea of this kind,
lying as it does at the bottom of the modern interpretation of all
scientific phenomena, if only dimly apprehended, is distinctly

better than none. These facts, handled in this way, involved the principles of classification in a broad sense, a true classification expressing ideas of genetic relationship rather than a convenient arbitrary system of cataloguing. And this view of the matter again, if indeed somewhat hazy, is better than a much more detailed one of an artificial arrangement. Thus we may say that, on the whole, the course made for very marked improvement in botany teaching, and this may be attributed in large part to the influence of the master teacher and investigator Huxley, who saw in plants as in animals materials of equal importance for education.

But, in spite of these very good points, there are grave defects in the type course if we consider it from our present point of view, quite apart from its place in a scheme of biological instruction in the college and university. **Defects of the Type Course.** For the secondary school it is deficient because, on the side of the science and of the needs of the pupil it is unrepresentative and insufficient. In its more extreme forms it neglects largely the physiological aspects of biology and ignores the experimental side entirely. It deals scarcely at all with the correlation of the morphological and physiological phenomena in such a way as to bring out the ecological or natural history phases of the study. This is true also of the economic, and with it, of the informational content, which are thus reduced to a minimum. It deals with a certain set of forms, and largely neglects the mass of materials more easily available, and so loses the out-of-doors point of view. On the side of method, while trying to insist upon comparison, and a broad interpretation of facts, the way in which these facts are obtained is by the process of verification in which the true comparative method is often obscured by substituting for it a comparison of plant and description. It therefore often falls into a fitting of the type to the book, and this, of itself, is little better than the similar business of the herbalist. The intellectual effort of the student is therefore often reduced to the attempt to see what the book calls for; they often do so, facts to the contrary notwithstanding. This has been true even of college work, and, as would be expected, much more so of that in high schools. It becomes a mere training of the senses, rather than of the powers of acquiring knowledge, — the power of searching out for one's self and of putting facts together.

It is obvious that the study of forms·in the more intensive way characteristic of the type method has, however, a definite claim on the time devoted in the high school to botany. In it lies the basis for a broad conception of affinities and hence of true classification. It supplies, therefore, a broad basis for the appreciation of the idea of evolution. For these reasons, if for no other, a series of types should be studied. I should, however, insist upon a physiological viewpoint, not only by the introduction of experimental work, but by the study of general adaptive characters, *e. g.*, of water and land plants, with an attempt to show some evidence for the supposition that is generally entertained that the former have been derived phylogenetically from the latter. Whatever the methods of change by which the forms of the present have been derived from those of the past, the fact of change is indubitable. The grand conception of a movement of advancing and retreating forms through unmeasured eons of time is one which is eminently worth while to have. To this end the idea of change must be constantly emphasized, and in the forms assumed by plants we must see the registration of this change. We come, therefore, to the point heretofore and repeatedly accentuated, that a dynamic viewpoint must be had. Just as the one who puts together the facts observed in the furrowed, rounded knobs of protruding rock, sees in imagination a glacier of thousands of feet in depth sweeping irresistibly overhead, so he who contemplates a series of types should be led to picture in his mind that current of life sweeping down from the past to the future, branching, eddying, changing, flowing together, but which is still going onward into an unknown beyond. Can this be done for him whose opportunity to receive this legacy of thought is

Some Study in the Type Method necessary in the High School.

perhaps limited to one year of the high school? Some will doubt it, but I believe that it can and should be done. The teacher's success depends upon the grasp of his mind, on the power of his own constructive imagination, and on his ability to turn on the light of inquiry upon the materials at hand.

Further matters of method will not at present be discussed. It is my purpose to return later to the question of what types may most profitably be used, the use which may be made of them, what the relation shall be between this part of botany and the other large divisions of the subject, and what the method of approach.

Another form of type course which was originally planned for introductory students in biology in the college should be mentioned here because of its adoption by some teachers into the high school, but not because of its real adaptability to secondary work. I refer to the course which is based upon the comparative study of two types of organisms, one a plant and the other an animal.[1]   No doubt that the Fern-Earthcourse can be made in the hands of a thorough worm Course. naturalist of good training in botany and zoölogy one of very great value and significance to college students under special conditions. That it should have been adopted as a high-school course is from the viewpoint of botany unfortunate for several reasons.

It is in the first place too difficult a course for pupils of the high-school age, both in technique and in subject-matter. In regard to the former there is relatively too great a proportion of time and effort expended upon microscopic work to which objections are urged elsewhere. It is also unsound pedagogically in beginning with an extended study of the cell.

The objections on the ground of the subject-matter are still more grave. The basis for the course is found chiefly in two types — one of plants and one of animals. This of course results in an extreme form of "type" study, with a disadvantage

---

[1] Sedgwick and Wilson, *General Biology*.

8

in developing in the pupil only a very inefficient and false point of view, a difficulty when dealing with high-school pupils scarcely to be overcome even by a skilful and competent teacher, while by a group of students of above the average intelligence with such a teacher some broad notions of the problems and scope of biology may be obtained. A general view of the plant and animal series, which cannot as an aim for high-school work be ignored, is well-nigh impossible unless the information is supplied by the teacher. But this defeats again the end desired, by supplying too narrow a basis in the experience of the pupil, with the result that the study tends to become an act of ordinary memorizing.

Furthermore, from the point of view of the botanist the representation of the plant kingdom by a fern has little in its favor. Anatomically the ferns are a widely aberrant group, and as the intensive study of the type brings much stress to bear upon the anatomy, it is obvious that quite wrong general impressions are received. These have usually been allowed to stand uncorrected, since the teachers who have adopted the course have usually been primarily zoölogists and therefore much more concerned with the animal side of the study. While the intention of those who originated the method was to compare animal and plant biology, the general effort of less able teachers has been to show by this comparison that the animal aspect of the study is the one really worth while.

Undoubtedly the one desirable feature of the fern as a type lies in the clear example it gives of alternation of generations in plants ; this subject, however, from a botanical viewpoint, can be little understood without a comparative study of different plants ; and when the comparison is with an animal such as the earthworm, where no such phenomenon is known to obtain, the produced contrast of positive and negative characters serves to isolate the types in the mind rather than to emphasize the lesson of a common field of inquiry.

Beyond this advantage, however, the fern as a type of plants in general little deserves an apologetic. It is a highly specialized and aberrant type. This is shown in the general arrangement of the vascular tissue and in the character of the scalariform elements. The stem of the type used, *Pteridium* (*Pteris*) *aquilinum*, is horizontal, and the growth of leaf from an apical cell is .not typical, nor in a wide sense is the similar growth of the stem. For the high school, therefore, we conclude that the fern-earthworm course has little to recommend it and is open to many grave objections. It is in no sense the kind of a course for young pupils who will presumably have no other opportunity for the study of botany.

A distinct advance upon the courses heretofore described came with the recognition of the importance of the principle that all parts of the science of botany should be represented by the study of their fundamental knowledge content. A very good expression of the attempt to do this is to be seen in the book of Barnes,[1] a brief survey of the plan of which will give the reader a good idea of the arrangement of such a course.

Various Parts of Botany separately represented.

Commencing with a study of the cell sufficient to gain an idea of its more obvious features, the pupil passes on to an examination of types from the simple to the complex, which are selected to illustrate the evolution of the plant body, commencing with the lower forms. Then follows the part treating of the physiology of plants, the subject of reproduction being dealt with separately from a morphological point of view, and in a manner analogous to the treatment of the plant body. Asexual and sexual reproduction are distinctly separated, and this leads to a clear distinction between them. In the final part the attention is directed to ecology, or the study of plant adaptation, while the matter of classification is practically laid aside.[2] In the briefer edition, for practical reasons

[1] Barnes, C. R., *Plant Life*. New York. 1898.
[2] Approximately the same sort of a course has been outlined by Clements and Cutter in *A Laboratory Manual of High School Botany* (Lincoln, Neb., 1900), for the schools of Nebraska, although I understand that it has proved somewhat too difficult for the majority of schools in that State.

less attention is paid to minute anatomy and to sexual reproduction.[1]

It will be seen at a glance that the author recognizes the importance of giving a fair and well-proportioned view of the field, and his efforts are successful so far as they go. The entire neglect of classification is regarded by some as an insufficiency, a criticism partly justified. And the insistence on the necessity of beginning the study of types with the unicellular form offers an objection which will be discussed beyond. Aside from these the only matter for consideration is the question of how the parts of the subject should be related to each other in the course. Of this, Barnes says :

" The work in plant physiology may be presented either in connection with the study of morphology or may follow it as an independent division of botany. In my judgment it makes little difference which of these two methods is pursued. Both have strong advocates, the former especially being the favorite of those who speak from a theoretical standpoint. It may be pointed out, however, that if one wishes to introduce the study of absorption after a consideration of the root, and to illustrate transpiration and photosynthesis after the examination of the leaves, there can be no serious objection to it, provided certain dangers of omission are guarded against. Too often thus the leaves are left out of consideration as absorbing organs, absorption being associated wholly with the study of roots. In reality, however, the absorption of gases by the leaves is of quite as much importance as any absorption by roots." [8]

We have already discussed in Chapter III. the issue here stated, and we shall meet it again in examining the claims of the course which we pass on now to examine.

The consideration of the reader is now directed to a third type of botanical course which is of later development than the preceding, and which offers advantages in scope and arrangement which have been wanting in the others.

---

[1] *Outlines of Plant Life.* New York. 1900.
[8] Barnes, C. R., Plant Physiology in the High School.

A course of this kind consists of the best knowledge which the science of botany has to offer in the fields of morphology, physiology, classification, and ecology, correlated in **The Synthetic Course.** such a manner that their interrelations are brought out. In this way, if the course is properly carried out, a dynamic viewpoint is made dominant. Such an arrangement of botanical study has been called by Ganong[1] "synthetic," and it has gained an increasingly wider acceptance as the best sort, largely through the use of the excellent book for high schools by Bergen,[2] and through the vigorous defence of the ideas involved by Ganong (*loc. cit.*), but while the fullest present expression of the method is due to the efforts of these two in the educational field, the idea has been more or less fully carried out, though not always in the same way, nor to the same degree of effectiveness, by Spalding,[3] Setchell,[4] and Atkinson,[5] in books which are adapted chiefly to the abilities of college students, but of which one (Atkinson) appeared in abridged and simplified form better adapted to secondary students.

The position of the advocates of this method has been recently materially strengthened by the acceptance of its essential features as embodied in a Report[6] of a committee appointed by the Society for Plant Morphology and Physiology by that body, and also by the adoption of this Report as a standard college entrance option by the College Entrance Board of the Middle States and Maryland.

The central motive of the synthetic course is the thought that the best results from the standpoint of general education and of training in the scientific methods of observation and thought, as well as of the best representation of the subject, are to be obtained by correlating closely morphological and

---

[1] *The Teaching Botanist.*
[2] Bergen, J. Y., *Foundations of Botany.* Last edition.
[3] *Introduction to Botany.*
[4] *Laboratory Practice for Beginners in Botany.*
[5] *Elementary Botany.*
[6] *School Science.* May, 1902.

physiological study, thus bringing together in the mind the things which stand in close relation to each other in nature, namely, form and structure and behavior and function. There are two types of the synthetic course determined by the dominant viewpoint held. In the one, the basis of the work is morphological, and those who adopt this method take the view with Ganong that "physiological experiments most profitably come along with the particular structures which they explain." [1] It is argued that the best results are obtained when the attention of the student is directed first to the structure and form. By careful observation an accurate notion is obtained of the machinery, and the question then follows in a natural way, why the machinery is arranged as it is, that is, what activities of the plant have produced a given form and structure, and what is the value of these to the plant.

Two Types of Synthetic Course.

The second type of synthetic course is one which reverses the relations of morphology. While the one regards morphology from the physiological viewpoint, the second regards physiology primarily and looks for morphological knowledge to come incidentally. The chief advocate of this method is Atkinson, whose defence I quote :

"The method which I have found successful is to begin with a study of the vegetative life processes of plants, or physiology, thus dealing largely with function. Since some knowledge of form must accompany a study of function, the pupil gains by necessity some knowledge of morphology while studying life processes." [2]

If we strike a balance of results attained by these two methods of dealing with a synthetic course, we should find very little to be said. In the hands of a good teacher, either would be productive of good results, since both are vitalized by a dynamic viewpoint.

Some differences are, however, to be noted, and these are of

---

[1] *The Teaching Botanist*, p. 37.
[2] Atkinson, G. F., '98.

considerable weight in determining which method is chosen. They are not necessary differences, to be sure, but rather such as have in practice characterized the carrying out of the methods by those who have adopted either one or the other.

Those who approach the subject on the morphological basis have usually chosen the seed[1] as the starting-point. The reasons for this are the following: First, it is urged that an elementary course, especially for young students, should begin with things of some degree of familiarity; that to begin with remote and unfamiliar or entirely unknown objects, *Spirogyra*, for example, as is proposed by the second method described, is to surround the pupil with so many difficulties, and to introduce him to so many strange things and ideas at once as to bewilder and discourage him, and this is obviously not improved by the necessity of using the microscope which introduces difficulties of interpretation which cannot be avoided.

Begin with the most familiar.

"To begin a course with objects needing the use of the compound microscope, that is, to introduce the use of the most special tool before eye and hand have had some training by themselves, is not only illogical in theory, but, as I and many other teachers know from experience, wasteful in practice. It produces a long and despairing floundering about from which balance and stability are but slowly regained. Moreover, it impresses a wrong ideal of scientific work, implying as it does that there is some sovereign virtue in elaborate instruments, thus tending to elevate these to a rank above their proper grade of mere aids to eye and hand."[2]

This argument is, of course, equally applicable to the "type course," which is begun by the study of simple forms of life first, as I have above shown. Certainly the argument is a good one if botany is given to pupils in the earlier high-school years, for the treatment in the *Elementary Botany* of Atkin-

---

[1] I have myself advocated beginning with the fruit. *Teachers College Record*, Vol. II., No. 1.

[2] Ganong, *The Teaching Botanist*, p. 34. see also the Preface to Huxley and Martin's *Practical Biology*.

son is without doubt too difficult and abstruse for them, a con-
cession implied in the later publication of his *Lessons in
Botany*, the treatment in which approaches more nearly that
of Bergen and Ganong, and which is better adapted to secondary students.

Secondly, it is held that the study of several types of seeds
or fruits gives a better training in simple, exact observation

and in the habits of comparison, by offering mor-
Seed the
Better Start-   phological problems of a fair amount of ease, but
ing-point?   demanding, nevertheless, careful discrimination of
essential and non-essential characters, and thus leading the
students to proper morphological conceptions based upon
comparison.   Of this Ganong says:

" Next among the scientific instincts I would place that for critical comparison and generalization, the morphological instinct.   It
consists both in a power to compare a series and eliminate what is
individual and unimportant from what is common to a number and
important, and also in a power, by comparison of different stages
of development, to trace back differing forms to their common
origin, or similar forms to their different origins, as the case may
be.   For training in this power, so important in all phases of
human activity, nothing is better than morphology, the introduction
to which is best made through forms which are large and plain
enough to need no tools, but only the unaided eye and thought.
For this the embryos in seeds, which show homologous parts under
the greatest diversity of size and form, are particularly good, especially since they may so easily be traced through stages of germination and growth where actual proof of their analogies and some of
their homologies may be found." [1]

At the same time, seeds and developing seedlings are
excellent material for use in exemplifying fundamental physiological processes on the one hand and adaptive movements
and structures on the other.   The co-ordinate treatment of
these various aspects of botanical study when based on these
materials is so natural and effectual, and can with no serious
difficulty and with no aspect of forcing, be made so interesting,

---

[1] *The Teaching Botanist*, p. 34.

that it is not easy to see how an introduction to botany could better be made. Nevertheless, some advance the objection that high-school boys will not regard seriously a course in botany to which they are led by beginning with seeds — that it does not appeal to them as worth while, and so they look at it with disrespect. This is probably true in the later years of the high school, more so even than of the earlier college years, and to overcome this calls for a strong personal equation in the teacher. And it might also be objected that some of the facts should be familiar to the pupil through his grammar-school work, which might very well be true. Neither of these objections can, however, be regarded as very weighty ones. The latter could be met in an ideal school by properly grading the work, and there is no doubt that this should be done. The former recognizes a supercilious attitude on the part of the pupil which should be overcome by the skill of the teacher.

It would seem, therefore, that a choice between these two methods will usually be determined according to the circumstances with which a teacher finds himself surrounded, and by his convictions as to what method of approach is the better. I am myself of the opinion that for the high school the method of beginning with the more familiar objects such as fruits or seeds is pedagogically the better of the two, especially if, as often happens, the course in botany extends only over half a year. The ideas which should grow out of high-school study must be scientific ideas, and these, in spite of some degree of familiarity with the material, are sufficiently unfamiliar to the student to give him vigorous mental work if he is properly led to it and if the right kind of problems are given him to solve. And I have decided on this course in spite of the unhappy experience of finding that students in many cases had the attitude towards work on seeds above mentioned. The method employed was in appearance to ignore the pupil's attitude, and to adjust the recitation so that the ignorance of such persons was laid bare. It is usually not long before they are disabused of their prejudices.

There have now been examined and criticised all the main

(**Summary and**   types of botany courses, or courses involving
(**Conclusion.**   botany, which have at any time had any large
amount of recognition.   These may, by way of summary, be
mentioned as follows:

1. The herbalist type — consisting chiefly of collecting a
   limited number of the flowering plants and of analyzing
   and naming them.   A small amount of text-book work
   on physiology was sometimes, though seldom, added.
2. The "type course," consisting of a study of a series of
   plant and animal forms, or of plant forms alone, selected
   to illustrate the course of evolution.   The order was
   sometimes reversed, and physiological matters were
   largely absent.
3. The plant and animal type course — making two forms
   studied comparatively the basis for a course in elementary biology.
4. The course taking up the great divisions of the science,
   morphology, physiology, classification, and ecology.
   Characterized chiefly by lack of co-ordination, and
   usually by the abeyance of classification.

The last three represent a reaction from the first type of
course.

5. The synthetic course, an advance upon (4) in that greater
   emphasis is laid upon the correlation of morphology and
   physiology.   Hence a dynamic point of view is taken
   and carried out, though this point of view is not necessarily absent from (4) or even from the others.   In point
   of fact, however, it usually has been.

Viewed historically, these courses stand in the order above
given, (1) being the oldest, (4) and (5) being modern expressions of practice and of differences of opinion.   It is not
my purpose to pass final judgment upon the merits of these
two as compared with each other.   Opinion and experience
among secondary teachers, and among those most competent
to judge, is clearly in favor of (4) or (5) as better than any of
the others for the high school.   I therefore conclude that the

present differences of opinion, and the reasons advanced in their support, should come under searching criticism on the part of the intending teacher. For my own part, I can say only that my own experience and judgment favors the synthetic course, beginning with the more familiar materials.

CHAPTER VI

USE OF THE METHOD OF THOUGHT IN TEACHING BOTANY

I PROPOSE now to take up for consideration certain points in the method of acquiring botanical knowledge, with a view to their bearing upon the teaching of this science. Belief in the efficacy of the " method of discovery " for the pupil is based upon the assumption that each of us must constantly re-discover for himself what those who have gone before have discovered. That the same method of knowledge acquisition is used by all is true in general ; but as regards the body of knowledge itself, it is certainly false to suppose that it is profitable or possible laboriously to attempt to repeat the experience of the race in a single life. What is accumulated experience good for ? And how is progress possible unless we can use previously deter- mined results ? It is significant that in teaching we *illustrate* well-established knowledge rather than *discover* new truth ; and much of this is necessary before any one of us may be fortunate enough to advance the limits of knowledge.

It will therefore be profitable for the teacher to examine the method by which botanical knowledge is gained, in order that he may be guided in his teaching to right pedagogical habits ; thus he may rather be the more truly a leader to his pupils than a setter of tasks.

The important desideratum in teaching botany, as in other objective sciences, is to make it possible for the pupil to realize the knowledge which is his by right of inheritance. To do this, however, he must, to some degree at least, repeat the experience of his intellectual forebears in the use of the methods by which they obtained their knowledge. This is quite a different doctrine from that of the method of discovery. Practically, it teaches that pupils should gain a thorough acquaintance with the method of acquiring botanical knowledge by using it. By learning how botanical knowledge has been gained, the results which have been obtained in other fields as well will have a proper significance for him. To do this, he must first be taught to observe. " To see a natural object as it is, correctly and completely," [1] is a scientific victory, without which none other can be gained. The immediate end in view is to form a mental image of the thing observed — not to remember statements about it, but the thing itself as having dimensions, a certain form, color, and other qualities.

How Botanical Knowledge is Gained.

Theoretically, the acquisition of facts is a perfectly simple operation and in an ideal condition of education we ought to be able to assume that pupils coming from the elementary school have pushed their ability in this direction to some considerable degree of perfection. The facts, however, do not permit us to assume this. There is repeated testimony that pupils of high-school grade and even beyond are usually completely lost when they are asked to form a clear notion of some simple, natural object. [2]

If this is even partly true it is idle, pedagogically considered, to require a beginner in botany to make his earlier observations with an instrument. It would seem to be beyond dispute that, if a student cannot use his unassisted senses to good effect, to introduce a system of lenses between the eyes and the object tends to confusion. It certainly does so in the majority of cases. Even if we pass by the technical difficulties of using the instrument, there is a psychological difficulty in the inability of a beginner to reconstruct, from a series of optical sections, an image of a solid object. This is a very great and real difficulty, unappreciated by the majority of teachers who forget their early difficulties. Thus a yeast cell, according to a beginner's observation, is an oval plane ; *Spiro-*

---

[1] Ganong's *Teaching Botanist.*

[2] Farlow, W. G., Biological Teaching in Colleges. *Popular Science Monthly*, **28** : 581. March, 1886.

gyra is a band or ribbon, and not a cylinder.[1] The difficulty is increased when the object is too large to be included in the field of the microscope, in which case the student must needs reconstruct in the directions of all the dimensions. In view of the difficulty of forming a notion of a single entire object, we must believe that we have in this a grave hindrance to the exercise of the operations of comparison — of distinguishing likenesses and differences, and of forming a notion of a type. For what we must aim at is not alone **Forming a** the seeing of a single object, but rather the con-**Notion of** struction of a general group of objects. Assum-**Type.** ing the object to be a seed or a leaf, what we desire is that a student shall study, not one specimen, and know that one, but that, by the study of several, he shall eliminate by comparison the non-essential differences, get at the constant elements of form, of structure, and the like, so that he shall thus obtain a type notion. This is the more necessary in view of the exigencies of teaching which lie in the possibility, in a short time, of giving the student an opportunity at every point of forming a type notion from his own observations. We must allow time at the beginning of a course for the student to culti-vate the ability to form the notion of a type from his own observations. But we have to use the mental attitude thus gained, in getting knowledge later on more rapidly. For example, in a course commencing with the seed, a good number of seeds of the same plant may be examined with fair speed, and a general idea may thus be formed. But in the later anatomical study of the stem the time is insufficient for the student to do the same thing for, say, monocotyledonous stems. The mere remark that there are exceptions means

---

[1] In training students, who are ready for such work, to get a mental image of three dimensions, one very good way is for them to study a cell of *Spirogyra*, and then to reconstruct an optical transverse section. Another method is to require students to reconstruct a piece of pine wood in three dimensions, from longitudinal, transverse, and tangential sections. This plan was first used by Professor W. G. Farlow.

nothing unless the exceptions are actually examined, unless some grasp has been gained of the value of comparison, and of the dependence we may place on a type, in point of usefulness. I should say that the early work of a course may be regarded as successful in this direction, if the pupil should ask to see other stems so as to test the validity of the type ; and further, that it would be good practice for teachers to be provided with drawings, photographs, lantern slides, or demonstration for several kinds of stems, and to show these to the class, following a careful study of the essential features of the specimens supplied.

We desire, then, that pupils shall get the ability to determine correctly the features of an object, to compare this with others of the same kind, and by comparison to get the facts common to a number of objects. In this way is gained the knowledge of a group as expressed in a type. This is, of course, not to be confined to closely similar objects ; the same process applied to objects of greater differences is more difficult and calls for greater mental grasp. Thus we may first study the fruits of one species, then of another species ; still again of a third ; but we must soon institute a comparison of these different fruits in order to lead the pupil to a somewhat comprehensive notion of the fruit in general. It is, furthermore, important that the materials shall be such as to offer fair conditions for observation. It is not just to ask a student to see things which are difficult for an accomplished observer to see ; as, for example, to compare two objects, unless with a fair amount of diligence, all the points of comparison may be made out, or may be seen to be absent in one or both. The seed of the onion, for instance, is far too difficult for a high-school student to study in comparison with, say, the pea. It is pertinent, also, to point out that the objections against the use of the microscope early in the course do not hold **Value of a** for the use of a simple lens. It is a common **Simple Lens.** experience that, having once seen some rather minute character with a hand lens, it becomes distinct enough afterward to the naked eye. I have found that, distinct as is the micropyle on a lima bean, it will often escape the attention until searched for and found with a lens. It is thereafter readily seen with the naked eye and the same feature will the more readily be found on other kinds of seeds.

Such morphological ideas as the above may be gained, as we have shown, by comparing different objects as to the cor-

How the Idea of Development is Gained. respondence or homology of their parts. But comparison has a further use, for when we apply this method to the same object or organism in different stages of its growth we gain an idea of development. Just as the rapidly passing pictures of a kinetoscopic series give, by the exact and rapid superposition of one on the other, the impression of movement of the elements of the pictures, so the superimposed images of a plant in various stages in its development supply the elements out of which the idea of change in form is obtained. This is most desirable, in order to the end, elsewhere specified, that students should get a dynamic viewpoint.

What has been said above in regard to acquiring knowledge of form, that is, of gaining morphological ideas, is equally true

General Physiological Ideas. with regard to physiological ideas. These also, in general form, can be obtained only by comparison. It would be unscientific after having observed the behavior of a given organ in one plant, to assert that the behavior of the corresponding organ in another plant is the same. Being familiar with the structure of corresponding physiological parts, we may infer that the functions of similarly constructed parts are the same. But this inference is possible only after the comparative study of function as of structure. For the pupil, however, much comparison is impossible. He must therefore be content with illustration of behavior, or, otherwise stated with a physiological type, chosen with due regard to its value as such.

There is, in physiology, a special application of the method of comparison in the control experiment, and it is of the highest importance that the teacher appreciates its value both as a means for gaining knowledge, and for efficient teaching. Essentially the method of control is simply the **Control** setting up of an experiment in duplicate, one **Experiment.** condition only being varied. Theoretically it is a comparison of the behavior of a normal plant and one under experiment. If, for example, we desire to know the behavior of a given plant in the absence of carbon dioxid, we must know what it is in its presence in normal quantities. But to determine the former, an apparatus is necessary, which may or may not cause the introduction of other abnormal conditions, such as extreme humidity. To bring this under control, therefore, a similar apparatus in which the normal amount of carbon dioxid is present must be set up, and both experiments must be surrounded by like conditions of light, temperature, etc. If this is properly done but one factor will differ in the experiment and control ; and upon this, differences in structure and in behavior will depend. The teacher will readily see the pedagogical advantage of the control experiment. Since it is only by such means that we can learn the exact truth, so also is it possible to teach scientifically only by the use of the same method.

Observation and comparison of their form and behavior are, then, the steps to knowledge of plants. We should not neglect to mention, however, the mental condition under which work of this kind may be accom- **Amount of Work in a** plished, namely patience. No one learns a lesson **Lesson.** in geometry in one step ; ability in use of language cannot be acquired at once. No more can a task in botany be comprehended at a glance. To be willing to see and acquire knowledge of facts as such is part of the scientific attitude. Pupils are very likely to become restive under a task in the laboratory, and this is due often to the apparent uselessness of the work. But this work of observation is unavoidable. It is, however, most true that we should not, as teachers, insist on the acquisition of a large number of observations without giv-

ing direction to the mind of the pupil. Making a lot of unnecessary drawings or of detail beyond a certain useful limit is
wasteful. Bootless fact-gathering is as bad in one place as
another. Patience and willingness to examine things and
make them out are begotten of success in using those already
attained. Success is the ground for faith that other facts
whose meaning is not at once clear will become related and
significant sooner or later. The patience of the real naturalist
is the expression of belief that, as his efforts to find the relations of facts have succeeded in the past, so further efforts will
succeed. But a high-school pupil has little or none of such
experience. The teacher must, therefore, make it worth while
to him, but without doing his work. The more the pupil finds
himself gaining the power of self-direction the more will his
work seem to him worth while. The indiscriminate observation of many facts is a far different thing from intelligent,
selective observation. That training may be regarded as successful in proportion as it stimulates the pupil to efficient self-
directed effort.

While it is highly important that the teacher should not demand the observation of too many or of unimportant facts, but

**Side-lights
on Labora-
tory Work**   should the rather skilfully use the fewer important
necessary ones, it does not follow that the pupil's
mind shall be completely excluded from the incidental consideration of accepted ideas or theoretical explanations of some of the more important features. The
scientist in the search for truth must be a dispassionate observer of facts apart from their meaning, and it is of great
educational value, as Ganong has well said, that students should
learn this. This is the ideal of which Darwin[1] was so complete a master. Nevertheless, it is just as true that it is a
perfectly normal operation of the mind to search all the while
for explanations; and whether these are ultimately proved to
be true or not, they are the product of the scientific imagina-

---

[1] See his autobiography.

tion, and they serve as stimuli to quicken the powers of acquisition and to give them direction.

Now my contention is that in the school we as teachers (should help students to think, and we can do this by indicating in some manner the significance of some of the facts with which they are dealing without disturbing certain definitely outlined problems. The truth of this position is indicated by the fact that interested students are constantly asking for explanations, and a refusal to illuminate their work is justified only when it really vitiates their problems for them. Furthermore, a good teacher can use such opportunities to illustrate, by his own answers, the judicial attitude of the real student of nature. This matter is illustrated by the treatment of the micropyle in the first studies of the seed. Such a constant and familiar structure often elicits inquiry as to its value, to which, in answer, one may say that it is regarded by some as a point for the rapid absorption of water, and it is certainly utilized in very many plants for the access of the pollen tube. The former explanation, the teacher may point out, is capable of immediate experimental examination. The micropyle may be sealed with soft paraffin, the seed placed in water, and the tissues watched. This should by all means be done. He may expand upon the second statement to indicate the extent of the problem, during which it may be said that, in some plants (*Cannabinaceæ*) the micropyle becomes closed by fusion of the perimicropylar tissues, which single fact will show that it is not a necessary condition, but one which may have been seized upon by the pollen tube as an advantage.

Not only, then, must the student, by his own labor observe and think and experiment. The teacher must by skilful guidance be an inspiration to his students. Above all things he need not be an encyclopædia, but rather a living example of skill in the use of the scientific method. This demands on the part of the teacher knowledge and good training.

Every course in botany should be a unit in the sense that every new lesson should take for its departure the point already

reached by previous studies. Each exercise should, therefore, be made the occasion (1) of acquiring new facts and
(2) of leading the student by comparison with previously
learned facts to formulate logical conclusions; *i. e.*, should
call for the exercise of the method of thought. That the
study of plants may not become merely a study of formal
morphology or of taxonomy, the ideas of the organism and
of its activities should be kept steadily in mind. We shall
now take up the problem of the early exercises in botany, and
see what materials we may choose and how these shall be
managed.

The majority of teachers in elementary courses have advocated beginning such with the study of the
seed. A fuller discussion of this point has been
given elsewhere. Ganong has especially advocated this pro-
cedure.

Early Lessons in Botany.

"There is nothing known to me better than large seeds, which
have the further advantages of being easy to obtain and in condition for study at all seasons, as well as a logical point of beginning for the study of the cycle of plant life. The correct sizes and
shapes of these seeds, the exact kinds and relative positions of all
of the markings on the coats and their relations to the parts of the
embryo inside, the number of the coats, the full number of parts
in the embryo, and the exact way they are put together, all afford
under the skilled teacher fine materials for practice in observation,
a failure to succeed in which cannot be laid to inability to use
instruments, or ignorance of how to begin work." [1]

I have myself, while agreeing with Ganong in principle,
taken a somewhat different position.[2] In the passage just
quoted the phrase " a logical point " has no particular force, since it admits that there are other
equally logical points for starting the study of
botany. One of these is the fruit, which, after some years
of experience with the other method, I have found to be

Beginning with the Seed.

---

[1] *The Teaching Botanist*, p. 35.
[2] The Course of Botany in the Horace Mann School. *Teachers
College Record*, Vol. II.

especially useful for the following reason. The largest and only really useful monocotyledonous type for the study of the development of the seedling, which is at the same time readily accessible, is the "grain" of Indian corn (*Zea Mays*). Besides being large, it germinates quickly, the parts are readily observable, and it is one of the most important of American food plants. The greatest objection to it is found in the fact that the "grain" is a fruit, the contained seed being devoid of seed-coats which have been lost by absorption, and being closely invested by the thin membranous pericarp. This circumstance gives trouble, not alone to students, but to many teachers, and I have often had evidence of this in the note-books of high-school pupils. The amount of success which sometimes attends the efforts to find the micropyle is quite remarkable. Of course it is not there, the seed-coats being absent. Even if the teacher is fully aware of the difficulties, explanations often go for nothing. The student does not have any facts at his disposal which will help him to form his own judgments. I lay particular emphasis upon this point, because it is at the beginning of a course that we must make especial efforts to give the student a chance to get clear ideas. This is entirely avoided if the fruit is made the point of departure, and I have used the pea or bean for this purpose. The treatment in detail will be seen upon examination of the outline in the eighth chapter.

Beginning with the Fruit.

A further point which I have been accustomed to emphasize in consonance with the dynamic idea of plants which has been discussed above is that of development. In the first few lessons on the seed as generally carried out no facts are brought out with this aim in view. By using two or three stages of development the relative growth of the different regions of the fruit and of the enclosed seeds can be made out, and the exercise has been found extremely useful in later work.

Compare Young and Old Stages of Development.

There is a difficulty which must be noticed at this point,

namely, that it is not possible for a beginner to make out in all the forms studied every feature which can be seen in some one fruit and its seeds.   For example, the micropyle is seen readily enough in the seed of the lima bean, of the pine, **Incomplete** but only with great acuteness of observation in the **Evidence.** castor-oil seed, and not at all in Indian corn, as above pointed out.   It becomes, therefore, an exercise in judgment on the part of the pupil in concluding from incomplete evidence that a given object is a seed in a morphological sense.

But on the other hand it has seemed to me that beginners may not be expected to understand the seed-coats at all, a point which is usually insisted upon.   Although there are two integuments in the types mentioned above except in the pine they become indistinguishable in the legume by fusion ; they do not separate from each other in *Ricinus* in their dividing plane (the test is, in fact, only a part of the inner integument) so that it is incorrect to call the inner integument the 'tegmen' or 'endopleura' and the outer the (testa).   In Indian corn they have been absorbed, and in the pine only one integument is present, the delicate membrane immediately surrounding the endosperm being a remnant of the nucellus.   The evidence is, therefore, so scanty and so difficult to get at that it is too severe and confusing a task for the beginner, and would therefore best be omitted.   In the later years of the high school or for more mature students in general an account of the behavior of the seed-coats illustrated by charts and microscopic propositions has in my experience proved of interest and instruction.

CHAPTER VII

GENERAL BOTANICAL PRINCIPLES TO BE EMPHASIZED IN TEACHING

BIBLIOGRAPHY

Agassiz, L. Method in the Study of Natural History. Boston, Houghton, Mifflin & Co. 1887.

Bailey, L. H. The Survival of the Unlike. New York, The Macmillan Co. 1897.

Spencer, H. Principles of Biology. New York, D. Appleton & Co. 1898.

Goebel, K. Organography, Part I. Oxford, 1900.

THE teacher of botany has before him in the choice of material a complex task. The management of these in the . class room is also difficult, since they offer so many points of interest and attack. The danger which a teacher is not unlikely to fall into is, therefore, that of touching on a great many facts, and of failing to keep in sight the broad ideas which are derived from the study. What these are I shall now attempt briefly to discuss.

According to the outline we shall adopt, the subject-matter of botany is divided into four parts: Morphology and anatomy, physiology, ecology, and classification. These may be arranged in two groups, structural and physiological, in order to see what the general ideas of plants are which these two classes of ideas should endeavor to deal with in the course. We take them in the order given.[1]

1. *Anatomy and Morphology*, the structure of organisms, in a broad sense.

---

[1] The student should consult Chapter I. of Parts IV. and V. . . . . in Spencer's *Principles of Biology.*

(1) The possibility of the type conception rests upon the observed fact of "uniformity" in plan or conformity to a type. Objective types are non-existent; but for practical purposes they may be chosen as expressing objectively, with more or less exactness, the subjective idea. The observed fact of "uniformity" in plan is that within limits plants possess similar organs of similar origin similarly placed, the obvious (sense-appreciable) results of similarly responsive reactions to similar stimuli. The idea of type is therefore a generalized notion arrived at by comparison, a point of method discussed above. The determination of similar parts and their similar positions (the criterion of which is largely similarity of origin) is the determination of homology.

Homology.

This explains the prevalence of the use of the words "type" and "typical" in the above outline, and it constitutes also the reason for the wise choice of types. These must be as generalized as possible, free from detail of specialization, *i. e.*, as little aberrant as may be.

(2) The fact that the origin of organs does not indicate their functions, and therefore (*a*) that homologous organs may serve widely different uses, and (*b*) that the same use in the economy of the plant may be subserved by organs of different origin, makes it necessary to determine by observation and experiment what the function of a given organ may be. We thus arrive at the idea of analogy in organisms. Examination of analogous organs discovers the fact that though unlike in some structural features they are alike in others, from which the important generalization is derived that the structure of an organ is connected with its function. Structure here means form as well as anatomy. It is a broad inference, but one growing in importance and recognition, that all morphological structures are the expression of function. The study of morphology cannot, then, be separated from the study of physiology. From these considerations we conclude that types chosen for study shall be such as to illustrate diver-

Analogy.

gence of function in homologous parts. We conclude, also, that in elementary education cognizance should be taken chiefly of the functions and activities of the organism and to a minor degree of the morphological and anatomical considerations connected therewith. Therefore, I hold that the introduction of experiment is of the greatest importance both for the determination of function and of emphasizing the dynamic phase of plant study.

(3) The organism passes through a cycle of change known as its life history or ontogeny. These changes are from a simple undifferentiated to a complex differentiated **Life History.** condition. The study of various stages · in the growth and development of individuals supplies the materials for getting a record of these changes. For this purpose types should be chosen which show some marked ontogenetic changes, which if possible epitomize the phylogeny and which are fairly rapid in their development. In plants, the embryological history is so much curtailed that comparatively few plants serve sufficiently well for elementary work, but among these the *Leguminosæ* are the best.

The study of the life cycle connects itself with that of reproduction in the process by which a new similar life cycle is started. A plant begets on the whole its like, from which there results a morphological stability. The fact that more or less aberration from the parent occurs, and that life cycles do not repeat themselves exactly as to individual differences in all instances, if in any, is of great importance from the viewpoint of evolution.

(4) Just as there is, in the individual, a series of changes from simple to complex, from the relatively undifferentiated to the differentiated (ontogeny), so, in the history of **Race History.** organisms, as a whole, have there been such changes (phylogeny). The descent of each particular organism is, theoretically, traceable through a series of successively more and more specialized forms. The evidence as regards s plant is, however, chiefly obtained from comparative study of existing

organisms, and to a less degree from fragmentary records of the past found in fossils, and it is not easy to arraign the evidence in elementary work. Nevertheless, the modern doctrine of evolution, which was arrived at first by the study of animals and plants, is a far too important generalization from the point of view of education as well as of science to be neglected in the high school. Furthermore, it is chiefly, if not entirely upon the courses in botany or zoölogy that the high-school pupil must depend for enlightenment in this direction. It therefore becomes necessary to choose the materials which, in as brief and clear a manner as possible, will serve best as a basis for illustrating the great generalization of modern biological science. The evidence in the study of living plants can be drawn most directly from the study of alternation of generations, and for this purpose beautiful material may be obtained among the *Bryophyta* (mosses and liverworts) and *Pterido-phyta* (ferns and fern allies).

We can, however, scarcely take the ground that in the high school there can be attempted more than a brief exposition of evolution and a summarizing of the more striking evidences, though it would seem that people should not be wholly ignorant of the facts of variation, mutation, adaptation, the struggle for existence and inheritance, nor inappreciative of the importance of these for the explanation of evolution. Nevertheless, the popular acceptance of the theory must rest upon its reasonableness rather than explicit and final proof. The study of the *modus operandi* of evolution is, I believe, not a subject for the high school. Concerning this, we can boast chiefly of our ignorance. It is theoretical and taxes the intelligence and the experimental ability of the most astute minds.

Difficult, however, as it may be to deal with the subject, the skilful teacher can find abundant opportunity for illustration and exposition. Field work is of especial value in this connection because by this means the pupil can be brought into contact with a large amount of material. This may be enhanced in its value to him by following up a judicious selection of reading.

It is, of course, not assumed that all these ideas shall be mastered by the pupil while studying the materials selected for this part of the course. As is seen from our discussion of these points, they depend upon and assume the work in physiology, ecology, and classification. But the adoption of these ideas as part of the aim of the course is expected to lead the teacher to a certain economy in the selection of materials, and to this we shall pass in the next chapter.

We have spoken above of differentiation and of adaptation. Both of these ideas are of prime importance, and we bring them before the reader again to em- **Differentia-tion and** phasize the importance of the physiological view- **Adaptation.** point.

The differentiation of organic structure is the result of physiological division of labor. A function becomes localized in the organism and at that point a special organ is developed. This differentiation is a response to the sum total of environmental conditions, and constitutes adaptation. The problem of adaptation, as also of the division of labor, is a physiological problem, and is to be studied as far as possible experimentally. I have elsewhere indicated the importance of this. This is the essence of the method of study in ecology, which is supplanting the method of the guesser, who, assuming design, assumes also that any subjective idea which appears to fit really does so. For this reason ecology is a difficult subject as well as a complex one, to the study of which all kinds of knowledge needs to be brought. There is always doubt about an ecological explanation which has not been subjected to some rigorous test, experimental so far as possible. In elementary education, time and other circumstances do not always allow much more than the emphasis of the viewpoint and method, unless many other features of interest are sacrificed.

It will be clear, it is hoped, that no consideration of morphological materials is possible, from the point of view of modern science, or profitable educationally, which is not directed from the physiological basis. This has been emphasized in the discussion of the nature of the synthetic course, especially by Ganong[1] and myself.[2]

2. *Physiology.* The outline of the work in physiology is sufficiently detailed to be for the most part self-explanatory. There are, however, some matters of general bearing which should receive consideration.

Aside from photosynthesis the fundamental physiology of plants and of animals is much the same. The activities in the two groups of organisms differ quantitatively. It is of fundamental importance educationally that the study of plant physiology be so managed as to strengthen and broaden the knowledge previously gained in earlier studies of physiology. It is equally important that the most fundamental point of difference — namely, the relation to food — should be studied both from the scientific and human viewpoints. The student should, therefore, be led to as full and complete a knowledge of photosynthesis as possible, since it is chiefly to this act that many of the most important plant adaptations are related. The only degeneracy in plants of fundamental importance is that of the loss of chlorophyl. The wide human interest of the process of photosynthesis has been discussed.

Correlation of Animal and Plant Physiology.

That the adaptations of plants are in very large measure correlated with their photosynthetic activity is explicable only as the organism acts as a unit. Its parts do not react independently, but with reference to the whole economy of the plant, and physiological activity must be so interpreted. Adaptation is seen, not alone in the form and position of parts, as the results of physiological activity, but in a wider and more exact sense

The Plant as a Whole with Parts in Mutual Interaction.

---

[1] *The Teaching Botanist.*

[2] Botany in the Horace Mann School. *Teachers College Record*, 2 : No. 1, January, 1901.

in the activities themselves. The study of adaptation therefore commences with the study of irritability, of stimulus, and response. We therefore again see the importance of studying adaptation experimentally. We are also led to see the weight attaching to the idea that every complex organism acts as a whole and not as a complex of independent activities. It is educationally not necessary to begin the study of physiology with that of the cell; a great deal of it can be learned without any knowledge of the cell as such. Not all, however. The study of the leaf as a mechanism is a most important part of anatomical and of physiological study, but is to be understood only by a study of the cell and of the behavior of protoplasm.

The conception of the organism as an expression of physiological activity, and the localization of special activities as a result of the establishment of special relations to the segregation of environmental factors, is of prime necessity in appreciating the idea of evolution. This has been mentioned in connection with the work in morphology.

Physiological Division of Labor.

The organism dies, but life is continuous. We cannot say that it will always be so, but for all practical ends it is. Each individual adapts itself to this condition by providing for a fresh life cycle, and so each generation begets a new one. The study of reproduction is simply the study of how this is accomplished, and its essential features may be studied with ease and very great clearness in plants. We have already discussed educational reasons why this should be done.

The Continuity of Life.

These four more important general principles are to be kept in view in carrying on the study of physiology. Further specification on other less general points will appropriately be left for consideration in connection with the discussion of the course in detail.

CHAPTER VIII

In a previous chapter the view has been adopted that the synthetic course in botany is the best adapted to the use of the high school. It is our present purpose to examine such a course with especial reference to the choice of materials and the best treatment of these in the laboratory. For this purpose we shall assume (1) that the principles laid down in the third chapter are agreed upon and (2) that the Report[1] of the Committee on a College Entrance Option in Botany, of the Society for Plant Morphology and Physiology in its latest form represents substantially the attitude of the botanists in this country in regard to the objective content of the course. We take this to be the case for the following reasons :

1. The report " is founded upon the two important reports of the National Educational Association, — the Report of the Committee of Ten (Washington, 1903) and the Report of College Entrance Requirements (Chicago, 1899)," from which circumstance it represents the culmination at the present time of the thought of leading teachers of botany upon the subject. It should be added, also, that the report in its latest form embodies so far as possible all the important suggestions and criticisms offered; so that in essence it will be found to express the opinion of a much larger circle of botanists than that included in the membership of the society before which it was presented. Trafton[2] has examined the opinion of sixteen authorities,

Basis of Discussion.

---

[1] Published in its latest form in *School Science*. May, 1902.

[2] Trafton, G. H., A Comparison of Recent Authorities on Methods of Teaching Botany. *School Review*, 10 : 138. 1902.

including as such the reports of committees of leading educational and scientific societies, and he showed that there is a consensus of opinion among these demanding a place in the course in botany for " physiology, ecology, general morphology (study of types), and gross morphology (study of the structure and modifications of organs of seed plants)." The report under discussion was one of those examined by Trafton, and we may therefore conclude that the agreement is sufficiently strong to warrant our assumption.

2. The report has been adopted by the Examination Board of the Middle States and Maryland, as the basis for its college entrance requirements. It constitutes, therefore, a recognized standard for high-school work which has not been opposed from above, but which is the product of the growth of general experience and opinion. It is assumed that the course in botany is a one-year course of four to five hours a week.

The specifications of the report including the fundamental topics of botany are here given with some slight verbal changes as follows:

A. In Anatomy and Morphology.

The seed. Four types (dicotyledon without and with endosperm, a monocotyledon and a gymnosperm); structure and homologous parts.

Food supply; experimental determination of its nature and value. Phenomena of germination and growth of embryo into a seedling (including bursting from the seed, assumption of position and unfolding of parts).

The Shoot. Gross anatomy of a typical shoot; including relationship of position of leaf, stem (and root), the arrangement of leaves and buds on the stem, and deviations (through light adjustments, etc.) from symmetry.

Buds, and the mode of origin of new leaf and stem; winter buds in particular.

Specialized and metamorphosed shoots (stems and leaves). General structure and distribution of the leading tissues of the shoot; annual growth; shedding of bark and leaves.

The Root. Gross anatomy of a typical root; position and origin of secondary roots; hair-zone, cap and growing point.

Specialized and metamorphosed roots. General structure and distribution of the leading tissues of the root.

The Flower. Structure of a typical flower, especially of ovule and pollen; functions of the parts. Comparative morphological study of six or more different marked types, with the construction of transverse and longitudinal diagrams.

The Fruit. Structure of a typical fruit especially with reference to the changes from the flower and from the ovule to seed. Comparative morphological study of six or more marked types, with diagrams.

The Cell. Cytoplasm, nucleus, sap-cavity, wall. Adaptive modifications of walls, formation of tissues.

B. In Physiology.

Rôle of water in the plant; absorption (osmosis), path of transfer, transpiration, turgidity, and its mechanical value, plasmolysis.

Photosynthesis; Dependence of starch formation upon chlorophyll, light and carbon dioxid; evolution of oxygen, observation of starch grains.

Respiration; necessity for oxygen in growth, excretion of carbon dioxid.

Digestion; digestion of starch with diastase, and its rôle in translocation of foods.

Irritability; Geotropism, phototropism, and hydrotropism; nature of stimulus and response.

Growth; localization in higher plants; amount in germinating seeds and stems; relationship to temperature.

Fertilization; sexual and vegetative reproduction.

C. In Ecology.

Modifications (metamorphosis) of parts for special functions. Dissemination.

Cross-Pollination.

Light relations of green tissues; leaf mosaics.

Plant Societies; Mesophytes, Hydrophytes, Xerophytes; Climbers, Epiphytes, Parasites (and Saprophytes), Insectivora.

Plant Associations, and zonal distribution.

D. In Classification.

A list of recommended types from which, or their equivalents, selection may be made:

A. Algæ. Pleurococcus, Sphærella, Spirogyra, Vaucheria, Fucus, Nemalion (or Batrachospermum or Polysiphonia or Coleochæte).[1]

B. Fungi. Bacteria, Rhizopus, Yeast, a rust (Puccinia) (or a Powdery Mildew), Mushroom.[1]

Bacteria and yeast have obvious disadvantages in such a course, but their great economic prominence may justify their introduction.

C. Lichens. Physcia (or Parmelia).

D. Bryophytes. In Hepaticæ, Radula (or Porella or Marchantia). In Musci, Mnium (or Funaria or Polytrichum).

E. Pteridophytes. In Filicineæ, Aspidium, or equivalent, including, of course, the prothallus.

In Equisetineæ, Equisetum.

In Lycopodineæ, Lycopodium, and Selaginella (or Isoetes).

F. Gymnosperms. Pinus or equivalent.

G. Angiosperms. A monocotyledon and dicotyledon, to be studied with reference to the homologies of their parts with those in the above groups; together with the representative plants of the leading subdivisions and principal families of Angiosperms.

I have already advanced reasons on page 123 for adopting the plan of commencing an elementary course with a study of the fruit and seed. This plan has given such satisfactory results that I shall give in detail the outline for laboratory study which I have elaborated.[2] The only disadvantage which is apparent is the difficulty of getting them in northern localities, where the castor-oil plant does not thrive sufficiently well to bear well-seeded fruits. Collecting bureaus would probably supply them. They may be kept in formalin and serve well the purpose in that condition.[8]

---

[1] The wording of the report is here reproduced. Differences in recommendation will be noted below.

[2] Those who are preparing themselves for teaching should study comparatively the outlines for study of the seed given in the various text-books, especially those of Bergen, Atkinson, Ganong, Stevens, Setchell, Spalding, and others. See Chapter X. for full titles.

[8] For further information concerning material, see Appendix B.

The field of study based upon fruits and seeds falls into three parts, morphology, with a small amount of anatomy, physiology and ecology. I believe it is of the greatest importance to carry out this part of the course very thoroughly and logically so as to lay the foundation for the rest of the work, which will be colored by the character of that of the first few weeks. The following outlines are given as examples of how the laboratory exercises may be worded.

Morphology and Anatomy of the Fruit and Seed.

Answers to questions are given in foot-notes and should not appear in students' outlines.

THE BEAN. *Materials.* — Very young and maturing but still green pods of lima bean (string or wax bean) and of pea. The pupil should examine two types comparatively.

Outline of Laboratory Study. — Examine an unopened pod. Is it divided into two similar halves, *i. e.*, is it bilaterally symmetrical? At one end may be found the stalk which supports the pod on the plant. This stalk (pedicel) is expanded at the point where the pod (fruit) is attached to form the *receptacle*. On its edge may usually be found the withered traces of the parts of the flower. This receptacle is a platform which supports the organs of the flower, of which the pod is one, enlarged and developed much beyond its original size. At the other end the pod tapers suddenly into the *style* which ends in a withered tip. The larger part of the pod is the enlarged *ovary*, containing the *seeds*, which make the sides of the pod bulge here and there. Compare the parts of the ripened fruit with those in the very young condition. Make drawings (side views) of the forms supplied, in the same *relative* position to the same scale. Label the corresponding parts.

At the upper and lower edges of the pods are two tracts along which the food, which is necessary for the growth of the pod and seeds, passes to these from the plant. The tracts are made up, for the most part, of special vessels through which passes the food in solution.

The pod is covered by a toughish membrane with striations. What is the direction of the striation? This fact is connected with the way in which the pod opens suddenly under oblique tension and forcibly ejects the seeds to a distance.[1]

With the scalpel cut the pod transversely through the middle of one of the seeds. The knife should pass through a seed. Is its attachment exactly in the middle plane of the pod?[2] We may now distinguish between the two *valves* forming the sides of the pod. Open a pod and decide by examination whether the seeds are all attached to one valve or the other. Verify in the transverse section. The stalk (funicle) of the seed expands at its point of attachment to the seed; from this point there spreads out, so as to envelop the plantlet (embryo) within, the *test* or seed-coat, which serves to protect the embryo after the seeds are scattered, and before germination. The two masses within each seed are the cotyledons or seed leaves. Make a good-sized drawing of the transverse section in the same relative position as the drawing of the pod.

Open a pod by splitting it along the sutures. Notice that each seed has a translucent lump near the stalk. What is the position of this lump with reference to the stalk?[3] Make a sketch to show the seeds and the pod, which shows clearly this relation.

Remove one of the seeds. Does the stalk come off with the seed?[4] The scar left by the breaking of the stalk is called the *hilum*. A seed of the lima bean may best be used for this point, as it is larger. On the same margin of the seed

---

[1] The relation should be determined by examining ripe pods during and after seed expulsion. Wild species must generally be used.

[2] The attachment of the seeds is alternately on one valve and the other, and not in the middle plane.

[3] On the side toward the receptacle. Loose seeds can be placed in their proper relative position in the pod if this point is determined.

[4] It is left attached to the pod.

as the translucent lump is a minute opening, the *micropyle*. The micropyle is of use in many plants as a way for the pollen tube to enter the young seed. Now remove the seed-coat, being careful to notice the *relative position of its outer markings and the inside structures* of the embryo. The mass within separates easily into three pieces, two big halves, the cotyledons,[1] seen above in the transverse section of the pod, and the young primary shoot. How are the cotyledons and the stem united?[2] Draw. The upper part of the shoot ends in a primary bud, the *plumule*. The lower part (hypocotyl) of the stem ends in the *rootlet* or *radicle*.[3] The cotyledons are joined to the stem at a point between the radicle and plumule. That part of the stem above the insertion of the cotyledons, *i. e.*, between these and the plumule, is the epicotyl. The part below the cotyledons is the hypocotyl. Make a drawing of these parts.

Passing a scalpel between the cotyledons, split another seed exactly into halves. The knife should pass through the middle of the shoot and divide it lengthwise. You can see in the shoot some translucent lines. Follow them out as far as you can. They are the vascular tissue, along which the water, with substances in solution, is transferred from one part of the plantlet to the other. Notice also a translucent tip of the radicle, the *root-cap*, a thimble-shaped mass of tissue which grows from within out, and so protects the root from injury as it bores its way down into the ground. Draw the exposed surface, showing the seed-coat and all the parts as they lie within, including the vascular tissue and *root-cap*.

---

[1] Certain recent views as to the homology of the cotyledons are not sufficiently substantiated yet to warrant discussion before elementary students.

[2] By the stalks of the cotyledons. The narrow portion should show clearly in the drawing made.

[3] There is likely to be some difficulty in determining the lower limit of the hypocotyl, but this can be made clear with the use of a solution of permanganate of potash, which does not readily stain the cuticularized hypocotyl, while the root on the other hand is deeply stained.

INDIAN CORN. *Materials.* — Mature sweet corn on the cob. Grains of field corn (flint corn preferably) and pop-corn ("rice" variety) ; very young grains of any kind of corn, with "silk" undisturbed.[1]

Outline of Laboratory Study. — 1. Compare several dry grains of "field" corn or "sweet" corn and note the variation in form. In what do fresh grains differ from dry ones?[2] The rough point is the place of attachment of the grain to the "cob" or stalk. At or near the end of the light, oval patch, away from the pedicel, one may find a small tubercle, the base of the withered style. Compare this ripe grain with a young one, taken when the corn is silking out. Make drawings of a young and of an old grain in the same relative position, to show the comparison.[3] Label all the parts. Compare with a grain of "rice" pop-corn and notice that the base of the style is *hollow*. Draw carefully a grain of pop-corn. The whole bean, pod and seeds, is termed fruit. What is a corn grain?[4]

2. The oval patch above referred to indicates the position of the embryo. From a soaked grain of "field" corn and of "pop" corn dissect off the outer tough membrane. To what does this correspond in the bean?[5] Now carefully dissect the embryo out of the hard yellow mass, which is a food tissue (here the endosperm). Draw the embryo from two points of view, to show all the external features. On the flat side, notice that a small cylindrical structure lies buried in a fold of a larger mass, the cotyledon. Dissect the embryo so as to fix in mind the relations of these two parts. That end of the

---

[1] See True, R. H., On the Development of the Caryopsis (*Botanical Gazette*, **18** : 212–226, 1893) for description of the integuments and their fate.

[2] They differ according to the relative amount of water; *e. g.*, sweet corn is shrunken when dry.

[3] Lateral views are necessary. The teacher should insist upon the importance of having the sketches in the *same relative position.*

[4] Inasmuch as the style is distinguishable, the grain evidently corresponds to the bean pod and included seeds, and is therefore also a fruit.

[5] To the pod.

cylindrical structure which is directed toward the style is the plumule. Where is the stem?[1]   Take three other grains ; cut two in halves longitudinally, one to be cut parallel to the broad face, the other to the edge, and the third transversely, through the middle point of the embryo.   Study the exposed surface in each case.   Draw and label the parts.   The endosperm and embryo together with a very thin membrane, difficult to recognize, are the seed.   What main points of difference are there between the fruit of the Indian corn and that of the bean plant?[2]   Which is the more similar to the bean fruit, the "field" corn or the "pop" corn grain, and in what way?[3]

CASTOR-OIL PLANT.   *Materials.* — Young ovaries and fairly mature fruits.   Seeds (variety *Zanzibarensis*) well soaked.

Outline of Laboratory Study. — 1.   Examine the features of a well-developed fruit.   Identify the parts which you have learned in connection with the other materials.   Compare the young and old condition of a fruit.   How does this differ as to the number and arrangement of parts with the bean fruit? Examine a fruit cut through the middle transversely.   Can you now see the partitions which separate seed cavities of fruit? How many?   How many seeds do you find?   Is there any unoccupied space in the seed cavities?   Is it more like corn or bean in this respect?   Do you find any sutures here as in the bean?   Examine a section of a fruit cut through the middle of a seed longitudinally.   Where is a seed attached to the wall?   Recall the relative position of the hilum and the micropyle in the bean, and find the micropyle in the castor-oil seed.   Draw to show the above points.

2.   Study the mature seed of the castor-oil plant.   The shape, color, and markings have been suggested as protective, through

---

[1] It extends from the plumule, between the folds of the cotyledon, to the root (radicle).

[2] The pod encloses one seed tightly in corn; in the bean the pod encloses several seeds loosely.

[3] The hollow at the base of the style in the rice pop-corn grain makes the comparison with the bean pod closer than in the case of the field corn grain, where no unoccupied space is to be found.

their mimicry of a beetle.[1] From the hilum along one side of the seed runs a low ridge (the *raphe*) ending at the other end of the seed, in the *chalaza*. Is this point in the same relative position as in the bean? Note that the micropyle is surrounded by a mass of soft, spongy tissue, which may be of use, though of what use is problematical. Crack open the hard shell or test. Notice at the point beneath the chalaza a reddish-colored area, from which run veins in all directions. These have served for carrying food to the developing embryo and endosperm. Examin the diagram which will help you to understand these points. Split open the kernel in its largest plane. The embryo will thus be discovered lying in a large mass of endosperm. The conical hypocotyl and radicle are at once seen. Are the cotyledons more or less leaf-like than in the bean? State your reasons.[3] Carefully remove an embryo from the endosperm, injuring it as little as possible. Is the nature of the food suggested to you? Make drawings which will show clearly the embryo and endosperm.

PINE. *Materials.* — Ripe cones of fir,[4] preferably; or of pine; young cones of same kind; large pine seeds.[5]

Outline of Laboratory Study. — 1. Examine first a cone of the pine or fir tree. Study a scale which has been removed. Look for a thin *bract* or leaf-like structure on the under side of the scale. Notice the two seeds and their wings attached

---

[1] A good chance is offered the teacher to scrutinize the value of this explanation.

[2] A diagram of longitudinal section through the micropyle and chalaza I find almost a necessity. This seed is quite difficult enough in any case. It is better for the student to be helped to get a clear idea of the seed than through lack of judicious help to get a meagre one. The structure of the test and tegmen may thus be made clear if the instructor goes into the matter. At any rate, it is very seldom that students can make out the micropyle satisfactorily, though they often think that they do. The diagram should therefore show this clearly, and should also show the chalaza pores.

[3] Thin, leaf-like venation evident.

[4] Fir is the best, since the scales fall away readily.

[5] Large kinds may be purchased from seedsmen.

to the upper side of the scale.   How does this arrangement differ from those in the three forms you have studied?[1]

2. Compare a young scale with an old one ; find all the parts, and draw by measure so as to show the old and young scales comparatively.   Which parts develop most as the scale grows?

3. Study a pine-seed and wing.   How is a seed attached to a wing?   Is the wing a part of the seed or of the scale?

Notice that the oval seed shows no external characters like those found in other seeds you have studied, save the micropyle which may be seen at the narrow end.   Split open the seed according to instructions[2] which will be given you, and you will then be able to make out the thickness of the hard seed covering, which, however, thins out toward the micropyle.   Make a drawing to show the characters.

By *carefully* dissecting the kernel find the embryo buried in the endosperm.   How many cotyledons does the pine seed have?[8]   If you split a kernel longitudinally you will be better able to make out the very big root-cap which covers the end of the root.   Draw.

Notes. — The above detailed outline of study calls for a fair amount of original work by the pupil.   It avowedly follows to some degree the verification method, without, it is hoped, freeing the pupil from the necessity of using his own abilities.   The question method is used to an extent sufficient to the purpose of leading him to do this.

The sequence of types which makes the Indian corn the second form studied is of advantage in instituting comparison, since but a single locule is present in the ovary of the first two types studied.   As to classification, no confusion appears to result, since the question is not taken up at the beginning.

---

[1] The seed is not enclosed within a pod, but lies on the upper surface of the structure which bears it.

[2] Whittle off a little from the edge of the seed, when a dark line — a suture—will be seen.   Carefully insert a knife point, resting the thumb on the seed, and pry open.

[8] According to the species.   *Pinus Coulteri* about fifteen.

The student should be guided to see essential things and to pass over non-essentials. For example, the protuberances on the *Ricinus* ovary are of no moment in this work, and time may be lost in trying to draw them. On the other hand, it may be contended that it is worth while to draw attention to such a prominent structure as the caruncle on the *Ricinus* seed, since every plant or part of a plant may have something more or less different from every other. There is a danger in studying types of forming an expectation that all plants will conform wholly to the types studied. This expectation is often too strong.

The knowledge gained by following the above outline is sufficient for a basis for some thoroughly good work in physiology and ecology. The experiments in these subjects may be carried on by the instructor and students while the laboratory work is being followed, and some observations and simple experiments may be done as home work. The following is a statement of these parts of the study.

Ecology.

The study of the outline above will give the pupil training in observation and comparison, and will also put him in possession of facts and a terminology for doing a good deal of interesting and valuable work in ecology and physiology. For convenience in discussion we give an outline of work in ecology first, but in practice it may be done, in part at least parallel to the work given above. Physiology and ecology — at least if the latter is taken in its modern and proper meaning — merge into each other, so that it is practically difficult to separate them.

The materials used for the studies here given are chiefly those already used above with some others indicated below.

1. Conditions under which germination takes place. Suggestions for experiments on this topic (air, water) are given in Bergen's *Foundations*, p. 10. This work may usually be carried on in the higher grades, or by pupils as home work.

2. Localization of absorption of water. The presence of an opening in seeds, as prominent as in the bean, is generally seized upon as an instance of adaptation for the entrance of water, and has been so interpreted in some cases. It is, however, capable of experimental investigation.

(a) Take bean seeds with unbroken tests. By applying a thin coat of soft paraffin with a warm needle, and placing in water, the failure of the test to expand whenever so protected from the water shows that paraffin prevents absorption.

(b) Seal the micropyles of a dozen seeds, place in water to examine at frequent intervals. The buckling of the test shows where the water is most quickly absorbed. Each pupil should record when and where the buckling first takes place, by using a diagram.

(c) The hilum and strophiole may be investigated similarly.

(d) The method of weighing at different times may also be carried out, but is on the whole no more instructive. The ultimate question is, Is germination delayed by such experimentation? This may be tried by planting seeds variously treated, in moist sphagnum or sawdust without previous soaking.

(e) Similar experiments may be tried on other seeds, e.g. castor oil: seal the chalazal pore, micropyle, caruncle.

(f) How does the test behave in some other seeds? (e. g. radish, flax).[1]

In discussion a beautiful case which is worth speaking of is the American mistletoe, though here, of course, the adhesive coat is derived from the pericarp.[2]

3. The rupture of the seed-coats (or pericarp in certain forms). The embryo is enclosed within a resistant test, and

---

[1] Rapidly absorbs water, and becomes mucilaginous.

[2] Von Schrenk, H., Notes on Arceuthobium pusillum, *Rhodora*, 2: 2–5, pl. 12, January, 1900. MacDougal, D. T., Seed Dissemination and Distribution of Razoumofskya robusta, *Minnesota Botanical Studies*, 2: 169–173, pls. 15, 16. 22 February, 1899.

so must do work in breaking it and thus emerging. Is this process constant in any particular form? This question may be answered intelligently by the pupil by careful examination of the earliest evidences of the rupture of the test, where it has taken place. The pea is a good one for such observation. The question is often put forward by a pupil in raising the point that the micropyle, being opposite the radicle, serves for a place for emergence of the radicle, and indeed is so explained in some books.

(a) Examine a dozen peas which are commencing to germinate. Does the rupture always occur in the same place? If so, where? How caused? Is the growth of the embryo localized?[1]

(b) Is the micropyle useful in the pine seed? After soaking well, wrap the micropylar end of the seed with fine wire and plant.

(c) What is the behavior of the pericarp in the Indian corn grain? Look for cases in which the behavior is not normal and describe results observed.[2]

(d) In the castor-oil seed, are the cracks in the test (which is very hard) constant in any particular? Is there any weak point in the test which throws light on the distribution of cracks?[3] Is there any localized growth in embryo or endosperm which stands in causal relation to the cracking of the test.

Careful observation and experimentation as above outlined lays a good foundation for the appreciation of such special forms as the squash.

(e) Place squash seeds in various positions, and allow to germinate. Does the position in which the seed is placed have any relation to the position in which the " peg " occurs?[4] (Correlate with the experiments in physiology on geotropism.)

---

[1] In the axis.

[2] Sometimes the pericarp does not split properly, and the coleoptile is quite hampered thereby.

[3] At the micropyle.

[4] Lloyd, F. E., The " Peg," or " Heel," in Seedlings of the Cucurbitaceæ. *Torreya*, 1 : 120. October, 1901.

(f) There may profitably be discussed the special adaptation, in the date (which may be grown readily in the laboratory) and cocoanut. In these forms there is a locally specialized area connected with the pushing out of the radicle. In some plants (date and many palms) a definite " plug " is formed. The common *Tradescantia* is a very good example of the same thing, and may easily be grown. Correlate these — using the date and cocoanut as special examples.

4. The behavior of seedlings in breaking their way upward through the soil. This may be made a good test for the morphological lessons learned, as well as one of adaptive behavior. Is the way in which the soil is bored through the same in all seedlings? In those in which the action is the same, are the same morphological parts involved in the same way?

(a) Indian corn. What part grows upward through the soil? (Straight plumule.) Get a good idea of the mechanism by determinating the rate of growth in the epicotyl and coleoptile (sheath leaf of plumule). Is the length of the first determined by the depth of the soil covering the grain? Plant at different depths; or, after the tips of the plumule appear, cover with cards (previously paraffined to prevent warping) with small holes for the shoot to grow through. Raise the card to different heights above the soil surface, excluding light from the sides. Is soil or light or moisture the determining factor? Mechanical advantage of this behavior, as indicated by the positions in which roots appear?

(b) What part of the pea embryo makes its way through the soil? Of the common bean? Of the squash? Is this behavior correlated with form and function of the cotyledons? Compare these with the castor-oil seedling (in which the cotyledons are thin, but are in contact with a bulky endosperm).

(c) Onion seedlings. Study carefully the germination and growth of some onion seedlings until a second leaf appears.

In what respect is this plant like others studied (pea, squash) in the way it comes through the soil? What is the function of the cotyledon in the onion and castor oil? Compare behavior of cotyledon in these with Indian corn, date, and cocoanut.[1]

The facts here brought out supply the starting-point for a study of digestion and food absorption, under physiology.

Plant onion seeds in sawdust and pretty firm soil at the depth of two cm. Does the curve which first appears look alike under the two conditions? The result may be interpreted as a form response to the mechanical conditions in the substratum. The cotyledon of the onion is a good example of an organ serving three functions, haustorial action, propulsion, and photosynthesis.

(d) Pine seedlings should be studied, and by comparing with the above types, it should be decided whether they conform to any or are different, and if the latter, in what regard?[2]

5. Compensatory growth after injuries. One of the most constant dangers to a young seedling is from predatory animals. How far a seedling may overcome such injury may be determined by the experiment of removing one or another part. *E.g.*, remove the plumule of the pea and similarly remove subsequently formed shoots. Remove the hypocotyl. Obtain

---

[1] In the castor-oil seed the cotyledons remain for some time in connection with the endosperm, and absorb food from it. They afterwards become exposed to air and light, functioning as foliage leaves. In the onion the cotyledon lengthens very considerably, curving, after the manner of the epicotyl in the pea and the hypocotyl in the bean, and, like these, breaking upwards through the soil. The portion of the curved cotyledon thus exposed to air and light then becomes photosynthetic, while the distal end still remains in contact with the endosperm, drawing food from it. In corn the sheath leaf (coleoptile), the homology of which is not agreed upon, grows straight upwards, pushing through the soil, but does not become photosynthetic, except, perhaps, to a very slight degree. In the date the first foliage leaf (the first leaf above the cotyledon) grows in the same manner, but becomes a functional leaf. In the cocoanut the first leaf has to bore through the husk, the cotyledon acting as a haustorium.

[2] The curve is in the hypocotyl, passing often into the cotyledons.

acorns and separate one of the cotyledons from the stem at the base of the petiole,[1] after the plumule is visible.

Field Work.

It is distinctly profitable to carry out some field work to enlarge the scope of the pupils' observations. Some useful suggestions for such exercises have been published by Robison.[2] It is well to have definite problems in mind, based upon the pupils' work. The following topics are suggested:

What general difference of behavior is there between many-seeded and one-seeded fruits when fully mature? Does dehiscence take place in dead and dried ovaries only? (The behavior in *Impatiens* should be carefully observed and recalled later under the subject of turgor.)

Observe particularly the movements of the valves of pea or bean fruits. What is the condition under which these take place? What does the direction of the striations (or grain) of the valves indicate in this connection? Look for other fruits (*e.g.*, castor oil) in which you find the same striation in the walls of the fruit, and compare the movements of dehiscence throughout.

Study other mechanisms from the point of view here gained.

Distinguish between active and passive methods of dissemination, and determine the relative effectiveness.

Examine the peduncles of young and old flowers and fruit of various plants, and observe the (carpotropic) movements which they undergo. Do the movements supplement in any way the other organs in the dissemination of the seeds?

Look for fruits with awns, *e.g.*, *Erodium*, *Stipa*. See how the awns behave under varying degrees of moisture. These suggestions may not all be followed, but are given to show the direction which may be profitably given to field work.

Pupils may be encouraged to collect materials and study

---

[1] Lloyd, F. E., Teratological Notes. *Bulletin Torrey Club*, 22: 396, pl. 247. September, 1895.

[2] Outlines for Field Studies of Some Common Plants, pp. 31–35.

them. As careful records should be kept of field observations as of other work.

Physiology.

The teacher must distinguish between experiments which teach special things about seeds, and those which illustrate general physiological truths. The work in physiology for high-school students may be for the most part taken during the first half of the course, which should constitute an introduction to the remainder.

It will be unnecessary to outline experiments which are elsewhere described, it being our purpose to indicate what may properly and profitably be done in connection with the above outlines on the morphology and ecology of the fruit and seed.

Expenditure of Energy by the Living Plant. — Aside from energy whose expenditure is not visibly demonstrative, that, namely, expended in metabolism, a large amount may be measured, which the plant uses directly in adjusting itself to its environment.

Growth is of course merely a form of movements in general involving the expenditure of energy. It offers a distinct pedagogical advantage to commence physiology by demonstrating that a living plant does expend energy. Growing seedlings may be used with great clearness of results.

1. Expenditure of energy by growth. (a) Show that the upward growth of the hypocotyl or other organ through the soil, involves lifting and pushing aside of the soil. Direct observation will furnish data.

(b) The pushing downward through the soil of a root is clearly another example.

2. Show that there are other (metabolic) processes going on which result in the expenditure of energy, *e.g.* heat. This may be done by registering the temperature of growing seeds.

In discussing the phenomenon of heat evolution, reference may be made to the heat produced in decaying compost and how it may be utilized, *e.g.*, in making beds in forcing-frames.

The determination of the fact of the expenditure of energy serves as a motive for tracing the source of energy for the growing seedling.

To do this one may proceed as follows :

(a) Remove the cotyledons from a young pea seedling. (1) Does it grow? (2) Does it therefore expend energy?

(b) Remove the endosperm from some young Indian corn seedlings. Plant some of these and affix to the cotyledon of each of several others a little mass of stiff cornstarch paste. Do these grow equally well and why?

The general conclusion arrived at will be that to grow, to do work, food is necessary. It is therefore the source of energy for the growing seedling. The parent plant as the source of food may be alluded to, but its activities in this connection are taken up later. The ecology of storage organs in the seed should also be brought up as well as the resulting value of seeds as food for man.

The question of physiological importance now is, by what means is food manipulated in the plant so as to make its energy available, *i. e.,* to accomplish its release.

This topic involves the matters of oxygenation, oxidation, and excretion of carbon dioxid and of the chemical and physical nature of foods. Perhaps the best way, certainly a very good way, is to take up first the gas exchange in growing seedlings.

1. Show that a gas exchange does take place when seeds are growing. Make the result more general by using also the petals of flowers (rose petals which are taken from large expanding buds), fungi (toadstools, mushroom, etc.).[1]

2. Determine what this exchange is by determining the resultant gaseous bodies.

(a) Shake up in a given volume of air some baryta water (barium hydroxid solution) and note degree of milkiness.

(b) Treat a like volume of air in which a taper has burned

---

[1] See MacDougal's *Elementary Plant Physiology*, Fig. 75.

a few minutes, to show that barium hydrate is an indicator, that after burning, a gas which causes the milkiness is present now in greater proportion.

The information must be given that the gas is CO_2 (carbon dioxid) indicating how this is determined.

(c) Pass the breath through baryta water to show that CO_2 gas passes off from the body.

(d) Show in the same way that plants excrete CO_2.[1] It may be inferred that an oxidation goes on in living organisms and that a plant produces heat by oxidation, and by analogy, other forms of energy. Show this to be so as follows :

(e) Seedlings will not grow unless they have oxygen.[2] They cannot therefore do any work. (Do movements occur in absence of oxygen? See if a root will bend in an atmosphere of hydrogen.)

(f) When they do grow, they produce a volume of CO_2 equal to the volume of oxygen used.[3]

(g) Some seeds will produce CO_2 when no free oxygen is present, *e.g.*, peas (intramolecular respiration). If two or three peas are placed, after soaking, in a small test-tube which has first been filled with mercury, and inverted so as to stand in a small vessel[3] the amount of CO_2 set free in a night will displace a good deal of the mercury. Introduce a particle of caustic potash. Note the rapidity with which the CO_2 is absorbed, the mercury again filling the test-tube, or nearly so. While it is probably not necessary to discuss the process of intramolecular respiration, the teacher should be fully cognizant of it.

Having shown that food is the source of energy for the plant, and that the energy may be obtained therefrom by oxi-

---

[1] See MacDougal's *Elementary Plant Physiology*, pp. 100–111, for an excellent brief presentation of respiration in its modern aspect.

[2] For further suitable experiments see Ganong's *Plant Physiology*, pp. 96, 97. Straight test-tubes will do if the seeds are supported by wire gauze.

[3] Use a test-tube just a little larger in diameter than the seeds used.

dation, a convenient opportunity is thus afforded to take up the study of the foods which occur in seeds. The object of such study is to determine the kinds of foods and their physical characters which have important physiological bearings. There is also the lesson which may be touched upon at this time of the great economic importance of seeds as sources of food of all kinds for man, not to mention other uses. Of course, the chemical nature of these foods is a matter which is too difficult for the high-school student, and such information as may be made use of later must be given.

The method of study here advocated is as follows: 1. Examine the various foods occurring in seeds by the method of extraction — the method of the physiological chemist — one which has been found to be very practicable both on account of the conclusive character of the results and on account of the removal of all but the simplest of the microchemical tests, which are generally not at all adapted to young beginners.[1] The tests should be made first on the substance, a well-known food, to be used as a criterion, and then upon the extracts.

2. Test the solubility and the diffusibility of some foods. It is not profitable to take up all of them, since starch, cane sugar, and grape sugar serve to illustrate well the principle involved.

3. Recall the anatomical conditions which are found in, e.g., the corn grain, in which the starch occurs in the endosperm, while the expenditure of energy is in the roots and shoots, together with the facts that (a) although the starch is removed from the endosperm it does not appear as starch in the root and shoot, and (b) that the haustorium (cotyledon, scutellum) is non-perforate, its surface being smooth and continuous.

4. Test the diffusibility of the product of starch and diastase and show it to be grape sugar, thus making clear the value of digestion.

---

[1] Lloyd, F. E., Botany in the Horace Mann School. *Teachers College Record*, 2 : 1–4, 30–59. January, 1901.

The outline for this work presented somewhat in detail is as follows:

Foods. — The kinds of foods and methods of determining their occurrence,[1] especially in seeds.

(a) Proteids. Demonstration of the reactions of an acknowledged proteid by applying the following tests to a weak solution of egg albumin in water:

Coagulation by heat. Test the coagulum with nitric acid and ammonia. Boil a little of the albumin in nitric acid, *cool* and add *slowly* ammonia.

Determine whether proteids occur in the seeds which have been studied, or in other seeds.

Grind up as finely as possible in a coffee-mill about twenty-five grams of dry seeds. Make extracts as follows:

(1) With water (100 cc.), allowing to stand for twenty-four hours. Test the extract obtained with the above tests, and compare the results with those obtained above with egg-albumin. Note the similarity of animal and plant albumin.

(2) Taking the same material, extract it with a 10 per cent solution of common salt. A second proteid, insoluble in pure water, will thus be thrown down. Obtain this in dry form by dialysing and drying. This may then be examined and tested as above.

(3) A third proteid may be obtained from wheat by taking the flour, making a dough, and then washing the dough in a cloth under the tap. The sticky substance — gluten — is a proteid which is insoluble in water, and should be tested with nitric acid and ammonia.

(4) Does gluten occur in peas? The question should be answered by applying the method in (3). It is, on the whole, preferable for this series of experiments to be done by the instructor.

(b) Starch.

---

[1] For a more detailed account of these methods, see MacDougal's *Text-Book of Plant Physiology*, Chapter IX.

Demonstrate the color reaction (blue) of starch with iodine by adding the latter (a very weak solution) to some *very thin* starch paste.

˙Examination by pupils of starch grains in the cells of the potato tuber, mounting the sections in very weak iodine solution.   Let one or two cells with contained starch grains be drawn.[1]

Application by the students of the iodine test to determine the presence or absence of starch in the seeds studied.

(c) Sugar.

Determine the color reaction of Fehling's solution and grape sugar, or glucose, by boiling them together and obtaining a red precipitate.   Ordinary sugar of commerce may be used, but has the disadvantage of being chiefly cane sugar, which, however, may be inverted by means of dilute sulphuric acid.

Test extracts of seeds for the presence of sugar.   If a negative result is obtained with Fehling's solution, add a little.acid to a small volume of the extract, after which repeat the grape sugar test.

(d) Cellulose (reserve cellulose).   It should be pointed out that this food substance does not occur in marked quantities in any of the seeds heretofore studied.   In this instance we must resort to the micro-chemical test.   It is not wholly necessary to introduce cellulose, but is worth while because of the instructive behavior of the date seedling.

Demonstrate the hard white reserve cellulose as it occurs in the date or persimmon seed.

Using a well-soaked seed, make a thin section with a sharp knife, place the section on a piece of glass in small drop of chlor-zinc-iodine.   The color reaction is characteristic.

(e) Oils.

Demonstrate the solubility of an oil (*e. g.*, cottonseed or olive oil) in ether.   Naphtha or benzine may be used, but are not so volatile and therefore rather less effective.

---

[1] To make good preparations of potato, cut freehand some thinnish sections ; rinse well in water, and mount in iodine-eosin.

Grind up some of each of the kinds of seeds studied, and extract them with ether. Place the extracts in glass vessels, and examine after the ether has passed off. The oil is easily recognized as such by its behavior on paper, or on a glass surface by its smear.

Digestion. — (1) Demonstrate insolubility of starch in cold water.[1] Test a very weak starch paste for grape sugar. Add a little diastase in solution and repeat the test in five to ten minutes.

(2) Demonstrate the indiffusibility of starch, by placing a little of the thin paste in a dialyser. Test the inner and outer fluid for starch. Add a little diastase to the starch mixture, and after an interval test the outer fluid for grape sugar. In making these grape-sugar tests, it is very necessary not to allow the deep color of the Fehling to mask the precipitate if slight. Obviously, the instructor must learn to manipulate his operations so as to detect small quantities, if he is working rapidly. It is well worth while to show that these changes are rapid.

(3) The fact that starch occurs in minute granules may throw open to some doubt its inability to move in the plant. In the absence of full anatomical demonstration of the continuity of the epidermis enclosing the starch, the objection may be met by showing that cellulose, also a food, occurs in the form of a continuous mass. In this way the date seed is especially good for making very clear the necessity of digestion. These seeds will germinate and produce, in about two months, good-sized seedlings. The gradual growth of the haustorium (the end of the cotyledon) and surrounding it, the zone of translucent endosperm where the action of the ferment (cytase) is taking place, are splendid evidences. For demonstration, a partly germinated cocoanut is very useful on account of the fine, large haustorium.

The wide significance of digestion is better appreciated

---

[1] The possible slight solubility of starch is a negligible matter, as will be seen by testing its non-diffusibility.

when some knowledge of the anatomical structure of plants is obtained from the study of the root and leaf.[1]

Irritability. — That plants expend energy, and that food is the source of this energy, furnish one aspect of physiology — the causal. That the structure and movements resulting from these are, on the whole, those which enable the plant to cope with the conditions in which it finds itself, furnish the telcological aspect. We have shown elsewhere that there is a good deal of danger that this phase of botany may be treated in an insufficient or even thoroughly unscientific manner, and we have tried to emphasize the principle that teleological interpretations should be, as far as possible, tested.

Adaptation in plants is possible only because of the adaptive responses of plants to stimuli, and is seen most clearly when the responses of a given organ are different under different conditions. The ability of a plant to perceive stimuli and to respond to them is called irritability. The behavior of seedlings towards various environmental factors illustrates this quality, and the results of the behavior give us the data for scientific teleological interpretation. Experiments on some of the various tropisms may be done with seedlings, and serve well for the purpose of study in adaptive response. The method of experiment need not here be given, as directions will be found in the references appended. The tropisms which may be studied are the following :

Geotropism of roots (primary and secondary), of the shoot and of leaves. (See below under Etiolation.)

Phototropism of root and shoot.

Hydrotropism of roots.

Chemotropism of roots. Separate a battery jar into two chambers with a piece of tin, with a good number of holes punched in it. Fill one chamber with finely chopped sphagnum well washed with water and rinsed with distilled water, and the other with sphagnum well dipped in nutrient solution.

---

[1] The subject of digestion is admirably treated in Green's *Physiology of Plants.*

All the sphagnum should be well squeezed out so that there will be no free water. Plant seeds upon the moss near the partition, and keep covered. When the roots are well developed note their distribution.

It is highly important that the general notion that the sum total of reactions such as these are expressed in the form of the plant as a whole. This point is generally neglected both in the books and by the teachers, but, after all, there is no significance in the different responses of the different organs except when these are viewed as parts of the whole. Thus the different kinds and degrees of geotropism of the members of the root system account largely for its configuration and for the advantageous arrangement of its elements. When other factors are unequally distributed in the substratum, advantageous modifications of this configuration result. Further, this may be applied to the parts above ground. The axis is frequently epigeotropic, the leaves diageotropic. This may be shown clearly by growing plants in the dark. The sweet potato is very good for this. Any change in the position of the axis results in a rearrangement of the leaf blades so as to keep them in a horizontal plane. After bringing the plant into a condition of one-sided illumination, the phototropic responses mask the geotropic response, but it must be concluded that the positions of these organs is the resultant of responses to two stimuli acting in different directions. Generalizing, we conclude that the whole organism is the result of responses to the stimuli of all environmental factors (both inner and outer) applied in various directions.

Etiolation. The subject of etiolation in large part in elementary work is, like that of irritability, useful in directing the attention to the teleological aspect of plant physiology. But it is very useful also in getting a point of view for the later study of photosynthesis. We have already indicated above the value of studying the plant in the dark for determining geotropic responses. Other points to be noticed are :

(1) The relative development of parts. In a particular

plant, what parts grow more, and what parts less than they would in the light. In some cases these facts may be interpreted as adaptive, as, for example, the behavior of the shoot of a seedling which is, in the dark, such as it would be if making its way through the soil, where it is, of course, also in the dark.[1] The frequent persistence of Sachs' curve, or its analogy as, *e. g.*, in the cotyledon of onion illustrates this.

(2) The color reactions. Most plants fail to produce chlorophyll in the dark. The exceptions are to be found chiefly in plants attuned to weak lights, as some forest-floor plants, *viz.:* ferns. Red color is usually produced, *e. g.*, in the beet, which, by the way, is a most beautiful plant for these experiments. The important relation of chlorophyll to light is thereby indicated. What this relation is may be treated in connection with the study of the leaf.

The outline suggested above should furnish the basis for work which when thoroughly presented may serve as an adequate introduction to botany. It should be well understood by the teacher that the bias of the whole course will be determined in the first few weeks, and it is therefore necessary that the right method of study shall be closely adhered to, even though it may seem that the pupils work rather slowly. Making haste at first will do no good ; if the student learns to work properly he will learn to work rapidly.

At some convenient point, either in connection with the study of each type of fruit and seed, or after the completion of the work up to this time, the early stage of germination should be studied to determine in addition to the points called for under "Ecology" (p. 153), the fate of the parts of the embryo. For this purpose it is advisable to have in addition to the material to be distributed, a lot of growing plants in pots or boxes, for observation from time to time in the living condition. This could well be made a part of the home

---

[1] The most exhaustive study of etiolation, one with which teachers should be acquainted, is by MacDougal, D. T. *Memoirs of the New York Botanical Garden*, Vol. II. 1903.

work, for which the pupil might be supplied with seeds and be held accountable for their growth and study. The following points should be worked out :

(1) What is the mode and direction of growth of the various parts of the embryo? What are their ultimate positions? These questions may be answered by a series of sketches. What is the color of the parts underground and of those exposed to light? Keep a record of all movements which may be noted in any parts.

The development of the root and shoot from the embryonic parts opens up a new field of study of the more intimate details of the organs of the plant. The most important general fact for the teacher to keep in mind in leading the pupil to the proper interpretation of the ecology of the highly differentiated plant is the stratification, so to speak, of the environments into two parts, with opposite characters as to the water content. The full appreciation of this will give the teacher a good viewpoint, and will give the chief point of contrast in the functions of root and shoot, and the grasp of this by students is a good thing to work for.

The Root.

It is convenient and logical to study first the root and work upwards, although, of course, this is not the only way. As a matter of fact, the plant as a whole must be kept in mind at all times, while in practice we have to study it in some orderly fashion.

The points which are generally understood to be of importance are so well worked out in the text-books that we need do no more than mention them, save to point out that in the study of the root-cap and of root-hairs there is a very good opportunity of getting a knowledge of the general structure of the cell. For this purpose I know no better material than the roots of the Wandering Jew (*Zebrina*), which are readily obtained in numbers by placing short cuttings of the plant in water, most conveniently in a shallow dish. The outer cells of the root-cap become exfoliated and retain their normal appearance, although separated from the plant. In this condition they show most beautifully the typical plant-cell structure. If the class is made up of third or fourth year students, they may, with profit, study the behavior of the cell during plasmolysis, for which good directions will be found in Atkinson's *Elementary Botany*. This topic is of fundamental importance in the understanding of the mechanical significance of turgor in the plant, and well repays the effort spent upon it, if the student is sufficiently advanced.

The outline for laboratory work should embrace the following points :

(1) *A typical root system.* — External features. Tap root,[1] root hairs, root cap. For the root cap, the roots of oats or of some small grass are very good, being small and transparent. The root cap in *Lemna* or *Spirodela* should also be used, and although somewhat unusual in their general character, help very materially in getting a good notion of the structure.

Secondary roots. — Their position, best studied by means of a root cage. Note how curvature in the tap-roots affects the distribution of secondary roots, and the ecological significance of this.

Anatomy. — Plan of structure of a tap-root — chosen on account of its convenience as to size — including cortex, stele : wood, cambium, and bast. Later, when studying the stem, attention should be called to the difference in the mechanical relations in the root and stem, this point affording a good point for comparison.

The endogenous origin, and the arrangement in orthostichies of new roots. The former can be made out by careful external examination, especially on larger roots. Sections, of course, help to make the matter clear and are necessary for the latter point, and these are easily made by hand through the first node of an Indian corn seedling, in which the endogenous

---

[1] As indicated, potassium permanganate may be used for delimiting the root from the hypocotyl.

origin is clearly shown. If the instructor has the requisite skill, hand sections of the tap root, which are necessary to show the structural relations, may be made after it has been hardened in alcohol. The large broad bean is very good for this purpose; the pea, although small, may be used. Otherwise microtome sections may be resorted to.

In working on the anatomy of organs, the student always finds a good deal of difficulty in deciding what to draw. Generally he will start to put in a lot of detail, and, finding it a long and usually useless job, he will make a lot of meaningless little circles for cell walls. It is much better for him to be told just what to do, namely, to make out the groups of tissues, representing these by a diagram, making no attempt at finer representation. If, however, the time and ability of the student warrant it, a careful representation of a few cells for each kind of tissue, as seen with strong magnification, will be best.

There is, however, a difficulty connected with the study of transverse sections with which the student meets readily overlooked by the teacher, that, namely, of getting an idea of the total form of the cell, a matter of great importance in understanding the movements of water and foods. It is necessary to study longitudinal views before this can be done. But it is not difficult to get these in a small root, by crushing it slightly, or teasing it. If, however, for lack of time, this point is allowed to pass with a word of explanation, depending on the experimental work to help clear the matter up, the whole subject may be understood later when the structure of the stem is studied.

The root hairs, as above indicated, may be studied carefully for the sake of getting a good notion of the protoplasm. It is important for the purpose that the roots bearing the root hairs, which are to be microscopically examined, should be free from air, and the best way to do this is to grow them in water as above indicated. The seeds of lettuce, radish, or any quickly germinating seed will produce great numbers of root hairs when grown on moist blotting paper, and each student may easily have good material to study.

Physiology. —·The function of water absorption by the roots ; wilting following injury or drying of the roots ; bleeding from a stem cut near the soil ; tracing out the path of water (and of contained materials) in the root, through root hair, cortex, and vascular tissue. Show that the work of raising water in a plant may, in part at least, be accomplished by the root by *osmotic* pressure (root pressure experiment).[1]

The study of the irritability of the root has been planned for above.

The secretion of acid by roots. A very simple and pretty demonstration may be had by planting some Indian corn grains which have just started to germinate so that the roots may lie in contact with blue litmus paper. This may be done by lining a plain glass tumbler with the paper and filling in with moist sawdust, which, of course, must be neutral. Put the corn grains near the top between the glass and paper. As the roots develop, the reaction will be obtained.

The ecological significance of the secretion of acid by roots is suggested in the experiment of arranging a growing seedling so that the roots may etch a piece of polished marble.

What materials besides water are absorbed by roots? The answer to this can be had by controlling the materials supplied to the roots, which may be done by means of water cultures. Elaborate cultures are generally difficult to carry out, and of no particular profit to an elementary class, since the whole problem of the functions of mineral salts is an abstruse one. The point of chief educational weight is the fact that such substances as starch, sugars, proteids appear in the plant, but not in the air or water of the culture. This conclusion, together with the physiological work on the seed, prepares the way for the work on photosynthesis.

Ecology. — 1. The mechanical rôle of roots : The ramifying

---

[1] For which the rubber-plant is very good.

root system; guy roots in corn. Organs of attachment in climbing plants: English ivy, trumpet creeper, poison ivy.

2. The modifications in the shapes of roots resulting from the storage of food materials. It must be remembered that in many cases, *e. g.*, radish, the hypocotyl takes part in the storage and therefore constitutes part of the enlargement. The result of artificial selection in producing useful food plants.

3. Haustorial roots of parasitic plants, *e.g.*, *Cuscuta*. Hand sections of alcohol-hardened material may easily be made. It is not difficult, also, to raise *Cuscuta* from seed and the very interesting habits of the seedlings may be watched. Coleus or Balsam make good host plants.

4. Symbiosis in roots. Mycorrhiza, the association of roots and fungi, *e. g.*, Indian pipe (*Monotropa*), hemlock, and many others: root tubercles in leguminous plants caused by nitrifying bacteria, and their very great ecological significance.

5. Air roots are most interesting if material may be had. The rapid absorption of water by the air roots of orchids through the specialized *epidermal tissue*, the velamen. If there is a green-house at hand, a trip is well worth while for the purpose of seeing these roots, and also the

6. Respiratory roots of many plants, *e. g.*, some palms, etc. Reference may also be made to the respiratory roots of swamp plants such as the mangrove, *Avicennia*, which grows in the tropics. Illustrations may be found in many books. Cypress "knees," "swell-butt" black gum; arched roots.[1]

7. Vegetative reproduction in roots as, *e. g.*, in sweet potatoes, the suckers of many trees and shrubs.

Field work on underground roots is, on the whole, rather less satisfactory than any other subject, although of itself of very great interest.

1. The clinging organs of climbing plants should be examined, and their position and origin determined, to decide

---

[1] Kearney, T. H., Contr. U. S. Nat. Herb. 5: No. 6, 1901.

whether they are roots or not.[1]   In what parts of plants are
adventitious roots most commonly produced?   Plant cuttings
of various kinds, and study the roots as they appear, noting
position.

2. Compare the roots of several land and water plants.
Correlate facts observed with water as an environmental
factor.   Plant various seeds with the roots submerged and in
moist air, and note development of root hairs.

3. Note the spongy texture of many submerged roots, due
to the development of aërenchyma (respiratory tissue).   (Sub-
merge willow twigs — aërenchyma from lenticels.)

4. If the opportunity is favorable, without the danger of
doing harm to wild flowers, it is a profitable exercise to determine the extent and distribution of roots of some plants.
Weeds, of course, may be sacrificed *ad libitum*.

The Shoot.

The shoot consists of an axis (the stem), which, itself a
complex of organs, produces lateral organs.   These are (a)
axes of higher orders, and (b) leaves of different kinds, of
which the foliage leaves are the typical photosynthetic organs,
and, while by no means exclusively so, are from the point of
view of nutrition of chief importance.

Recall the plumule (the primary chief-shoot) of which the
pupil should get a clear idea.   Dissect a large bud, marking
out the axis and the lateral organs of various shapes.   It is
well worth while to demonstrate longitudinal sections [2] through
a shoot tip to show the young lateral organs, the origin of
which is superficial.   Compare with roots in this regard.

---

[1] Teachers should, of course, be watchful, on account of the danger
of poisoning from the poison ivy.   Robison (*Field Studies*, p. 22) suggests that the stems and leaves should be enclosed in glass, and thus
studied without the necessity of touching.   This should be done before-
hand, and particular attention should be directed to the similarity and
differences of the virginia creeper and poison ivy.

[2] Good free-hand preparations of Elodea stem tips will serve also.

External Anatomy and Morphology. — The scars of scale and foliage leaves on twigs; annual growth increments. The relative position of buds and leaves as indicated by the leaf scars.

The relative position of leaves — *i. e.*, their phyllotactic relations — in, *e. g.*, maple (or ash or horse chestnut), in oak, hickory ($^2/_5$), and in ailanthus ($^3/_8$). Relative positions of branches; the growth or suppression of the chief bud, and production of monopodial or sympodial type of tree.

The age of a twig as indicated by the "rings" formed by the closely packed scale-leaf scars of terminal or chief buds.

The inflorescence as a branching system of shoots. I have found that a good dynamic view of this usually dry and terminological part of botany may be gained by studying in this connection two or three types, avoiding, however, those (*e. g.*, *Datura*) which show displacement, and so become too difficult for elementary work.

For this purpose a raceme (*Capsella*) an umbel (wild carrot), and a cyme (chickweed). A good brief treatment of this subject will be found in Bergen's *Foundations of Botany*, p. 186. The teacher should emphasize the phylogenetic aspect of this topic, showing how one type of inflorescence may be derived from another by the different relative development of parts.

Other superficial characters of twigs — especially the lenticels. Study portions of the stem of various ages, and note the splitting of the epidermis. At what points does it begin? How long does the epidermis remain intact? What is the ultimate result? (The epidermis will be found to split at different ages in different trees. The splitting is the beginning of the exfoliation of the epidermis, which ends in laying bare the cortical tissues. The bark is therefore made up of originally internal tissues which, secondarily, become protective, being highly resistant to the entrance of parasitic plants.) Can any evidence of activity be discovered in the epidermis and bark of trees? (In spring and early summer new exposure of bark can be seen in the bottom of rifts. Constant falling of bark scales, etc.) Poplar is especially good for this topic. which is well adapted for field work.

Internal Structure. — For getting a clear idea of the primary structure of the dicotyledonous stem, the twigs used above are not good for beginners. The stem of *Clematis* is excellent. The stem of the Dutchman's pipe (*Aristolochia*) is most frequently used, since it is easily obtained and shows very distinctly the following structures : In a transverse section of a growing internode, the epidermis, cortex, central cylinder : vascular tissue (*phloem, xylem*), cambium, medulla, and medullary rays. In a three or four year old internode, make out the following secondary changes. Exfoliation of the epidermis (of which the expanding radish hypocotyl offers a good illustration), formation of bark (correlate with work on *lenticels*), splitting of the cylinder of mechanical tissue (commonly, but unfortunately called " hard bast ") ; annual increments of phloem and xylem, persistence of cambium cylinder.[1] The pupils' attention should be directed to the observation of the relative thickness of the cell walls in the xylem, mechanical cylinder, and epidermis as compared with the remainder of the cells of the stem.

Peel off the epidermis or bark from any young stems, and note the green tissue beneath. This point is to be referred to during the study of photosynthesis in the leaf. For the study of the monocotyledonous stem, corn is, of course, good, the chief points of contrast with the dicotyledonous stem being the absence of a continuous cambium and scattered bundles.

Annual increments of growth in trees. Pupils should verify their conclusion as to the ages of twigs determined by observation of scale scars by counting the annual growths of wood. Method of determining the age of trees, and possible sources

---

[1] It is very easy for the pupil to get a false impression by talking about the cambium " ring," without understanding the conditions aright. The cylinder, of course, appears as a ring in a transverse section, but the appearance should be properly interpreted from the first.

of error. Age of a tree = age of the sapling of the height of stump, plus number of wood layers ("rings"), allowing for possible reduplication of growth within a year.

Physiology. — 1. Growth. Determine, by the marking method, where the regions of maximum elongation are in a dicotyledonous and in a monocotyledonous stem. Correlate the mechanical adaption of the cylindrical leaf base in grasses, etc., with the growth of the axis.

2. Movement. Circumnutation, especially marked in vines, accompanied by torsions. A very simple and instructive experiment may be done by wrapping a thick solder wire about a round stick spirally, after first making a row of ink dots along one side of the wire.

3. Bending movements (geotropic). Where do such movements take place, and how far do these coincide with regions of maximum growth? Determine by marking method. That such movements are responses to the stimulus of gravity can be shown by means of a simple clinostat experiment. Young radish hypocotyl is good for this experiment.

4. Lenticels as organs for aeration of the stem. Place twigs in water in a moist chamber, and watch for the signs of growth in the lenticels. Arrange a twig so that the cut end shall project beyond the upper end of a cork, the upper end being plunged into water in a bottle. Bore another hole for a bent tube, through which the air in the bottle may be exhausted by means of an aspirator or air-pump. The cork should, of course, be tight. The air will escape through the lenticels.

5. Mechanics of the stem (a) maintenance of rigidity by means of turgor. Tissue tension, and effects of plasmolysis on herbaceous stems (rhubarb petioles illustrate this well, though of course they are not stems). Wilting in plants (see Atkinson's *Lessons in Botany*, and *First Studies in Plant Life* for a very good treatment of this topic).

(b) Rigidity attained by means of thickened cell walls. Compare the rigidity of two fresh stems, herbaceous and

woody, of similar dimensions, by the support of weights while
in a horizontal position. Allow them to dry, and note results.
Turgidity in young tissues, which later become woody, indicating the limit of adaptive value of turgor in a mechanical way.
The study of this topic may, of course, be extended to other
parts — especially leaves, which offer many beautiful examples
of adaptation. The full appreciation of the mechanical value
of turgor in cells in giving rigidity to the plant body can be
had only when such work is done as is suggested by Atkinson
(*Elementary Botany*, pp. 13–21). When this is not possible,
it is still worth while to do the work outlined above.

6. The function of the stem in transporting water. Place
some translucent plant (*e. g.*, balsam) in eosin water (red ink),
and determine the course of water throughout the entire plant.
As far as possible this experiment should be done also quantitatively; *i. e.*, the rate of the ascent of water should be
made out.

7. Transpiration experiments may be introduced here, or in
connection with the leaf. There are three available methods
of determining the loss of water, (a) by watching a moving
bubble, (b) by the use of cobalt chlorid, and (c) by weighing. The first of these is the most difficult to set up, but is
very instructive.[1]

The cobalt chlorid method requires care, but is not difficult. Filter paper, wet with a ten per cent solution of cobalt
chlorid, and thoroughly dried, must be closely applied to a
leaf surface, and protected from the action of the air by a bit
of glass. The reddening [2] will go on more or less rapidly,
according to the amount of transpiration. The transpiratory
activity of surfaces of the same leaf and different leaves may
thus be compared within a brief space of time ; and the results
make a very vivid impression on the mind.[3] Atkinson (*First*

---

[1] MacDougal, *Text-Book of Plant Physiology*, p. 210.
[2] Cobalt paper is blue when dry, but reddens on access of the slightest
trace of moisture.
[3] Lloyd, F. E., Botany in the Horace Mann School.

Studies, p. 97) has planned another form of this experiment, which serves for demonstration before a class as a whole. There is an advantage in each member of a class doing the experiment for himself, and it is so easy to do, in spite of impressions to the contrary, that it is a pity not to do it. The leaves of *Zebrina* serve very well for the purpose. They are easy to obtain and keep well, after being removed from the plant, for a long enough time at least for distribution to a class, and for experimentation.

The method of weighing is the commonly used experiment, and is a thoroughly good one. It should be carried through several days, and the amount of water lost each twenty-four hours placed in a vial for comparison, and for the purpose of making the results vivid. Thus if a plant in transpiring loses twenty-four grams, twenty-four cc. of water should be measured out. The method of determining transpiration by means of a hygrometer may also be used. For a simple form, see MacDougal's *Elementary Plant Physiology*, p. 74.

Ecology. — 1. The part that phyllotaxy, apart from other factors, plays in bringing about the light adjustments of leaves. Study cases of marked dorsiventrality, — *e.g.*, Beech, etc., — and decide whether the phyllotaxy is in itself expressive of dorsiventrality ; and find instances of dorsiventrality produced in spite of radial symmetry in the axis itself. In such, what other factors bring this about?

2. Where on the twigs of various trees do the biggest buds occur? Determine the cause of this, so far as may be possible, by noticing the environmental relations of a given twig. What are the ecological results? Where are the twigs most numerous? and the leaves? Is there an advantage to the plant in this? What do we learn about the art of pruning fruit trees and shrubs? Analyze the " habit " of trees, referring it to the different types of development as far as possible.

3. Chief shoots are sometimes replaced by lateral shoots. Is this due sometimes to accident? (*Coniferæ*.) Recall experi-

ment of excising the plumule in the pea. Does this take place regularly in some trees? (*Sassafras*, sympodium.)

4. Examine vines and shrubs, with the view of determining (1) whether any torsions occur in the stems and (2) whether there has been any ecological significance in bringing about light adjustments in the leaves.

5. Study the stems and other supporting parts, such as petioles, etc., with reference to the various arrangements of mechanical tissues. Annuals, biennials, and vines afford the greatest variety of instructive examples. A hand-lens may be sometimes necessary. Diagrams should be made. (See Kerner-Oliver's *Natural History of Plants.*)

6. Stems which are modified by the storage (a) of water, as adaptations to xerophytic conditions, *e. g.*, cacti, *Salicornia*, etc. ;[1] (b) of foods, as adaptions for vegetative reproduction, *e.g.*, potato tuber, *Arisæma* (or crocus) corm, etc.

7. Stems as climbing organs (tendril stems) as in *Ampelopsis*.

8. Vegetative reproduction : (a) by separation of twigs in crack-willows; (b) by runners and the like, *e.g.*, strawberry, blackberry, etc. ; (c) by suckers (stems produced from roots). The condition of a neglected orchard.

These topics on the ecology of the stem are especially appropriate for field work, and should be, as far as possible, carried out in this way. While given here as work strictly on the stem, it cannot be separated wholly from the study of leaf ecology, and indeed should not be. This applies especially to topics 1, 4, and 5. Further suggestions will be found in Robison's *Outlines for Field Studies*, pp. 17–31.

If circumstances allow, the elements of the theory and practice of grafting should be taken up. A very thorough account may be found in Sorauer-Weiss, *Physiology of Plants*, and in Bailey, L. H., *The Grafting Book*, also *Cyclopædia of Horticulture.*

---

[1] MacDougal, D. T., Some Aspects of Desert Vegetation, *Plant World*, 6: 249–257, Illus. November, 1903. *Bulletin*, No. 19, *The Carnegie Institution.*

The Leaf.

External features of a foliage leaf. — Form and venation of a monocotyledonous and dicotyledonous type. The structure of the epidérmis and of stomata and the distributions of the latter. (Correlate with transpiration, using cobalt chlorid method.)

Internal structure. The epidermis and mesophyll; palisade and spongy chlorenchyma.

The lesson on the structure of the leaf offers, in this part of the course, as Ganong has pointed out, a very good opportunity for training in anatomy, and for material the leaf of the rubber plant is very satisfactory because of ease of cutting sections by hand. A half-dozen narrow strips taken parallel to the secondary veins may be held together, and sections made very rapidly. The epidermis is, however, compound, and the stomata rather highly specialized. As a matter of fact, however, it is rather too difficult a task for high school pupils to make out the structure of a stoma in transverse sections, although a good student will often succeed in this. The class may then be allowed to examine the successful preparation. The pupil should, however, make out the intercellular spaces and the form of the chlorenchyma cells, and correlate these facts with the positions of the leaf, the insolation and the distribution of stomata. The thick cuticle should be understood as a protective arrangement to prevent undue loss of water. This may be demonstrated by slicing off a bit of the cuticle from a rubber plant leaf with a sharp scalpel, and noting the results. The morphology of the leaf parts is best studied in developing buds of various kinds, in which different parts serve as protective coverings in the winter bud.

Physiology. — 1. The path of water in the leaf blade, traced by means of eosin (see above under " Stem ").

2. Determine, by marking with indelible ink, the regions of growth in a monocotyledonous (*e. g.* onion,) and dicotyledonous leaf. Correlate with form of venation.

3. Determine the responses of leaves to gravitation. Sweet

potato vines are very good, and when excluded from light show very regular diageotropic responses.

4. Transpiration (see above, on p. 178, the cobalt chlorid test).

5. Photosynthesis. Show (a) that green leaves fail to form starch in the dark; (b) that the non-green parts of leaves (geranium "Bijou," coleus, white-striped grass or white-striped wandering jew, not, of course, the silvery-striped variety) do not form starch in the light, and (c) that the green parts of leaves do. To apply the iodine test most successfully use a chloral-hydrate-iodine solution upon leaves from which the chlorophyll has been removed by alcohol. Leaves may, after treatment, be rinsed, stretched upon glass and dried, when by transmitted light a beautiful result will be seen. Such preparations will keep for a long time, so that they may be used repeatedly if the teacher has to have them for numerous and large classes.

That photosynthesis demands CO_2 (carbon dioxid) may be easily shown by taking a cutting of geranium, which has been in the dark twenty-four hours, and, after enclosing it in a bottle provided with a CO_2 absorber, exposing it to light. (See Ganong, *Plant Physiology*, p. 89.)

6. Respiration. What is the behavior of the leaf toward the air when in the dark? Answered in part by testing (with barium hydrate solution) the air surrounding leaves placed in a bottle kept in the dark, for excreted CO_2.

7. Excretion of water by leaves. Atkinson (*First Studies in Plant Life*, p. 103) describes a good arrangement for experimenting on this point.

8. Secretion of nectar by extrafloral nectaries found on leaves, *e.g.*, cherry, brake (seen well when the "crosiers" are unfolding),[1] elder, castor-oil plant. Set up an artificial nectary with a carrot, potato, or any such fleshy part.[2] Try to make

---

[1] Lloyd, F. E., Extra-Nuptial Nectaries in the Common Brake, Pteridium Aquilinum. *Science*, II., 13: 885-890. June 7, 1901.

[2] MacDougal's *Elementary Plant Physiology*, p. 50.

an artificial nectary on a large petiole, by scraping the cuticle and putting a few grains of sugar on the surface.

Ecology. — 1. The distribution of mechanical tissues and their relation to the support of the leaf blade. Bulrush (*Typha*), etc., pine, corn (relation to stem). Experimental test by cutting the prominent veins.

2. Leaf surfaces : waxy or hairy coverings and the like.

3. The forms of leaves. Degrees of dorsiventrality in branches and the part played by the form of the leaf in bringing about the result (correlate with phyllotaxy). Torsions in petioles. Leaf mosaic : relative size and length of leaf blades and petioles. The mosaics formed in compound leaves by the pinnæ, stipels, stipules, etc.

4. Leaf movements. How far are the positions in which leaves are found due to movement of the leaves themselves out of the position assumed when deprived of light? In what part of the leaf does such movement take place? Can any special organs be found which accomplish the movements? Are there any periodic movements of leaves? Test the "sleep" notion, by seeing if the so-called "sleep-movements" may be induced in any other way, as *e.g.*, by temperature changes. (Some further good points for experimentation may be found in Atkinson's *First Studies in Plant Life*, Chapter XX.)

5. Find instances of nectar-secreting organs on stems or leaves. Do these attract insects? Can any evidence be found that the insects are of any benefit to the plant?

6. Study instances of vegetative reproduction from the leaf; *e.g.*, walking fern, bryophyllum, begonia, peperomia, etc. If there is a greenhouse available, there is usually opportunity for seeing propagation by leaf cuttings.

7. High specialization in leaves. (a) For climbing, as tendril leaves, *e.g.*, pea. (b) Pitcher leaves (*Sarracenia*), and other forms of insect traps (*Drosera, Utricularia, Frullania*).

8. The preparation of trees and shrubs for winter by shedding leaves, caused by cellular activity, for which any material

with a large leaf base is good.   Note the condition of the leaf
scar, when the leaf falls; is it an open wound, or protected?

The Bud.

It is scarcely necessary, perhaps, to treat this topic separately, except to indicate how it may be treated as a whole.
All that naturally falls to high-school work in this subject has
been already suggested above; much that is actually done in
such schools is much more appropriate to the grades, such,
for instance, as the recognition of different kinds of winter
buds, and the gross features of their early development.   Buds
are, of course, the young ends of shoots, which may or may
not enter into a resting condition, according to circumstances.
The upper end of the primary shoot above the cotyledons,
called technically the plumule, is a bud, and it is perhaps
better to call it so in the early work on the embryo rather
than to use the term plumule.   This fact suggests a line of
thought regarding the behavior of the bud somewhat as follows.
In herbaceous annual plants, does the bud develop continually?
In some examples (pea, rubber plant, geranium, fuchsia, etc.)
what is the disposition of the leaf parts in the bud?   What
leaf parts chiefly enclose the bud?   Is their position favorable
to the protection of the inner structures, and are these latter
of such texture as to need protection?   What kind of protection?   In plants subjected to the rigors of unfavorable climate the buds enter upon prolonged resting periods.   When
resting buds are formed, what are the more obvious changes
which take place in the component parts?   Are these related
to water, temperature changes, or mechanical dangers?   At
what time are winter buds formed in various plants?   Do all
the shoots of the same plant (*e.g.*, *Ampelopsis*, blackberry)
form winter buds?   Trace out the homologies in the leaves of
expanding winter buds.   The resting buds (hibernacula) of
water plants, *e.g.*, *Utricularia Elodea*.   Buds which serve in a
special manner for vegetative reproduction (onion, bulbils of

various plants), and cultural bud modifications, which serve as food (Brussel sprouts, cabbage). The use of buds in grafting.

Determine whether food materials are present in buds and adjacent portions of the stem.[1] (Horse-chestnut.)

The experimental proof of the value of winter buds would be a subject of interest. To do this remove the bud scales, and see whether the young parts can withstand the exposure, apart from temperature changes (*e. g.*, drying action). Remove the scales from frozen buds and bring treated and untreated buds indoors and subject to rapid thawing. Most of this study is adaptable to field work, and should, if possible, be made so.

The flower is not treated here.

The course up to this point may properly be regarded as introductory in the sense that, in addition to training in the scientific method as applied in botany, it brings to the attention of the student the chief ideas of morphology and the principles of physiology, involving the notion of adaptive response. At the outset of such a course, which will occupy a half-year's work, the teacher should have the whole matter in his mind; it should, as it were, stand out as a picture, so that so far as possible the bearings of one part on another are clearly apprehended. To this end, it is well to examine critically the treatment found in various elementary text-books. This should be done to determine, for example, what the morphological content is, and how it is brought into relation with the rest of the work.

When the student has fairly appreciated this body of knowledge, he is in some degree prepared to pass on to do the work in types — to get some idea of a series of forms, which represent the evolution of the vegetative body and of the methods of reproduction. The second half of the school year is better adapted to this part of the work on account of the greater

---

[1] Halsted, B. D., Reserve Food Materials in Buds and Surrounding Parts. *Memoirs Torrey Club*, **2** : 1–26, No. 1. 1890.

ease of getting appropriate materials. It may be conceded, too, that in view of the extent and nature of the training of the first half-year, it will not be amiss to commence with a study of lower forms first, if this is preferred by the teacher. Either method is consistent, and one is as logical as the other. For younger pupils, it is probably better to commence at the top of the scale. The time of the year and availability of materials will have a practical bearing on this point. Early in the year, in February and March, algæ and fungi are easily obtainable, the following three months bringing the higher plants in abundance.

A detailed account of the study of type forms is, of course, not called for here; and it would occupy too much space to point out how the dynamic viewpoint is to be emphasized at all points.

In the following outline, therefore, I shall not attempt to do more than mention the most available and advantageous materials for the high school, and add such notes and suggestions as seem of particular value. It may be emphasized here that the most valuable asset that a teacher can have for this part of the course is a wide knowledge of forms, without which it is well-nigh impossible to present the matter in a well-balanced fashion.

The teacher will find many additional suggestions of value in Chamberlain's *Methods in Plant Histology;* in Caldwell's *Suggestions to Teachers,* and in Bergen's *Teachers' Hand-Book.*

Cryptogams (Flowerless Plants).

The more immediate aims of the teacher should be to help the student: (1) to get a fair notion of the appearance and habits of the plants of the different large groups; (2) to appreciate the physiological contrast between chlorophyllous and non-chlorophyllous plants, *e. g.*, algæ and fungi, and their correlated life habits. The economic importance of the lower plants stands in close relation to the facts connected therewith; (3) to get a good idea of alternation of generations by contrasting the relative development and complexity of the gametophyte and the sporophyte ; (4) to gain a knowledge of the essential features of sexual and non-sexual reproduction. For the first of these aims, the school should be provided with a well-selected set of specimens for use in demonstration. By the method suggested in Chapter IX, it is possible to make use of a great deal of herbarium material, while mostly a school herbarium remains unused. Thus it is usually impossible for high-school students to study, say, lichens, in any detailed way. Their anatomy is very difficult to make out, and only a very small amount of microscopic work is profitable. The pupils should, however, see enough of at least three well-chosen types to get a fair notion of their appearance, and a field lesson may well be added to the school exercise, for the purpose of exercising the ability of identification.

The subject of alternation of generations may be exemplified most profitably by the Bryophyta and Pteridophyta. In connection with the Thallophyta, the question is too abstruse and academic in character for young students. I would therefore not attempt to bring the topic to their attention until the Hepaticæ are examined.

On the other hand, the most fascinating subject of life habits, and the significance of chlorophyll, is most clearly to be appreciated by the study of the algæ and fungi. The subsidiary topics of symbiosis, saprophytism, degeneracy, and the like are here naturally prominent. For getting a satisfactory knowledge of reproduction, in a wide sense, we find abundance of favorable material among all the groups, and for sexual reproductive methods especially so. The most available forms are mentioned below.

Myxomycetes.

Although these forms are questionable in their affinities, the behavior of the vegetative body, the plasmodium, is very instructive and is easily handled. Abundant material may be found and grown in the laboratory, and the reactions to light and moisture studied. If the teacher can manage to get a preparation which shows the movements of the protoplasm,[1] it is well worth while to take time enough for each pupil to see it. The others may be busied the while with an examination of the sporangia of a few types, which are quite easily preserved in a dry state. During field work in the early autumn, material may be found in abundance on rotting logs, leaves, etc. Shaded corners of old fences are favorite localities for some of these forms. I have found a half dozen different kinds in as many minutes in such a place.[2]

Schizophyta.

Bacteria (*Schizomycetes*). — The great practical importance of these forms is the justification for some study of them. Outside of the examination of stained preparations of a few of the more striking forms, and of a large motile form (*Spirillum*), microscopic work is of no further importance. The chief interest in the study of these organisms is physiological, pathological, and technical, and even their classification is based upon physiological characters. The work should therefore be chiefly experimental.

The most useful forms for demonstration are as follows :

Hay bacillus and a small motile *Spirillum* may be obtained in hay infusion two or more days old.

A spore-forming bacillus occurs on raw potato which has been kept moist for two or three days. Spore formation never fails to take place.

A very large *Spirillum*-form may be obtained in old alga cultures, especially on addition of a small amount of $CaSO_4$ (Calcium sulfate).

The drippings of steam exhaust pipes on engines usually

---

[1] For directions, see Stevens's *Introduction to Botany*, p. 103. Macbride, T. H., The Slime Moulds, *Rhodora*. April, 1900.

[2] For discussion of affinities, see Bessey's *Briefer Course*, last ed.

furnish iron bacteria — useful for connecting morphologically the bacteria and blue-green algæ.

In old cultures of *Nitella, Cladothrix* may be found.

For other suggestions see *Outline for Bacteriology for High Schools*, Frost, W. D., and Hastings, E. G.[1]; Stevens's *Introduction to Botany*, p. 254 ; Peabody's *Laboratory Exercises in Anatomy and Physiology*, p. 67.

Discussions. — The instructor may very profitably give a brief sketch of the history of bacteriology, referring especially to the work of Leeuwenhoek, Lister, and Pasteur ;[2] Biogenesis and abiogenesis ;[3] Infection and immunity ;[4] Plant and Animal Diseases ;[5] the great importance of hygienic conditions and habits.

Note. — The outline above given for work with bacteria is probably too long to form a part of a regular course in Botany. Such work is, however, without doubt, most valuable informationally, aside from the value as training. In some high schools (*e. g.*, in the Boys and Girls High School, of New York) bacteriological work forms part of a course in physiology, and has been carried on very successfully. There is no reason why, if a course in general physiology is given in the eighth grade, it should not be made part of the plant physiology work.

Blue-Green Algæ (Schizophyceæ). — The blue-green algæ are very common and easy to get, and some, *e. g., Oscillatoria,* on account of their movements, are instructive objects for study. They present, however, no feature of any great impor-

---

[1] *Jour. App. Micros.*, **6**: 2205. March, 1903.

[2] Pasteur's original classical paper on the presence of organized bodies in the atmosphere is available, in German, as a reprint published by W. Engelmann, Leipzig.

[3] An admirable brief discussion, a model for the teacher, is to be found in T. J. Parker's *Lessons in Elementary Biology.* London, Macmillan Co. 1891. Lesson 9.

[4] See Sternberg's *Infection and Immunity.*

[5] Much valuable literature is to be obtained from the United States Department of Agriculture.

tance for high school work, and they may, therefore, be treated very briefly, or omitted if time is lacking.   If a greenhouse is available the root tubercles formed on cycadean roots in which a symbiotic fission-alga may be examined.   The remarkable case of *Azolla* and its algal symbiont serves as an interesting example for brief discussion ; the case of the liverwort *Blasia* scarcely less so.

The chief reason for referring to these plants is their economic importance as agents in the contamination of water supply.[1]

Thallophyta.

Algæ. — The green and brown algæ are of great educational importance on account of the clearness with which the sexual process of reproduction may be studied.[2]   For this purpose *Spirogyra* and *Vaucheria,* among the green algæ, are the best types ; among the browns, *Fucus.*   They are common, and the sexual organs may readily be obtained.   A rather careful microscopic study of Spirogyra and Vaucheria is amply justified.   If time permits *Fucus* may be added, since the living material may be shipped by express from the seaboard.[3]   Preserved material may be used, but is not so valuable.   Alcohol should be used.   This will shrink the thallus, and harden it. The sections will swell up when placed in sea-water which can be made artificially if not otherwise obtainable.

It does not appear profitable to spend time in the study of

---

[1] See Farlow, W. G., On Some Impurities of Drinking-Water caused by Vegetable Growths.   Massachusetts Board of Health, First Annual Report. 131. 1880.   Moore, G. T., The Contamination of Public Water Supplies by Algæ.   *Yearbook of United States Department of Agriculture.* 1902. p. 175.

[2] A good general account on The Origin of Sex in Plants, by B. M. Davis, can be found in *Popular Science Monthly,* November, 1901.   Also The Evolution of Sex. *Ibid.* February, 1903.

[3] Material has reached Kansas from New York, and has then been used to demonstrate fertilization.

the minute structure of the algæ beyond that of *Spirogyra*. This plant, howéver, is remarkable both in structure and for its beauty, and is, too, a splendid test of the ability to interpret what one sees. This on account of the spiral chloroplasts. Species with not more than three or four chloroplasts should be chosen, as otherwise the structure becomes obscured. Very beautiful results may be obtained by staining with a watery solution of iodine (KI and I) and eosin. If this stain is of proper strength, the nucleus and cytoplasm will be stained pink, and the starch in the pyrenoid blue, the chlorophyll remaining for some time green.

The reconstruction of a transverse section of a *Spirogyra* cell taken through the nucleus is the best possible test of the student's ability to interpret what he sees through the microscope. In such a drawing the nucleus, chloroplasts, cytoplasm (threads radiating from the nuclei and peripheral layer), and cell wall should appear. It is well worth while, if time and other conditions allow the introduction of these studies at all, to do the work on *Spirogyra* in a thoroughly satisfactory manner.

Conjugating material should be collected and preserved in a chrome-alum-formalin mixture. Enough preparations for demonstration may be prepared in a short time.

Vaucheria is valuable for the contrast it shows in comparison with *Spirogyra* in regard to the reproductive elements. In Spirogyra the sexual cells are structurally similar, while physiologically there is a difference seen in the motility of one of them. In *Vaucheria*, the structural difference is marked, the egg being large and well supplied with food, and the sperm cell small and highly motile. Beyond the study of this point it will hardly pay to go in high-school work, since *Vaucheria* is not typical in its anatomy. It belongs to the *Siphoneæ*, a curious aberrant group of plants.

The carposporic type of reproduction is, I believe, too difficult for very elementary pupils, since it involves too delicate observation and interpretation. However, it may be pointed out that *Batrachospermum* (growing in running streams) and *Nemalion* (marine) are good forms for class work. Material may be obtained from dealers.

Fucus is most useful for demonstrating the process of fertilization, and is so hardy that young plants will grow slowly for a month or more in watch-glass. The only precaution necessary is to see that the normal salinity is maintained by adding fresh water as the water in the watch-glass evaporates.

In order successfully to see the sperm cells actively swimming about the eggs, a diœcious species (*Fucus vesciculosus*) should be chosen. The male and female plants should be separated and kept fairly warm in the dark (in a tin box) and moist, but not under water. When the eggs and sperms have oozed out from the conceptacles, they are ready for use. They should be mixed in a watch-glass or on a slide. This is possible only from November to January on material from the eastern coast.

For the study of zoöspores, the best material of wide distribution that I know of is *Drapanaldia,* which may be obtained in early spring in slowly running streams attached to stones, leaves, etc. If plants are brought in and placed in vessels over night, the next morning the whole process of zoöspore formation may be watched with great ease. This form is well worth introducing into all elementary work, for no one can fail to be interested in the process. *Ulothrix,* which occurs in brackish waters, is exceedingly good. *Ulva,* which can be kept in aquaria, may also be used.[1]

Other forms which may be studied are diatoms (for their shells and movements) ; *Pleurococcus* (arrangement of cells) ; *Sphærella (Hæmatococcus) lacustris* [2] ("red snow" plant).

Œdogonium, Nitella (for the movement of protoplasm. A

---

[1] See also Coker, W. C., Algæ and Fungi for Class Work. *Jour. App. Micros.,* **6** : 2411. July, 1903.

[2] A full description of this interesting plant, by Hazen, T. E., Sphærella lacustris. *Memoirs of the Torrey Botanical Club,* **6** : pp. 211–244; 2 colored plates. 1899.

very instructive object, especially if there happens to be a binocular microscope available). *Coleochæte* has been recommended by Atkinson as illustrative of the beginnings of alternation of generations. It is, however, like *Nemalion* and *Batrachospermum*, not adapted to young students, and is hard to obtain, except through dealers. It appears, however, to be obtainable by allowing cultures of algæ to stand for a considerable period — about five or six months.[1] It is suggested by W. C. Coker[2] that cover glasses be suspended in culture jars on the side away from the light, since the common form is hard to remove from the surface of the glass without breaking.

The laboratory exercises should be supplemented with an opportunity for the pupils to examine a good series of herbarium material of the algæ, for the sake of getting a general idea of their appearance. Many forms may also be grown in small aquaria including the marine form — *Ulva*, and some others.

Fungi. — The wide range of adaptation and the very great economic importance of fungi make them important objects of study. The classification, except in a very broad sense is, however, difficult and not pertinent for elementary work. In point of fact, the recognition of the fungi as a group is based on a wholly physiological character, and it would be just as logical and true to the facts to regard the Indian Pipe (*Monotropa*) as a fungus, while really it is a flowering plant, as every one knows. The fungi, then, are not a continuous series ; as in the algæ, the three types of reproduction are to be found.

If the subject of reproduction is taken up at all, the following are the best and most available materials.

Sporodinia grandis may be obtained in the autumn by collecting some of the firmer kinds of toadstools and keeping

---

[1] Hickman, Mary A., A Method of Raising Coleochæte. *Jour. App. Micros.*, **6**: 2256. April, 1903.

[2] *Jour. App. Micros.*, **6**: 2411. July, 1903.

them under glass covers to prevent drying out.   It will be very certain to produce zygospores.[1]

The *Cystopus* on the common ragweed will illustrate the oösporic type.   The sexual elements are easily obtained.

The ascosporic type cannot be studied by elementary students except so far as they can examine the result in the " fruit."

The pretty red *Lachnella,* found very commonly on decaying wood, is good for illustrating the *Peziza* type.   At this point it is profitable to compare with the *Peziza* cup, the "fruit" of the Lichens (refer to, or introduce here, *Pleurococcus*) for which the common *Physcia stellaris* is a good type.

Of the powdery mildews, *Microsphæra* (on lilac leaves, very common late summer and autumn) is very interesting on account of the beautiful anchors radiating from the fruit, and *Uncinula* (common on maple leaves) scarcely less so, though possessed of simple hooks.

The work on the Basidiomycetes, including the puff balls, should be chiefly of the natural history character, and this is true also of the rusts and smuts.   These latter should, however, not be neglected because of their great economic importance.   The teacher can profitably refer to the early (1760) Massachusetts legislation against the barberry, before its relation to wheat was understood.[2]   The great annual loss to this country on account of corn smut, amounting to over $2,000,000 annually,[3] certainly warrants reference to this plant.

Educationally, the fungi have practical advantages in their abundance, in many cases their ease of culture, and in their availability for field work.   It seems therefore reasonable to emphasize in the high school the study of the more obvious

---

[1] Coker, W. C., *loc. cit.*

[2] Plowright, C. B., *British Uredineæ and Ustilagineæ.*   London. Kegan Paul, Trench & Co.   1889.   p. 47.

[3] *United States Year-book Department Agriculture.*   1902.

characters of a good number of kinds, rather than to expend too much time in details. It should be pointed out, however, that there is a good deal of such work, which is at present done in the high schools, which could be done as easily in the elementary schools, as, for instance, the recognition of the chief kinds of the large forms of toadstools and mushrooms, and the relations of many of these to diseases in trees. Even the more obvious rusts and mildews on common plants and the common saprophytic kinds, in their gross features recognizable to the naked eye, or with a large reading lens, might be studied in the higher grades. If this were done, much time would be saved for the high-school course, and better and more intensive work there done.

It is very easy to grow many common forms, including Mucorineæ, *Penicillium*, coprophilous fungi,[1] etc. Almost any substratum will produce something worth observing.

The following topics for discussion and reading may be suggested.

Absence of chlorophyll and correlated life habits. Rôle of fungi is underground plant parts (Symbiosis). Plant and animal diseases, and the great loss and distress caused by fungi, *e. g.*, famine in Ireland caused by *Phytophthora infestans* of potato rot.

Method of entrance of fungi into the higher plants (correlated with anatomy of leaf).

The teacher will find a good account of the fungi in L. M. Underwood's *Moulds, Mildews, and Mushrooms.* Also Conn, H. W., *Bacteria, Yeasts and Molds in the Home.*

Lichenes. — As suggested above, the fungal character of the lichens is indicated by the peziza type of " fruit." [2] Further anatomical work other than the demonstration of the algal

---

[1] For a monograph of these, see Griffiths, D., The North American Sordariaceæ. *Memoirs Torrey Botanical Club,* **11** : pp. 1–134, 19 plates. 1901. $1.75.

[2] The Basidiolichenes need not be taken into account here.

element need not be done. The pupil may, however, be led
to distinguish the chief common types, especially as to habit
(crustaceous, foliaceous, fruticose). A great help to both
teacher and pupil are the well-illustrated papers by Mrs. C. W.
Harris, in the *Bryologist* (from Vol. IV on). A handy manual
is Schneider, A., *A Guide to the Study of Lichens.*

Bryophyta.

These plants and the ferns are especially useful in the study
of symmetry and alternation of generation, since in all of
them the sporophyte and the gametophyte are well enough
developed to be readily studied, even without the help of the
compound microscope. The subsidiary topics which are connected with the understanding of the evolution of the sporophyte are : (1) The relative persistence of the sporophyte and
gametophyte in each group and in the different groups. Connected with this is the mode of development of the sporophyte
in each group ; (2) The degree of complexity, as indicated by
their organ-forming power, of sporophyte and gametophyte.
Anatomical evidence is, perhaps, less available in elementary
work, chiefly on account of lack of time and the necessity of
technique.

Hepaticæ (Liverworts). — For the above-named purposes
no materials are more varied and interesting, and at the same
time more easily studied than the liverworts. The temptation
is to spend too much time on them. While most of them are
rather small, they are not so much so that they are not studied
readily with hand lenses, or at most with low powers of the
microscope. They are, moreover, easily obtained, and may be
preserved dry. Their small size favors the storage of a great
deal of material in small space. After thorough wetting[1] the
individual plants may be separated and placed in water in small

---

[1] In some it is a little difficult to get rid of air bubbles, but this may
be done with a brief immersion in boiling water or alcohol.

white dishes (small sauce or butter plates), and each pupil may then have abundance of good material.

It is singular that these plants, particularly the foliose hepaticæ, have been so little made use of in elementary courses, but the reason appears to be that they are so little known and they are, therefore, supposed to be difficult to find and to study, which is contrary to fact.[1] Many of them are readily grown in the laboratory if kept in a reasonably moist atmosphere,[2] on well-drained soil. Especially instructive is material (*e. g., Pellia*) collected in very early spring when the sporogonia are small. These will develop in the laboratory and the whole behavior of the capsule may be watched with ease.

Generally *Marchantia* has had chief attention, but there is no doubt that it is among the least useful of the liverworts for general study, inasmuch as it is a very highly specialized type, both anatomically and physiologically. It is far too difficult to study, except as regards its general features. The gemmæ are, of course, useful on account of their size, and the ease of experimenting on dorsiventrality for which purpose also the gemmæ of *Lunularia*, so common in greenhouses, are equally good.

For the study of archegonia the liverworts are not quite so good, perhaps, as mosses, and if such study is undertaken by pupils individually, which I think cannot be done, the mosses would better be used. *Marchantia*, however, offers advantages in this detail. The antheridia are comparatively easy to manage in both mosses and liverworts. In the former especially the living sperm cells may readily be observed. It would be better, I believe, for the teacher to make use of well-prepared

---

[1] The series of articles in the *Bryologist*, by W. C. Barbour, will be found useful, as also Underwood's systematic treatment in Gray's *Manual*, by means of which the genera, at any rate, can be easily named.

[2] Too moist an atmosphere will produce unusual reactions, which disturb the usual appearance. Such reactions, however, are instructive to the student.

sections and of charts and diagrams. The stages of the sporophyte may, however, be studied without much difficulty, if a clearing agent (lactic acid is very good) is used. Total preparations mounted in glycerine jelly may also be used, and can be kept in sufficient numbers of duplicates for classes. Thus time will be saved.

The most readily obtainable types are the following: *Radula* and *Porella* (on tree trunks), *Cephalozia* (on borders of swampy places, hummocks, decaying logs), or *Scapania* (on moist, shady banks; a beautiful large species grows in hilly places), are good for general characters, as they produce sporophytes abundantly. *Frullania* (common on tree trunks) is interesting on account of the pitcher leaves, and fruits abundantly. A little field experience will discover many others equally good in one feature or another.

Musci (the true mosses). — The points of general interest in comparison with the liverworts are the occurrence of an extensive protonema (dimorphism of the gametophyte), the radial symmetry in the gametophyte (absent in the Hepaticæ), the mode of development of the sporophyte (the younger tissue at its top), the specialization of capsular tissues, of which the elaborate peristome, annulus, and chlorenchyma are the result, and the secondary elaboration of the archegonium wall to form the calyptra, which serves to protect the young tissue of the sporophyte during the lengthening of the seta.

The more useful types are *Polytrichum*, or Hair-moss, for general characters. The antheridia are especially easy to get at, and can be seen with the naked eye on pulling apart the male "flowers." It is very good for sectioning. *Philonotis fontana* is also good for antheridia; for antheridia, and especially for archegonia, *Mnium* is very good. *Pogonatum tenue* is especially valuable for its extensive protonena, and is common on shaded clay banks. The calyptra is similar to that of the *Polytricha*. *Georgia* (*Tetraphis*) *pellucidia* for gemmæ and for a simple peristome. *Funaria*, for general characters, and especially for the beautiful peristomic movements, and the shedding of the annulus, when the capsule is immersed in water. To do this successfully, material should be gathered, usually in June, when well ripened and dried. The pupils may place a few dry sporophytes in water, in a small vessel, and observe the movements of the seta, the exfoliation of the annulus and the loss of the operculum. Upon drying, the capsules may be attached to slides with paraffin, so that the peristome is directed upwards. On applying the lower power, the hygroscopic movements of the peristome teeth, when breathed upon, are quickly displayed.

The adaptation of leaves as in *Sphagnum*[1] and *Leucobryum*, for holding water; the elaborated chlorophyll bearing laminæ in *Polytrichum* leaves, the occasional secondary bilaterality, as in *Fissidens*, and the methods of spore dissemination, are topics of interest for the teacher to elucidate.[2]

Pteridophyta (Ferns and Fern Allies).

The extent to which the structures of these forms may be studied is so well understood that but little need be said. The ground covered in such text-books as that of Stevens, of Bergen, and of Andrews represents fairly what may usually be done, and the teacher will by consulting these get helpful suggestions.

The true ferns may be grown indoors easily. *Lycopodium* must be collected. Dried material of this genus, if it has not been pressed too hard, will, upon boiling, be restored to its usual appearance, color excepted. *Selaginella* can be grown

---

[1] The economic value of Sphagnum as a peat-forming agent should be touched upon.

[2] For an interesting series of papers, see Grout, A. J., The Peristome. The *Bryologist*, April, 1901, 5: 53, 73, 94. 1902, etc. Also his Mosses with a Hand Lens (very good for beginners), and Mosses with a Hand Lens and Microscope. Many other papers appear from time to time in the *Bryologist*.

indoors as easily as the ferns, but needs a moister air. They should, therefore, be covered with glass. *Equisetum* must be collected in early spring. Fern prothallia may be grown readily.[1]

It is hardly possible for pupils to make out much about the antheridia and archegonia. With a little skill, however, the teacher may demonstrate the antherozoids. To do this a mature prothallium must be taken after it has remained for twenty-four hours without watering, and with no free water. It should be mounted upside down, in a very small drop of water, covered with a cover glass and after a while pressed lightly. Generally such treatment will be rewarded. The objection to this kind of work is that it does take a good deal of time ; but I believe that it is worth it if the teacher is skilful. Other work may engage the attention of pupils who are not occupied by the demonstration, so that it need not mean loss of time for any of them. If the number of students is so great as to make the demonstration of· living sperms impossible, a good preparation may be made by fixing and staining the sperms with iodine-eosin, taking care that the amount of potassium iodide is not great enough to cause collapse of the sac.

In the true ferns, the points of study may be somewhat as follows : Sporophyte : relative position of stem and leaf. Form of leaf : the venation of several types to discover general character ; position of sorus with reference to venation and form of three types of indusium in different genera. Absence of indusium (*Polypodium*) ; false indusium (*Pteridium*). For elementary work, there is no value in the study of the stem anatomy. General structure of sporangia (*i. e.*, especially the annulus), and their movements, demonstrated by the use of glycerine.[2] Or a piece of a leaf rich with ripe sporangia

---

[1] For excellent directions for growing prothallia, see Chamberlain's *Methods in Plant Histology*, p. 104. Also Andrews's *Botany all the Year Round*, p. 254.

[2] Atkinson's *Elementary Botany*, pp. 171-173.

may be wet thoroughly and then allowed to dry, lying with the sporangial surface up, on a piece of white paper. As the sporangia dry, the spores will be expelled to some distance, which may be measured. Herbarium material collected just before the sporangia are completely matured is best. Study growing prothallia and some which have young sporophytes. Make up a series showing the development so far as can be made out with a hand lens. Demonstrate sections of prothallia showing archegonia and antheridia. Enlarged photomicrographs would be useful here.

Equisetum. — Examination of fertile and sterile shoots, spores, and their movements by means of the elaters. Prothallia may be grown from fresh spores and early stages demonstrated.

Herbarium specimens of *Lycopodium* and *Selaginella* may be exhibited. Additional points of study in *Lycopodium* are the spores (all of one size), and the differences between foliage leaves and sporophylls. In *Selaginella*, the two different sizes of spores (heterospory).

At this point a brief sketch of the geological history of the pteridophytes should be given, attention being called to the character of the vegetation of the coal period, and the nature and origin of coal. For this reason, it is especially important for the pupil to become acquainted with *Equisetum* and *Lycopodium*, as remnants of a once widespread and huge vegetation.

The following types may be demonstrated by means of museum preparations. Nothing more than an examination sufficient to get a general idea of the form of the plants should be required. This is therefore to be done very briefly. *Isoetes, Marsilia* (venation, leaf unrolling), *Pillularia*, not in North America generally (leaf unrolling), *Salvinia, Azolla.*

In order to continue the study of alternation of generations, and especially to direct the attention to the evolution of the sporophyte, a very good method is to point out its simple anatomical and physiological character in the liverworts and the early development of the sporangium. In the true mosses, the sterile tissue is much more extensive relatively, and the sporangium develops later, and there is found even in the capsule a relatively large amount of photosynthetic tissue and a complicated mechanism for setting free the spores. The teacher will keep in mind, of course, that the liverworts, mosses, ferns, and the fern allies do not represent a direct line of development. We may, however, see in them advancing stages of complexity in development, which enable us to form a legitimate notion of evolution. In the ferns, forms such as *Aspidium*, *Onoclea*, or *Osmunda*, *Marsilia* beans, and *Selaginella*, followed by the pine scale, lead up well to the understanding of the sporophyll in the Angiosperms.[1] In *Aspidium*, only a small amount of the tissue is spore producing, the green leaf (photosynthetic tissue) having full development. In *Onoclea*, the whole of certain fronds becomes considerably reduced in extent, and contracted into organs enclosing the sporangia. In *Marsilia*, the highly specialized organ produced on the leaf, which enclosing the sporangia offers an illustration of a step in the direction of the development of the ovule, which here contains two kinds of spores. These may be seen easily by placing the beans in water until the gelatinous ring swells discovering the spores.[2] In *Selaginella* the two kinds of spores are found in separate sporangia, and the leaves which produce them are small. The ligule is of no importance here. The general correspondence to the condition in Pinus or other Pinaceæ is readily seen, and the step from the gymnospermous to the angiospermous condition, involving the evolution of the flower, is then not difficult to understand in a general way. It is to be noted that all the work by the pupils on these interesting plants may be done with a hand lens.[3]

[1] Coulter and Chamberlain, *Morphology of Angiosperms*, Chapter II.

[2] Material may be obtained through dealers.

[3] A most useful volume, for teacher and pupil alike, is Waters' *Ferns*. If one book on ferns for the pupils' reference shelf is to be chosen, it should be this.

The introductory chapters to Underwood's *Our Native Ferns and Their Allies* constitute a first-class essay on general matters pertaining to the Pteridophyta.

Phanerogams (the flowering plants).

Gymnosperms. — If the outline above suggested has been followed, the structure of the cone will be already understood, but may be briefly reviewed in this connection. The pollen of the pines is well worth microscopic examination, on account of the special adaptation in the bladdery appendages, which are connected with the wind as the agent for pollination. Field work should, if possible, be arranged for at the time of flowering, especially if the conifers are abundant in the region.

A very large amount of pollen is often to be found in some regions, making the ground yellow. When not so abundant it may still be seen forming yellow streaks about the bases of rocks from which it has fallen or been washed by the rain. Both kinds of cones should be sought for, and the arrangement of the scales for catching the flying pollen examined. Attention may also be directed to the position of the cones at flowering, and later in the season to the carpotropic (anthotropic) movements, which occur in some kinds (*Picea, Pseudotsuga, Tsuga,* etc.). Seedlings may be looked for, and a good piece of field work done in elementary forestry by determining the number and age of seedlings which have grown in or near a wooded area, and so whether they germinate and develop least in the forest or in the open. By studying the branching, very close estimates of the age of conifers may be made, if they are not too old. The length of time the leaves persist may be made out, together with the general character of the foliage. It will be good training to learn to recognize the different genera by their leaf characters, the leaf regarded as a whole and in transverse sections. The morphology of the fascicles in Pine and Larch offer good simple morphological exercises.   Interesting and valuable, too, is the study of wound healing.[1]

Especially practical will work in elementary forestry prove, and for the guidance of the teacher there are good books.[2]

Search for signs of disease and determine the causes as far as possible (see under Fungi), whether animal or plant.

Angiosperms. — It is obvious that, if any real attention is given to such work as has been suggested the time for the study of the flowers of the higher plants will be limited. There is practically a choice between the more thorough study of a small number of types to be supplemented, if opportunity offers, by a more superficial identification of a number of others in the field, and a less thorough examination of a larger number. I believe the former the better, for it will conduce to greater interest and a more searching attention on the part of the pupil. In order to justify this part of the work educationally in a broad sense, the teacher must keep in mind the point of view which has been repeatedly urged. The flower must be chiefly regarded as a mechanism, and its parts must be studied, therefore, in their relation to pollination. This should be done, too, not in a speculative way, but as far as possible by actual observation of the objects in the field.[8] With some experience of this kind, the pupil may establish enough first-hand knowledge, which may be used in interpretation of peculiarities of form and development in many flowers. The teacher will do well to have a small collection

---

[1] See Fernow, B. E., Age of Trees and Time of Blazing determined by Annual Rings. Circular 16, Division of Forestry, United States Department of Agriculture, illus. 1898.

[2] Pinchot's *Primer of Forestry*, and Roth's *First Book of Forestry*. Excellent monographic studies of the white pine (V. M. Spalding) and of the timber trees of the Southern United States have been issued by the United States Department of Agriculture. The *Wood Sections*, sold by R. B. Hough (Lowville, N. Y.), are very useful.

[3] A very good chapter on the flower is one in Stevens's *Introduction to Botany*, and excellent suggestions for field work are to be found in Andrews's *Botany all the Year Round*. See also Müller's *Fertilization of Flowers*.

of good illustrative materials[1] exemplifying the different types of flowers.

The most difficult part of the study of flowers to understand is the development of the embryo sac and embryo, and it is pretty generally conceded that it is beyond the scope of the elementary student to do more by his own effort than to get a good idea by means of experimental evidence[2] of the necessity of pollen.[3] The pollen itself may be studied in germination, many of the larger kinds producing tubes quickly in sugar solution. This must, however, be done by way of demonstration. The fact of alternation of generations may be pointed out, and the structures of the ovule and the development of the embryo explained by means of diagrams[4] and demonstrated by means of preparations. The three types of ovules (Tulip, *Capsella*, and *Polygonum* are good for anatropous, campylotropous, and orthotropous ovules, respectively) may be studied.

If a collection of dried plants is required of the pupil, these should be very carefully prepared, and to this end fewer specimens should be asked for, since it is very much better educationally to do this well than to gather together a lot of poor, scrappy specimens. Hence the motive for the work must be right, and for suggestions in this direction I can do no better than to refer the student to the excellent essay of Ganong[5] and to the directions and suggestions by Bailey.[6] Far better than the usual method of collecting indiscriminately a lot of plants from here and there, without a directive idea, is to col-

---

[1] Various large flowers in longitudinal sections, and the various structures taken separately, may be displayed in specimen jars affixed by means of gelatine to a piece of ordinary glass, and preserved in 5 per cent formaline, with a little alcohol (15 per cent). The structures may then be examined from either side.

[2] Thus it is quite possible to pollinate geranium flowers in the laboratory, and test the efficacy of pollen.

[3] See Andrews, *loc. cit.*, pp. 226. Stevens, *loc. cit.*, pp. 162–201.

[4] See Stevens, *loc. cit.*, pp. 296, 297.

[5] *Teaching Botanist*, pp. 95–118.

[6] *Lessons with Plants*, pp. 437–444, especially the " Suggestions."

lect those of a particular habitat, or those of the same species growing under different environmental conditions, or those illustrating similar habits of activity, etc.   In the case of a collection of different kinds of plants of the more usual kind, the pupils should at least be required carefully to dissect the flowers, and to arrange their parts, after they are dried, in their relative positions, rather than to resort to the floral diagram, which in my experience is not sufficiently well comprehended by the average pupil.   Nor is it necessary to confine the collection to the higher plants.   Ferns, mosses, liverworts, lichens, algæ, and fungi, all may be sought for and preserved, and this will prove the more instructive and interesting when the initiative for collection comes from the pupils themselves. The teacher's work is to show them how to collect intelligently, and get the most out of their collections.   The best material collected should, if the pupil is willing, be properly labelled and contributed to the museum collection, and the practice of constantly eliminating the less instructive specimens should be followed.   In making the choice the teacher should exercise such strict judgment that the pupil whose work is chosen may feel it a real distinction to be thus singled out.   The school collection will in this way be made an especially fine one, every specimen being as nearly perfect as it is possible to make it.   More important still, it should be much used, which is generally not the case.

Geographical Botany and Physiographical Plant Ecology.

Within recent years there has been an increasing tendency to make the elementary study of vegetation a part of a course of botany for high schools.   This is indicated by the space devoted to it in the text-books of the last few years, notably those of Atkinson, Bergen, Caldwell, Bailey, Coulter, Clements and Cutter, Stevens and of Andrews.   The movement in education toward the recognition of this part of botany may be referred to the great activity among American botanists, and indicates a commendable spirit among teachers who have seized upon the outdoor, dynamic phases of botany with much eagerness. The attempt to gain recognition in this direction has not been wholly successful, partly because of the inherent difficulties of the subject-matter itself, and partly because of the failure of most teachers to manage with young pupils such imperfect knowledge as we may be said to possess.

It is obvious, for reasons elaborated elsewhere, that the work that is done must be field study, and of such a kind that it is related to the physiology. It is, however, quite reasonable, and sound educationally, to give to a class such information about the chief types of vegetation as will lead them to appreciate what the appearance of these are. This can be based directly upon field observations; for it is seldom true that the topography of a given region does not supply illustrations of all three leading vegetation types, — xerophytic, hydrophytic, and mesophytic. But every teacher should know that these terms are very misleading, if they are assumed to stand for some rigid relation in the economy of nature. As plants individually change, so do plant associations, and it is therefore equally important to hold to the dynamic interpretation here as elsewhere. It is certainly good advice to say that a teacher ought to put himself through a course of training, in fact make it the hobby of the summer vacation, and work over some area before attempting to teach the subject. For this purpose, it would be a good plan to take some one of the published papers [1] and try to repeat the study. This will have a very healthful effect in demonstrating the working value for a class, of this kind of study, as well as widening the horizon of the teacher. For the reason that, as Cowles has well put it, " The facts of physiographic ecology are widespread rather than local, it becomes possible for secondary schools " (or the

---

[1] For a complete list of papers published on North American plant geography, see Cowles, H. A., Recent Contributions to American Phytogeography. *Botanical Gazette*, 24: 383. November, 1902.

teacher at least) "to take up local problems with the assurance that they will have much more than local importance." [1]

Some suggestions for study have already been given in the outline above under the head of ecology. It will hardly be profitable to do here more than to indicate to the student the best sources for other suggestions. By the translation of Schimper's splendid *Pflanzengeographie* it is now possible for the teacher to have a thoroughly first-class reference work at hand.

Andrews, E. F.   Botany all the Year Round, pp. 248, 249. . Suggestive of a good method of setting problems, and of questioning.

Bailey, L. H.   Lessons with Plants, pp. 410–414.

Caldwell, Otis W.   A Laboratory Manual of Botany, Chapter IX.

MacDougal, D. T.   The Nature and Work of Plants, Chapter X.   A series of very pertinent topics, with directions for study.

---

[1] Cowles, H. A., A Comparison of Land and Marine Beeches as to Ecology of the Vegetation, *School Review*, 10 : 48. 1902.   See also Gloss (*ibid.*) ; Whitford, H. N., Physiography and Botany, *School Review*, 10 : 45. January, 1902.   Harshberger, J. W., Geographical Biology, *Education*, 14 : 513. April, 1894.

CHAPTER IX

THE LABORATORY, ITS EQUIPMENT. MATERIALS FOR STUDY AND FOR DEMONSTRATION

General Laboratory Equipment.

FOR the teaching of biology by proper methods a good laboratory is a necessity. The character of the desks and the arrangements for seating and lighting of an ordi- **Laboratory a** nary class room are entirely inadequate and may **Necessity.** be permitted only when no other place for work is to be had. A good laboratory is one with good lighting, ample space for comfortable work, places for storing the equipment, and room for aquaria and vivaria. I shall attempt in a brief way to point out the most important things to look out for in planning a laboratory. It will not be necessary to give working plans, since any given problem will probably be different from all others. For the convenience of any to whom the task of planning a laboratory falls, we append below a list of papers describing plans, from which suggestions may be obtained.

By far the best illumination is obtained by a northerly exposure. If possible, all ordinary laboratory work should be done by the light of north windows, and if this **Lighting.** condition is attended to, the prime necessity is fulfilled. Direct sunlight is an intolerable nuisance, since it cannot be used for illuminating the microscope. White shades become necessary, and when these are used on partly cloudy days the light is part of the time too weak, and so the shades have to be raised and lowered every few minutes. On the whole, northerly and easterly exposure are the best, since sufficient direct sunlight may be had for growing plants and for other purposes from the east windows, while the north windows may be used as specified above. The windows should be amply large in any case, but it is impossible to specify the size unless the arrangement for seating is first decided upon.

In schools, where large numbers of pupils have to be provided for, the problems of seating and table space is a difficult one. The most acceptable method, when space is available, is to have tables arranged with their longer axes at right angles to the wall, and placed opposite a window. If the longer sides of the tables are oblique, as recommended by Bessey, there results a double advantage of non-interference of light and economy of floor space, matters of prime importance, the former to the pupil, the latter to the teacher. Few things are so wearing on the teacher as to have to crowd between chairs in order to get to the individual student, and V-shaped tables obviate this. This arrangement has been found by experience to be a very satisfactory and comfortable one. A table with sides nine feet long, fifty-five inches on the broad and thirty inches on the narrow end, will seat six or seven persons comfortably. Four such tables may therefore be made to seat twenty-eight persons, and five, thirty-five persons, the highest number that one instructor should be expected to handle. Each pupil should have at least thirty inches of space on the table edge. This form of table is not, however, well adapted when the pupils have to retain their places for recitation, but this should be avoided if possible. If the room can be planned so as to leave beside the working tables a lecture table and seats for a class of normal size, this is a much better arrangement. Otherwise the tables must be disposed so as to get the best illumination possible for each of the students, who by turning 90 degrees or 180 degrees may then face the teacher, who must, of course, have a wall at his back. In this case, parallel tables twenty inches wide, having thirty inches floor space between, with the pupils arranged in quincunx order, are the most economical of floor space.[1]   Revolving stools fixed to the floor have also this advantage, since chair backs occupy a good deal of space.   Stools should be resorted to, however, only as a last resource, since a comfortable seat is necessary.

The finish of the laboratory table tops is a matter of importance, since it must be such as to protect the wood from damage, and keep it clean and smooth.   Many prefer a black finish, to obtain which the following method gives good results.

Make up solutions :

(1) Copper Sulfate ($CuSO_4$) . . .	625 grams.	
Potassium Chlorate ($KClO_3$) .	625	"
Water to make	5 liters.	
(2) Anilin Oil	300 grams.	
Hydrochloric Acid (HCl) . . .	450	"
Water to make	2500 liters.	

Apply solution (1) followed immediately by (2) several times, until the wood becomes dark green, allowing the applications to dry each time.   The darker the tone reached the better.   The wood must then be washed thoroughly with soap and hot water, applied with a brush.   This is necessary in order to remove the superfluous salts.   The table is finished with oil and will then be dead black.[2]

For a natural wood finish, an oil or paraffin finish are the best.   (1) Boiled linseed oil, with dryer in it, applied thickly, and the superfluous oil rubbed off, leaves a good surface resistant enough for ordinary purposes.   The tables should receive an annual cleaning with sal soda and then be re-oiled. · (2) Paraffin (the hardest obtainable) must be ironed into the woodwork with a hot flat-iron, and rubbed off with a cloth while hot.

---

[1] I am indebted to Mr. J. E. Peabody for data of the arrangement of the seats of the Laboratory of the Boys and Girls High School, New York.

[2] I am indebted to Dr. E. B. Livingston for the details of this process which he has applied with success.

Caldwell, O. W.   Laboratory Manual of Botany, New York, 1902, p. 5 (plans for laboratory table).

Dodge, C. W.   Laboratory Tables.   JOURNAL OF APPLIED MICROSCOPY, I : 121, 122.   July, 1898.

The teacher's desk or lecture table should be of good size (two feet six inches broad), solidly built, and provided with **Teacher's Desk.** drawers and cupboards for the equipment which is needed at hand.   If possible it should be provided with running water and gas.   The size of the desk should admit the setting up of physiological experiments to run several days and its stability, for this purpose, is an obvious necessity.

The pupil's equipment should be very simple, and consist **Pupil's Equipment.** of the following :

1. A sharp penknife or scalpel.

2. Two dissecting needles.   Penholders with strong needles pushed in eye-end foremost.

3. A small pair of forceps (may be dispensed with if appropriation is too limited).

If a compound microscope is used, there will be needed also :

4. Pieces of cheapest filter paper, for taking up excess of water on preparations.

5. Glass slides and cover-glasses ; a dozen of each.

For making laboratory records :

6. Pencil (Dixon's 4H, or one of similar hardness and quality) and paper for sketches.   If sheets are used separately, they should be cut of uniform size with paper for making notes and doing essay work.   These may then be fastened together in a suitable cover.   A bond or ledger paper is good for general laboratory purposes.   Bound note-books are found by many teachers more satisfactory.   Since many times pupils spoil their sketches, these may be made on good paper, cut out and pasted in in a suitable arrangement.   It is generally difficult for pupils to foresee what a page will look like when filled.   A bad result may, however, in this way be avoided.

The wall behind the teachers should have blackboard space, and chart racks which may be raised and lowered. Simple strips of light wood (two inches by one-half inch) supported by firm cotton cords reeved through **Chart Racks.** screw-eyes answer every purpose. The curving of lower edges of charts hung on such a strip may be prevented by attaching light strips to them with clips. More elaborate racks hardly present enough advantage to justify the extra expense. Any other available wall space may be utilized for the hanging of charts. Another advantage of the light strip is that it may be suspended almost anywhere obliquely across a room corner, for example. Charts may be suspended by some form of clip hook.

A desideratum of great importance is the provision of storage room for pupils' materials and for equipment. For each pupil, room for a note-book and a few simple implements must be provided. This, however, is **Storage of Equipment: Pupils'.** necessary, in order that much needed things, as pencils, will be there when wanted. For the purpose, small cloth-covered pasteboard boxes answer well. The name and table number of the pupil can be printed plainly on a label, and this slipped into a thin brass label holder.[1] The boxes when not in use may be stacked on a convenient shelf, near the entrance to the laboratory, so that the pupil may get them on entering and replace them on retiring. This arrangement renders costly cabinet work unnecessary, and allows of any practical degree of expansion.

It is very necessary to keep the microscopes in a dust-proof closet under lock and key, and it is better to dispense with the usual cases which accompany the instruments, **Of Microscopes.** an item of expense which may be saved. In order to keep the instruments in good condition, it is well to keep them tagged, so that the same persons will use a particular instrument each time. The source of damage can thus be

---

[1] Obtainable from the Cambridge Botanical Supply Company.

better traced. When the number of microscopes is large enough only for their use in demonstration this precaution is unnecessary. Other optical instruments, such as extra lenses and dissecting microscopes, may be kept with the microscopes.

Every laboratory should have another storeroom with plenty of shelf-room, for the storage of glassware, chemicals, and implements of all kinds, and for plant and animal materials for study. Some simple method of classification will be necessary and a card index, with a record of cost, dealer, and other useful data will be found very useful. To get rid of useless materials and keep the rest clean and in order is an important rule applying to a storeroom. The materials for study which are kept in fluids may be arranged in order of use — probably the best way if large numbers of pupils are to be provided for. For the same reason it is better to have in the general stock an abundance of the materials to be used than small amounts of many kinds, excepting, of course, for special reasons. In the absence of a stockroom, cases or shelves in the laboratory must be used.

Of Glassware, Chemicals, Instruments, and Materials.

Charts must, of course, be kept in a suitable case. One form suggested by Ganong[1] consists of an upright case, attached to the wall and opening on the front and top. Less economical of space, but more useful, is a series of shallow drawers, in which the charts may lie flat and be more easily examined. Rolled charts, such as the Leuckart series, are kept most conveniently on end in a rack or box.

Of Charts.

Much plant material may be kept dry, to be soaked previous to use. This may be kept in envelopes, loose or attached to sheets of paper, and placed, according to a system, in pasteboard filing boxes,[2] or it may be kept on the usual size of herbarium paper, uniform with sheets of flowering plants. The small-sized ones are, however, easier to handle, and the boxes can be used for such things as fungi,

Dried Materials.

---

[1] *The Teaching Botanist*, p. 117.
[2] The largest size made by the Library Bureau are very good.

which refuse to be flattened out. And again for general school use, smaller herbarium sheets, one-half the standard size (11½ by 16¾) are large enough.

For keeping living materials, stock aquaria of galvanized iron strengthened with heavy wire made to any size desired are most useful. Wire covers can be made **Living Materials.** to prevent the escape of animals. Strips of galvanized iron can be placed so as to partition off the interior when necessary. Battery jars are the cheapest form of glass aquaria, and it is always well to have a good number of these. Half-barrels (oak) make fine aquaria, especially for larger water plants, fish, etc. For keeping potted plants, etc., in good condition, a small conservatory built as a bay window[1] and roofed with glass is the best arrangement. A conservatory, however, may be built, against a window or two, inside the laboratory, and may be heated by a small hot water system. Some heating arrangement independent of the general heating plant, is, of course, necessary if it is desired to keep materials growing in cold weather. A "Vulcan" hot water heater[2] and a hot water radiator will keep up the temperature, which may be controlled by a Powers Temperature Regulator[3] controlling the supply of gas. A small pilot flame must be kept burning. The "by-pass" of the Powers three-way cock may be closed or opened, according to the exigencies of the climate. When this is impossible, a Wardian case, as described by Ganong, will do good service.[4]

Another convenience is a dark room in which physiological experiments may be conducted. Of course, it is a simple enough matter to etiolate plants under covers, but **Dark Room.** it is most valuable, educationally, to be able to run experiments on growth, *e. g.*, in continuous darkness. For

---

[1] See bibliography below. Mast, S. O.

[2] Crane & Co., New York. Price about $7.00.

[3] The Powers Regulator Co., New York, 111 5th Ave.; Chicago, 40 Dearborn St.; Boston, 224 Franklin St.; Philadelphia, 922 Real Estate Trust Bldg.

[4] See *The Teaching Botanist*, pp. 83–85.

students to be able to go into a dark room, and see the plant by a small amount of illumination, makes a deep impression on the mind. The same room may be used for photographic purposes, or better, if it is large enough, may be partitioned off. Ventilators which will be light-tight should be provided.[1]

Brooks, S. D.   The Biological Laboratory in the Small High School. JOURNAL OF APPLIED MICROSCOPY, 5: 1603–1608. January, 1902.

Elliot, L. B.   Representative American Laboratories. 1. Cornell University. JOURNAL OF APPLIED MICROSCOPY, 1: 23–32. February, 1898.

Ganong, W. F.   The Teaching Botanist. New York, The Macmillan Co., 1900. Pp. 80, 81.

Ganong, W. F.   Plant Physiology. New York, H. Holt & Co., 1901. Pp. 23–30.

Ganong, W. F.   The New Laboratory and Greenhouse for Plant Physiology at Smith College. SCIENCE, II., 15: 933–937. 13 June, 1902.

Herrick, F. H.   Biological Laboratory of Western Reserve University. JOURNAL OF APPLIED MICROSCOPY, 3: 949–955. August, 1900.

Lloyd, F. E.   The New Laboratory for Plant Physiology of the Agricultural Academy in Poppelsdorf-Bonn. JOURNAL OF APPLIED MICROSCOPY, 5: 1829–1835. June, 1902.

Marsh, C. D.   The New Biological Laboratories of Ripon College. JOURNAL OF APPLIED MICROSCOPY, 4: 1149–1155. February, 1901.

Mast, S. O.   The Description of a New Biological Laboratory. Proceedings of Michigan Schoolmasters' Association. 49. March, 1902.

McClung, C. E.   Laboratory Equipment for beginning Course in Zoölogy. JOURNAL OF APPLIED MICROSCOPY, 5: 1677–1679. March, 1902.

Murbach, L.   The Biology Work in the Detroit Central High School. JOURNAL OF APPLIED MICROSCOPY, 2: 425–435. July, 1899.

Peabody, J. E.   Physiology in the Peter Cooper High School, New York City. JOURNAL OF APPLIED MICROSCOPY, 3: 917–932. July, 1900.

Treadwell, A. L.   The Biological Laboratory of Vassar College. JOURNAL OF APPLIED MICROSCOPY, 5: 1717–1725. April, 1902.

Woolman, A. J.   Laboratories for the Duluth High School. JOURNAL OF APPLIED MICROSCOPY, 2: 353–359. May, 1899.

Wylie, R. B.   The Biological Laboratories of Morningside College. JOURNAL OF APPLIED MICROSCOPY, 5: 1949–1954. September, 1902.

---

[1] Ganong, W. F., *Plant Physiology*, New York, 1901, p. 27. (A good construction for a dark room, which may be modified to peculiar conditions.)

Other Laboratory Equipment.

Microscopes should be strongly made of the Continental type on account of its solidity and simplicity. Two objectives are necessary, one of quite low power (two or three) and one of fairly high power (five to seven, pref- erably five). Optical Apparatus. A nosepiece will prevent loss of time, and will save wear and tear on the lenses, which should be parfocalized. Oculars one and three will be sufficient. A coarse rack and pinion adjustment is also very much to be desired, since the manipulation of the draw-tube by hand leads often to mishap. This, of course, heightens the cost. From twenty-five to thirty dollars will provide a suitable instrument. A japanned base keeps a good clean appearance the longest. A large mirror, revolving diaphragm, and fine adjustment conclude the necessary specifications.

Magnifying glasses of an amplification of ten diameters, on a suitable stand as, *e. g.*, the Barnes dissecting stand, are of constant value. Three-legged affairs are troublesome. A good lens (achromatic, with a large flat field) is worth the cost, which is not great.

A camera lucida is found by some teachers to be a valuable aid in teaching, since the teacher can make a quick sketch of any object being studied, for control of the class work.[1]

A horizontal microscope is useful but not a necessity. A very good one is made by Leitz. One may be improvised by fixing an ordinary tube to a retort stand.

The outfit of a good laboratory should include also a small paraffin oven and a microtome. The latter need not be of the expensive type. The teacher should be able to make hand sections of much of the material used, but a microtome will often be found useful.

Charts are exceedingly valuable helps in teaching if properly used, but the amount of dependence placed on

---

[1] Bergen, J. Y., *Teachers' Handbook*, p. 19. Boston, 1901.

them will vary with the teacher. A well-made, attractive chart can hardly fail to arouse and to keep interest. In elementary work those which show developmental stages are especially valuable. But no set of charts which will be found in the market will be likely to meet all the peculiar needs of individual teachers, and at any rate, teachers ought not to have to depend on them. Especially should money not be wasted on charts of things so simple that a few strokes of the crayon will duplicate them — and every teacher should have facility in the use of the chalk and blackboard, and he should be able to make special charts for himself when he may need them. The series of charts (approximately size, 84 by 68 cm.), which can be bought and which are here recommended, are the following :

Charts.

1. The Kny Series of 100. Cost, 320 marks, unbacked.
2. The Errera-Laurent Series of 15. Cost, 40 marks, unbacked.
3. The Frank-Tschirch Series of 60. Cost, 180 marks, unbacked.
4. The Peter Flower Series of 50. Cost, 125 marks, unbacked.

Series 1, 2, and 4 are the most valuable. They should be ordered through dealers, and should be backed with cloth in Germany, as it can be done there more cheaply and better.

" Home-Made " Charts always mean more to the teacher and can be made at small cost. The materials which may be used are as follows : Black " pattern paper " ($3.25 per roll, three hundred yards), using chalk for lining, fixing the same with gum mastic.[1]

Muslin, common unbleached or roller shade cloth, or detail

---

[1] Harshberger, J. W., Natural History Charts and Illustrations. *Education,* **7**: 493. April, 1899. See also Heald, H. P., A Method of Making Biology Wall Charts. *Journal of Applied Microscopy,* **4**: 1172. February, 1901. Tracy, M., A Simple Method of Making Wall Charts. *Journal of Applied Microscopy,* **6**: 2114. January, 1903. Bessey, C. E., Home-Made Wall Charts. *Journal of Applied Microscopy,* **4**: 1195. March, 1901.

paper, with lines of paraffin pencil in various colors. Oil colors may be applied to the cloth if preferred. A much more refined material is muslin-backed drawing paper. The lines may be made with marking pens, using waterproof ink, and water colors may be applied. Cheap and effective when they are made on unbleached muslin, they are practically indestructible and require no particular care in handling. I have some charts which were made by this method in 1893, which are as good as new to-day. An arrangement for illustrating the structure of flowers as represented in floral diagrams is made by cutting pieces of colored card into diagrammatic shapes. These may be attached upon a piece of soft board, painted black, in the relative positions by means of thumb tacks.

Frost, **W. D.** A Rack for Exhibiting Charts. JOURNAL OF APPLIED MICROSCOPY, 5: 1993, 1994. October, 1902.
Ganong, **W. F.** Teaching Botanist, p. 86.

Of certainly equal value with charts are large photomicrographs, which have the advantage of appearing much as the original object does to the eye. They are, therefore, often a very great help in enabling the teacher to clear up misunderstandings arising from the inability of the pupils to interpret what is seen in the microscopic field. They are, however, rather expensive. The best made are those by Samuel F. Tower, purchasable through Ginn & Co., $2.75 each. A list of these may doubtless be had on application. A partial list may be found in Bergen's *Teachers' Handbook*.

A stereopticon is a most useful piece of apparatus for the cursory study of general matters. An occasional talk of general interest, illustrated with good lantern Projection slides, is an educational treat which can be made Apparatus. to do good service. The danger of overdoing the lantern business is one which every sensible teacher will beware of; but there can be no harm and often much good, accruing from a judicious use of optical projection. One point of importance educationally is that the teacher himself should manipulate his slides, standing by his apparatus, and becoming, as it were, a part of the audience.   He has in this way an additional point of advantage of being in a good place to manage his class.   Of very great value, also, is the use of microscopic projection,[1] but this will generally be beyond the limits and possibilities of most teachers.

Lantern slides are sold by: Wm. H. Knapp, Bausch and Lomb Optical Co., Chicago, Ill.   A set of twenty-five, of excellent quality, in box, $12 net ; W. B. McCallum (Department of Botany, University of Chicago, Chicago, Ill.) and S. M. Coulter (Shaw School of Botany, St. Louis, Mo.) at a cost of $17 the set of fifty, or three sets for $50.   Six sets are offered, each on one of the following topics : General morphology, general ecology, physiographic ecology, general physiography, pollination, types of trees.

The apparatus needed for elementary plant physiology consists of set pieces of apparatus and of general glassware, tools,

Apparatus for Plant Physiology.
etc.   It is quite unnecessary here to indicate the latter in detail.   An examination of a modern text-book will generally be sufficient (see bibliography below).   As to the set pieces, the problem is rather more difficult.   Fortunately these are few in number, a clinostat and an auxanometer being the principal ones.   The forms of these articles at present on the market may be purchased through general dealers, and from Stoelting (see list).   I am informed that some pieces, designed by Ganong, are soon to be placed on sale.   A modified form of an auxanometer of my own will also soon be purchasable from the "Home-Made" Apparatus Co.   A set of double-walled bell jars is also very desirable.   For small colored light chambers see Ganong, *Plant Physiology*, p. 109.

The following references will be found useful, especially to the teacher who is inclined to put together apparatus himself:

[1] See Cole, A. H., The Projection Microscope — Its Possibilities and Value in Teaching Biology.   Proc. N. E. A.   1902.   771–778.

Arthur, J. C. BOTANICAL GAZETTE, **22** : 463–472. 1896.

Ganong, W. F. BOTANICAL GAZETTE, **27** : 255. 1899.

Ganong, W. F. Plant Physiology for the High School. SCHOOL SCIENCE, II., **3** : 382. January, 1904, *et al.*

Ganong, W. F. A Laboratory Course in Plant Physiology.

Ganong, W. F. The Teaching Botanist.

Lloyd, F. E. A New and Cheap Form of Auxanometer. TORREYA, **3** : 97–100. July, 1903. SCHOOL SCIENCE, **3** : 345. December, 1903.

MacDougal, D. T. Elementary Plant Physiology.

Murback, L. A. Simple Auxanometer. SCHOOL SCIENCE, **2** : 346. December, 1902.

Reed, Howard S. Methods in Plant Physiology. JOURNAL OF APPLIED MICROSCOPY, Vols. V. and VI.

Richards, H. M. A Modified Form of Respiration Apparatus. TORREYA, **1** : 28. March, 1901.

Stone, G. E. Botanical Appliances. BOTANICAL GAZETTE, **22** : 258. September, 1896.

Stone, G. E. Physiological Appliances. TORREYA, **4** : 1–5. January, 1904.

Dealers in Microscopes and General Supplies.

ARTHUR, J. C. Purdue University, Lafayette, Ind. Apparatus for Plant Physiology, described in *Botanical Gazette*, **22** : 463–472.

BAUSCH & LOMB OPTICAL CO., Rochester, N. Y. Manufacturers of microscopes, and dealers in general laboratory supplies.

CAMBRIDGE BOTANICAL SUPPLY CO., Cambridge, Mass. All kinds of supplies useful to botanists. Plant materials.

DRURY, MISS E. M., 45 Munroe St., Roxbury, Mass. Photomicrographs, microscopic preparations.

EIMER & AMEND, New York, N. Y. Chemical Supplies, glassware. General importers.

THE "HOME-MADE" SCIENTIFIC APPARATUS CO., Mechanicsburg, Ohio. Simple apparatus for physiology, etc., including a cheap form of auxanometer designed after a model by Lloyd.

ITHACA BOTANICAL SUPPLY CO., Ithaca, N. Y. Plant materials ; microscopic preparations.

KNY-SCHEERER CO., 225 4th Ave., New York, N. Y. General dealers and importers. Natural history materials ; living plants.

KRAFFT, WM. 411 West 59th St., New York ; Boston ; Chicago. Importers of Leitz microscopes, and of general laboratory supplies.

QUEEN & CO., Philadelphia, Pa. Dealers in general laboratory supplies.

SPENCER LENS CO., Buffalo, N. Y. Microscopes.

C. H. STOELTING CO., 35 W. Randolph St., Chicago, Ill. Auxanometer, clinostat.

THORBURN, J. M. & CO., 36 Cortland St , New York City. Seeds.

Tower, S. F., Boston English High School, Boston, Mass. Photo-micrographs.
Walmsley, Fuller & Co., 134-136 Wabash Ave., Chicago, Ill. Photomicrographs.
Whitall, Tatum & Co., New York, N. Y. Glassware.
Williams, Brown & Earle, Philadelphia, Pa. Beck microscopes, general supplies. .

The Preservation of Plant Material for Laboratory Use.

For the purposes of elementary work, the preservation of materials is quite simple, and does not in the least involve the more elaborate methods of the advanced botanist. It is therefore my purpose here to mention the ordinarily useful methods. If special methods are needed, directions may be found in the literature which is readily available. Chamberlain's book, mentioned below, will meet special requirements.

Some materials may be preserved dry, in the same manner as herbarium specimens, and when moistened are perfectly satisfactory. A general rule to follow in pressing such plants as may be treated in this way is to apply as light a weight as possible, the object being to preserve the material in good condition, in a dry state, rather than to press it, so as to make flat herbarium specimens. Specimens which receive this treatment will expand well if soaked in water over night, or if boiled, the former being the better plan. Very small plants, such as mosses, liverworts, and many fungi, will expand fully in a few minutes. On account of its simplicity as well as economy, this method is recommended as especially available for those who do not have funds at their disposal. Even flowers and fruit may be managed in this way, and although fresh materials are always to be preferred, and used whenever possible, the teacher will always do well to have a good stock of materials on hand. This of course is especially true of the lower forms, which are less likely to be obtained fresh when wanted.

Other plants may be kept in living condition. Outside of various house plants, including ferns, which get along fairly well indoors, water plants, including algæ, may be kept in aquaria. Some mosses, selaginellas, fern prothallia, etc., will grow well if the air about them is kept moist by means of glass, and if they are well drained, which is of very considerable importance. For this purpose charcoal answers the best. If pots are used, they should be half filled with coarsely broken bits of charcoal. This preserves the looseness of the soil, and does not allow it to get soggy with water.

For preserving the natural form and appearance (color often excepted) of plants or plant parts, the most useful fluid is a formalin solution. This is a one per cent to five per cent solution of the commercial formaldehyd in water, and serves well for all ordinary purposes. Three per cent and five per cent solutions are most commonly used.

A solution of formalin, one per cent, and chrome alum, one per cent, in water is especially good for algæ, sea-water, of course, being used for marine forms. It is also recommended for flowers, as it does not make them brittle.

For very delicate plants, especially those with large size and little substance, such as fungi, the addition of glycerine to raise somewhat the specific gravity of the fluid, is sometimes an advantage, as it buoys up the specimens.

Alcohol would better be used for hardening and preserving materials for anatomical work. A strong (80 to 95 per cent) mixture with water is necessary.

List of Materials and Method of Preservation.

Myxomycetes. — Living Plasmodium, on decaying wood, kept dark and moist, not wet.[1] Sporangia dry, pinned to bottoms of boxes (*e. g.*, cigar boxes with cork fastened to the bottom).

Algæ. — Marine algæ in chrome-alum-formalin solution made up with sea-water. For fresh-water algæ the same made up with fresh-water. Many blue-green algæ, diatoms, desmids, and other green algæ may be grown in aquaria. Usually they

---

[1] Macbride, T. H., The Slime Moulds. *Rhodora*, April, 1900.

must not be allowed too much·sunlight. Keep cool as possible. Aquaria always do better if covered with glass. Materials to show special points (*e. g.*, conjugation in *Spirogyra*)
should be kept on hand in preservatives.

Fungi. — All the smaller kinds may be kept dry, but this
of course does not need to apply, in practice, to the moulds
which grow abundantly on decaying substances (bread, tomatoes, etc.). The larger fleshy forms are readily preserved in
formalin. Woody fungi are kept dry.

For preserving soft fleshy fungi, as recommended by B. O.
Longear : [1]

    1. Alcohol 1 part, water 2 parts.
    2. Formalin 1 part, water 10–20 parts.

This for firmer kinds. Does not succeed so well with the
softer ones.

Bryophyta (*Mosses and Liverworts*). — Plants bearing
gemmæ (*Georgia pellucida, Scapania, Marchantia, Lunularia,*
etc.) are better kept in formalin. Other material may be kept
dry. Soak mosses over night preferably. A few moments
boiling drives out air. Lactic acid is especially good for
clearing temporary mounts for microscopic examination.

Pteridophyta. — Many hardy ferns and *Selaginella,* may be
grown ; or fresh materials may be obtained from florists. *Lycopodium* and *Equisetum* may be kept dry. Prothallia may be
grown.

Gymnospermæ. — The young and immature cones, both male
and female, are best preserved in alcohol, since the resin is not
soluble in watery solutions. Formalin may be used and the
material placed for a while in alcohol previous to use.

Ripened cones are kept dry for the purposes of elementary
study. The cones of some species of Fir (*Abies*) are the
best. Failing these any of the other forms will answer ; and
the larger they are the better. Fresh foliage material should
always be used, if possible.

---

[1] Some suggestions for the beginner in collecting and studying fleshy
fungi. *Journal of Applied Microscopy,* 6: 2369. June, 1903.

Angiospermæ. — For the study of the flower, fresh material should always be used so far as possible. ˙ It is more attractive and easier to manage. Nevertheless, a stock of preserved material should be kept on hand. For preserving, formalin one per cent, with chrome alum one per cent.

Material for the anatomical study of the leaf, stem, etc., are best preserved in alcohol, or if in formalin they must be hardened in alcohol before sections are cut.

Seeds are, of course, kept dry. Young and nearly mature stages of the fruit should also be kept in formalin. Mature fruits, dry.

Bergen, J. Y. TEACHERS' HANDBOOK. (To accompany the FOUNDATIONS OF BOTANY.) Ginn & Co., Boston. 1901.

Caldwell, Otis W. Suggestions to Teachers. (Designed to accompany Plant Structures.) New York. D. Appleton & Co. 1900. Pp. 1–26.

Chamberlain, C. J. METHODS IN PLANT HISTOLOGY.

Harshberger, J. W. Home and School Window Gardens. EDUCATION, 18 : 555. May, 1898.

Dealers in Plant Materials.

THE CAMBRIDGE BOTANICAL SUPPLY CO., Cambridge, Mass.

ITHACA BOTANICAL SUPPLY CO., Ithaca, N. Y.

GALEN, JAMES. Bonview, Pa., R. F. D., No. 1. Cable address, McCall's Ferry, Pa. Twigs, wild plants, seeds, etc.

KNY-SCHEERER CO., 225 Fourth Ave., New York. (Will supply living materials within suitable limits of distance at very reasonable rates.)

Materials for Demonstration.

No teacher can afford to depend solely upon the materials which the pupil himself handles. It is impossible for him to use but a very small part of the available material. His direct observation may, however, be very greatly widened, by the use of a well-selected collection of specimens, properly mounted and arranged so as to illustrate definite points. It is well to include in such a collection even those materials which the pupils use, so they may, if necessary, supplement their work.

15

Museum materials for demonstration can be made of very great value, too, in the presentation of various topics, and should be fully drawn upon.

Demonstration specimens may be preserved in fluids, or dry, according to the nature of the materials. It is, of course, wasteful to use fluids and glassware, when the dry material is just as good.

Particularly instructive are series of developmental stages. The specimens are properly arranged, surface water removed, and affixed, by means of a thick gelatine solution used warm, to a piece of picture glass,[1] which has been cut to fit the glass jar to be used. As soon as the gelatine hardens the whole is plunged into the fluid.[2] If no more gelatine has been used than is necessary, it will hardly be noticed at all, so that the specimens may be viewed from either side of the glass with equal facility. Even such small objects as prothallia, *Selaginella* embryos, and the like can be so managed, and beautiful illustrative preparations be made. The following are suggested as a useful list of such preparations :

Developmental (germination) series of pea, bean, castoroil, squash, Indian corn, date, onion, and of the fruits of these, including a series of the ear of Indian corn. A partly germinated cocoanut to show the large haustorium is a very instructive preparation. Series of fruits for comparative morphology of the receptacle, *e. g.*, rose (cultural varieties), raspberry, strawberry, the fig ; some of the larger compositæ, etc. Series of fleshy fruits, *e. g.*, pepper, tomato, cucumber, etc. Also types of flowers which show the more striking adaptations for cross pollination by insect agency. These should be cut in such a manner as to show the flower in longitudinal section, or in some other desired way. Plants with thick parts, or forms which lose their shape or instructive appearance if dry or under pressure. Root systems, showing root tubercles of some typical leguminous forage plants.

---

[1] Opaque glass, black or white, is seldom to be preferred.
[2] Formalin 5 per cent, alcohol 15 per cent in water.

Many kinds of plants, however, show their general features quite well as herbarium specimens, if carefully prepared, and when this is true they may be attached to herbarium sheets, or, still better, to cards, which may be covered with glass or, better, with transparent xylonite,[1] and bound with passe-partout strips. The xylonite is practically indestructible, and is stiff enough to protect the specimens. Any number of duplicates of suitable subjects may be made up on a uniform size of card, and these can often be used in the laboratory for the pupils' study, especially when large classes are to be provided for. The specimens may be labelled if desired, or if to be used as laboratory material, left unlabelled, but provided with an index number. In most cases I prefer not to label parts, but rather to make use of them as problems. Full labelling has its place in public museums, but may be easily made to defeat the aims of the laboratory. The kinds of specimens which show up well mounted in this way are those which show leaf homologies, climbing organs, and so on; seedlings to show ontogenetic leaf series, or different forms of cotyledons; thin parts of plants showing parasitic fungi, lichens, algæ, and bryophytes (though these are better treated as below).

Then, too, if herbarium sheets are to be handed around a class for demonstration, they may be placed in a cover made of a stiff card and xylonite, which will serve to protect the specimens from damage;[2] such a cover is lighter than one in which glass is used, and is practically unbreakable. Some specimens can be best mounted in glycerine jelly, either between sheets of glass or between glass and xylonite, or between two sheets of xylonite bound with passe-partout paper. I have used for two years a large thin transverse

---

[1] The kind I have used is described thus: Color, No. 301; Thickness, $\frac{10}{1000}$; Finish, AA. Obtainable from the Celluloid Company, 30 to 36 Washington Place, New York. A sheet 20 by 49 inches costs $1.20.

[2] For further suggestions as to the kinds of collections to make for these purposes, see Ganong, *The Teaching Botanist*.

section of sugar-cane mounted between pieces of xylonite for demonstration and it remains in good condition. It may be viewed either with the naked eye or with a magnification of three hundred diameters with sufficient clearness to see details. A preparation of this kind may be bent considerably without damaging the specimen. Mosses and liverworts may be similarly treated. Microscopic preparations of the rough sort, say of stem sections, when cytological details are not desired, may be covered with thin xylonite, such as is used for photographic films. This method obviates the usual breakage of cover glasses, and the xylonite is better than mica optically, and is not so easily damaged by splitting. Much may be said, also, in favor of glycerine jelly as a mounting medium for demonstration preparations, instead of balsam, since this hardens and becomes brittle. In some cases when the tissue is very delicate, it cannot be used, nor is anything but glass suitable for covering. It is obvious that any method of saving time, energy, and material from breakage is of great value when large numbers of pupils are involved.

This method is especially valuable for thin specimens of some delicacy, the parts of which curl when dry, as *e. g.*, mosses, liverworts,[1] fern leaves, to show different forms of sori and indusia, many sections, etc.

A more elaborate method of mounting herbarium material, adaptable especially to making attractive museum specimens, is by means of the Riker Natural Science Mount, obtainable from The Sydney Ross Company, 48 Vesey St., New York, from whom a descriptive price-list may be obtained.

Ganong, W. F.   *The Teaching Botanist.*
Lloyd, F. E.   Handling Herbarium Specimens in Classes. TORREYA, 2: 40. March, 1902.
Richards, H. M.   New Methods of Drying Plants. TORREYA, 1: 145. December, 1901.
Stone, G. E.   Formaline as a Preservative of Botanical Specimens. JOURNAL OF APPLIED MICROSCOPY, 2: 537. 1899.

[1] Sphagnum, *e. g.*, must be mounted in fluid in a bottle for best results.

CHAPTER X

BOTANICAL LITERATURE FOR THE USE OF TEACHERS AND STUDENTS

THE following lists of books have been arranged with reference to their most apparent usefulness, and include the most important of those published in the English language. Books in other languages have usually been omitted. Some are out of print, but are mentioned because of their value. Such, for example, is von Sachs' *Physiology of Plants*.

The chief purpose in giving this bibliography is to direct the attention of the intending teacher to the modern literature bearing closely upon the teaching of botany with which he should be conversant. It represents, also, a good working collection of books. A smaller number which at the same time would answer well for a school library is indicated by asterisks. Naturally the choice of taxonomic works will depend upon locality.

Abbreviations.

Al. Allyn & Bacon, Boston, Mass.
Am. American Book Co., New York.
Ap. D. Appleton & Co., New York.
B. Baker & Taylor, New York.
Clar. Clarendon Press, Oxford, England.
G. Ginn & Co., Boston and New York.
H. D. C. Heath & Co., New York.
Ho. H. Holt & Co., New York.
K. Knight & Millet, Boston, Mass.
L. Longmans, Green & Co., New York.
M. The Macmillan Co., New York.
Pr. Preston & Rounds Co., Providence, R. I.

Text and Laboratory Books for Students' Use.

*Atkinson, G. F.   Elementary Botany. Ho. 1898. 23 + 444. $1.25.

Atkinson, G. F.   Lessons in Botany. Ho. 1900. 15 + 365. $1.12.

Atkinson, G. F.   First Studies of Plant Life. G. 1902. 12 + 266.
60c.

*Andrews, E. F.   Botany all the Year Around. Am. 302. 1903.
$1.00.

Bailey, L. H.   Lessons with Plants. M. 1898. 31 + 491. $1.10.

*Barnes, C. R.   Plant Life, Considered with Special Reference to
Form and Function. Ho. 1898. 10 + 428. $1.12.

Barnes, C. R.   Outlines of Plant Life. Ho. 1900. 6 + 308. $1.00.

Bergen, J. Y.   Elements of Botany. G. 1896. 8 + 275. $1.10.
With flora of North and Middle States. 57 pages.

*Bergen, J. Y.   Foundations of Botany. G. 1901. 10 + 257. With
flora. $1.50.

*Bessey, C. E.   The Essentials of Botany. Ho. 1896. 7 + 356. $1.12.

*Caldwell, Otis W.   A Laboratory Manual of Botany. Ap. 1902.
9 + 107. 50c.

Clark, C. H.   A Laboratory Manual of Practical Botany. Am.
1898. 271. 96c.

Campbell, D. H.   Elements of Structural and Systematic Botany for
High Schools and Elementary College Courses. G. 253. $1.12.

Gray, Asa.   How Plants Behave. Am. 1875. 8 + 46. 54c.

Gray, Asa.   Lessons in Botany. Am. 1875. 12 + 236. 94c.

Hunter, G. W., Jr., and Valentine, M. C. Ho. 1903. 7 + 215. 60c.

Leavitt, R. G.   Outlines of Botany for the High School Laboratory
and Class Room. Am. 1901. 6 + 272. $1.00. With Flora, $1.80.

Macbride, T. H.   Lessons in Elementary Botany for Secondary
Schools. Al. 1896. 11 + 233. 80c.

*MacDougal, D. T.   The Nature and Work of Plants. M. 1900.
17 + 218. 80c.

Pepoon, Mitchell and Maxwell.   Studies of Plant Life. H. 1900.
12 + 95. 50c.

Robison, C. H.   Outlines for Field Studies of Common Plants.
Published by the Author, Oak Park, Ill. 1902. 39   25c.

Setchell, W. A.   Laboratory Practice for Beginners in Botany. M.
1897. 14 + 199. 90c.

*Stevens, W. C.   Introduction to Botany. H. 1903. With Flora,
$1.50 ; without Flora, 10 + 436, $1.20.

Reference Books for Students.

*Bailey, L. H.   Botany. An Elementary Text-book. M. 1900.
14 + 356. $1.10.

Bailey, L. H.   Lessons with Plants. M. 1899. 491. $1.10.

Beal, W. T.   Seed Dispersal. G. 1898. 89   35c.

Clements, F. E., and Cutter, I. S.   A Laboratory Manual of High School Botany.   University Publishing Co., Lincoln, Neb.   1900.   4 + 123.   75c.

Conn, H. W.   Bacteria, Yeasts, and Molds in the Home.   G. 1903.   6 + 293. $1.00.

Coulter, J. M.   Plant Relations.   Ap.   1899.   7 + 264. $1.10.

Coulter, J. M.   Plant Structures.   Ap.   1900.   9 + 348. $1.20.

*Coulter, J. M.   Plants.   A Text-book of Botany.   Ap.   1900.   7 + 348. $1.80.

Coulter, J. M.   Plant Studies.   Ap.   1901.   9 + 392. $1.25.

Macmillan, C.   Minnesota Plant Life.   Minnesota Survey Botany. Series III.   1899.   25 + 568.

*Pinchot, G.   A Primer of Forestry.   Part I.   The Forest.   BULLE-TIN, No. 24, United States Department of Agriculture, Washington, Government Printing Office.   1900.   88 pages.

Sargent, F. L.   Corn Plants.   Houghton, Mifflin & Co.   1899. 5 + 106.   75c.

Education and Method of Thought.

Cramer, F.   The Method of Darwin.   Chicago, A. C. McClurg & Co.   1896. $1.00.

Elliot, C. W.   Educational Reform.   The Century Co., New York. 1898.   9 + 418. $2.00.

Ganong, W. F.   The Teaching Botanist.   M.   1899.   11 + 270. $1.10.

Huxley, T. H.   Science and Education.   Volume III. of his Collected Essays.   Ap. $1.25.

James, W.   Talks to Teachers on Psychology.   Ho.   301. $1.50.

Mivart, St. J.   The Groundwork of Science.   G. P. Putnam's Sons. New York.   1898.   18 + 328. $1.75.

Pearson, K.   Grammar of Science.   M.   1900.   18 + 548. $2.50.

Spencer, Herbert.   Education: Moral, Physical, and Intellectual. Ap.   283. $1.25.

Spencer, Herbert.   Principles of Biology.   Ap.   1901.   Vol. I., 12 + .706.   Vol. II., 12 + 663. $4.00.

Natural History of Plants. Evolution.

Arthur, J. C., and MacDougal, D. T.   Living Plants and Their Properties.   B.   1898.   9 + 234. $1.25.

Bailey, L. H.   The Survival of the Unlike.   M.   2d ed.   1897.   515. $2.00.

*Bailey, L. H.   Plant Breeding.   Third edition.   M.   1904.   13 + 334. $1.00.

*Campbell, D. H.   The Evolution of Plants.   M.   1899.   8 + 319. $1.25.

de Candolle, A.   Origin of Cultivated Plants.   Ap.   1886.   10 + 468. $2.00.

Darwin, Charles.   The Effects of Cross and Self Fertilization in the Vegetable Kingdom. Ap. $2.00.
*Darwin, Charles.   Different Forms of Flowers on Plants of the Same Species. Ap. $1.50.
*Darwin, Charles.   The Origin of Species. Ap. $2.00.
*Darwin, Charles.   Insectivorous Plants. Ap. $2.00.
*Geddes, P.   Chapters in Modern Botany. Scribner. 1893. 201. $1.25.
Haberlandt.   Eine botanische Tropenreise. Leipzig. Engelmann. 1893. 9.25 marks.
*Kerner-Oliver.   Natural History of Plants. Ho. 1896. 4 volumes, $15.00. 1903. 2 volumes, $11.00.
Lubbock, John.   Flowers, Fruits, and Leaves. M. 147. 1884. $1.25.
Lubbock, John.   On Buds and Stipules. London, Kegan Paul, Trench, Trübner & Co. 1899. 15 + 247. $2.00.
Lubbock, John.   British Wild Flowers in Relation to Insects. M. 1893. 16 + 194. $1.25.
Müller, H.   The Fertilization of Flowers. Translated by Thompson. M. 1883. 10 + 669. 21s.
*Schimper, A. F. W.   Plant Geography upon a Physiological Basis. Translation by Fisher. Clar. 1903. 30 + 839. 4 volumes, $12.00.
Thomson, J. A.   Science of Life. Herbert S. Stone, New York. 1899. 10 + 246. $1.25.
Wallace, A. R.   Darwinism. M. 1889. 494. $2.25.

Books on Taxonomic Botany (for Teachers).

Beal, W. H.   Grasses of North America. Ho. 2 volumes, $7.50.
Britton, N. L.   Manual of the Flora of the Northern States and Canada. Ho. 1901. 10 + 1080. $2.25.
Britton, N. L., and Brown, A.   An Illustrated Flora of the Northern United States, Canada, etc. Scribner. 3 volumes, index, $10.00.
Chapman, A. W.   Flora of the Southern United States. Am. $4.00.
Coulter, J. M.   Manual of the Botany of the Rocky Mountain Region. Am. 16 + 453. $1.62.
Eaton, D. C.   The Ferns of North America. K. 2 volumes, $40.00.
Engler and Prantl.   Natuerliche Pflanzenfamilien. 16 volumes (yet incomplete), $75.00 (about). Leipzig. Engelmann.
Gray, Asa.   Manual of the Botany of the Northern United States. Am. $1.62.
Gray, Asa.   Field, Forest, and Garden Botany. Am. $1.80.
Greene, E. L.   Manual of the Botany of the Region of San Francisco Bay. San Francisco, Cubery & Co.
Grout, A. J.   Mosses with a Hand Lens. Published by the Author, 360 Lenox Road, Brooklyn, New York City. 11 + 74. $1.10.

Grout, A. J. Mosses with a Hand Lens and Microscope. Part I. Ditto. 86. $1.00.

Howell, T. Flora of Northwest America. Portland, Ore. Published by the Author.

Macbride, T. H. The North American Slime Moulds. M. 1899. 17 + 231. $2.25.

Murray, George. An Introduction to the Study of Sea-Weeds. M. 16 + 271. $1.75.

Schneider, A. A Guide to the Study of Lichens. K. 1904. 12 + 234.

Small, J. K. Flora of the Southeastern United States. 1903. 10 + 1370. $3.60. Published by the author, New York Botanical Garden, Bronx Park, New York.

Underwood, L. M. Our Native Ferns and Their Allies. Ho. 1900. 10 + 158. $1.00.

Underwood, L. M. Moulds, Mildews, and Mushrooms. Ho. 1899. 5 + 236. $1.50.

Waters, C. E. Ferns. A Manual of the Northeastern States. Ho. 1903. 362 pages. $3.00.

Warming, E. A Handbook of Systematic Botany. Translated by Potter. M. 1895. 12 + 620. $3.75.

Wettstein, R. von. Jena. G. Fischer. 1898.

Laboratory Guides, Technique (for Teachers).

Arthur, J. C., Barnes, C. R., and Coulter, J. M. Handbook of Plant Dissection. Ho. 11 + 256. $1.20.

Bailey, W. W. Botanical Collector's Handbook. 14 + 139. G. A. Bates, Salem, Mass. 1881. 75c.

Bower, F. O. A Course of Practical Instruction in Botany. M. $2.60.

*Chamberlain, C. J. Methods in Plant Histology. Chicago. The University of Chicago Press. 1901. 8 + 159. $1.50.

Groom, Percy. Elementary Botany. London. G. Bell & Co. 1898. 10 + 252. 90c.

Huxley, T. H., and Martin, H. N. A Course of Elementary Instruction in Practical Biology. 279 M. $2.60.

Johnston, A. Botany. A Concise Manual for Students of Medicine and Science. Ap. 1891. 14 + 260. $1.75.

JOURNAL OF APPLIED MICROSCOPY. 6 volumes, 1898–1903 (now discontinued). Rochester, N. Y.

Poulsen, D. A., and Trelease, W. Botanical Micro-Chemistry. S. E. Cassino & Co., Boston. 1884. 18 + 118. $1.00.

*Spalding, V. M. A Guide to the Study of Common Plants. H. 1894. 23 + 246. 80c.

Strasburger, E., and Hillhouse, W. Practical Botany. M. 1889. 24 + 425. $2.60.

*Zimmerman, A. Botanical Microtechnique. Translated by Humphrey. Ho. 1893. 12 + 296. $2.50.

Books on Plant Physiology (for Teachers).

Davenport, C. B.   Experimental Morphology.   M. Vol. I. 1897. 14 + 280. $2.60. Vol. II. 1899. 18 + 588. $2.00.

*Darwin, Charles.   The Power of Movement in Plants. Ap. $2.00.

*Darwin, Charles.   Movements and Habits of Climbing Plants. Ap. $2.00.

Darwin, F., and Acton, E. H.   Practical Physiology of Plants. M. 1895. 19 + 326. $1.25.

*Detmer, W.   Practical Plant Physiology.   Translated by Moor. M. 1898. 19 + 555. $3.00.

*Ganong, W. F.   A Laboratory Course in Plant Physiology especially as a Basis for Ecology. Ho. 1901. 6 + 147. $1.50.

Goodale, G. L.   Physiological Botany. Am. 1885. 21 + 499 + 36. $2.00.

*Green, J. Reynolds.   An Introduction to Vegetable Physiology. J. & A. Churchill, London. 1900. 20 + 459. $4.00.

Green, J. Reynolds.   Soluble Ferments and Fermentation. M. 1899. 14 + 480. $3.00.

Haberlandt, G.   Physiologische Pflanzenanatomie. Leipzig. Engelmann. 1896. 550.

*MacDougal, D. T.   Text-Book of Plant Physiology. L. 1901 14. + 352. $3.00.

MacDougal, D. T.   Elementary Plant Physiology. L. 1902. 11 + 134. $1.20.

*Pfeffer, W.   The Physiology of Plants.   Translated by Ewart. Oxford. Clar. Vol. I. 1900. 12 + 362. $7.00.

Sachs, J. von.   Lectures on the Physiology of Plants.   Translated by Ward. Clar. 1887. 14 + 836.

*Sorauer, P.   A Popular Treatise on the Physiology of Plants. Translated by Weiss. L. 1895. 10 + 256. $3.00.

Verworn, M.   General Physiology.   Translated by Lee. M. 1899. 16 + 615. $4.00.

Vines, S. H.   Lectures on the Physiology of Plants. M. 1886. 10 + 710. $5.00.

Ward, Marshall.   Timber and Some of its Diseases. M. 1889. 8 + 295. $1.50.

General Texts — Anatomy and Morphology.

Atkinson, G. F.   The Study of the Biology of Ferns by the Collodion Method. M. 1894. 12 + 132. $2.00.

*de Bary, A.   Comparative Anatomy of the Vegetative Organs of Phanerogams and Ferns.   Translated by Bower and Scott. Clar. 1884. 16 + 659. $5.50.

*de Bary, A.   Comparative Morphology and Biology of the Fungi. Mycetozoa and Bacteria.   Translated by Garnsey and Balfour. Clar. 1887. 10 + 525. $5.50.

Bennett, A. W., and Murray, G. A Handbook of Cryptogamic Botany. L. 1889. 8 + 473. $5.00.

Bessey, C. R. Botany for High Schools and Colleges. Ho. 1885. 10 + 611. $2.20.

Bonnier et du Sablon. Cours de Botanique. P. Dupont, Paris (not yet complete).

Campbell, D. H. The Structure and Development of the Mosses and Ferns. M. 1895. 6 + 544. $4.50.

*Campbell, D. H. A University Text-Book of Botany. M. 1902. 15 + 579. $4.00.

*Coulter and Chamberlain, C. J. Morphology of the Spermatophytes. Vol. I. (Gymnosperms). Ap. 1901. 10 + 188. $1.75. Vol. II. (Morphology of the Angiosperms). Ap. 1903. 10 + 348.

Curtis, C. C. Text-Book of General Botany. L. 1897. 8 + 359. $3 00.

Farmer, J. B. A Practical Introduction to the Study of Botany. L. 1899. 8 + 274.

*Goebel, K. Organography of Plants. Part I. translated by Balfour. Clar. 1900. 16 + 270. $3.10.

*Goebel, K. Outlines of Classification and Special Morphology of Plants. Translated by Garnsey and Balfour. Clar. 1887. 12 + 515. $5.25.

- **Gray, Asa.** Structural Botany. Part I. of Gray's Botanical Text-Book. Am. 12 + 442. $2.00.

Gregory, Emily L. Elements of Plant Anatomy. G. 1895. 8 + 148. $1.25.

*Strasburger, E., Noll, F., Schenck, H , and Schimper, A. F. W. A Text-Book of Botany. Translation of 5th German edition. M. 1903. 5 + 671. $5.00.

Scott, D. H. An Introduction to Structural Botany. M. 1894. 2 parts (Flowering Plants, 288, and Cryptogams, 312), each $1.00.

Vines, S. H. A Students' Text-Book of Botany. M. 1886. 16 + 821. $3.75.

Vines, S. H. An Elementary Text-Book of Botany. M. 1898. $2.25.

Westermaier, M. Compendium of General Botany. Translated by Schneider. John Wiley & Son, New York. 1896. 10 + 299. $2.00.

History of Botany.

*Sachs, Julius von. History of Botany. Translated by Garnsey and Balfour. Clar. 1890. 15 + 563. $2.50.

Botanical and General Periodicals.

BRYOLOGIST. Illustrated bi-monthly. 100 pages, $1.00. 78 Orange St., Brooklyn, N. Y. Mosses, Liverworts, Lichens.

*BOTANICAL GAZETTE. Illustrated monthly. 900 pages, $5.00. University of Chicago Press, Chicago, Ill.

BULLETIN OF THE TORREY BOTANICAL CLUB. Illustrated monthly, 700 pages, $3.00. Columbia University, New York.

FERN BULLETIN. Illustrated quarterly. 100 pages, 75c, Binghamton, N. Y.

NATURE STUDY. Illustrated monthly. 150 pages, 50c. Manchester, N. H.

*PLANT WORLD. Illustrated monthly. 300 pages, $1.50. P. O. Box 334, Washington, D. C. Official Organ of the Wild Flower Preservation Society of America. A department for teachers in botany.

RHODORA. Illustrated monthly. 250 pages, $1.00. 150 Commercial St., Boston, Mass.

*SCHOOL SCIENCE. Illustrated monthly. 550 pages, $2.00. Ravenswood, Chicago, Ill. Especially for secondary science teachers.

SCIENCE. Weekly. 2000 pages, $5.00. Official Organ of the American Association for the Advancement of Science, of which the dues are $3.00 annually.

TORREYA. Illustrated monthly. 200 pages, $1.00. Torrey Botanical Club, Columbia University, New York.

THE TEACHING OF ZOÖLOGY

INCLUDING

HUMAN PHYSIOLOGY
IN THE SECONDARY SCHOOL

By MAURICE A. BIGELOW, Ph.D.

Adjunct Professor of Biology in Teachers College, Columbia University

Prefatory Note

NUMEROUS important problems relating to the teaching of zoölogy in the secondary school are still unsolved, and concerning these there is wide divergence of the opinions held by teachers who are specialists in this science. As to the method of teaching zoölogy, there is general agreement that the modern laboratory practice is all-essential, but with regard to the special application of this there are, as we shall see, differences of opinion. But the greatest uncertainty is concerning the subject-matter to be taught, and on this point there is far wider disagreement than in the case of any other science commonly taught in high schools. In the last ten years great changes in subject-matter content have been made, but general agreement seems more distant than ever and further changes are inevitable. In short, zoölogy for secondary schools must on the whole be regarded as still in an undeveloped state.

In dealing with the many problems of secondary-school zoölogy, the writer is conscious of not having succeeded in keeping his personal opinions in the background. However, it has been attempted in all cases to give reasons in justification for the position taken on debatable questions, and to examine in all fairness the opposition views. Even with all possible care in examining the pros and cons of propositions it is not to be supposed that final conclusions can be drawn from mere discussions. There is a vast difference between the theory and the practice; and in the light of new experience the writer himself will in the future undoubtedly revise some opinions which from the present viewpoint seem best. All that can be claimed for the present chapters is that they aim to present the teaching of zoölogy in secondary schools as variously practised at the present time and attempt to point out those things which seem to lead the way towards greater efficiency and uniformity for the future.

The fields of zoölogy and botany are so closely allied that in considering some fundamental questions this second part of the volume undoubtedly repeats in essentials discussions which in Part I refer directly to botany. Such repetition seems unavoidable if the teaching of zoölogy is to be given unity and breadth in treatment. Aside from consultation regarding general outlines, the two parts of the volume have been written quite independently; and hence the apparent repetition in certain parts will have the advantage of affording the possibility of comparison from the viewpoints of specialists in botany and zoölogy respectively. Moreover, it has seemed best to discuss with special reference to zoölogy certain topics, particularly in Chapter I, which in terms of science in general have been discussed in the first chapter of the preceding part of this volume. Finally, there is special justification for any slight overlapping in that very many teachers who use one part of this volume may not be specially interested in the companion part, and therefore each part should aim to be as complete as possible in itself.

The writer acknowledges great indebtedness to his wife, Anna N. Bigelow, whose criticisms and suggestions, based on a personal experience in teaching biology in both school and college, have in no small measure influenced many parts of this work.

The

Teaching of Zoölogy in the Secondary School

CHAPTER I

THE EDUCATIONAL VALUE OF ZOÖLOGY AND THE AIMS OF ZOÖLOGICAL TEACHING IN SECONDARY SCHOOLS

BIBLIOGRAPHY

· **Bessey, C. E.** Science and Culture. Proceedings National Educational Association, 1896, pp. 934-942.

Eliot, C. W. Essay: What is a Liberal Education? In Educational Reform (New York, 1898). Value of Natural Science on pp. 109-112. Also in CENTURY MAGAZINE, n. s., Vol. VI., pp. 203-212. June, 1894.

· **Forbes, S. A.** Pedagogical Contents of Zoölogy, pp. 28-78, in Educational Papers by Illinois Science Teachers (Peoria, Ill., 1891). Also in EDUCATIONAL REVIEW, Vol. I., pp. 328-336. 1891.

Ganong, W. F. Essay: The Place of the Sciences in Education and of Botany among the Sciences. In The Teaching Botanist. New York, Macmillan. 1899.

Geikie, Sir Archibald. Science in Education. 'POPULAR SCIENCE MONTHLY, Vol. LIV., pp. 672-686. March, 1899. Also in NATURE, Vol. LIX., pp. 108-112. June, 1899.

Harvey, N. A. The Pedagogical Content of Zoölogy. Proceedings of National Educational Association. 1899. Pp. 1106-1112.

Huxley, T. H. Science and Education Essays. New York, Appleton. On the Educational Value of Natural History Sciences (1854). On the Study of Biology (1876). On the Elementary Instruction in Physiology (1877). On Science and Culture (1880).

Jordan, D. S. Science in the High School. POPULAR SCIENCE MONTHLY, Vol. XXXVI., pp. 721-727. April, 1890.

Mill, John Stuart. Inaugural Address at University of St. Andrews (1867). Quoted by Youmans in Culture Demanded by Modern Life (See below.)

Mann, Horace. The Study of Physiology. Sixth (1842) Report of Secretary of the Board of Education of Massachusetts. Also in Vol. III., pp. 129-229, of Life and Work of Horace Mann. Boston, Lee & Shepard. 1891. Also in COMMON SCHOOL JOURNAL, Vol. V., pp. 229-352. Boston, 1843.

Mivart, St. G. The Groundwork of Science, A Study of Epistemology. London, Bliss, Sands & Co. New York, Putnam. 1898.

Paget, J. On the Importance of the Study of Physiology. A Lecture before Royal Institution of Great Britain. Reprinted in Culture Demanded by Modern Life. Edited by E. L. Youmans. New York. Appleton. 1867. Pp. 149-184.

Payne, Joseph. Lecture on The True Foundation of Science Teaching (1872). In Lectures on the Science and Art of Education. American edition, Kellogg & Co., New York. 1887.

Pearson, Karl. Grammar of Science. Second edition, London, A. & C. Black. 1899. (The first chapters touch upon the educational value of science in general.)

Sedgwick, W. T. Educational Value of the Methods of Science. EDUCATIONAL REVIEW, Vol. V., pp. 243-256. March, 1893.

Spencer, Herbert. Education: Intellectual, Moral, and Physical. London, Williams & Norgate. New York, Appleton. 1861. (See chapter on " What Knowledge is of Most Worth ? ")

Thomson, J. Arthur. Study of Animal Life. Third Edition. New York, Scribner. (See Appendix I b.)

· Wilson, E. B. Aims and Methods of Study in Natural History. SCIENCE, N. S., Vol. XIII., pp. 14-23. January 4, 1901.

Youmans, E. L., Editor. Culture Demanded by Modern Life. New York, Appleton. 1887. (A collection of essays and addresses by prominent men of science and education.)

The teacher will first be interested in the essays by Huxley, Spencer, Eliot, and Forbes.

THE place of natural science in education has been well advocated by many excellent essays with which there is now general

Science in Education. agreement in both theory and practice, and it may seem unnecessary to attempt again a review of the aims and value of any particular science, such as zoölogy. Time was, in the earlier days of Huxley, Spencer, and other great leaders of scientific education, when it was necessary to emphasize the aims and value of sciences for the purpose of gaining their recognition in educational systems; but these pioneers in scientific education presented the claims of science so convincingly that it has come to be generally recognized as an absolutely essential part of education.

But aside from attempting to give further support to the

right of any science in educational curricula, frequent considerations of its educational contents are certainly
profitable in that they tend to keep the attention
of teachers centred upon the great essential facts
and principles as viewed from the combined standpoints of science and education. This leads the way towards
organized instead of lawless and haphazard teaching into which
science has often drifted in the past ; and, therefore, considerations of any science in its educational aspects are certainly
important in advancing its influence in education. The present
state of advancement of science teaching is due largely to the
fact that science has slowly entered every phase of education,
every advance being made only by definite and decisive results
which have gained for the sciences recognition of their importance in education. It has therefore been the good fortune,
not the misfortune as it has often seemed, that it has been
necessary to demonstrate the value of sciences in order to gain
their admission as essentials in all education. Other subjects
have for a long time held their place in the educational systems
through the power of historical associations, and without a
question as to their value, but sciences have been introduced
and will remain in general education only on the basis of
demonstrable results of superior quality. Herein should lie
the source of a powerful stimulus towards the development
of the highest possible efficiency in science teaching, and to
this end it is well that from time to time science teachers
should renew the critical examination of the educational value
and aims of the science which they teach ; it is in this way that
we can estimate progress, perhaps discover evidence of some
retrogression, and establish a definite goal towards which future
advances will be directed. It seems clear, then, that renewed
discussions of the educational contents of any science have
their justification aside from defending the place of that science
in education.

But with the educational value of science in general we are
not here directly concerned. For the purpose of this chapter

Importance of Discussions of Educational Contents of Sciences.

it will be taken for granted that science is generally recognized by educators as deserving a place in general education. The arguments pro and con have been written often and the reader is referred to the writings of prominent men of science and education, some of the best of which are mentioned in the list of references accompanying this chapter.

It is the primary purpose of this chapter to re-examine the question of the educational value of zoölogy in order to lay

The Aim of this Chapter. down some principles for guidance in our later discussions of the teaching of zoölogy, particularly in secondary schools. Obviously many of the arguments for the value of zoölogy might with slight modifications apply to science in general, but it seems more profitable to limit the following discussion closely to the science with which we shall deal in later chapters.

For the purpose of later application it will be most profitable to consider the value of zoölogy in general education from two

Educational Value of Zoöl-ogy as Disci-pline and as Information. standpoints, namely, (1) its value as discipline, and (2) its value as information ; and finally at the end of this chapter it will be attempted to deduce from the educational contents of zoölogy the leading aims which should govern the teaching of the science in the secondary school.

I. The Value of Zoölogy as Discipline.[1]

The disciplinary value of the study of zoölogy, as indeed of any other science, is found in that it may contribute to the

Discipline afforded by Science Study. development of a scientific attitude of mind, by directing various mental processes, such as those involved in scientific observing, classifying facts, reasoning on the basis of demonstrated facts, exercising judg-

---

[1] On the value of sciences in general as intellectual discipline, see Karl Pearson's *Grammar of Science* (revised) ; Spencer's *Education*, pp. 73-79; Huxley's *Essays on Science and Education*, especially those on Science and Culture and on Value of Natural History; and the essays by Bessey, Geikie, Sedgwick, and Payne. With direct reference to zoölogy see the references to Harvey and Cramer in Chapter III.

ment and discrimination, and learning to appreciate demonstrated knowledge. I do not propose to review here the well-known discussion of the value of the mental training to be derived from the above processes in science study. For our present purposes it is sufficient to indicate the general bearing of the disciplinary aspect of zoölogical teaching.

It is evident that the discipline in scientific method is not to be advocated as peculiar to zoölogy. It is now well recognized that all the sciences furnish materials for developing the chief elements of a general scientific attitude of mind. In the teaching of every science in a secondary school no occasion should be neglected for giving training in scientific observing and scientific thinking. Many educators now regard such training as far more important in liberal education than the knowledge of the facts of any science. "Science should hold its place in the schools," says President Jordan, "by virtue of its power as an agent in mental training, not because of the special usefulness of scientific facts, nor because knowledge of things has a higher market value than the knowledge of words." And along the same line Huxley has said: "You must not be solicitous to fill him [the pupil] with information, but you must be careful that what he learns he knows of his own knowledge. . . . Pursue this discipline carefully and conscientiously, and you will make sure that, however scanty may be the measure of information which you have pounded into the boy's mind, you have created an intellectual habit of priceless value in practical life."[1]

Scientific Discipline of Zoology not Peculiar.

Professor S. A. Forbes, of the University of Illinois, sees value in the study of zoölogy both for discipline and for information: "The pursuit of this science may tax to its utmost, it seems to me, every power of mind, and the knowledge of the life it leads to has a great and primary value and interest to us all. It will not do, consequently, to look on it as an apparatus for mental gymnastics

Zoölogy for Discipline and for Information.

---

[1] From essay on Scientific Education.

only, and neither will it do to look at it, for our purposes, as a body of valuable knowledge and nothing else. We must see both what it contains that our pupils ought to know, and what the pursuit of it requires that they ought to learn to do." In all this I agree with Professor Forbes ; for I believe there is no serious conflict between discipline and information, and aiming at one does not necessarily exclude the other, as many people seem to think. It is not necessary in teaching a science with scientific training as one leading aim that its essential facts should be at all neglected, for the training depends primarily upon the method of teaching rather than upon the subject-matter. The best of discipline may be given along with information concerning the essential facts and principles of zoölogy which have value along the lines discussed in the following pages. To accomplish this the method of teaching must be the general method of modern science — the laboratory method ; but the quality of the training depends entirely upon the way in which the laboratory work is directed. If the disciplinary aim of zoölogical teaching is to meet with the greatest possible realization, it must be kept prominently in mind while planning a laboratory course in zoölogy, for very much depends upon the manner in which problems for solution are presented to the minds of the pupils. A consideration of the fundamental principles of the laboratory method and its special application to zoölogical teaching need not here involve our discussion, but it will be referred to in Chapter III.

II. The Value of Zoölogy as Information.

Aside from the training in mental processes which the study of zoölogy, like all science studies, may give the pupils, there is the important phase in which zoölogy stands upon its own merits as a science with a peculiar subject-matter, some knowledge of which is believed to form a valuable part of a liberal education. In this aspect of its educational value, zoölogy is quite distinct from the physical sciences ; but it is often impossible to draw any sharp line between zoölogy and the sister-science botany, which in fundamentals stands upon the same basis.

For the purposes of later application we may consider the information side of zoölogy from the following points of view : (*a*) The direct utilitarian value of zoölogical knowledge, or zoölogy as applied science ; (*b*) the intellectual value of zoölogy considered as pure science ; (*c*) the æsthetic value of zoölogy ; and (*d*) the moral value.[1]

Zoölogical Knowledge from Various Viewpoints.

a. Utilitarian or Practical Value of Zoölogical Knowledge.

The utilitarian value of knowledge of zoölogy, that is, zoölogy as applied science, will be made evident by a general review of the lines in which zoölogical knowledge is of direct practical use in human life.[2]

Beyond question the most important of these is the physiological side in which zoölogy touches directly upon human life and health. In anticipation of the chapter on human physiology; it may be said that this subject is at basis closely related to general zoölogy, and its study is best pursued from the viewpoint of the science of animal life. In the physiological phase of zoölogy and its bearings upon human health the science of zoölogy has strong justification in support of its place in general education, and in so far as the science has such a practical relation to human life it should be an essential part of the education of every individual.

Physiological Aspect of Zoölogy.

A second argument for the utilitarian value of zoölogy is found

---

[1] I find that this division, which was suggested to me by Huxley's essays, corresponds with Professor Forbes's classification of zoölogical knowledge, "according to its industrial, its emotional, its ethical, and its intellectual values."

[2] This practical value of zoölogical knowledge is touched upon by Huxley in essays on Educational Value of Natural History, On the Study of Biology, and in various other incidental references in his *Science and Education Essays*. See also Forbes, *loc. cit.* Especially important are the essays by Horace Mann, Huxley, Herbert Spencer, and Paget, on the importance of human physiology in general education.

in the relations of animals to man along economic lines. We

Economics of Zoölogy. need only mention some of these relations in order to suggest the great practical importance of some economic aspects of animal life.

Most important of these is the value of animals in the food-supply of man. Of course this value does not argue directly in **Animals and** favor of the study of animals in general education. **Food-Supply.** The value of animals in the food-supply is not directly affected by widespread knowledge of zoölogical science, for at most such knowledge would be of direct practical value only to the relatively few who are able to apply it in the supplying of animals for food. But the problems of the food-supply are of such importance that we must believe that there is general interest in them and especially in the attempts to increase the supply by the application of scientific principles gained from the study of animals. A knowledge of the general facts of zoölogy will do much towards making the average citizen appreciative of the work in this line, especially that of governmental departments such as the United States Department of Agriculture, the United States Fish Commission, and the various State agricultural stations and fish commissions.

Besides the value of animals in the human food-supply, there **Domesticated** may be mentioned the useful domesticated ani-**Animals and** mals and the animal products other than food.[1] **Animal** **Products.** These are aspects of animal economics which should arouse at least an intelligent interest on the part of educated citizens.

Then there are the numerous animals which are directly op-**Injurious** posed to the interests of man. The economic im-**Animals.** portance of this aspect of zoölogical knowledge is evident when one inquires into the monetary value of crops and

---

[1] As summaries of these aspects of economic zoölogy, Simmond's *Animal Products,* Shaler's *Domesticated Animals,* and Wood's *Dominion of Man* are suggested. See full biographical references under " Economic Zoölogy " in chapter on " Zoölogical Books."

domesticated animals which are annually destroyed by such animals as insects, rodents, and parasites.[1]

Thus in the broader outlines we see that the economic relations between man and animals are manifold and of great utilitarian significance; and we cannot but believe that such knowledge concerning animals is of general interest because of economic relations. It is true that the great majority of citizens may make little direct practical application of knowledge of the economic relations of animals, but indirectly all are concerned; and on the ground of intelligent interest alone this would argue for the study of animals in general education. This is to my mind exactly the same line of argument which we have long accepted as the chief justification for the study of the commercial aspect of the geography of foreign countries. Very few persons have opportunities for making direct practical application of the facts in this line which are commonly taught in our schools, but the general interest in the economics of commerce is regarded as sufficient justification. Likewise, zoölogical knowledge has great utilitarian value from the standpoint of human life in general, but for the masses of individuals it is of importance, not on account of direct application, but because of interest in animals as they may affect man.

General Interest in Economic Relations of Animals.

We have seen that from the practical standpoint a strong case can be made out in favor of zoölogy in education. But while this utilitarian view is in harmony with the materialistic tendencies of our commercial age, it is not to my mind the strongest argument for this or for any other science in general education. In fact, we have seen that the utilitarian arguments, with the exception of the unquestioned value of "physiology," apply specifically

Practical Value not the Strongest Argument for Zoology.

---

[1] For accounts of injurious animals, see Harris's *Insects Injurious to Vegetation*, Smith's *Economic Entomology*, Miall's *Injurious Insects*, Sanderson's *Injurious Insects* (references in chapter on "Zoölogical Books"). Also numerous reports and bulletins of the United States Department of Agriculture.

only to the special education of the few who may practise certain phases of "applied zoölogy." Hence, aside from the question of general interest of most citizens in the zoölogy of commerce in its widest sense, the practical value of knowledge of the science cannot be held to justify its place in general education. In reality this applies only to technical education, especially in its agricultural phase.

Clearly the science of zoölogy requires some more general justification than that of its industrial application, and this we **Cultural Value** find in its cultural value, which includes all which I **of Zoölogy.** have in this essay discussed under "disciplinary," "intellectual," "moral," and "æsthetic" values. It is for this aspect of zoölogy, as indeed for science in general, that we must stand. This opinion has been expressed by many writers from Huxley to the present time. Especially to the point are the addresses by Sir Archibald Geikie and by Professor C. E. Bessey, who strongly protest against the mere utilitarian views as to the value of science and argue for its cultural value. In Professor Bessey's words, " that culture is best which so prepares a man that whatever fact presents itself to him, he will be able to arrange it accurately with reference to others. This ability to classify facts is of far more importance than mere acquaintance with facts, however extended the latter may be."

b. Intellectual Value of Zoölogical Knowledge.

The intellectual value depends upon the relation of zoölogical knowledge as pure science to that of other sciences and to still other phases of knowledge.

With regard to the relation of zoölogy to other sciences, we must note first that its greatest generalizations are intricately **Relation of** bound up with those of botany in the fundamental **Zoölogy to Other** principles of the general science of life — biology. **Sciences.** Hence to a large extent we cannot discuss the intellectual value of zoölogy entirely apart from that of botany. Considering, then, the relation of biology to other sciences, it has been pointed out by Huxley, Spencer, and others that the subject-matter of the biological sciences stands midway between the physical sciences concerned with matter and energy and those dealing with the mind and society.[1] We recognize four orders of facts in science and four groups of sciences, namely, physical sciences dealing with matter and energy, biology with life phenomena, psychology with mind, and sociology with society. " Each of these depends upon its predecessor. The student of organisms requires help from the student of chemistry and physics ; mind cannot be discussed apart from body ; nor can society be studied apart from the minds of its component members. Each order of realities we may regard as a subtle synthesis of those which we call simpler. Life is a secret synthesis of matter and energy ; mind is a subtle form of life ; society is a unit of minds." [2] In essentials this is the idea of the central relation of facts of biology to other sciences which has been expressed by many writers. It is clear, then, that knowledge of the biological principles must be especially important as a foundation for studies of the more complex sciences dealing with mind and society.

Owing to its central position among the sciences, biology has exerted a great influence upon many important problems which came forward during the last half of the nineteenth century. Cosmic philosophy, theology, ethics, and sociology especially have undergone radical changes **Relation of Biology to Philosophic Problems.** in the light of the theory of organic evolution as it was set forth by Darwin's epoch-making *Origin of Species*, and Spencer's *Synthetic Philosophy*.[8]

---

[1] See Huxley, On Educational Value of Natural History; Spencer, Relations of Biology, Sociology, and Psychology — *Popular Science Monthly*, Vol. L., p. 163 (1896) ; J. A. Thomson, *Study of Animal Life*, third edition, pp. 348–350.

[2] Thomson, *loc. cit.*, p. 349.

[8] The influence of the theory of evolution upon modern thought along the above-mentioned lines is evident to the reader of such works as Fiske's *Cosmic Philosophy* and the later series beginning with his *Destiny of Man*, Le Conte's *Evolution and Religious Thought*, and Huxley's *Evolution and Ethics*. (See full bibliographical references in chapter on " Zoölogical Books.")

Now, while the theory of evolution is broadly biological, deriving its support from both plants and animals, it is the animal

Evolution and Man's Relation to Animals. side which makes the strongest appeal to general students of biology. Man's relation to animals has made the great law of evolution seem overwhelmingly full of philosophical significance, and it is therefore but natural that general interest should be appealed to by the zoölogical evidences of evolution, especially by those which appear to throw light upon the relation of man to nature. This is why the evidences of evolution among vertebrates are so interesting to general students who are led to consider the facts pointing to the place of man in the back-boned series. It was the suggestion of man's descent in the *Origin of Species*, afterwards expanded into the *Descent of Man*, that first brought the theory of evolution prominently to the attention of scholars in general. It is this same natural interest in man's relations which is sure to continue to be of absorbing interest to each succeeding generation of beginning students. Even without regard to interpreting facts of animal structure and function in terms of evolution, interest in the science of biology, and especially in zoölogy, is profoundly influenced by the similarity of structure and vital phenomena of man and other organisms. This similarity has always affected, perhaps sometimes unfortunately, all phases of biology ; and on the animal side there has been a decided tendency towards interpreting structure, functions, and especially nervous phenomena from the human standpoint. We find, then, one great difference between the animal and plant phases of biology, namely, that the evidences of evolution and many general principles of biology are for the general student more interesting and more convincing on the animal side because of man's relation to the animal kingdom. It follows that any arguments for the value of biology which are based on the relations of its greatest generalizations to other phases of knowledge, apply with special force to the zoölogical side of the general science of life.

From these outlines of the relation of zoölogy to other phases of human knowledge, it is clear that the intellectual value of the science must be regarded as a strong argument favoring its place in general education. The relation of the theory of evolution to modern thought in general alone offers a sufficient argument for general knowledge of the science which most clearly and convincingly illustrates the principles of organic development.

With regard to application of the above discussion to secondary education, it must be admitted that pupils of the high-school age do not have the mental development which will enable them to grapple with the great generalizations to which reference has been made. Nevertheless, high-school pupils are able to appreciate a large number of the underlying facts, and it seems reasonable to suppose that even an elementary course of biology in the high school may give the pupil an appreciation of the relations of facts and a viewpoint which in later years may be important in giving the proper perspective to philosophic studies, which are commonly of interest to liberally educated men. But of course the biological work in the secondary school should not digress in order to attempt pointing out the bearing of biology upon other fields of knowledge. This must come from future development; but I believe that the foundation may be laid even as early as the secondary school. We may therefore conclude that the arguments for the intellectual value of zoölogical knowledge are applicable to the secondary phase of general education.

Intellectual Value as Applied to Secondary Education.

c. The Æsthetic Value of Zoölogical Knowledge.[1]

" In all animals there is something to admire because in all there is the natural and the beautiful." — Aristotle, " Father of Natural History."

We now pass from considerations of the value of zoölogical information viewed as facts and principles of natural science to

---

[1] The æsthetic value of zoölogy is referred to by Huxley, Thomson, Geikie, Forbes, Wilson, and Bessey, in essays already cited. Also see Pearson's *Grammar of Science*, pp. 34-36.

that of its relation to æsthetics — the science of the beautiful. Huxley, the master to whom we frequently turn for ideas on science in education, has thus advocated the importance of the bearing of biology on our appreciation of the beautiful:

" There is yet another way in which natural history [biology] may, I am convinced, take a profound hold upon practical life, and that
Huxley's   is, by its influence over our finer feelings, as the great-
View.   est of all sources of that pleasure derivable from
beauty. I do not pretend that natural history knowledge, as such, can increase our sense of the beautiful in natural objects. . . . But I advocate natural history knowledge from this point of view, because it would lead us to seek the beauties of natural objects instead of trusting to chance to force them on our attention." [1]

That there is educational value in cultivating an appreciation of the beautiful in natural objects we may accept as demonstrated by the students of æsthetics and by our own personal experiences. However, this has often been neglected in weighing the value of science in education, because its field has no direct relation to that of pure natural science. The æsthetical appreciation of natural objects has little significance from the standpoint of pure science which the emotional must not be allowed to influence, nor from that of applied science with its formal demand for material results, but it is full of meaning when our outlook upon life and nature is that of Sir John Lubbock in his *Beauties of Nature;* of John Van Dyke in his *Nature for its Own Sake;* of Gilbert White in his *Natural History of Selborne;* of Ruskin; of our American nature-lovers, Henry Thoreau and John Burroughs; and of many others who have helped us to appreciate beauty in nature.

With direct reference to the animal side of biology, the strongest reason for advocating on æsthetic grounds the study of animal life is found in that the appreciation of the beautiful in animal form, colors, and movements has in all times and

---

[1] Huxley, On the Educational Value of Natural History, p. 63, in *Science and Education Essays.*

countries been the chief source of a general interest in animal life. "To many animal life is impressive, not so much because of its amazing variety and numerical greatness, nor because of its intellectual suggestiveness and practical utility, but chiefly on account of its beauty. This is to be seen and felt, rather than described and talked about."[1] This is the explanation of the popular interest in birds, insects, shells of mollusks — all forms with splendid coloration and other attributes which appeal strongly to the æsthetic sense. The same is true of the very many animals which have long been under the care of man primarily because of their beauty, — for example, gold fishes in Japan, numerous birds and other so-called ornamental animals. On the other hand, there has never been general interest in such animals as are commonly considered repulsive ; but to the man of science some of these despised forms are of great interest and from the study of some of them much light has been thrown upon important principles of zoölogy. It therefore seems clear that popular interest in animals is in no small measure determined by æsthetic rather than by strictly scientific considerations.

The Beautiful in Animals, the Chief Source of Popular Interest.

We find further evidence of the existence of a general tendency towards interest in the beautiful in animals if we examine books on animal natural history which have been popular with general readers. These books have not aimed to present the cold scientific facts which mean most from the standpoint of pure science, so much as they have emphasized those things which appeal to the æsthetic sense. This is especially true in the recent illustrated books which have had unparalleled popularity. The secret of the great wave of interest in these is not, I believe, to be found in their descriptions of animals — in many cases these are not to be compared in literary charm with many older books ; but modern methods of illustration have made it possible for the first time

The Æsthetic in Books on Animal Natural History.

---

[1] Thomson's *Study of Animal Life*, p. 15.

to represent, with considerable approximation to the natural, the beautiful in animal form and color. Heretofore the beautiful in animals has been expressed only in words, but now their almost perfect likenesses are given a setting which appeals strongly to the æsthetic sense. This, I feel sure, is the chief reason for the widespread interest in our modern nature books as contrasted with earlier works, and the popularity of representations of the beautiful in animals is only another proof of a general tendency towards interest in animals because of their appeal to the æsthetic sense.

Still further evidence of the appeal to interest by the beautiful in animals may be obtained by studying the attitude **Interest of Young People in the Beauty of Animals.** of young pupils, and even many college students, toward such animals as butterflies as compared with less beautiful specimens, such as earthworms. Or in some great museum notice the interest of visitors in the beautiful animals, and this alone convinces one that great interest in animals, especially that of young people, is in no small degree influenced by beauty.

I have emphasized the general interest in the beautiful in animals for two reasons. First, because it suggests the importance of cultivating an appreciation of animal beauty **Importance of Emphasis on the Æsthetic.** for its own sake, and second, because I see in the general interest in the æsthetic side of animal life an opportunity for enlisting and developing interest in the study of animals from the standpoint of pure science.[1] For these two reasons I would urge that æsthetical considerations should be recognized by teachers as offering important arguments for the study of animals and plants in general education, and as suggesting the nature of studies aiming to cultivate the æsthetic appreciation of animal life. The æsthetic value is, I believe, not secondary in its importance in education, but equal to those which I have grouped under "practical" and "intellectual."

----

[1] See Wilson, *loc. cit.*, p. 22.

d. Moral Value of Zoölogical Knowledge.[1]

As evidence of the moral value of the knowledge of animals, many writers have been fond of pointing out that various inter-relations of animals — *e. g.*, in social life, parasitism, struggle for existence, and mutual aid — have a suggestive bearing upon human life and conduct. Without here questioning the soundness of such direct comparison between man and animals, there can be no doubt that in their broad application certain facts and generalizations of biology do affect human ethics. For example, we need only mention the biological laws of evolution and heredity which in the hands of Herbert Spencer and other ethical writers of the evolutionary school have led to the interpretation of the science of conduct from an entirely new point of view.

Relation of Biology to Ethics.

However, the philosophical deductions of students of ethics from biological facts really belong to the intellectual value of zoölogy. Here I wish to limit the discussion to the influence of knowledge of animals upon human conduct directly through sympathetic acquaintance, rather than by way of any formulated ethical principles. It is in developing sympathetic appreciation of animals that the chief moral value of the study of zoölogy in general education is to be found. "The peculiar ethical effects of zoölogical study," says Professor Forbes, "are to be drawn chiefly from that side of it which deals with the lower animals as alive; from a knowledge of them as sentient, often intelligent, and sometimes thoughtful beings, which tends to greatly broaden and enrich the pupil's sympathetic interest." These results, like those on the æsthetic side, are not measurable by examinations, but I believe they may be

Moral Value of Sympathetic Acquaintance with Animals.

---

[1] Special references: H. Spencer on the Moral Discipline of Science, in *Education*, p. 79. A. B. Buckley's *Moral Teachings of Science* (Humboldt Library of Science) is suggestive, but her comparisons between human and animal life often seem extreme.

made a very real and important addition to the educational value of zoölogy.

Certain critics of the modern method of zoölogical study, which oftentimes necessarily involves the killing of animals, **Moral Effect** would have us believe that the courses of zoölogy **of Method of** as now commonly conducted tend to lessen rather **Studying** **Animals.** than increase the sympathy of pupils for living animals. Perhaps this criticism is often justified as applied to particular cases, but for these individual teachers are responsible. With the laboratory work properly conducted by a teacher who has the true scientific spirit, along with interest in living animals, there seems to be no reason why pupils should learn to value animal life lightly, even if for the sake of science study some few individuals must be sacrificed. But unfortunately some amateurs in science teaching have the false impression that to be ruthless and careless in taking animal life is proof of scientific attainments; and as a result the zoölogical laboratory is sometimes turned into a veritable slaughter-house. There is no justification for the wanton waste of material which is sometimes the outgrowth of the teacher's lack of appreciation of living animals. The effect upon the pupil is bound to be bad, both morally and in scientific training. As opposed to such reckless practices, I would urge that it is the duty of the teacher to discourage by example and by words the ruthless and unnecessary sacrifice of animal life; and pupils should be led to get the greatest possible results from a minimum of materials. Especially is this important in the case of the higher animals with which our sympathetic relations are most direct.

But in addition to such indirect work against possible loss of appreciation, I would urge the importance of direct effort **Direct Effort** towards increasing sympathy with living animals. **to Develop** The attitude and the example and the incidental **Sympathy.** suggestions of the teacher have the greatest influence; and besides the reading of certain books which deal with animals as living should be encouraged, especially books on birds and mammals.[1] Special mention should be made of Shaler's *Domesticated Animals*, especially the introduction and the chapter on Rights of Animals; Kropotkin's *Mutual Aid among Animals*; also his articles in *Nineteenth Century*, Vol. XXVIII., pp. 337, 699, 1890; Thomson's *Study of Animal Life*, Part I.; Sharp's *Wild Life near Home*, and the selections from this in *A Watcher in the Woods* (Century Company). Aside from the question of scientific accuracy, the animal books by Kipling, Thompson-Seton, Long, London, and other imaginative writers, are certainly to be commended as stimulating the interest and the sympathy of readers. With the explanation that they are stories, I can see no possible harm, but much good, in the moral effect which may come from putting such books into the hands of pupils old enough to read them. However, such books should not be erroneously classed under natural history.

We have seen that from several points of view the study of zoölogy has value in general education. Further, it has been indicated that in all those aspects wherein the science is important in liberal education it is applicable to schools below the grade of college. Clearly, it is desirable for such schools because the masses of citizens never have opportunity for studying the subject in college. *All above Values applicable to Schools below College.*

From the educational contents of zoölogy we may formulate two aims which should govern the teaching in the secondary school. First, the aim to teach zoölogy so that it will afford good scientific discipline should be the very foundation of zoölogical teaching. Second, it should be aimed to present the information — practical, intellectual, æsthetic, or moral in its bearing — which seems most valuable for liberal secondary education. Equal emphasis should be given these two aims which, as already suggested, are in no sense necessarily conflicting, for the one stands for methods and the other for materials. These two general aims *Aims for Zoölogy in the Secondary School.*

---

[1] See list of books on " Animal Natural History " in Chapter X.

include the minor aims which various authors have suggested, and into these they will later be analyzed. A consideration of the disciplinary aim in its relation to the laboratory method can best be made after some selection of the materials which are demanded by the second aim, and with such selection the next chapter deals.

CHAPTER II

THE SUBJECT-MATTER OF ZOÖLOGY FROM THE STAND-POINT OF THE SECONDARY SCHOOL [1]

"The main object of teaching biology as part of a liberal education is to familiarize the student not so much with the facts as with the ideas of the science."—T. JEFFREY PARKER.

BIBLIOGRAPHY

Forbes, S. A. Pedagogical Contents of Zoölogy. In Educational Papers by Illinois Science Teachers (Peoria, Ill., 1891), pp. 38–48. Also in EDUCATIONAL REVIEW, Vol. I., pp. 328–336. 1891.

Bigelow, M. A. Introduction to Outline of a Course of Zoölogy in Horace Mann High School. TEACHERS COLLEGE RECORD, Vol. II., No. 1, pp. 4–15. January, 1901. Also in SCHOOL SCIENCE, Vol. I., Nos. 2 and 3, pp. 68–72, 131–138. April, May, 1901.

Davenport, C. B. Zoölogy as a Condition for Admission to College. High School Bulletin, No. 2, University of State of New York, Albany. 1899. (Followed by discussion.)

Report of Committee on Zoölogy. Proceedings of National Educational Association, 1899, pp. 805–808.

Report of Committee of New York State Science Teachers' Association, on Secondary School Course in Zoölogy. High School Bulletin, No. 7, University of State of New York, pp. 528–548, 743–777. April, 1900. (Obtainable from secretary of the University, Albany, N. Y. Price 35 cents.)

Prefaces to text-books by Needham, Davenport, Jordan and Kellogg, Harvey, Kellogg, and Colton. See list in Chapter X.

IN selecting the subject-matter for an elementary course in zoölogy for secondary schools, the field of zoölogical knowledge should be viewed from the standpoint of liberal education, as distinguished from special or technical education. The field is wide, and at best only a glimpse of animal structure and life can be given in a single course. Bearing in mind that the great majority

Zoölogy from the Standpoint of Liberal Education.

---

[1] The leading views expressed in this chapter may be regarded as essentially the development of some suggestions in *Teachers College Record*, Vol. II., No. 1. January, 1901.

of secondary pupils can never follow more than one course of instruction in the subject, the problem is to fill that one course with *those zoölogical facts and ideas which have the closest relation to the every-day life of a liberally educated man.* In the future it must be recognized more clearly than it has been in the past that many phases of the science of zoölogy which are of interest and of importance to the specialist may have no definite meaning to a man in other walks of life. Many teachers of zoölogy in secondary schools do not seem to have examined the subject in this light, and as a result elementary zoölogy has been too often taught as if it was the aim to train the pupils for professional work in zoölogy or in some of its direct applications, such as medicine. This special or technical training is the proper work of colleges, and has no more place in the secondary school than have higher applied mathematics. In the college system the student may be expected to acquire much technical information while he is getting a general view of the field of zoölogy. In the secondary school the technical matter is undesirable, but the general view is of great importance. These wide differences between the aims

Different Aims in College and Secondary School. which govern the zoölogical teaching in colleges and those which should underlie the work in the secondary school need to be strongly emphasized, for already there have been too many attempts to transfer college courses and books into the secondary school. The problem of high-school teaching is not a question of how near an approach can be made to the college technical courses in zoölogy, but a question of the value of such work in liberal secondary education. Is it the most valuable which can be selected from the wide field of zoölogy? This is the really vital question which apparently has been overlooked by many who have prepared outlines of study for elementary zoölogy in secondary schools, but upon the answer will depend whether in the future zoölogy justifies its right to a place in the secondary curriculum. To a discussion of this problem of the essentials of zoölogy this chapter will be devoted.

The field of zoölogical knowledge is so wide that, as a matter of convenience, naturalists recognize the subdivision of the general science into special sub-sciences or phases, **Divisions of** each dealing with a peculiar aspect of animal **Zoölogy.** structure or life, and all necessarily involved in any wide and comprehensive view of the general field of zoölogy. Among these sub-sciences we must consider the following : anatomy (including histology), dealing with animal form and structure ; palæontology, treating of animal fossils; systematic zoölogy or classification ; physiology, dealing with functions of organs ; and the science of animal environmental relations, ecology. The first four are based on structure and hence are commonly regarded as sub-divisions of morphology in the strict use of that term, although we sometimes find it used quite synonymously with anatomy. Physiology and ecology, the first referring to functional relations within the organism, the second to relations between organisms and its environment, are to be looked upon as aspects of general physiology, which with morphology constitute the science of zoölogy.[1] Before considering the educational contents of these sub-divisions of the strict science of zoölogy, we must examine the so-called " natural history," which during the past few years has aroused so much interest in connection with the high-school study of animals, and point out its general relations to zoölogy as a science.

The limits of the field of animal natural history as now understood cannot be defined sharply, since its materials may be drawn from several of the sub-sciences involved in **Relations of** zoölogy. In fact, it may be said to be a general **Natural History and** superficial survey of animals, especially from the **Zoölogy.** standpoints of their external structures and adaptations, general

---

[1] The relations of these sub-sciences are well presented in the introductory chapters of Sedgwick and Wilson's *General Biology* (Holt, New York), and in Hertwig's *General Principles of Zoölogy : translation by Field* (Holt). The relation of physiology to ecology is clearly pointed out in the first chapter of Semper's *Animal Life* (Appleton), in which " physiology of organisms " (ecology) is compared with " physiology of organs " (physiology as commonly understood).

classification, life-histories, habits, and economic relations to
man. As now applied to elementary study of animals, natural
history has the same relation to zoölogy which the two had to
each other in the historical development of our knowledge of
animals. In the time preceding the eighteenth century, there
was accumulated a vast mass of facts about animals, especially
concerning their external structure, classification, and life-histories. In all this mass of material there was little order
because facts stood more or less isolated, and to all this the
term " natural history " was literally applicable.[1] But with the
laying of the foundation of modern comparative zoölogy in
the latter half of the eighteenth century, the accumulated facts
from twenty-five centuries began to take their places in the
science of zoölogy ; and few, indeed, were the facts of the old
natural history which had not some definite relation to the
science as it was organized long before another century had
passed. Such was the transition from the natural history
("records of researches ") of animals to the modern science
of zoölogy. It was the result not alone of the rapid accumulation of new facts or of the nature of these, but rather of the
classification and organization of facts on the basis of the
generalizations which constitute the foundation of zoölogy as
we know the science to-day. The established principles are
the distinguishing features of modern zoölogy as compared
with the old natural history of animals. The same difference
obtains between natural history as we now apply that term to
certain elementary studies of animals and zoölogy in the strict
sense. By the first we mean now, as historically, a general
survey of animals for the sake of acquaintance with the facts,
and with little or no organization of these facts on the basis of

---

[1] The phrase "natural history," as applied to animals, appears to
have originated from the Latin translation of the title of Aristotle's
work, which in the original Greek meant "records of investigations on
animals." The natural history of animals, before its development into
modern zoölogy, was chiefly a mass of "records," without organization
into science.

generalizations. Zoölogy, on the contrary, in education as in the pure science, involves as an essential the idea of comparisons leading to generalizations upon which to classify the facts. Such I conceive to be the difference between natural history and zoölogy considered historically, and so they should be understood as applied to education at the present time. In this volume the term natural history will be used in its historical sense to refer to mere accumulations of facts about animals — chiefly the more obvious facts observable in the living animals — while the term zoology will be applied to the study of animals from the standpoint of the modern science, with the principles, comparisons, and generalizations which make it organized. With this understanding of the relations of natural history and zoölogy, we may consider the place of the former in education.

We can best understand the present natural history in secondary schools after briefly reviewing the history of formal instruction concerning animals. From the earliest records of such teaching in the last part of the eighteenth century until sometime in the eighties of the nineteenth century, the common instruction was along the lines of the old natural history, consisting chiefly of descriptions of external form, life-histories, classification, and relations of animals to man. Such instruction was designed simply to give the pupils acquaintance with the most interesting facts about animals, and involved no aim for scientific discipline.[1] But all this was changed by the advances in the instruction in colleges along the lines laid down by Huxley.[2] Between 1885 and 1895 the laboratory method became extensively applied to the teaching of zoölogy in our high schools. Practical studies

Natural History in Education.

[1] For a more complete account of this early instruction, see History of the Teaching of Zoölogy in the Secondary Schools of the United States, by Marion R. Brown, in *School Science*, Vol. II. October and November, 1902.

[2] Especially in Huxley & Martin's *Practical Biology* (1875), and in essay On Study of Biology (1876).

came to constitute the chief part of the work ; and, as an opposite extreme from the study of the old natural history, books
were neglected. In the very nature of things structure of
animals was best adapted to such exclusive laboratory studies,
and the work became almost entirely anatomical, involving
much dissection and use of the compound microscope.

As will appear later, there are many serious objections to
such exclusive limitation of studies of animals to the anatomical

**Present Posi-
tion of Natu-
ral History.**
work, and the criticisms which have been made
against such study have within the past five years
led to a reaction and a decided tendency towards
abandoning many of the characteristic features of the anatomical
course and returning towards the former   natural-history
course. This reaction is best expressed by the Davenports in
the *Introduction to Zoölogy*,[1] which was planned as " an attempt
to restore the old-time instruction in natural history." Such
a course as presented by these authors has nothing to do with
the study of internal structures of animals which is a prominent
feature of all courses in zoölogy. Obviously there can be no
scientific consideration of the fundamental physiological processes, and there is no attempt to present the general principles
of zoölogy as a science. Emphasis is placed on the study of external form, classification, movements, habits, and life-histories
of animals. In short, this and other recent courses in the natural
history of animals are in essentials modern restorations of the
· old-time instruction, and in subject-matter are very similar to
text-books which were used fifty years ago. The chief difference between the old and the new teaching in natural history
is not essentially one of facts but rather one of methods ; for it
is now proposed to subordinate the recitation to personal observation by the pupil who will learn some facts from the natural
objects instead of exclusively depending upon books, as formerly.

---

[1] This text-book may be regarded as the full development of an Outline of Entrance Requirements in Zoölogy, Lawrence Scientific School,
Harvard University. 1898.

With regard to the value of natural history, suffice it to say here that such a general survey of animals is generally regarded as very interesting to those who cannot go deep into the science of zoölogy.[1] "What the ordinary citizen needs," says Professor Davenport, "is an acquaintance with common animals." It is not to be denied that giving such acquaintance should hold a place in the zoölogical instruction in schools below the grade of college, but just what is its proper place in such schools is a question which we shall consider in Chapter IV. In the present connection it is only necessary to say that it may well be doubted whether a course devoted exclusively to natural history is altogether the best for secondary work. Especially in the omission of all reference to the general facts of internal structure in all animals the reaction from the purely anatomical course has been too extreme. In a succeeding section of this chapter there will be discussed the value of physiological study, and from this it will appear that many general facts of internal structure of *some* animals are from the physiological standpoint essential in an elementary course in zoölogy. Hence, in not presenting internal structure the strictly natural-history course is inadequate. It gives a view of animal life which is almost as limited, even though more interesting, as the anatomical work which it is proposed to supplant. We must not lose sight of our aim to present the important general facts and principles of zoölogy; and we must conclude that while a general acquaintance with animals is needed by the average citizen, exclusive attention to such popular and somewhat desultory studies leads to the omission of facts of morphology and physiology which are of great importance in secondary education. Enough has been said to indicate that natural history does not in itself give that view of the principles of the science of zoölogy which are demanded for general education. It is undoubtedly well

Value of Natural History.

Criticism of Natural History.

---

[1] See Davenport, *loc. cit.* (1899), p. 463. Also preface to the *Introduction to Zoölogy.*

adapted for giving the general acquaintance with animals which is desirable as preliminary to the study of zoölogy as a science, but such preliminary study should have limitations which will be pointed out in the introduction to the chapter on "Beginning Work in Zoölogy."

Rejecting natural history as in itself inadequate for general secondary education, we may now consider the educational **Educational** contents of the general science of zoölogy with a **Contents of** view to selecting the subject-matter valuable for **General** **Zoölogy.** secondary education. It will be most convenient to regard it as separated into its various phases or sub-sciences, although in actual practice in elementary study no such division lines can be drawn ; and we shall discuss in succession : anatomy, physiology, ecology, classification, embryology, palæontology, philosophical zoölogy (evolution), economic zoölogy, and the history of zoölogy.   It is from these phases of zoology considered as an organized science that we must draw the facts and principles for a general course.   To a great extent our selection of facts must be guided by the principles which they illustrate ; for " the main object of teaching biology as part of a liberal education is to familiarize the student not so much with the facts as with the ideas of the science."[1]

Anatomy.

The 'study of anatomy, gross and microscopical, is obviously the foundation for that of all other phases of zoölogy ; for classi-**Anatomy** fication, physiology, embryology, and ecology rest **fundamental.** upon a basis of structure.   It follows, therefore, that anatomy is an absolutely essential part of any elementary course in the science of zoology, and there is no other way of beginning except by giving considerable attention to structural facts as the basis for classifying, determining functions, studying life-histories, or interpreting environmental relations.   Anatomy, then, is the foundation of zoölogical study.   It is in the very na

---

[1] Parker's *Elementary Biology*, preface.

ture of things the beginning, but should it be also the end in a course in elementary zoölogy ? This is essentially the question concerning the teaching of zoölogy in secondary schools which in recent years has aroused much discussion.

As has been incidentally stated, the course in elementary zoölogy which from about 1885 to 1898 was followed in the majority of the more prominent secondary schools consisted largely of the detailed comparative study of the structure of a series of animals. This was a very close imitation of a common introductory course in comparative anatomy for college students, which was introduced in 1875 by the well-known *Practical Biology* by Huxley and Martin. The introduction of this line of work into high schools was undoubtedly an attempt on the part of the teachers to transfer into the secondary schools the course of study and the methods in which they had been trained at college. In fact, this tendency towards duplicating the first college course in the high school led to the use in some schools of such laboratory manuals as Huxley and Martin's *Practical Biology*, and Marshall and Hurst's *Practical Zoölogy*.[1] Even Boyer's *Biology*, which was especially prepared for high-school work and for many years extensively used, erred in the same direction and was scarcely less technical and as completely anatomical as the common manuals for college work in comparative anatomy.

With college courses in zoölogy we are not here directly concerned, for the secondary school offers quite independent problems. However, it will be of interest to turn aside long enough to note that the introductory college course in zoölogy from the anatomical standpoint leads to other courses in which other phases of zoölogy are considered, and in the end *some few* students may gain a broad view of the field of zoölogy, and learn to think of animals in the

High-School Anatomical Course.

College Anatomical Course as Introductory to Zoölogy.

---

[1] Even as late as 1901, at least two prominent colleges mentioned these books in their catalogues as the basis of high-school work leading to their college-entrance examinations.

various aspects of their structural and functional relations. Clearly, even the colleges need a general introductory course offering a broader view for the great mass of students who cannot spend more than one year on a single science. Such a course seems to be gaining favor, and especially is there being manifested a decided tendency to study morphology and physiology in their natural relations. This is the reason for the growing popularity of books such as Parker's *Elementary Biology*, Sedgwick and Wilson's *General Biology*, and Parker and Parker's *Practical Zoölogy*.

Within the past five years the value of the study of animal structure as presented in many high-school courses has been very much questioned;[1] and it has frequently been criticised because very much of the subject-matter is so technical as to be of very doubtful value to a liberally educated man who has no special reason for being learned in the details of anatomy. Moreover, when such exclusive attention is given to structure there is no time for the pupil to learn anything about the other phases of zoölogy; and since the practical work in anatomy is usually conducted with preserved specimens, it is far from being inspiration to the study of animal life. This objection to the narrow view offered by anatomy has been well stated by Professor Needham, of Lake Forest University: "It has been a popular delusion that a term of dissections constitutes a proper elementary course. Such a course was an improvement on former methods; the study of dead animals is far better than no contact with animals at all. But to study animals with nature and life left out is to omit a phase of the subject of deepest scientific interest, of highest educational importance, and of greatest pedagogical utility."[2] It is evident that an anatomical course will give pupils who follow it an *extremely narrow view* of the animal kingdom in its varied aspects.

Criticism of Anatomical Course.

---

[1] See High School Bulletin, No. 2, University of State of New York (1899), pp. 459–476; Proceedings N. E. A., 1899, pp. 806–808.

[2] From preface to Needham's *Lessons in Zoology*.

Still another objection to the anatomical course of the high schools is that it involves too much dissection, the extensive practice of which in such schools no one has suc- **Objection to** ceeded in justifying. This work is more or less **Dissection.** distasteful to many young pupils, it is very time consuming, the skill acquired is of technical value only — these are the chief objections which have been urged against dissection. The practice is surely growing in disfavor so far as the secondary schools are concerned; in fact, there have been indications of the coming of the other extreme in which internal structure of all animals is to be excluded from elementary courses on animals.

In defence of the course in anatomy it is often urged that the working out of details of structure tends to give valuable scientific training. This is certainly true ; but much **A Defence of** of this is purely special training, and the facts of **Anatomy.** detail are only of technical value. There is a growing belief among naturalist teachers that much of the anatomical study in secondary courses can be replaced with more important subject-matter, and this with no loss so far as efficiency in developing scientific observing and thinking is concerned.

Summarizing, the foregoing considerations lead to the conclusion that in so far as anatomical study deals with the great facts of structure, both internal and external, in **Summary.** several typical common animals, it has many good features which commend it for secondary education ; but in so far as stress is placed upon details and comparisons of number, minute structure, exact extent and position of organs in some dozen types of animals all requiring dissection or sectioning, the study must be regarded not only as of minor importance in liberal secondary education but also as using time which should be devoted to other important phases of zoölogical study. But since the study of general anatomical structure, internal as well as external, of some animals is important as giving a basis for other phases of zoölogical study, especially physiology, therefore it is necessary that this much of the anatomical work should be retained in an elementary course in the secondary school.

Physiology.

It is now generally recognized by naturalists that the study of animal structure and that of function are closely inter-related. In the words of Professor Whitman,[1] of the University of Chicago:

Relations of Structure and Function.

"Morphology and physiology are two quite distinct sides of biology, each with definite and constant peculiarities of method and aim; but these two sides are only the statical and dynamical aspect of one and the same thing; one presents the features, the other the expression. It is only as a matter of convenience that these two aspects are dealt with separately; they are complemental, and have their full meaning only when united.

"The history of morphology and physiology is one continuous illustration of their interdependence. When the famous Harvey was asked what led him to think of the circulation of the blood, he at once referred the original suggestion to one of the morphological features of the vascular apparatus — the valves and their arrangement. The hint furnished by structure was then followed up and tested by experiment, and the result was a discovery that brought the position of valves, pulsation of the heart, effects of ligatures, and other facts, into rational relation to one another."

It is true that Professor Whitman had especial reference to the relation of morphology and physiology as applied to the studies of advanced students and particularly to original investigations. But the work of the beginning pupil in biology is more a difference of degree than of kind; and, even in the most elementary nature-study of animals, structure and function should be, and naturally are, considered together. The pupil in the elementary and secondary school is intensely interested in finding that the structure of the grasshopper's leg is connected with the power of jumping, but the pure morphology of the insect leg would to the child be unattractive and valueless. The structure of a dead frog's leg would be the basis of an unimportant lesson for the young pupil

Correlation of Morphology and Physiology.

---

[1] Fifth Report of Director of Marine Biological Laboratory (Boston, 1892). Also in *American Naturalist* (1892).

who is not led to consider the organ as in action. Still another illustration is the case of the structure of the blood-system and the circulation of the blood ; as Professor Whitman pointed out, morphology and physiology were closely related in the original discovery, and they should likewise be related in the re-discoveries of pupils who study these organs in the laboratory ; otherwise the experience of the pupils may largely repeat that of those students who preceded Harvey. This is one example of numerous opportunities for combining anatomical and physiological study in their natural relations.

In advocating the introduction of physiology into elementary zoölogy for high schools, it is here intended to include the essential processes in the general metabolism of the animal body, and not to limit the study to the observation of movements and responses to stimuli, **Physiology in High-School Zoölogy.** which is the chief characteristic of the " physiological " study referred to in outlines of several elementary courses that in recent years have been prominent. The value of the study of movements and responses to stimuli must be recognized in that this is a very practical way of giving the pupils some idea concerning the methods of strictly physiological experimentation. On the other hand, study of fundamental physiological processes obviously admits of very little practical work in a direct line, and the essential facts must be presented by text-book and teacher. But the morphological and experimental basis for such study can be strictly practical, and a logical presentation should lead the pupils from observed facts to conclusions, so that the discussions of the subject of general physiology of animals may be of far greater value as discipline and as information than a mere didactic exercise.

The usual objection to physiological work in secondary schools is that the subject, unlike morphology, cannot be presented by a strictly laboratory method. But how much knowledge of the fundamentals of the physiology of general nutrition does the college student **Objection to Physiology for High Schools.** get directly from his own laboratory studies as compared with

18

what he accepts on the authority of teacher and books? In how many colleges is the laboratory method strictly and exclusively applied even in morphological teaching? Certainly the college methods do not support any objection to physiological teaching which has a basis in practical work, even though it is not possible for pupils to depend exclusively upon their results in the laboratory.

The importance of interpreting the activities of the human body from the comparative standpoint seems sufficient reason for advocating the consideration of the fundamental

Human Physiology from the Comparative Standpoint. principles of physiological action in connection with the study of elementary zoölogy. No other phase of zoölogical study arouses a deeper interest and appreciation or is more spontaneously applied by the pupils in connection with the study of their own life-activities. It is scarcely necessary to offer a stronger reason for including physiological study in an elementary course of zoölogy.[1]

In combining physiology with morphological work of the course in zoölogy, it is important that the two phases of study

Morphology and Physiology should be closely related in Teaching. be closely related throughout the course. The few text-books and teachers' outlines which merely suggest the tendency towards a union of these two phases of zoölogical study seem to show that in general the attempt is to teach physiological ideas in the form of abstract generalizations with little of concrete application to particular animals which are studied morphologically. Sometimes these generalized principles of physiology are introduced before the pupils have progressed far in the practical study of animal structure, but more often after the completion of a purely morphological course. An example of the latter is the text-book and manual of elementary zoölogy by Kingsley, in the last chapter of which there is an excellent statement of the principles of comparative physiology; but there is no specific

---

[1] This will be further developed in discussing the teaching of human physiology in Chapter XII.

concrete application of those principles. Such a method of presenting, the principles apart from concrete application is open to serious objection. In the light of experience it may well be doubted whether such presentation gives pupils a clear conception of general life-activities. A physiological principle may be formulated in a generalized way, and as such may be memorized by the pupils; but that they do not grasp the ideas involved is shown by the fact that they usually fail in application when concrete cases are placed before them. Every zoölogist knows in personal experience how indefinite and unsatisfactory are the ideas gained from reading generalizations if he cannot easily recall and connect them with the specific underlying facts; and in order to appreciate the attitude of the elementary pupil, it is only necessary to recognize the fact that even at the close of a year's course the pupil has not the definite remembrance of the details of structure which are necessary for concrete illustration and application of the principles of physiology. In order to give the clearest possible conception of physiological principles it is essential that structures and functions should be studied in their natural relations. The principles of physiology should be introduced with the first animal which is studied morphologically, and each principle as introduced should receive concrete application. The study can easily and quickly be made comparative as successive types of animals are taken up; and finally such specific and comparative studies may be made to lead to a direct application of the principles of comparative physiology to the activities of the human body.

Animal Ecology.[1]

Still another important phase of zoölogical study which has recently become prominent in education is that of animal

---

[1] Ecology, ethology, bionomics, and natural history have been used within recent years quite synonymously. Natural history has been used in so many senses (see Huxley's essay On Study of Biology) that to apply it to a special phase of zoölogy would lead to endless confusion;

ecology — the science dealing with the relation of animals to
their environment.   Although an attempt to classify definitely

Rise of Ecology.
and explain in terms of physiology and psychology
the facts of animal relation to environment marks a
quite recent stage of the development of zoölogical science,
and hence animal ecology is popularly regarded as a new
science, the truth is that a vast mass of information in this
line has long been in existence as a prominent part of the so-
called "natural history."   In fact, long before there was any
exact science of zoölogy ecological facts were being accumulated by patient observers of animal life in its familiar forms;
and many a popular old-time book bearing the title *Natural
History* owed its charm largely to the accounts of animals as
living creatures with interesting habits of life and life-histories
adapting them to their environmental conditions.   It is true
that such books also contained much information concerning
structure, especially external; but this, too, largely derived
its interest from ecological considerations.

The psychological phase of the study of animal life, dealing
with nervous activity, instincts, and intelligence, is obviously

Relation of Psychology and Ecology.
closely associated with problems of ecology; in
fact, these nervous phenomena constitute to a
great extent the fundamental basis for relation
between animals and their environment.   It is this psychical
aspect which makes animal ecology so much more intricately
complex than plant ecology.   A "plant society" may be
analyzed from the standpoint of its chemical and physical
relations to the environment, but the ecology of social animals
is vastly more complicated by the added nervous or psychical

---

and there is now general agreement that it should be applied only to
general accounts of animals, as defined in the earlier part of this chapter.
At present there is no agreement as to choice between ecology, bionomics, and ethology.   In favor of animal ecology is that the phrase
corresponds to plant ecology just as plant physiology to animal physiology; but in opposition it has been urged that the problems of the
animal side are not parallel to those offered by plants.   See article by
W. M. Wheeler, in *Science*, N. S., Vol. XV., No. 390, pp. 971–976.   1902.

factors which at times seem to refuse to be governed by the chemical and physical environment. The principles underlying these phenomena associated with the internal working of the nervous mechanisms are for the advanced student most conveniently considered under psychology, independently of ecological applications. But, aside from the questions of the relations between the psychic life of lower animals and man, it is in the application to animal ecology — to the behavior of animals under natural environmental conditions — that the advanced student finds intensely interesting applications of the principles presented in psychological works such as those named in the chapter on "Zoölogical Books."

Ecology is so closely related to other phases of zoölogy that so far as elementary instruction is concerned it is often impracticable to draw any sharp division line. The problems of ecology are centred around the living animal in relation to its surroundings, but obviously even the elementary considerations of the activity of any part of an animal necessarily involves at least the external structure of the organ. For illustration, let us take the characteristic adaptive structures and movements of the legs of the grasshopper. The internal structure, with its mechanism of muscles and the hidden activities involved in the production of the movements expressed externally, furnishes problems which belong to the domains of morphology and physiology. With these internal phenomena ecology is not as directly concerned as it is with the external structure which visibly stands in direct correlation with the characteristic adaptive movements ; but it is evident that ecological problems are closely related to the facts of internal structure and physiology in which in the ultimate analysis explanations are to be sought. These intimate relations between ecology and other phases of zoölogy lead to some suggestions regarding the study of living animals, for animal ecology is characteristically the study of animals alive under natural conditions, and as such in decided contrast to the anatomical and physiological phases of zoölogy.

Relation to other Phases of Zoölogy.

In conducting ecological study external structure must be considered as a basis for the ecological interpretation. Meas-

Structure the Basis for Study of Ecology.

uring the distance over which a grasshopper can jump or observing other activities of animals is an exercise of scientific value only when correlated with knowledge concerning the general external structure of the animal so that the adaptations will be evident.   Logically, then, some knowledge of a structure should precede inquiry into its function or adaptation; but in elementary teaching the principle of interest may demand a reversal of this order. Probably most young pupils will be more interested in a grasshopper's leg after they have witnessed its activity.   However, observations on the adaptive structure and function should be carefully correlated.   Unless they can be studied hand in hand, as when living animals are available for use in the laboratory, it seems better to precede the ecological study with some anatomical work.   The best preparation for the appreciation of study of any animal in the field is a preliminary examination of external structure and activities so far as these can be determined from living and preserved materials in the laboratory. Such preparation will add greatly to the scientific significance of a study of animals in their native haunts; and there is evidence that it intensifies rather than lessens interest.

As to the value of the study of living animals in their ecological relations, we might defend it on the ground of

Value of Study of Ecology.

economic importance of the knowledge obtained, notably in the case of insects; and also in that the facts of environmental relationships aid the advanced student in interpreting some great problems of zoölogy, and especially are they full of significance in relation to the questions of organic evolution.   With reference to the value of animal ecology for the general student of animals, the preface to Jordan and Kellogg's well-known *Animal Life* is especially to the point when it is stated that :

" The beginning student should know that the whole life of animals, that all the variety of animal form and habit, is an expression of the fitness of animals to the varied circumstances and conditions of their living, and that this adapting and fitting of their life to the conditions of living come about inevitably and naturally, and that it can be readily studied and largely understood. The ways and course of this fitting are the greatest facts of life excepting the fact of life itself. In this kind of study of animals every observation of fact in animal structure or behavior leads to a search for the significance, or meaning in the life of the animal, of this fact. The veriest beginner can be, and ought to be, an independent observer and thinker. It is this phase of the study of zoölogy which appeals most strongly to the beginning student, the phase which treats of the why and how of animal form and habit."

But aside from any practical value of ecological knowledge and the relation of its facts to those of other phases of zoölogy, its place as an important part of elementary zoölogical instruction may be justified on the ground that it is undoubtedly the most interesting part of all *General Interest in Ecological Facts.* zoölogy not only for young pupils but also for the majority of citizens of liberal education. As has been said, it is the ecological phase which constitutes the essence and the charm of the popular books on natural history, and the widespread interest in these is sufficient proof of the general demand for information about animal life. Of all the phases of zoölogical study, it is the ecological which is directly concerned in the æsthetical and moral values discussed in the preceding chapter; and from these alone we may derive sufficient justification for emphasizing in all elementary courses the ecological phase which brings the pupils so directly into contact with animals as *living* creatures.

Teachers will find valuable suggestions for practical work in this line in the following books: Needham's *Lessons in Zoölogy* and *Outdoor Studies* (A. B. Co.); *Suggestions to Teachers*, accompanying Jordan and Kellogg's *Suggestions for Teachers.* *Animal Life* (Appleton); Comstock's *Insect Life* (Appleton); Chapman's *Bird Life*, Popular Edition, 1901 (Appleton); Chapters XXXI. to XXXIII. in Kellogg's *Elementary Zoölogy* (Holt); French's *Animal Activities* (Longmans); and Colton's new *Practical Zoölogy* (Heath).

The methods and point of view of teachers of plant ecology are often suggestive to the teachers of the animal side. The ecological materials in Coulter's *Plant Relations* (Appleton), and Bergen's *Foundations of Botany* (Ginn), and their accompanying handbooks for teachers, should be familiar to all teachers of animal ecology.

For pupils' supplementary reading in the line of animal ecology Thomson's *Study of Animal Life*, Part I., and Jordan and Kellogg's *Animal Life* are unsurpassed. Many other books named in the lists on natural history and ecology in the chapter on " Zoölogical Books " are valuable for both teachers and pupils.

Reading for Pupils.

Classification.

For many years the study of classification of animals has not been fashionable in most colleges and consequently in most high schools. The term has unfortunately become popularly associated with the memorizing of polysyllabic scientific names of animals. On this side of classification I have comparatively little to recommend for practice in secondary schools ; but I wish to call attention to another aspect which has been generally overlooked by teachers. I shall quote the exact words of Professor S. A. Forbes of the University of Illinois.

" That a study of the classification of animals is not only possible, as every one admits, but may be made highly profitable to the common school pupil, if properly conducted, I have long been perfectly sure. We must beware, however, of confusing two quite distinct and very different things: the mere learning of a correct classification based on all the facts of morphology as interpreted by the highest zoölogical authorities ; and the effort to classify made by the pupil himself, as a practice in generalization. I have yet to learn where in the common school course this training in generalization, this practice in the forming of large and complicated concepts out of concrete materials, in tracing from point to point the threads of the web of relation by which unlike things are unified and made into larger wholes again capable of being compared among themselves, and so built up into higher and higher concepts, — I have yet to learn where this in-

Forbes's View.

valuable part of a sound education is now commonly provided for. The doing of this first on things and then on ideas, is a most profitable exercise, and the habit of doing it spontaneously is a large part of the education of the thinking man."

An objection to the study of classification recorded in the report [1] of a committee of the National Educational Association deserves attention: **Objection to Study of Classification.**

" The systematic method involves the detailed study of a group or groups in the most careful manner from the taxonomic standpoint. This plan has the advantage of bringing the pupil in contact with the objects studied, and trains powers of discrimination and analysis, but it gives the student an exaggerated idea of the importance of certain structural parts and of limited animal groups, and fails to develop general biological ideas."

With regard to this objection it may be urged that it applies particularly to exclusive and excessive dependence upon the systematic method — a common tendency among the teachers who make any attempt at teaching classification. But that there is great value in classification studied in the way suggested by Professor Forbes no one will deny, and limitations of the work to certain of the more favorable groups (*e. g.*, insects, decapods, crustaceans) will avoid the dangers which have been supposed to lurk in the study of systematic zoölogy.

There are some taxonomic names which are so commonly used in general literature that they deserve to be emphasized in teaching zoölogy. The names of all phyla except **Some Important Names.** the modern sub-divisions of the " worms " ; the names of prominent classes of arthropods, mollusks, and vertebrates, but not those of "worms," protozoans, and I feel very doubtful about echinoderms and cœlenterates; the names of some familiar orders, especially of insects and vertebrate classes— these are about all the names in general classification which should be especially emphasized in high-school work. But I would make the pupils familiar with the general classification of

---

[1] Proceedings N. E. A., 1899, p. 806.

animals as illustrated by the arrangement of systematic treatises like Parker and Haswell's *Text-book of Zoölogy*, and this in order to teach pupils how to use zoölogical books of reference. In order to familiarize pupils with names of species and genera and larger groups I should use both the technical and common names of every animal studied, but I see no reason for insisting upon memorizing them.

For the basis of practical studies of classification, as suggested by the above quotation from Forbes, I should use decapods, **Practical** starting with the crayfish as suggested in Huxley's **Studies.** *Crayfish ;* or vertebrates, starting with the frog and following the thought of the last chapter in Part I. of Parker and Parker's *Practical Zoölogy;* or representatives of insect orders. Using the actual animals from one of these groups, I should lead the pupils to compare and group the animals on the basis of resemblances, thus laying their own foundation for ideas of classification.

Embryology.

The study of animal development has rarely been emphasized in elementary courses in zoölogy for secondary schools. Ordinarily that phase of life-history which deals with the **Embryology commonly** development of the egg into the individual animal is **neglected.** passed over hastily ; and, in fact, it is no uncommon thing to find that high-school teachers carefully avoid reference to sex and reproduction of animals. As an example, a well-known laboratory manual prepared for use in secondary schools omits all reference to reproductive organs in animals above Hydra — even in describing an earthworm with dorsal body-wall removed. This was probably an intentional — not accidental — omission ; for in an accompanying handbook for teachers there is this explanation : "The question of sex has been left largely to the tact of the teacher. We do not believe in presenting the play of Hamlet with Hamlet left out, but there are serious objections to giving this question adequate place in a manual prepared for mixed classes of young people. The studies have been arranged in such a way that it is hoped no one's false modesty will be shocked, and it has been left for the individual teacher to make any desired additions rather than to be obliged to pass over in silence some parts of the text."

The teacher of biology in high schools must recognize the widespread existence of a so-called "false modesty" whose dictates, if obeyed, would force avoidance of dis- **Essential** cussion of the subject of animal reproduction. Of **Facts should** course, there are no such limitations in the science **be taught.** of biology, but pupils are not specialists in science. Even at the high-school age they have acquired something of the "false modesty" which the teacher must avoid "shocking." However, I regard the above quotation as expressing an extreme attitude. "False modesty" is an outgrowth of human life, and in the minds of young pupils has little real existence with reference to lower forms of life. I have seen many classes of "mixed" pupils studying and reciting about essential facts of reproduction in Hydra, earthworm, crayfish, and frog, and rarely have I seen any indication that any pupil regarded these facts as any more "forbidden" than knowledge of other organs and processes. It is true that some few individuals show some evidence of embarrassment at the first mention of sex or reproduction, but all soon learn to have respect for such facts as an essential part of the science which they are studying — a result which is certainly valuable. A sincere and serious teacher who *delicately* but firmly handles the essential truths about the reproduction of animals, and who shows the same scientific spirit which is manifested in dealing with the other systems of organs will impress upon the pupils the fact in the realm of biological science all facts are important and worthy of serious consideration. On the other hand, any attempt to avoid all reference to the facts of animal reproduction is sure to give pupils the false impression that even in scientific study there is something "indelicate" about even the lower forms of animal life. The reproductive process is necessarily prominent in zoölogy and cannot be entirely overlooked by the pupils.

Here is an opportunity for science study to work against the very common misunderstanding of a subject about which every liberally educated citizen should have some scientific knowledge ; and I would urge that the *essential facts* of the reproduction of animals, as illustrated by selected types, should constitute an integral part of any course in zoölogy which aims to give the information most valuable for general education.

With regard to the function of text-books in teaching this subject, I cannot agree with the authors quoted above. If

Attitude of the Text-book. there is any difficulty in presenting the subject, surely a printed account is better than the explanations of teachers who may be amateurs in science teaching. At any rate the attitude of the text-book may well prepare the way for the " tact " of the teacher.

Considering in detail the facts to be taught, all teachers will agree that the secondary course is not the place for the detailed

The Facts to be taught. examination of cleavage, germ-layers, etc., which characterizes the embryological work in colleges. However there are many important and interesting facts of animal development which may be profitably presented in an elementary course in high school. Such facts as those relating to spontaneous generation ; asexual reproduction in lower forms ; the general principles of sexual reproduction, involving the leading facts about development from a one-celled egg ; the nature and effect of fertilization ; parthenogenesis among arthropods ; cell-division in development ; the heredity of general resemblances, — these are examples of topics about which some knowledge is at least as useful to liberally cultured citizens as that from any other phase of zoölogy. All these and more may be presented in a form elementary enough for the high-school pupil, notwithstanding that this is the approach to some of the profoundest problems of zoölogy. I would recommend that some of the great general principles of embryology be introduced early in the course, preferably in connection with the study of some invertebrate. These general principles should be briefly applied to each animal studied. The general features of the embryology and life-history of crayfish, earth-worm, Hydra, fish, frog, bird, and finally viviparous salaman-ders, snakes, and lizards will lead up to the internal development of the mammals. In mixed classes it is best to stop here ; but the tactful and thoughtful teacher will have no difficulty in briefly but clearly indicating that the mammals offer no exception to the great general principles which apply to the development of the individual animals of the lower forms previously studied.

All.this study of animal development, likewise all other ele-mentary zoölogical study, should be conducted to the end that the great facts may come to have in the pupils' mind a profound significance in relation to the sum-mit of the animal series — man. And concerning the bearing of zoölogical study upon the great facts which relate to the beginning of the individual human life, I find my views in complete agreement with those of Professor W. S. Hall,[1] of Northwestern University :

Life-History of Man.

> "Questions of life history, reproduction, whence, how and whither would better not be discussed. The courses in botany and zoology have sharpened the senses and incited the thoughtful questioning of the pupil. When he comes to the study of man, leave him alone with his thoughts in these deeper and more delicate questions, and he will arrive at the truth."

Palæontology.

The palæontological phase of zoölogy has rarely been referred to in connection with elementary courses for secondary schools. The limitations of time make it impossible to under-take any scientific study of fossil animals ; but I wish to emphasize the importance of including in a zoölogical course some simple general facts. It requires very little extra time to call attention to the methods by which the animal remains were preserved, the fact that probably few in-dividuals were fossilized, and some general facts about the different ages represented by animal fossils.[2] After such an

Some Impor-tant Facts of Palæontology

---

[1] In *School Science*, Vol. I., p. 61. April, 1901.

[2] Part III. of Brigham's *Text-Book of Geology* (Appleton) is valuable

introduction to the general principles it is easy to turn aside for a few minutes occasionally in order to call attention to the forerunners of existing animals, illustrating whenever possible by means of fossils, models, or pictures.

Philosophical Zoölogy — Evolution.

The question whether the doctrine of evolution should be generally taught in schools first attracted widespread attention **Teaching Evo-** owing to some criticisms by Rudolph V. o , of **lution in** Berlin, in an address on " Freedom of Science in the **Schools.** Modern State " delivered at the fiftieth meeting of the German Naturalists and Physicians, in 1877. While Vir- . chow did not then directly repudiate the theory, he distinctly stated that it was not proven and therefore should not be taught authoritatively to young people. In a prefatory note to the English translation of Ernst Haeckel's famous reply, " Freedom in Science and Teaching " (1878), Huxley expressed the following opinion:

" Far be it from me to suggest that it is desirable that the incul-cation of the doctrine of evolution should be made a prominent **Huxley's** feature of general education. I agree with Professor **Opinion.** Virchow so far, but for very different reasons. It is not that I think the evidence of that doctrine insufficient, but that I doubt whether it is the business of a teacher to plunge the young mind into difficult problems concerning the origin of the existing condition of things. I am disposed to think that the brief period of school-life would be better spent in obtaining an acquaintance with nature as it is ; in fact, in laying a firm foundation for further knowledge which is needed for the critical examination of the dogmas, whether scientific or anti-scientific, which are presented to the adult mind. At present education proceeds in the reverse way ; the teacher makes the most confident assertions on precisely those subjects of which he knows least ; while the habit of weighing evi-dence is discouraged, and the means of forming a sound judgment are carefully withheld from the pupil."

---

for reference and supplementary reading by pupils, and is an excellent introduction to palæontological facts which deserve a place in a course of elementary zoölogy.

Within recent years there has been a growing tendency to advocate that some of the leading points of the general doctrine of organic evolution should be taught in our second- What may be ary schools. Nevertheless, most American zoölo- taught concerning Evo- gists will, I think, agree with Huxley that it should lution. not be made a prominent feature because the problems are too difficult for the young mind. It is to be noted that this objection refers simply to evolution as a formal doctrine, and does not necessarily apply to the evidences, some of which may be suggested even by very elementary study. We may urge the importance of marshalling the materials so that pupils must be led to see resemblances between animals. As an explanation of such similarity, we may point to blood relationship by which in our every-day life we naturally explain resemblances between human individuals. But I seriously doubt whether it is advisable in secondary work to carry the interpretation beyond the authoritative statement that naturalists now regard such evidence as pointing towards common descent of animals. I know that it is a subject which often arouses the thoughtful questioning of some of the brighter pupils, but these often lead teachers far into discussion of many highly theoretical problems which are certain to be confusing to young minds ; and it seems to me far better to adhere firmly to study of actual conditions where some facts may simply point in the direction of evolution. This will lay the best foundation for later studies of theories of evolution, which, as we have already seen in Chapter I., are of general interest.

Considering more specifically what should and should not be taught concerning evolution, we note first that the decapods, insects, and vertebrates are certainly best for com- Anatomical parison intended to bring out the anatomical re- Resemblances. semblances between allied animals.[1] The pupils should be led to see the homologies in the external structure, particularly .

---

[1] I shall later (p. 346) refer to the value of such study of a limited group as compared with that of a series of phyletic types.

in the appendages of decapods and insects and in the skeletons of vertebrates. For such studies of affinities the lobster, crayfish, prawn, and various species of crab form one good series ; the grasshopper, cricket, and cockroach a second ; these compared with insects of other orders form a third ; and skeletons of frogs, lizards, birds, bat, dog or cat, and man a fourth series.

These anatomical comparisons suggesting relationship may be reinforced by reference to the similarities of embryos. The **Embryological Resemblances.** long abdomen of the young crab, the bifurcated walking-legs of the young lobster, the gill-slits and general similarity of external structure in vertebrate embryos of all classes — these are simple embryological facts suggestive of evolution which are intensely interesting and may be comprehended in a general way by pupils in the secondary school.

Occasional facts on the palæontological side may be brought incidentally to the attention of pupils in order to indicate the **Palæontological Evidences.** progressive development of animals in the past history of the earth ; but time and the age of pupils will not permit more than general suggestions.

More than these suggestions of evidences of evolution is **Limitations.** not, I believe, profitable in the secondary school. Obviously it is useless to attempt to demonstrate relationships between the various phyla ; and it is no more than the truth to point out that great differences of structure exist. For high-school pupils there is a great gap between vertebrates and lower forms ; and let it remain so rather than attempt to bridge the chasm with the debatable hypotheses which are comprehensible only by advanced students. In short, I do not believe that high-school work in zoölogy should attempt demonstration of evidences of evolution except within the boundaries of a few limited groups where the leading facts can be discovered by the pupils themselves.

On the side of the factors of evolution the subject is clearly beyond high-school pupils. Evidences of the struggle for exist-

ence and consequent survival of the fittest, adaptation to environment in relation to this struggle and survival, variations of individuals, and the influence of man's selection in Factors of
domesticated races — these are the leading points Evolution.
concerned with the factors which it may be profitable to notice
in a secondary school; but little more than suggestions in these
lines are possible.

" Does evolution mean that man came from mon- Descent of.
keys?" This is always asked when the subject Man.
of evolution is touched. Here is uncertain ground for the
teacher, for any discussion of the evolution of man is likely to
lead into most intricate problems. If the subject is brought
forward by the pupils, I believe that it should be dismissed with
the single statement that the undoubted structural resemblances
between man and apes suggest descent from a common auces-
tor, but that mentally there are vast differences which are not
yet understood.

Finally, I believe that it is undesirable that the teacher should
appear to stand in the position of an advocate attempting to
convince pupils of the truth of evolution. Whether
or not the pupils accept the theory on authority is Teacher not
an Advocate
of no consequence, but it is important that they get of Evolution.
a glimpse of the lines of evidences which may lead them later to
a broader view of nature and natural processes.

For further suggestions regarding facts of evolution which
may be presented in a secondary school see Chapter XXX. in
Kellogg's *Elementary Zoölogy;* page 264 in Need- References for
ham's *Lessons in Zoölogy;* Chapter XVI. in Jordan Teachers.
and Kellogg's *Animal Life;* Romanes's *Scientific Evidences of
Organic Evolution* and his *Darwin and after Darwin,* Vol. I.
The illustrations in the latter volume are especially instructive.
Other books for general readers are named in the chapter on
"Zoölogical Books."

Economic Zoölogy.

The importance of the economic phase of zoölogy in general
education has been discussed in a general way in the preceding

19

chapter, and here we shall consider specifically the nature of the work in this line which may be profitably undertaken in a high school.

The chief general topics in economic zoölogy are: useful domesticated animals (such as mammals, birds, honey-bee, and **Important** silkworm, considered as sources of food and cloth-**Topics.** ing and as pets and beasts of burden); useful animals not domesticated (chiefly for food and clothing); injurious animals (such as insects, parasites, rodents, poisonous and carnivorous species); animals beneficial because destroying those which are injurious (for examples, insectivorous animals, predaceous insects and arachnids, amphibians, reptiles, some mammals). Considerations of animals along any of these lines are full of interest to the average pupil, and I am inclined to believe that emphasis upon these relations of animals to the interests of man is bound to lead to deeper interest in zoölogy in general.

With regard to the methods of conducting studies in economic lines, field work should be supplemented with reading and **Methods of** lectures. The field work will be naturally associ-**conducting** ated with the ecological studies; and insects and **Studies.** birds are the most important groups for observations in this line. However, within the limits of time for zoölogy in the secondary school it is not possible to go far into the practical side of the economic work; in fact much of this is better conducted in the elementary school as part of the nature-study. Probably supplementary reading is the most feasible way of giving in connection with the high-school zoölogy a general view of this phase of the science. A commendable plan is to have brief reports prepared by the pupils basing these upon books and especially the governmental publications which are referred to under " Economic Zoölogy " in the chapter on " Zoölogical Books."

For other suggestions on economic zoölogy see the following: Proceedings National Educational Association, 1901, p. 584; Barrows in *School Science*, Vol. III., May and June,

1903; Gage on Study of Domestic Animals, in *Science*, Vol. X., p. 305; and references under "Utilitarian Value of Zoölogy," in the preceding chapter.

History of Zoölogy, and Biography.

Although not essentially a part of the subject-matter of the pure science of zoölogy, pertinent historical and biographical facts should, I feel sure, have a place in an ele- History of mentary course. The history of the development Zoölogy. of a science throws a flood of light upon the present state of the science, but probably of greater significance from the standpoint of the high-school pupil is the interest derived from historical facts. In elementary work historical references would often prove confusing if carried far into fields where the development of knowledge has passed through radical changes; and it is only to the epoch-making stages in the history of the science that it seems profitable to call the attention of beginning students. Such noteworthy achievements as the discovery of the circulation of the blood, the announcement of the cell-theory, the publication of the *Origin of Species*, the development of the germ-theory of disease, and other important landmarks of zoölogical history deserve mention in any general course which pretends to give a survey of the science of animal life.

Nor should the important contributions to zoölogical knowledge be divorced from the great names associated with them. It is unfortunate that in the elementary teaching of Biography. zoölogy so little attention has been given to the personal aspect. The student of elementary physics and chemistry becomes acquainted with names such as Newton, Priestley, Lavoisier, Helmholtz, Galvani, and Tyndal. These are commonly associated with great principles treated in even elementary text-books. As a decided contrast, few indeed are the elementary books of zoölogy which give prominence to even such names as Darwin, Agassiz, Pasteur, and Huxley. This should not be so. "A body of correlated scientific truth can hardly be studied apart from the personality of the names inseparably linked with it."[1] Zoölogy will take a deeper hold on the student if it is presented with due attention to the biographical aspect.

With regard to the teaching in this line, the historical and biographical points will naturally be supplemental to the regular zoölogical work. Notes by the teacher, brief biographical sketches prepared by pupils, exhibition of books and photographs, reading of selections from original works, lists of important discoveries and books with dates — these topics suggest ways of supplementing the work in pure zoölogy with intensely interesting historical and biographical material. For sources of such materials the great encyclopedias are always useful, but better are the special books and papers named under "Historical" and "Biography" in the chapter on "Zoölogical Books."

Summary.

We have seen that in each sub-science of zoölogy there are facts and principles contributing to the general view of animals which seems most desirable for liberal secondary education. From this we conclude that the elementary course, which for the vast majority of high-school pupils will be the only instruction they will ever receive in zoölogy, should be planned to present the fundamental facts and principles of each of the sub-divisions of the science. It may be objected that such a wide survey of the science of zoölogy, however desirable, involves an amount of work which is impossible for an elementary course ; but it must be understood that this has reference to only the general facts and ideas of the various divisions ; and as indicated on preceding pages, it is not intended that along any line the study should go far into details. It is obviously impossible to include all important points in one course, and it rests with the teacher to teach those which seem to have the greatest general importance from the point of view of liberal education.

Essential Facts in each Phase of Zoölogy.

---

[1] Carhart, The Humanistic Element in Science. Proceedings N. E. A., 1896, p. 946.

A second conclusion growing out of our examination of the subject-matter of zoölogy is that as far as practicable the various phases of zoölogy should be studied in their natural relations. A strictly pedagogical arrangement according to the scientific divisions — morphology, physiology, ecology, etc. — is at once impossible and undeŝirable. In the preceding discussions it has many times been noted that the various divisions of zoölogy are so closely inter-related that one depends upon another. It follows that elementary presentation of the science develops most naturally when the study of the various phases go hand in hand.

Study of Phases in Natural Relations.

The outline of a course in zoölogy given in Chapter VIII. is based upon the views expressed in this chapter, and it will concretely illustrate many points which have necessarily been discussed here in a very general way.

CHAPTER III

THE LABORATORY AND THE SCIENTIFIC METHOD IN THE TEACHING OF ZOÖLOGY IN THE SECONDARY SCHOOL

♪ " True Science-teaching consists in bringing the pupil's mind into direct contact with facts, in getting him to investigate, discover, and invent for himself. ' — JOSEPH PAYNE (1872).

" In order to get the fullest benefit from a scientific education, the teacher should endeavour to bring his pupil face to face with the great problems of Nature as though he were the first discoverer. He should, in fact, teach his pupil to face the great pro blems o Nature as if they had never been solved before." [1] — KEMSHEAD.

BIBLIOGRAPHY

Most of the references in Chapter I., especially the writings by Huxley, Forbes, Payne, Pearson, Sedgwick, and Mivart, bear more or less directly upon the subject of this chapter. In addition, the following are of interest:

Armstrong, H. E. The Teaching of the Scientific Method and other Papers on Education. London, Macmillan. 1903. Pp. 476. (Received too late for use in this chapter, but mentioned here for sake of greater completeness of the bibliography.)

Cramer, F. The Method of Darwin, A Study of Scientific Methods. Chicago, McClurg. 1896.

Cramer, F. Logical Method in Biology. POPULAR SCIENCE MONTHLY, Vol. XLIV., p. 372. 1894.

Forbes, S. A. The Scientific Method in High School and College. SCHOOL SCIENCE, Vol. III., pp. 53–67. May, 1903.

Harvey, N. A. The Pedagogical Content of Zoölogy. Proceedings of National Educational Association, 1899, pp. 1106–1112.

Harvey, N. A. Classification as an Element in Education. SCHOOL SCIENCE, Vol. I., pp. 451–455. February, 1902.

· **Murbach, L.** Method in Science Teaching. SCHOOL SCIENCE, Vol. II., pp. 12–18. March, 1902.

Saunders, S. J. Value of Research in Education. SCHOOL SCIENCE, Vol. II. March, 1902.

---

[1] Quoted by Payne in essay on True Foundations of Science Teaching.

Saunders, S. J. Value of Research in the Training of the Science Teacher. Read before New York State Science Teachers' Association. In High School Bulletin, No. 17, Univ. of State of New York, Regent's Reports, 1902.

Welch, W. H. Evolution of Modern Scientific Laboratories. Smithsonian Report, 1895.

The Annual Discussions of the American Society of Naturalists in 1898 and 1899 contain much of interest in this connection. The subject in the year first named was "Advances in Methods of Teaching" (abstracts in SCIENCE, Jan. 20, 1899). The papers of the second year discussed "Universities and Investigation." SCIENCE, Vol. XI., pp. 51–66. January 12, 1900.

1. The Place of Laboratory Work in Zoölogical Teaching.

NECESSARILY much of the discussion which is here directed specifically to zoölogical teaching would apply to the teaching of any other science by the laboratory method. However, for our present purpose it seems best to keep the discussion closely limited to zoölogy, although a broader application will often be obvious.

The extensive application of the laboratory method to the teaching of classes in zoölogy was first made by Huxley between 1860 and 1870, the *Practical Biology* (1875) being the result of his experience. The influence of this volume was widespread, and its careful directions for a course of practical study prepared the way for general adoption of the laboratory method for zoölogy in colleges. However, it should be added that the way had already been prepared for the acceptance of Huxley's method by the practice of Louis Agassiz in this country and other biologists in Europe ; but it should be noted that these men were aiming to educate specialists, while Huxley's work related to the general student seeking liberal education rather than special training for the naturalist's career. It is to Huxley, then, that we trace directly our now almost universal practical method of teaching the fundamental principles of biology as part of general education. But the foundation of the practical method of science teaching was laid long before

Huxley's time, and he simply worked out for use in general educational practice certain methods which had been developing for over two hundred years. In fact, as long ago as 1657 *The Great Didactic* of Comenius urged the teaching of science by " actual perception of things themselves."[1] This, of course, was but the logical application to scientific teaching of the method of scientific research which Francis Bacon so successfully presented in his *Novum Organum*, in 1620. It is now so generally accepted that the laboratory method is all

Principles of Laboratory Method are important. essential in the teaching of zoölogy that analysis of its educational value may seem unnecessary. Nevertheless, inquiry into the underlying principles of laboratory study is of great importance to the teacher who seeks guidance in the management of laboratory work, and we shall therefore consider it particularly with reference to the two general aims of zoölogical teaching which have been discussed in Chapter I., namely, the study of zoölogy as (1) information, (2) as discipline.

With regard to the acquisition of zoölogical information, it has often been urged against the laboratory method that it is

Laboratory Method and Information. very time consuming. This will be admitted by all who had been students or teachers in a zoölogical laboratory. Many more facts can be obtained from an hour of reading than from many hours of laboratory study; and so far as the quantity of the information is concerned the study of books about animals is more profitable than laboratory study of the actual animals. But what of the value of the facts gleaned exclusively from books? Harvey's dictum as quoted by Huxley[2] furnishes an answer : " Those who read without acquiring distinct images of the things about which they read, by the help of their senses, gather no real knowledge, but conceive mere phantoms and idola." ´ Huxley

---

[1] See Monroe's *Comenius*, p. 98 (New York, Scribners, 1900). Also Keatinge's translation of *The Great Didactic* of Comenius. (London, Black. 1896.) Chapter on " The Method of the Sciences, Specifically."

[2] *The Crayfish*, p. 5.

himself urged the value of information acquired by practical study :

"Nobody will ever know anything about Biology except in a dilettante 'paper-philosopher' way, who contents himself with reading books on botany, zoölogy, and the like ; and the reason of this is simple and easy to understand. **Huxley.** It is that all language is merely symbolical of things of which it treats; the more complicated the thing, the more bare is the symbol, and the more its verbal definition requires to be supplemented by the information derived directly from the handling and the seeing and the touching of the thing symbolized : — that is really what is at the bottom of the whole matter."

"You may read any quantity of books, and you may be almost as ignorant as you were at starting, if you don't have at the back of your minds the change for words in definite images which can only be acquired through the operation of your observing faculties on the phenomena of nature." [1]

The above quotations express the views now generally held by scientific men that for the learner " the true foundation of physical science lies in the knowledge of physical facts gained at first hand by observation and experiment to be made by the learner himself." [2]

But it is not to be understood that the student must get all his scientific facts from his own studies in the laboratory. To advocate this would be absurd. Such a limitation to the time-consuming laboratory work would make **Information not Exclusively from the Laboratory.** it impossible for the average student to acquire anything like a general view of the science. Some fundamental facts having been acquired by personal observation, such original knowledge may be the basis on which to build facts acquired from other persons through the media of art and language. With this supplementary work we shall deal in the following section, "On Relation of Laboratory Work to Book Work." In the present connection it is suffi-

---

[1] *Science and Education Essays*, p. 282.
[2] Payne, *Essays on Education*.

cient to have emphasized that scientific knowledge at first hand is essential as a basis for facts received from others, and that while scientific facts may be crammed from text-books and dictations by teachers, even considering science study as a source of useful information, the teaching is vastly more efficient when based upon the pupils' personal knowledge gained by direct study of natural phenomena.

So far we have considered the laboratory method in its relation to information only, but a more important aspect of the laboratory method is in its relation to scien-

Laboratory Method and Discipline. tific discipline. Now there is no question among scientific men of to-day that the laboratory method of science study is the one sure way of giving training in those mental observations which are essential to the scientific method. " There is very little profit," says President Eliot, of Harvard, " in studying natural science in a book, as if it were grammar or history ; for nothing of the peculiar discipline which the proper study of science supplies can be obtained in that way, although some information on scientific subjects may be so acquired." [1]

We may safely follow the now universally accepted opinion expressed in this quotation. But from the active teacher's

Analysis of Scientific Method Needed. standpoint there is little satisfaction in being told dogmatically by the great authorities in science teaching that laboratory study of zoölogy, or of any other science, gives a peculiar discipline. More than this the teacher should understand just what is involved in this discipline which is called " scientific " and how it may be best advanced by proper management of the laboratory study. To make such an analysis of the scientific discipline as involved in the study of zoölogical materials is the purpose of the next section. It is well worth while as teachers to stop to analyze the scientific method as it is related to the materials of zoölogy, for as Professor Forbes has well said :

---

[1] From essay on " What is a Liberal Education," in *Educational Reform* (Century Company). Also in *Century Magazine*. June, 1884.

" Our science teaching may be materially strengthened and be made practically more valuable if we will give much more attention and thought than hitherto to the rational action of the mind in science work, especially in the matter of inductive inference; if we will bestow as much care, ingenuity, and skill upon the selection, adaptation, and arrangement of materials for the training of the mind in the processes of logical reflection on the products of experience as we have heretofore used in equipping laboratories, and in teaching our students how to see, to manipulate, and to describe." [1]

2. The Scientific Method as Applied in Teaching Zoölogy.

What do we understand as involved in the general scientific method? In answer to this Huxley has said that "the great peculiarity of scientific training, that in virtue of which it cannot be replaced by any other discipline whatsoever, is this bringing of the mind directly into contact with fact, and practising the intellect in the completest form of induction; that is to say, in drawing conclusions from particular facts made known by immediate observation of Nature." [2]

What is the Scientific Method?

In brief, then, the fundamental basis of the general method of science is observation of particular facts and drawing conclusions from them. This is induction as a process of logic; and its prominence in science has led to the use of the term "inductive" method as synonymous with "scientific" method. But in this liberal use of the term inductive there is, unfortunately, a liability to misunderstanding, for the scientific method involves in addition to the logical process of induction those of deduction and verification. In fact, in the development of our greatest generalizations of biology, deduction has played an important part, but induction directly from observed facts has been the foundation. The relation of these processes — observation, induction, deduction, verification — has been illustrated by

Induction in the Scientific Method.

---

[1] From *School Science*, Vol. III., p. 66.
[2] From *Science and Education Essays*, p. 126.

Huxley, in his essay On Educational Value of Natural History, by reference to the circulation of the blood. Every teacher of science should be familiar with this essay, but for our present purposes the following points will suffice : Observation and experiment give the facts which lead to the conclusion by induction that the blood circulates in the particular animals studied. If it is wished to apply this to a new animal, it might be deductively reasoned from general similarity that there is circulation of the blood. But this deduction would not be secure until confirmed by verification, which would consist in making on the new animal all the observations and experiments involved in the original induction. Even then it would not be scientifically sure to conclude deductively that other animals which are structurally similar have a circulation, for as Huxley has pointed out, even those deductions which seem founded on the widest and safest inductions need verification.

This brief analysis of the scientific method as applied to a case in zoölogy gives us, for the purposes of the teacher, **Scientific Method in Great Generalizations.** sufficient insight into the principles involved. It would be interesting to trace the steps in the development of some great generalizations of biology through the stages of accumulation of facts by observation and experiment, then induction to hypothesis, then deductive application of the hypothesis to other particular cases, and finally attempts at verification ;[1] but this would be of little value so far as it might throw light on our practice in teaching in elementary courses. The greatest generalizations of science are the outcome of such a complicated interplay of observation, induction, deduction, and verification, that it is clearly impracticable that they should be presented to the pupils by the strictly scientific method, repeating that applied in the original formulation of the generalization.

---

[1] For such extended analysis of the scientific method see the references to Cramer, Forbes, Huxley, Pearson, and others, at the beginning of this chapter. Cramer's *Method of Darwin* is especially interesting to the biologist.

This leads us to recognize the distinction between two orders of reasoning : first, that followed in the original discovery of a truth ; and second, that followed by way of proof Two Orders or argument after the investigation has reached an of Reasoning. established conclusion. It is really this second order which we are forced to adopt in most biological teaching in which we attempt to lead the pupil to see the grouped evidence so that he will be convinced by the proof. This is essentially the order of most of our biological text-books, and few indeed are those which give the student even a glimpse of the steps which must have been passed over in the original investigation. For example, the circulation of the blood is usually stated as if it were axiomatic, and in the absence of the proofs the student may well wonder where there was anything remarkable in the original discovery.

So far as high-school laboratory work in zoölogy is concerned, only the simplest problems could be worked out by pupils following more or less closely the order of Order of Discovery; but no opportunity for making the pupil Teaching. the discoverer of even the minutest point in the historical order should be neglected. "The teacher should endeavor to bring his pupils face to face with the great problems of nature, as though he were the first discoverer." This is the key-note to the most efficient science teaching, for it is this attitude of the teacher which tends to direct pupils' minds in the order of discovery, involving in logical series observation, induction, deduction, and verification.

But although only the simplest problems are feasible for high-school practice in applying the complete scientific method in the order of discovery, students may get prac- Order of tice in some of the fundamental processes of the Proof. scientific method even from the order of proof. To illustrate : The individual pupil could not as a re-discoverer repeat all the steps in the development of a great principle like the cell-theory ; but it is perfectly possible for him to follow the order of discovery in many steps. First, through his own first observations of the microscopic structure of some simple tissue he will discover cells. Later he will discover cells in the other tissues, and will arrive at the conclusion that in the body of the animal studied there are cells in all tissues. This may be deductively applied to other animals, but without verification by further observation the deduction would not be scientifically secure. A limited amount of such verification may be made ; but of course no individual could repeat the vast number of verifications which have been made by investigators since Schleiden and Schwann announced the theory in 1838–1839, and in our teaching there comes a point where the established generalization must be given to the pupils. Thus, in a very condensed way the teacher might lead the pupil through some of the foundation steps in the re-discovery of the cell-theory. It is clear, then, that even in the cases of some of the widest generalizations, such as the cell-theory and the principle of evolution, the pupil's own experience with the underlying facts may be the foundation for the statement and illustration of these generalizations ; and certainly such first-hand acquaintance with facts leads to a proper appreciation of the history of the original discovery and to confidence in the truth of the principle.

The main point in this discussion which I wish to emphasize particularly is that in order to make the study of zoölogy most valuable as discipline in the scientific method, **Summary.** the essential processes and their relations must be kept constantly in mind by the teacher who directs the practical studies ; and it should be the constant aim of the teacher to lead the pupils to apply as far as possible the principles of the scientific method in discovering truth for themselves. To be sure all this is time consuming, and there is the ever-present vision of examinations and requirements of subject-matter ; but the emphasis upon scientific discipline is well worth more than one-half the time of a course. Perhaps some day those responsible for the requirements in knowledge of subject-matter, particularly those who set college-admission requirements, will come to take account, not simply of what facts a pupil holds in memory, but also of what scientific training has been received while getting the facts.

With the foregoing understanding of the general principles of the scientific method as applied to the study of zoölogy, it will be useful to examine the current teaching with **Subject-** regard to the actual application of the principles, **Matter and** especially in the relation between selected subject- **Method.** matter and the use of the scientific method.

The morphological aspect as it must be presented in an elementary course is most valuable for training in observation, and this is the training to be derived from the **Morphology.** great mass of the laboratory work in zoölogy as it is commonly taught.[1] Now observation, the very foundation of the scientific method, is valuable ; but we can lead to this through nature-study in the elementary school, and for the high school we need more of the scientific method.

It is to the physiological and ecological phases of biology that we must turn for material most suitable for training in scientific reasoning ; and the recent introduction **Physiology** of these into biological courses in the secondary **and Ecology.** school must be regarded as not only valuable for the wider view of the facts of the science, but also for the more complete training in the scientific method. As an example of such training afforded by simple experimental problems in physiology, we may mention the well-known experiments to determine some conditions of growth of yeast and bacteria. The following experiment with yeast is a fair sample of the possibilities in this line.

Take four test-tubes and fill one-half full of the following : No. 1, distilled water ; No. 2, 10 per cent solution of sugar in water; No. 3, Pasteur solution without sugar ; No. 4, Pasteur **An Experi-** solution with sugar. Add to each tube a drop of **mental Prob-** water containing living yeast, keep under conditions **Physiology.** favorable for growth. Examine twice daily for several days and

---

[1] See article by Forbes in *School Science*, III., p. 59.

compare as to turbidity (indicating growth), effervescence and odors (indicating fermentation). Write careful notes (1) describing the experiments, (2) on observation of changes which occur, (3) conclusion which you draw concerning the materials necessary (*a*) for growth of yeast and (*b*) for fermentation.

From this simple experiment, which should be repeated until sure of constant results, pupils may be expected by strict

Its Scientific Results. application of the scientific method involving observation, experiment, and induction, to arrive at the following facts and conclusions :

Facts : — Tube 1, No growth or fermentation in distilled water. No. 2, Some growth and fermentation in sugar solution. No. 3, More growth in Pasteur solution without sugar than in pure sugar solution. No fermentation. No. 4, Most growth and fermentation in Pasteur solution with sugar.

Inductions from these facts : No. 1, Distilled water lacks something necessary for growth of yeast. No. 2, Sugar is one substance which supplies the necessary materials for growth and fermentation. No. 3, Pasteur's without sugar contains other substances which are sufficient for growth ; but evidently without the sugar this solution is not sufficient for fermentation. No. 4, Pasteur solution with sugar contains substances for growth, but there is more growth than in tubes 2 and 3, and therefore the combination of the other substances and sugar is most favorable for growth. Also comparing 3 and 4 it is evident that sugar, not the other substances, undergoes fermentation.

As an example of simple deduction we might reason that since certain other plants — the moulds and bacteria — are

Deduction. in many ways similar to yeast, therefore the above conclusions derived from yeast are applicable to them. To make this sure would require the repeating the above experiments (verification) with the plants to which the conclusions are deductively applied. Even if time be not taken for deduction and verification the steps of such reasoning are worth pointing out to the pupils.

It is evident that such an experiment as that above offers opportunities for training in scientific reasoning which few of the usual morphological problems can furnish. It is true that this experiment is rather exceptional for the discipline which its careful solution may give, but in numerous small problems of physiology and ecology pupils may be led along similar lines of the scientific method.

Another illustration of the application of the scientific method is in the use of chemical tests for starch, proteids, and sugars. The common practice is essentially as follows : The pupil is directed to apply iodine **Another Illustration of Application of Scientific Method.** to various samples of starch, and a definite color appears. From this single observation the scientific conclusion is, of course, that starch is changed in color by the action of iodine. But this is not the point where the pupil's reasoning is stopped, for he is directly set to test for starch in unknown substances — a process involving (for the pupil) the unverified deduction that iodine produces the particular reaction in starch and in no other substance. Now the individual pupil could not verify this which has been established by the experience of thousands of chemists working with many thousands of different substances, but for the sake of practice in the first steps in the scientific method the pupil should follow his test of starch by tests of other substances — such as sugar, fats, and proteids — with iodine. Then make clear to him that the results of his own limited experiments are in line with the results of thousands of such experiments.

The same tendency of science teaching to take the short cut from facts to generalization is exhibited in numerous cases in which negative results are entirely ignored. As an example, the experiments on the digestion of **Negative Results Important.** foods, as given in most published books, are nothing more than verifications of the positive statements in the book. Experiments are made to show that pepsin and acid together digest proteid, but few authors suggest that it be tested whether pepsin alone or acid alone produces the same effect, or whether pepsin will digest foods other than proteids. From the standpoint of the scientific method these negative aspects are as

20

important as the positive. The really scientific presentation of gastric digestion in the laboratory would not be by an experiment "to show that gastric juice digests proteid," but rather by a series of experiments to determine the part which gastric juice plays in digestion of the various kinds of foods. In this particular case I know by experience that the more scientific method takes much longer for the experiments on digestion, but the time cannot be spent more profitably.

This last illustration of the scientific method brings to our attention two distinct methods of directing laboratory work in biology. The first is the mere verification of what **Two Methods of Directing Laboratory Study.** the book says, the second involves the setting of problems to be worked out. These two ways of directing the laboratory studies of students of biology are associated historically with the teaching of two famous naturalists, Agassiz and Huxley. The method of Agassiz consisted essentially in placing the materials before the student and leaving him with the minimum of direction and suggestion which will lead him to discover facts for himself. This we may call the "investigation" method, or since the suggestion of a problem would often take the form of a question, it has been called the "interrogation" method. The other method was characterized by the teaching of Huxley and is well illustrated by Huxley and Martin's *Practical Biology*. In this we find descriptions so complete that there is nothing for the student to do except to verify the printed statements. This we may call the "verification" method. Obviously, it has an advantage in that the students can rapidly gain a personal acquaintance with the facts, and hence, so far as zoölogy teaching is viewed from the side of information, this method is the best. But from the standpoint of scientific discipline, the "investigation" method has great advantages.

For the sake of a close comparison of the two methods of laboratory direction, I give here two outlines **Comparison of the two Methods.** which cover the same points regarding the external structure of the earthworm.

1. (*Directions for "Verification."*) " Notice that the body is cylindrical along the greater part of its length, flattened in its hinder part. It is pointed in front and blunt behind, and is thickest about one-third of its length from the anterior end. The general color of the animal is darker on dorsal and paler on ventral surface of the body."

2. (*Directions for "Investigation."*) " Notice living worm as it moves and determine anterior, posterior, dorsal, ventral. What is the general form of the body? Describe, illustrating with sketches, the form of both ends of the body. Compare the color on the dorsal and ventral surfaces of the body."

Now, comparing these two forms of laboratory directions, planned to lead the student to the same results in information, we note that in the first outline the pupil is given a complete description. This might be verified on a preserved specimen, and so far as the pupil is concerned there would be no evidence except authority that it is true, for the pupil cannot really know that the pointed end is anterior and that the paler surface is ventral until he has studied the movements of the living worm. On the other hand, the second method sets a problem for the pupil and gives the minimum of directions which will point in the direction of the correct answer, thus avoiding the wasting of time. Determination of the four points of orientation (anterior, etc.) in this case are easy problems for a pupil who has learned the meaning of the terms as applied to a crayfish, an insect, or a frog. Moreover, the second method requires the pupil to use his own language in describing the form of the earthworm, whereas the first method requires only reading and verification which may be so hasty as to be of little significance. So far as information gained is concerned there can be in practice little essential difference between these two methods. As regards time required, the second will take longer. But from the point of view of scientific training there can be no question about the superiority of the second ("investigation") method, for one of the simplest possible exercises is here presented in a form to give practice in true scientific investigation. Suggestions and questions start the pupil on the road, and he is left to proceed independently on the way to the discovery and testing of truth concerning the points in question.

It is to be noted that application of the "investigation" method is not always so easy as in the above example. To illustrate : the term cylindrical will be quickly applied to the body of the earthworm in answer to the question about its shape, but trials with several classes showed that few pupils would spontaneously apply the term "triangular," which is used in several books in describing the shape of the head of the frog. This is a case where the descriptive term should be given for verification ; and such cases are very common in zoölogy. Again, many questions and directions apparently attempt to avoid the verification of descriptions, and yet without explanation for guidance they are generally meaningless to the pupils. " Identify the liver," "Observe the arrangement of the blood vessels," " Do you find the kidneys? " " Locate the green gland," — these are common examples. Such directions apparently set problems for solution, but they do not help in the cultivation of scientific habits of study. Most of the problems as briefly stated are impossible of solution by a beginner, and are likely to lead to indefinite and uncertain results, and hence such directions are not to be commended for scientific study. Many such directions not uncommon in books lead to guessing and nothing more. It is clear that these are cases where the "verification" method has advantages; it will at least give good results in the line of information, whereas the "investigation" method will fail both in discipline and in information.

Limitation of "Investigation" Method.

Summarizing, we must conclude that there are advantages in both the "verification" and the "investigation" methods of laboratory study in zoölogy. The first is best from the standpoint of acquiring information about the science ; the second unquestionably affords the best training in the method of scientific study. Since the aims of

Summary.

zoölogical teaching are in this volume taken as both disciplinary and for information, it follows that neither method should
be adhered to exclusively. Whenever possible the laboratory
outlines should take the form of definite statements of simple
problems which it is *reasonable* to suppose can be solved
under the existing conditions of time, material, and advancement of the pupils. Note the conditions. They have been
too often overlooked by authors who have attempted strict
adherence to the "investigation" method. If these conditions are unfavorable to the "investigation" method in the
study of any topic, which in the majority of cases is true, let
the "verification" plan be adopted. Acceptance of this suggestion will lead to a combination of the two methods; for
much of the usual laboratory study for beginners is best accomplished by the "verification" method, but there are
hundreds of little problems which may be set for investigation
by the pupils. But whether the special method of teaching
the details takes the form of "verification" or "investigation,"
the general attitude of the teacher at all times should tend to
inspire the pupils to independent and original work — to lead
them as far as possible "to face the great problems of Nature
as though they had never been solved before."

It will be of interest to append to the above discussion of
method of laboratory study a list of the manuals which illustrate each. Among manuals for college work,
Huxley and Martin's *Practical Biology*, Marshall **Books following the Two
Methods.**
and Hurst's *Practical Zoölogy*, Parker's *Zoötomy*,
Parker and Parker's *Practical Zoölogy*, Brooks's *Handbook of
Invertebrate Zoölogy*, — all adhere closely to the "verification"
method, that is, these books are simply descriptions arranged
in a form for convenient verification in the laboratory. The
"investigation" method has received extreme application
in Dodge's *Biology* and Walter, Whitney, and Lucas's *Studies
of Animal Life*. Good examples of reasonable combination
of the two methods of study are Kingsley's *Elements of Comparative Zoölogy* and Needham's *Lessons in Zoölogy*.

3. The Relation of Laboratory Work and Book Work.

When the great advantages of the laboratory method both as a basis for scientific information and in mental training

Historical. began to be generally recognized some years ago there was developed a tendency to limit the teaching of zoölogy in secondary schools almost exclusively to practical work. This was partly the result of enthusiasm over the results obtained from the method then new to secondary education and partly due to the fact that laboratory guides long preceded suitable modern text-books of zoölogy for secondary schools. But in recent years there has been a gradual readjustment, and now both laboratory work and book work are generally recognized as having important places in zoölogical instruction.

From the conclusion in the preceding section of this chapter that knowledge obtained through personal investigation is the

Laboratory Study the Basis. proper foundation for zoölogical study, it follows that definitely planned laboratory exercises should be the basis of a course in elementary zoölogy. If we reverse this order and make the text-book the basis, then the laboratory work becomes largely verification of the text-book. From the combined standpoints of discipline and information laboratory work should be the basis and book work should be closely correlated so as to supplement, explain, and verify the very limited information which the pupil gets from his own studies of the actual objects. At present such correlation between laboratory work and book work rests entirely with the teacher, for a book which satisfactorily combines laboratory directions and supplemental reading for an entire course is not in existence. In fact, it may be doubted whether such a book is a desideratum, for several recent books furnish excellent material for collateral reading and it is simply necessary for teachers to select the appropriate topics. A difficulty which arises here is the impossibility, owing to cost, of pupils purchasing more than one book. Clearly this one book should be a good reference book which pupils will care to keep after the course is finished; and if laboratory manuals are to be used for directing the practical work they should be owned by the school. A set of twenty would be sufficient for one laboratory and with protective covers would last for years.

The recent revival of book work in teaching zoölogy in high schools is not without its dangers. The temptation to neglect the laboratory in order to give time to the recita- Dangers of tion is strong in those teachers who feel the im- Book Work. portance of *amount* of information, overlooking the at least equally important disciplinary aspect of zoölogical teaching. Especially are such teachers likely to err in the use of books such as the excellent volumes, *Animal Life* and *Animal Forms*, by Jordan, Kellogg, and Heath; for in the text of these there are no definite suggestions for close correlation with laboratory work. In fact, it is not at all clear to the present writer how these particular books, like all other books which deal with zoölogy in the form of a systematic treatise on the science, could be read continuously in close correlation with a series of elementary laboratory exercises. To attempt the use of such books as a *basis* of the course of study is sure to lead towards too exclusive dependence upon the text-book. Already there has been manifested in the use of *Animal Life* in some high schools a tendency to drift back to the old-time recitation method. Against such extreme use of this or any other text-book protest must be made.

Again I wish to emphasize the statement that if the most valuable results, both in discipline and information, are to be obtained from the study of zoölogy, the laboratory The Proper exercise must be the basis and the book work must Relation of be correlated as supplementary, not as anticipatory, and Book material. A properly organized course in zoölogy Work. must be primarily and fundamentally a series of laboratory exercises around which centre lectures, recitations, reading, and other supplementary work as sources of information.

4. Minor Problems of Laboratory Work in Zoölogy.

Space here will not permit more than a general discussion of principles underlying the practical working of the laboratory ; Sources of   but many valuable details will be found in the fol-
Suggestions.   lowing : Various school text-books (see list in Chapter X.) ; the laboratory manuals in morphology and physiology (see chapter on "Zoölogical Books ") ; *Suggestions to Teachers* accompanying Jordan and Kellogg's *Animal Life* (Appleton) ; *Teachers' Book of Suggestions* accompanying Walter, Whitney, and Lucas's *Studies of Animal Life* (Heath) ; and Report of Committee on Zoölogy to New York State Science Teachers' Association, *High School Bulletin*, No. 7 (1900), pp. 528, 743–777, obtainable from Secretary of University of State of New York, Albany ; price, 35 cents.

a. Form of Directions to Pupils.

Chief among the minor problems of the laboratory confronting the zoölogy teacher are those relating to giving directions
Oral and   to the pupils.   These, of course, may be oral or
Written   written, each with certain advantages.   The ad-
Directions.   vantages of the first are that the personality of the teacher comes into full play ; and also, it is possible to push the class rapidly over a given piece of work.   Its disadvantages are that all pupils do not work with the same rapidity, and the rapid ones set the pace with the result that a large percentage of the pupils are continually leaving tasks incomplete. This is such a serious objection, tending as it does to interfere with the individual work which is fundamental, that the method is of little value except for isolated demonstrations.   On the other hand, the value of written directions is just on this point, namely, that they encourage independent and individual work. If properly prepared, written directions economize time and keep the pupils continuously at work on definite problems. The teacher is left free to use his time for helping individuals over difficulties.   It should be recommended, then, that

written directions be used for all continuous work, reserving the general oral directions to classes for special points, which may come up unexpectedly, and for occasional isolated exercises.

With regard to the form of written directions, mimeographed [1] sheets are undoubtedly best because they can be adapted by the teacher to local conditions of outline of course, time, and available materials. In this respect most printed directions in books are inferior, for some flexibility is absolutely essential. In the absence of printed books and sheets, directions on the blackboard must be used. With large classes it is often difficult to arrange this so that all pupils can see; and necessarily the directions are very abbreviated, which is often undesirable.

b. Distribution of Apparatus and Materials for Study.

The aim should be to distribute material so as to save time for pupils and not unnecessarily burden the teacher. This is a problem not unworthy of serious planning by the teacher. The writer has seen some laboratories *Saving Pupils' Time.* where less than five minutes in an hour sufficed for the orderly distribution and collection of materials and apparatus, while in other schools much time was wasted because of obvious lack of system. The detail of this must be worked out to fit local conditions. Only some general suggestions may be useful here.

First, the same apparatus — microscopes, dissecting tools, etc. — must in most schools be used by pupils of several classes, and in order to place responsibility for *System Necessary.* care some system is necessary. The following scheme has been found satisfactory in several schools. All

---

[1] In the absence of a mimeograph or similar copying apparatus requiring a stencil, the simple method of printing from a pad of gelatine is not expensive and requires no special skill in manipulation. One of the best of these duplicators is the Hektograph made at 42 Murray St., New York, by the Hektograph Co. It will make forty or fifty good duplicates from a single copy made with pen or typewriter, using special inks.

large instruments, such as microscopes, are numbered and assigned certain places in lockers and on tables and to certain pupils. Smaller instruments in regular use which belong to the laboratory are kept in boxes or drawers, also numbered to correspond with the microscopes. Each pupil upon entering and leaving the laboratory must examine apparatus assigned to him and report any damage or loss. Thus pupils are easily held responsible for the proper use of the property of the laboratory, and aside from protecting the property of the school, the system is worth more than it costs in trouble to the teacher in giving pupils training in methodical habits.

With regard to distribution and collection of apparatus, it should be so systematically placed in lockers, drawers, or **Apparatus.** closets that pupils, moving in definite order, can obtain and return their own apparatus. The appointment of one or two pupils for the distribution of apparatus to each table will often save confusion in large classes. Sometimes when the same apparatus is to be used by a class immediately following, time may be saved by leaving it in place on the tables.

Materials to be studied should be distributed systematically, as in the case of apparatus. In large, roomy laboratories it is **Materials for** best to have supply-tables convenient to the work-**Study.** tables on which materials, properly labelled, may be placed by the teacher. As an almost ideal plan, I know of one laboratory with eight tables, each for six students, in which there are four supply-tables, with sinks and running water and closets for dissecting pans and other dishes, so arranged that no student is over fifteen feet from a supply-table. Some such arrangement saves time and energy for both teacher and pupil. However, in the absence of such conveniences, it is no great task to make systematic arrangements, so that pupils can do a large part of the work involved in distributing and collecting their own materials for study.

c. Amount of Time for Laboratory Work.

Five periods (from forty to fifty-five minutes) per week are usually assigned to zoölogy, as is the rule in other sciences. The division of this time between recitation and Time for Laboratory and Recitation. laboratory work varies with different teachers, but three periods for laboratory work and two periods for recitation or lecture seems to be the most common arrangement. Personally I have found the most satisfactory division of time to be four periods for laboratory work and one period for recitation or lecture, using in addition the closing minutes of many of the laboratory periods for recitation or lecture in order to clinch the essential points in the practical lesson.

With regard to the credit for laboratory work, most colleges regard two periods of laboratory work as equal to one period of recitation, the laboratory work not requiring the Credit for Laboratory Work. time for preparation which is demanded for the recitation period. This is impractical in most high schools, for the reason that the hours of attendance at school are usually so limited that all recitation hours must be credited. In a few academies and private secondary schools four periods of laboratory work and two periods of recitation work are credited as four periods, and four periods of laboratory work and one period of recitation as three periods. However, the most practicable plan for most secondary schools is five periods credit for an equal number of periods in recitation or laboratory work, and the assignment of supplementary reading and outside work so as to make the laboratory work require the same amount of preparation as does the recitation period. In this way a five-period course in biology may be made equivalent to one of equal time in other subjects, such as the languages or mathematics.

Double periods (ninety to one hundred and ten minutes) are preferable for laboratory work for the reason that the ordinary forty-five minutes' session is too short for performing many experiments, making of drawings, etc. Two double periods and one single period is an excellent arrangement for a five-period course. Unfortunately the double period is difficult to articulate with the regular school program, so that daily single periods are usually necessary in public high schools.

d. Drawings and Notes.

The ideal record of laboratory work in zoölogy should consist of both drawings and notes. Excessive attention to the morphological aspect of zoölogy has tended in both schools and colleges to over-emphasis upon drawings, which as a rule are certainly best for recording results derived from study of structure. I have already (p. 303) pointed out that morphology alone gives little opportunity for scientific training in induction, for the study is primarily observational ; and that for materials for training in induction we must draw upon other phases of zoölogy, particularly experimental physiology. Now, drawings like the structures which they represent lend themselves chiefly to the training in observation. For sound training in induction we must have notes — not simply the usual notes describing drawings and with the same disciplinary value, but clearly written, logical accounts of observations, experiments, and conclusions. The experiments already referred to on yeast (p. 303) as an example of a laboratory exercise affording more than training in observation are also good examples of work whose results cannot be expressed adequately by drawings alone. In such cases involving experiments the notes should clearly state : (1) The problem or what the experiment is designated to test. (2) Description of apparatus (with sketches) and of the experiment. (3) Results of the experiment. (4) Conclusion drawn.

Aside from notes for the sake of biological training in logical reasoning, descriptions of things observed and even of structures represented also by drawings give valuable training, not only in a literary way, but especially in accuracy in use of language — an invaluable part of the training which science study may give.

The Ideal Record of Work.

Another Value of Notes.

It is generally agreed that simple outline drawings only should be encouraged in regular laboratory work in zoölogy. Most pupils are not able to make more elaborate **Kind of** drawings, and the majority of those who have **Drawings.** artistic talent tend strongly to an impressionistic style which is not at all adapted to scientific work. In order to show beginners in the laboratory just what is meant by outline drawings, I know of no better way than to exhibit the illustrations in Morse's *First Book in Zoölogy*, which are ideal outline drawings of great simplicity and will give pupils valuable suggestions about representation of animal structure. In fact, I think that there is truth in Professor Morse's advice that beginning pupils should practise copying the drawings from the book. But this copying should supplement, and not supplant, drawings from nature. Copied drawings from any source should be placed beside original ones in the note-book, and the source labelled upon them in order to distinguish them from the pupil's original work. In laboratory note-books there is always a chance for some pupils to trespass upon their intellectual honesty, and the teacher must attempt to impress upon them the difference between original work and that which is derived from other sources; and the note-book should be so labelled that any one who may examine it can tell at a glance just what is original.

Against this recommendation that some drawings may be copied, some writers have advised that all books with drawings be kept out of pupils' hands, at least until after **Copied** animals are studied and drawings made. I cannot **Drawings.** agree to this because experience teaches that pupils do not give critical attention to figures in books after they have completed their own sketches. It is much better to allow them to examine drawings freely while studying materials and thus get the benefit of suggestions for their own sketches. In order to avoid direct copying while drawing from the actual object studied, reference books may be kept on special tables where they may be consulted from time to time.

Note-books.

There are in common use several good methods of keeping drawings and notes on biological work : (1) A note-book of good firm paper (ordinary paper for ink is not satisfactory for drawings) in which alternate sheets (or pages) are left unruled for drawings. The disadvantages are that often more paper for notes is needed, substitutions or rearrangement cannot be made, and the inconvenience of drawing in a book is great. (2) An ordinary note-book is used for notes; sheets of firm paper (linen-ledger or Bristol board) for drawings which are kept, dated and numbered in order of making, in manila envelopes. The advantages are economy in drawing paper and greater convenience in drawing on a loose sheet, but the objection arising from keeping notes and drawings separated is a very serious one. (3) Loose-leaf note-books with both ordinary paper for notes and special paper for drawings. These can be arranged as the relative proportion of drawings and notes demand. Obviously this has the advantages of the other methods combined. The chief objection to loose leaves for both notes and drawings is that pupils may substitute copied drawings or notes for those made in the laboratory. This is easily prevented by the teacher requiring that all drawings and notes made during a session be dated, numbered, and left on the teacher's desk. Before the next session they should be stamped or marked so that a substitution is rendered impossible, and it may then be állowable for pupils to make additions or corrections as the teacher may suggest.

A good book, with firm paper ruled on one side, bound in cloth, 100 and 150 pages, is sold by the Cambridge Botanical Supply Co., Cambridge, Mass., at about 45 and 55 cents.

A similar note-book, 100 pages, alternate blank pages, 9¼ x 5½ inches, strong binding, is sold by Chicago Laboratory Supply Co., price 40 cents.

Among note-books with loose leaves, the most popular in college circles is the " University Cover," made by the National Blank Book

Forms of Note-books.

Co., Holyoke, Mass. The No. 2 cover (size 6½ x 8½ inches) with perforations at side of sheet are the most convenient for laboratory notes. The ordinary paper (ruled or unruled) accompanying the cover should be used for notes and the same sized sheets of good quality, firm linen-bond paper, or two-ply Bristol board, should be used for drawings. The cost is about the same as that of the bound books mentioned above. Lemcke and Buchner, Broadway and 118th St., New York, sell the No. 2 cover (cloth) with 100 sheets of note-paper and 40 sheets drawing-paper at 50 cents.

Another good cover for laboratory notes is the " Perfection," No. 5, flat opening, sold by E. Pennock, 3609 Woodlawn Ave., Philadelphia.

The Chicago Laboratory Supply Co. makes a " Biology Tablet," containing 40 sheets (7 x 11 inches) of ink paper and 24 sheets drawing paper, in blocks, accompanied by an adjustable cover; price, 50 cents.

CHAPTER IV

ANIMAL NATURE-STUDY AND HUMAN PHYSIOLOGY IN THE ELEMENTARY SCHOOL AS RELATED TO ZOÖLOGY IN THE SECONDARY SCHOOL

BIBLIOGRAPHY

The following books and articles have proved most helpful to teachers of nature-study in elementary schools, and may therefore be referred to as representing the kind and scope of studies of animals which are practicable below the high school.

Bailey, L. H. The Nature-Study Idea. New York, Doubleday. 1903. Pp. 159. $1.00. (A collection of essays dealing with nature-study as a phase of education. Full of practical suggestions for teachers. Indispensable.)

Hodge, C. F. Nature Study and Life. Boston, Ginn. 1902. Pp. 514, figs. 196. $1.50. (Deals chiefly with the materials for nature-study, with special reference to animals. No other book so well presents the animal aspect. Full of inspiration and practical suggestions.)

Hodge, C. H. Foundations of Nature Study. Article in PEDAGOG-ICAL SEMINARY, Vols. VI. and VII.

Scott, C. B. Nature Study and the Child. Boston, Heath. 1900. (Primarily a discussion of aims and principles of nature-study. Also has practical suggestions for lessons.)

Lange, D. Handbook of Nature Study. New York, Macmillan. 1899. Pp. 329.

Jenkins, O. P., and Kellogg, V. L. Lessons in Nature Study. San Francisco, Whittaker & Ray. 1900. Pp. 191. (A collection of lesson plans, many of them on animals.)

NATURE-STUDY LEAFLETS, published by Cornell University.

Jackman, W. S. Nature Study for Grammar Grades. New York, Macmillan. 1899. Pp. 407. (Several books with similar titles are by the same author, but this one gives a fair view of the nature-study for which he stands.)

Wilson, Mrs. L. L. Nature Study in the Elementary Schools. Teachers' Manual. New York, Macmillan. 1899. (A series of practical suggestions for lessons in nature-study.)

Howe, E. G. Systematic Science Teaching. New York, Appleton. 1894. Pp. 326. $1.50. (Suggestions for a series of progressive lessons in nature-study, involving the biological, geographical, and physico-chemical aspects.)

Hall, W. S. School Science, Vol. I., p. 60. (Refers to nature-study as preparatory to high-school biology.)

Discussion on nature-study by Professors Beal, Packard, Coulter, Gillette, W. M. Davis, Verrill, Jordan, and Macbride. Science, n. s., Vol. XVI., pp. 910–913. December 5, 1902.

1. The Relation of Nature-Study to High-School Zoölogy.

Starting at the very foundation of nature-study for elementary schools, we note that the most fully developed type of nature-study stands for the following aims, which **Aims of** we here apply directly to the animal aspect of the **Nature-Study.** subject : (1) To give the pupils acquaintance and sympathy with common animals ; (2) To lay the foundation of scientific education by leading the pupils to gain some knowledge through their own observations on animals, and to appreciate the knowledge so gained ; (3) To give the pupils useful knowledge about animals, especially in their relation to man.[1]

Assuming that these aims meet in practice with a fair degree of realization — and the writer is convinced that this is true — it is clear that animal nature-study must be **Its Impor-** important in general education. That the aim **tance in Edu-** for acquaintance with animals stands for something **cation.** full of interest for intelligent people need not be argued in these days when there is such a great popular demand for books purporting to help in identification of animals. The aim for sympathy finds its support in the arguments on moral and æsthetic lines. The second aim, standing as it does for scientific seeing and thinking, requires here no special defence ; for such training is now universally accepted as valuable in all education, and the tendency of recent years has been to em-

---

[1] This order of statement is not intended to indicate the order of importance. On this point authors disagree ; but the writer's personal view is that all are important and should receive attention, for there is really no conflict. Bailey (*loc. cit.*) emphasizes the first aim, Hodge lays stress on the third, and all authors insist that nature-study must be taught on a basis of observation (the second aim).

phasize the necessity for special training in observation.[1] The third aim is for information which is useful and interesting for its own sake and which may later come into relation with advanced studies.

With this view of the relation of nature-study to general education, we may now discuss the first of the special problems Nature-Study and Zoölogy in the High School. of this chapter, namely, the relation of the animal nature-study of the elementary school to the study of zoölogy in the high school. For this purpose we must first consider the relation of nature-study to the so-called " natural history " of animals which has been referred to as constituting a very prominent part of many high-school courses in zoölogy.[2] Our inquiry must now be whether this is the proper place for this work; and in considering this question I shall attempt to show that much of the natural history properly belongs in the elementary schools as part of the nature-study.

Examining the contents of the natural history which is now common in secondary schools, we find that the work consists Natural History in High Schools. largely of observations on the external structures, habits, life-histories, and economic relations of common animals. The aims of such work may be well expressed by quotations from Professor Davenport, whose leadership has inspired and guided the return to the old-time instruction in natural history. He wrote in the preface to the *Introduction to Zoölogy* :

" What an ordinary citizen needs is an acquaintance with the common animals that may be the companions of his country walks, and that may even stray into Wall Street, Dearborn Street, or Commonwealth Avenue. He wants to know where else over the world the common animals of his State are to be found and, as a legislator or as a taxpayer, he wants to know how animals affect man. It is more important for him to know these matters than to

---

[1] See especially Eliot's *Educational Reform*, p. 112.
[2] Natural history in the high-school course is discussed in Chapter II., and its relation to the college work in zoölogy in Chapter XI.

know the location of the pedal ganglion of the snail, or to be able to recite the various ingenious hypotheses of the ancestry of echinoderms. Our conviction is, we feel sure, the common conviction of college teachers of zoölogy, who have often occasion to deplore the ignorance that their students show about common animals. It is the conviction of many other thoughtful men also who have recognized that an interest in nature is a powerful agent in making men more moral, more capable of appreciating the world they live in, and of finding satisfaction in living."

It is to be noted that emphasis is placed upon acquaintance with common animals, their economic relation to man and interest in nature. Such a statement of the aims and nature of the subject-matter suggests great similarity between the natural history of common animals in the high school and the nature-study of the elementary school. But general statements may mislead, and a more specific examination of natural history is necessary.

The common animals which have been introduced into the natural-history work of the secondary school are : grasshopper, butterfly, beetle, fly, crayfish, myriapod, spider, Scope of Natearthworm, slug, clam, fish, newt, frog, lizard, bird, ural History in High and mouse. As to the scope of natural-history Schools. studies of these animals, reference must be made to the outlines in published guides for practical work. Davenport's *Introduction to Zoölogy* (pp. 341–367) gives for most of the above animals directions for observations on the living animals. Likewise, Needham's *Lessons in Zoölogy* gives numerous suggestions for observations on common animals, especially in the field ; and still other books for secondary schools which emphasize natural history are French's *Animal Activities* and Colton's new text-book and guide.

In all these books a large percentage of the suggested studies of living animals are so simple that they are well within the capabilities of pupils in elementary grades. In Natural History fact, many of the simple experiments and observa- tory for Elementary tions suggested in these books have already been Schools. successfully introduced into elementary work as part of the nature-studies. There is no reason inherent in the nature of the materials and methods why a considerable part of the simple observations on common living animals along the line of natural history should not be done in the elementary school. In fact, I am inclined to believe that the pupil who has passed through a well-organized system of nature-study in the ele- . mentary school has that general acquaintance with common animals which is regarded as desirable for entrance upon the elementary zoölogical work of colleges. But at any rate all will agree that so much of the natural history as can be well done in the nature-study should be placed there, instead of in the high school.

From the point of view of zoölogy in the secondary school it would be a decided advance if the simple natural-history work could be transferred to the nature-study of the elementary school. There would be a gain (1) in that the high-school pupils would be prepared to begin the serious study of the science of zoölogy without any preliminary work designed for training in observation, stimulating interest, and giving acquaintance with common animals,[1] and (2) in that the nature of much of the work makes it better adapted to elementary than to high-school pupils. The first point will be granted without discussion, but the second requires explanation and defence.

Effect upon High-School Zoölogy.

It is the experience of many teachers that secondary pupils do not undertake certain studies of living animals with the enthusiasm and earnestness which characterize nature-studies in the elementary school, and to the average secondary pupil studies of living animals are not part of serious science work. In fact, since the advent of the purely natural-history courses in high schools there are many indications that the pupils who study physical as well as biological sciences, tend to regard

Natural History well adapted to Elementary School.

---

[1] See discussion on natural history as a preparation for high-school zoölogy in the chapter on " Beginning Work in Zoölogy."

biology, and especially zoölogy, as an "easy" subject which has scarcely the dignity of the other sciences, like chemistry and physics. I am inclined to agree with the pupils on this point. I doubt whether it is possible to present a high-school course dealing exclusively or even largely with natural history which will lead pupils to the serious attitude demanded by all the other sciences. This is the result of the very nature of the materials. A trained naturalist may see problems of profound significance in the wriggling of a worm or the jump of an insect, but to a beginner in zoölogy there can be little more to gain than some isolated facts, which may be interesting, but with little apparent significance, for in such studies the accumulated facts of a series of observations on living animals do not seem to the pupil to lead in any definite direction to a principle or generalization. In short, the facts of natural history are largely unorganized and unorganizable by high-school pupils, and for this reason they do not appeal as seriously to pupils as do the usual studies of other sciences, or even of other phases of zoölogical study. These objections do not obtain in the elementary schools. Experience shows that the young pupils become seriously interested in many little problems of natural history which the average high-school pupils regard as not worth their while. This is because the younger pupils are still in the stage where they are content to take each little fact for its own sake without reference to its broader relations. In fact, the simplest problems, and often those with little significance, are usually very interesting to the pupils of the elementary schools, and these are often the most valuable from the standpoint of the leading aims of nature-study. Thus, the movements of an animal are entrancing for most children in the lower grades, and offer a great opportunity for developing interest and giving training in accuracy of observing; but on the other hand such a fact as cross-fertilization of flowers, which is full of biological significance, means nothing very interesting to the pupils in the elementary school. These conditions are just reversed in the secondary school. The

pupil who has come to grapple with the problems of mathematics beyond arithmetic, with those of physics and chemistry
and with the intricacies of the syntax of classical languages, is
not likely to see much else than recreation and entertainment
in the study of grasshopper's jumps and similar animal activities.   Of course there is great significance in these, but the
specialist in zoölogy who sees this must not deceive himself
into believing that the high-school pupil agrees with him in
taking such studies seriously.   The fact is that the pupil demands something which directly appeals to him as significant
and worthy of serious attention.   This is offered him in most
of the studies of the high school, and the time has come
when zoölogy too must be taught on the same basis.   It is no
longer justifiable to teach zoölogy in the high school simply
for the sake of interest in animal life, for this can be done and
far better done in the nature-study of the elementary schools.
In the secondary school zoölogy must be presented for the
sake of the principles which, like those of physics and chemistry, will appeal to pupils because of their value as knowledge ;
and for the teaching of the more or less isolated facts of
natural history for the sake of interest and general acquaintance with animals we must look to the nature-study of the
elementary schools.

In opposition to the position here taken, it will probably be
pointed out that as yet few elementary schools have developed
An Opposing   nature-study so as to be able to do the kind of
Argument.   natural history which we have been considering,
and that here is an argument for including this in the general
course in zoölogy for high schools.   It is true that this fact
must largely govern our present practice ; but with nature-
study for the elementary school already in a state of rapid
development we must begin to look forward to the time when
a large part of the natural history now commonly assigned to
the high school will be finally placed in the elementary school.

Summarizing the foregoing considerations, it is urged that
teachers of biological science in high schools should recognize

the importance of the natural-history studies of common animals in the elementary school, for the reasons that (1) the results to be expected from such studies are more satisfactorily obtained with the younger pupils than **Summary.** in the high school, and (2) the secondary-school work in zoölogy should be relieved of much of this kind of work which when made prominent interferes with the serious study of zoölogy as a science. Upon all teachers interested in zoölogy for the high school there is the duty of aiding in every possible way the development of the animal nature-study in the elementary school, thereby making a freer field for the high-school course in serious zoölogy and at the same time gaining an important preliminary to the high-school studies. Finally, to guard against any possible misunderstanding, let it be repeated that we must regard the present prominence of natural history in the high school as a temporary necessity, but with the coming development of nature-study in the lower schools natural history in high-school study will deserve a place as incidental and supplemental to the study of the elementary principles of zoölogy — a position which it often has even in college courses.

2. The Relation of "Human Physiology" to Nature-Study and Zoölogy.[1]

Probably it will not be disputed as a general principle that the biological work of the public schools should be a continuous development from the nature-study of the earliest grades of the elementary school through- **Continuity in Biological Study.** out the courses in botany and zoölogy in the high-school. In discussing the relation of the elementary nature-study to the zoölogical courses of the secondary school, we have already seen that the elementary study may contribute to

---

[1] In the first pages of Chapter XII. it is pointed out that "physiology" taught in our schools is more than the science of functions referred to in Chapter II. The quotation marks in this section will avoid possible confusion.

this result by preparing both in discipline and in knowledge for the more advanced science work, especially the biological. From the same point of view let us now consider the relation of the "physiology" of the last year [1] of the elementary school which in the ordinary curriculum stands between nature-study of the lower grades and the science work of the high school.

In disciplinary value "physiology" as usually taught differs radically from all other biological science work in the schools,

Continuity in Discipline.
for both nature-study and the courses in botany and zoölogy in the high school are commonly based upon the pupil's own observations and experiments, rather than upon a text-book. The common method of teaching "elementary physiology" from a text-book makes a serious break in the continuity of the scientific discipline to which all science study should contribute.

· With regard to the general relation of the subject-matter of "physiology" to that of nature-study on the one hand and

Continuity in Subject-Matter.
high-school biology on the other, "physiology" as presented in most text-books is characteristically subjective, whereas the nature-study of the elementary school and the biological courses of the high school are decidedly objective. "Physiology" is centred around an introspective study of the human body viewed as quite independent of external nature. From this extreme difference in point of view there results a breach of continuity in the development of the subject-matter, and so we find nature-study and "physiology" commonly regarded by educators as two distinct and quite independent phases of elementary science. Such a division may have its use in a schedule of

---

[1] This is not the place for discussing the relation of physiology to the curriculum of the elementary school, and in explanation of this reference to the "last year" I may say in brief that for many reasons I decidedly favor not attempting physiology before the last year of the elementary school. For earlier years I regard simple lessons in hygiene — not as separate lessons, but in close connection with nature-studies — most satisfactory.

the school program, but in the outlines of courses there should be no such sudden transition from the nature-study to " physiology," and from this back again to external nature as presented in the biological work of the high school.   On the contrary, I believe that much advantage would result from making the introduc- Physiology as the Out- growth of Nature- Studies. tion to the study of the human body a natural outgrowth of the nature-studies of the earlier years.   The suggestion referred to in the last footnote, that all references to the hygiene of the human body during the first six or seven years of the elementary-school course should be in the line of correlations growing out of the nature-studies, is an important step in the direction of giving to the study of the human body an outlook upon the relations of man to external nature.   And this should continue to be the viewpoint in the " physiology" which in the last year of the grammar school leads the pupils into the study of the internal life-activities of the human body.   The introduction to this course in " physiology " should be made as a gradual transition from the earlier nature-study, by showing first the relations of man to the objective world, both the living and the lifeless, and to the end of the course these relations should be a leading thought worthy of all possible emphasis and illustration.

To put the above ideas into practice is not to attempt teaching by formulated statements that there are certain relations between man and the external world, or that the study of man is one link in a chain of sciences dealing with nature of which man is a part.   Such word formulas would, of course, be valueless; but a well-organized course of study with a basis of observation and experiment on animals and plants may bring pupils to some definite realization of Physiology from the Viewpoint of Biology. many essential facts concerning the relation of man to nature by showing that the study of the human body makes direct application of many of the earlier naturestudy lessons and derives many of its facts from studies of living and lifeless things in the objective world.   All the earlier nature-study should have led the way to this, for it will already have given the child some idea of his relation to nature. The study of the human body is then a culmination of nature-study. Along these lines, I believe we should look for the continuous and logical development of biological study from the work of the lower grades through the study of "human physiology" to the more rigidly scientific study of the biological sciences in the secondary school. This involves nothing more in essentials than teaching "physiology" from the viewpoint of the science of biology which emphasizes the relationships of organisms to each other and to the lifeless world. With this as a guiding principle, it is not difficult to teach "human physiology" as biological science, for even the most elementary study offers abundant opportunities for pointing to the relationships between man's structure and functions and those of the living and lifeless things in his objective world. Especially is all this readily accomplished when the basis of the teaching is in practical study of other living and lifeless things which help us to interpret man's structure, life-activities, and relations.

CHAPTER V

THE POSITION AND RELATIONS OF ZOÖLOGY IN THE HIGH-SCHOOL CURRICULUM

BIBLIOGRAPHY

Ward, H. B. Zoölogy in the High School. Proceedings N. E. A., 1897, pp. 953-958.

Report of Committee on Zoölogy. Proceedings N. E. A., 1899.

Papers on Sequence of Sciences in the Secondary-School Curriculum, read before the New York State Science Teachers' Association. 1899. In High School Bulletin, No. 7, Univ. of State of New York, Regents' Reports, 1900.

1. Relation of Botany and Zoölogy.

THE question of the position of zoölogy in the secondary-school curriculum is so closely involved with that of its relation to botany that we must first consider whether these two aspects of biology are to be regarded as independent sciences, each requiring a year's course, or whether a single continuous course should combine the study of animals and plants. An answer to these questions depends largely upon our understanding of the relation of all the sciences to the general curriculum.

It is first to be noted that three other sciences — physics, chemistry, and geography with geology — are commonly taught in high schools. It will be admitted beyond dispute, I think, that each of these offers training and information which are of importance from the point of view of liberal education. Moreover, it will probably be generally admitted that it is quite impossible to decide between the importance of these and the two biological sciences, for all have their strong points and all touch somewhere upon every-day human life, which insures that the elements of each are bound to be of interest to the average cultivated citizen. The ideal science curriculum, then, would appear to be one which gives a place to each of the five sciences, and in which these are so arranged that all pupils may have offered them the opportunity to get a general survey of the field of each science.

This, then, is the situation: There are four years of the secondary school in which the pupil may learn the elements

Four Years of Sciences and get a glimpse of the field covered by the sciences. It is generally admitted that the presentation of a science course requires at least a year of four or five hours weekly. This means that four courses in science will use over one-fourth of the total time of the secondary school, and the remainder of the time must be distributed between the languages, literature, history, mathematics — all of undoubted importance in liberal education. A larger proportion of science would certainly result in narrowness no less open to criticism than the extreme specialization in languages which formerly prevailed, and our conclusion is that four courses in science is the maximum allowable for liberal secondary education.

Now biology, uniting zoölogy and botany, is only one of the four sciences under consideration. Does it deserve more than

One or Two Years for Biology? one-fourth of the time allotted to the sciences? In support of an affirmative answer to this question it is sometimes urged that since biology presents the two phases, botany and zoölogy, the science should have two years of the four in the secondary school. This, of course, necessitates either the omitting of one other science or else overreaching the limits of four years of science work by the very unsatisfactory arrangement of two courses of science work in one of the school years.

In answer to the argument for two years of biology it may be urged that the ground for this division of biology seems not

Biology a Unified Science. to be well taken, for it is a unified science and the division of subject-matter into botany and zoölogy is largely arbitrary. "The study of living bodies," says Huxley, "is in reality one discipline, which is divided into botany and zoölogy simply as a matter of convenience."[1] Essentially there is no wider gap between the methods of study and the subject-matter of botany and zoölogy than between the so-called organic and inorganic aspects of chemistry, or between the various phases of physics. So far as any sharp demarkation of subject-matter and methods of study are concerned there is, then, no sufficient reason for regarding zoölogy and botany as two distinct sciences, each claiming a place in the secondary curriculum.

A more reasonable argument favoring the subdivision of biology into two separate courses of zoölogy and botany arises from the impossibility of covering the field of biology in one year of five hours per week. But it is likewise impossible to "complete" chemistry, physics, or geography in a single year. At best high-school science courses are simply an introduction to the general methods and principles of the sciences, and anything approaching mastery of even limited phases of the subject-matter is impossible. The fact, then, that both the animal and plant phases of biology cannot be completely presented in a single year offers no convincing argument for departure from the ideal plan of offering in secondary schools four years of science of which biology counts as one. If the subject-matter as presented by specialists in either botany or zoölogy is too extensive for such time limitation, a concentration of attention upon essential principles and selection of the most important material is surely needed.[2] The teacher of chemistry does not attempt to instruct a high-school class about the chemistry

Field of Biology Extensive. Selection Necessary.

---

[1] Preface to *Practical Biology*, by Huxley and Martin.

[2] "Zoölogy is still an arduous and extensive study, which must be reduced by selection, until even whole classes, not to speak of Natural Orders, Genera, and Species, are left unrepresented in a tolerably extended course. Still the groundwork may be laid for following out the subject, which is all that teaching can do, or should attempt, for many of the most fruitful regions of knowledge." — Alexander Bain, *Education as a Science*. 1878. Appleton's Edition, p. 302.

of all the elements; on the contrary, there is selection of the most common ones and these are used to illustrate the general principles of the science. But in the teaching of elementary biology we have yet to learn concentration of attention upon important and fundamental principles, and to spend less time upon the details of which organisms present unlimited variety. In biology, as in the physical sciences, we must come to select a limited number of common types as a basis for general principles; and other forms of animals and plants will be presented to the pupils simply for the sake of acquaintance. Viewed from this standpoint there seems to be no good reason why the important facts of animal and plant life may not be incorporated into a year's course in biology, which shall have a place in the curriculum equal with that held by the other three sciences, chemistry, physics, and geography. It is probable that the advantages of such a course would be generally recognized at once were it clearly worked out in some text-book and laboratory guide; but unfortunately high-school biology yet awaits the coming of an author who will be able to develop a course of general principles adapted to that grade of work as well as Parker's *Elementary Biology* and Sedgwick and Wilson's *General Biology* solve the problem of one general course for college students who cannot take more than one general course in biological sciences. But sooner or later such a book dealing with the essentials of the science will be written, and when it comes we shall see clearly that our present special books in botany and zoölogy deal with vast masses of details which are unessential to the general view of the great ideas of the science of life.

So far no reference has been made to possible specialization in any science at the choice of the pupil, for some individuals will prefer a certain science and will choose to pursue it to the exclusion of the others. Shall advanced elective courses be provided for such as these? I believe that as a rule such provision for specialization should be discouraged in all science departments in the average

Advanced Elective Courses.

secondary schools. Of course there are exceptional cases, as in special high schools which emphasize certain applied sciences. At any rate, the question of encouraging specialization by offering elective courses in any or all of the sciences is one which concerns only a limited number of individuals and schools, and this can be provided for independently of a general scheme which applies to the great majority of pupils. For the masses of pupils and in most high schools the general introductory courses in each science alone are needed, and the question of advanced electives should not be allowed to influence the general arrangement or scope of the science courses in the regular curriculum.

It is sometimes urged that if a year of biology is to be ranked with equally extensive courses in each of the other sciences, that year should not be divided between animals and plants, giving each phase one-half year, but that pupils should be allowed a choice between a year of botany and a year of zoölogy. The argument for this is that a half-year is insufficient for either botany or zoölogy and that a year in biology is equivalent to two distinct half-year courses with a serious break at the middle of the year when the transition from the study of animals to that of plants, or *vice versa*, is made. In answer to the first part of this argument, it has already been pointed out that so far as the essential facts and principles are concerned the ordinary courses in botany and zoölogy are capable of great condensation ; and with regard to sudden transition, there is no great difference in subject-matter and methods. It is possible to correlate the zoölogy and botany work of the two half-years, so that the result is a general course in biology involving a wide survey of animal and plant life. Moreover, there is a strong argument against the proposition of allowing a choice between a year of botany and one of zoölogy and in favor of one in biology. It is this : either of the separate courses fail to give the well-rounded view of life phenomena which is desirable in liberal education ; and since compara-

Half-year Courses combined.

tively few pupils can take both courses without omitting one of the other important sciences, we are again led to decide in favor of an introductory course which includes a summary of zoölogy and botany in a continuous year's course. Along these lines we may then defend the course consisting of two half-year courses in zoölogy and botany which, in the absence of suitable guides for close unification, teachers are now forced to follow ; but in doing so we must emphasize the importance of continuity and correlation between the two half-year courses. All this, however, is merely suggesting a temporary compromise looking forward to the time when a unified course in biology will make it unnecessary and quite undesirable to draw any line between botany and zoölogy, as the present arrangement of separate text-books and guides now practically require in most high schools.

Another objection to a year's course in biology for the high school is that most colleges which accept botany and College Admission Credit. zoölogy for admission require full-year courses in either botany or zoölogy in the last years of high school. However, the fact that this applies to comparatively few pupils should prevent it from having any weight in the consideration of a general scheme of courses. Furthermore, there are signs that the college demand for separate courses in botany and zoölogy is weakening, and several important steps have been taken towards recognizing for college admission a course involving both plants and animals.

As a compromise with the present college requirements, advanced elective courses in zoölogy and in botany in the A Second Course as a Compromise. fourth year will provide for those *few* pupils who wish to offer these sciences for college admission. This arrangement will provide, also, for those whose interest may lead them to more study of the life-sciences than was given in the general introductory course. A plan similar to this has recently been adopted for the public high schools of Greater New York ; a course in biology (botany, zoölogy, and human physiology) in the first year for all pupils may in the fourth year be supplemented by an elective course presenting botany and zoölogy as separate subjects.

The conclusion of our inquiry concerning the amount of time which should be assigned to biological science is (1) that it should be one in four years of science courses in biology, geography, physics, and chem- **Summary.** istry, and (2) that both the animal and plant phases should have representation in this course. Again it should be emphasized that these conclusions apply to the general conditions in secondary schools, and that such an arrangement suited to the great majority of pupils is not at all opposed to advanced elective courses in botany and zoölogy as separate subjects. These may be taken after the general introductory course in biology, if it is desired to allow more than four sciences, or encourage specialization in one science at the price of omission of others.

2. Position of the Biological in Relation to other Sciences.

Reviewing the leading views and most common practice, we find that there is a wide difference of opinion as to whether biology should come early or late in the high- **Biology in** school curriculum; or in other words, whether it **Early or Late** **Years of the** should precede or follow the other sciences. In **Curriculum.** favor of one of the two earlier years is the present practice in a large number of high schools and the recommendation of several important committees, particularly at the 1899 meeting of the National Educational Association. On the other hand, there is much in the nature of the subject-matter which makes it desirable for the pupils of the later years of the high school. It has often been advocated that the physical sciences should precede the biological for the reason that the latter, especially in the physiological phase, deal considerably with principles of chemistry and physics; but in discussing the position of human physiology in the high school (Chapter XII.) it is pointed out that so far as secondary work is concerned only the simplest principles of the physical sciences are needed and that these can be taught in connection with the biological course. It follows that the sequence of the biological and physiological sciences in the secondary school cannot be determined upon the basis of considerations regarding correlations of subject-matter.

The chief argument which has been advanced for zoölogy in the earlier years of the high-school course is the claim that the

Interest of Pupils in Early Years. younger pupils have more interest in the study of animals. This, I am convinced, involves a question of the kind of work. We must remember that the argument for this position of zoölogy has come forward in these later years when natural history has become a prominent part of the high-school work. That interest in this line comes early is the main thesis in Chapter IV.; and there is no doubt about the advisability of placing a course consisting largely of natural history in the first year of the high school rather than in a late year.

But in discussions in Chapters II. and IV. we see reasons for regarding natural history as inadequate in itself for high-school

Third or Fourth Years for Zoölogy as a Science. study of animals. The essential question, then, is concerning the position of a course in the general science of zoölogy which is defended in Chapter II. It is reasonable to expect that interest in principles will be greater on the part of pupils of the later years, and certainly the work leading to the principles is difficult enough to demand all the attention of the older pupils. For these reasons the writer favors the third or fourth years for a course in the science of zoölogy, or for a course in the principles of biology such as is advocated in the preceding section of this chapter.

But if local conditions make it impossible to place zoölogy, or biology, in one of the last two years of the high school, then

First Year, if Necessary. I should still advocate the same kind of a course for even the first year. Of course, it would necessarily be modified in the direction of greater simplicity, but I should aim to teach essentially the same general ideas of the science. The line of work covered in the outline given in Chapter VIII. is in my opinion best adapted to third or fourth year pupils, but in its essentials the writer has in actual experience found it more satisfactory for average first year pupils than work limited to natural history.

By way of summary of statements made in this and incidentally in earlier chapters, I wish to say that from my present point of view the most satisfactory arrangement of biology in schools below college would include (1) nature-study, presenting natural history of common animals, in the elementary school; (2) a year's course in physiology — drawing materials from animals and plants and with special application to the human body — in the eighth grade when some simple laboratory facilities are available, otherwise in the first year of the high school; and (3) finally a year course in the principles of general biology in the third or fourth year of the high school. This, in brief, is the general scope and arrangement of the biological work which I consider adapted to the needs of the majority of schools and pupils.

CHAPTER VI

THE BEGINNING WORK IN ZOÖLOGY

IN a previous discussion of the aims of zoölogical teaching in secondary schools, emphasis has been given those relating to scientific discipline and to knowledge of the great principles of the science of zoölogy. Satisfactory fulfilment of these aims depends, I believe, in no small measure upon the start which pupils are given in their zoölogical studies. This opinion leads me to give prominence to a discussion of the beginning work; and in this chapter it will be considered under the following topics :

Importance of the Beginning Work.

(1) The place of natural history in beginning work, (2) the introduction to physiological study, (3) unicellular and multicellular animals as introductory types, and (4) introduction to zoölogical principles by the study of one animal from the points of view of general zoölogy. · ·

1. Natural History in beginning Zoölogy.[1]

"The study of natural history [*i. e.*, zoölogy] should begin, as it does naturally begin, in childhood, and as it began long before there was any exact zoölogy, with the observation of animal life in its familiar forms." In these words the author of the charming *Study of Animal Life*, Professor J. Arthur Thomson, of Edinburgh, has expressed a general opinion of naturalist teachers. Few, indeed, are they who deny that the first study of animal life should be a study of living animals along the lines of natural history. It has been stated that the ecological aspect, the

Natural Interest in Animal Life.

---

[1] Here, as elsewhere, the phrase natural history is used, in the absence of a more precise term, to indicate a general superficial survey of animals for the sake of interest and acquaintance.

central feature of natural history, is to the young mind the most interesting side of animal life. Children have much interest in haunts and habits and life-histories and activities, but very little in structure except as it evidently relates to the life of animals. Recognition of this has led teachers to the view that the study of the science of zoölogy should begin along these lines of natural interest, for " a circuitous course of study, followed with natural eagerness, will lead to better results than the most logical of programmes if that take no root in the life of the student." [1]

The general recognition that natural history interests the average young pupil has within recent years brought about the prominence of the study of living animals in secondary schools. But without reference to the movement towards limiting all high-school zoölogy to the natural history (which is discussed in Chapter II.), we must here note that the latter has an important relation to beginning work. Recommendations to begin the study of zoölogy with this aspect of animals are now common in text-books and reports of committees; and I believe it is true that in the great majority of high schools the beginning work in zoölogy is at present natural history.

Under the existing conditions beginning the high-school work with natural history meets the needs of the pupils, for the reason that in the as yet incomplete state of development of nature-study in the elementary schools a large proportion of the pupils entering **Relation to Nature-Study.** high school are ignorant concerning the natural history and even the very existence of many common animals. So long as this situation remains unchanged it seems advisable that the first weeks in every elementary course of zoölogy in secondary schools should be devoted to the study of common living animals in the natural-history aspect. However, when nature-study becomes more firmly established in the elementary school, it will then be profitable to proceed directly in the high school with the study of zoölogy as a science, incidentally

---

[1] From Thomson's *Study of Animal Life*, 3d edition, p. 361.

introducing natural history when opportunity offers. The present recognition of natural history in the beginning of the high-school course may, then, be regarded as a temporary compromise which will become unnecessary, because the introduction to animals will come to be made through the nature-studies of the elementary school.

In Chapter II. it has been urged that there are important facts and principles in each phase of the science which should

Beginning Work in Science of Zoölogy.

be presented in their natural relations, and that this representation of the general field constitutes a course in the science of zoölogy in the strict sense. It is with the beginning work of such a course that we are primarily concerned here, and to a consideration of the problems involved in introducing the principles of the various phases of the science we may now turn.

2. Introduction to Physiological Study.

The first problem which demands attention is that of combining work in morphology and physiology. It has been

Correlation between Morphology and Physiology.

stated in a general way that morphology and physiology should be closely related throughout the course of zoölogy, introducing the principles of physiology with the first animal which is studied morphologically and later applying the principles to other animals so as to make the study comparative. It will now be of interest to consider in some detail the nature of the physiological facts to be taught in the introductory work and the methods of presentation.

Every text-book of zoölogy for secondary schools which has touched upon physiological principles has failed to begin at

Physiological Principles in Text-books of Zoölogy.

the basis of physiology. Many of the authors appear to have assumed that pupils intuitively understand such processes as digestion, respiration, excretion, etc. ; and without definition these terms are used freely. Thus, without explanation one book informs the beginner that "the kidneys are the excretory organs of the toad," and similar examples may easily be found. Now the truth is that even the majority of pupils who have studied "human physiology" in four or five years in elementary schools have no scientific conception of the essential meaning of even such a process as digestion, not to mention the more difficult excretion, respiration, and assimilation. The majority of pupils entering high school would define digestion as a process of preparing food "for nourishing the body," which is quite true, but hardly a strictly accurate scientific definition. It is necessary, then, that the essential principles of physiology should bē clearly presented at the beginning of the high-school zoölogy; and we may not assume that the pupils have brought from the elementary school any accurate knowledge of physiological principles and processes.

In teaching principles of physiology in connection with zoölogy, teachers should guard against the loose expressions which unfortunately have been allowed to creep into many elementary books on "human physiology." We are all familiar with unscientific explanations, such as, "Food and blood are needed to keep the body alive." There are many such phrases which even some authors of recent elementary text-books of zoölogy for high schools have been guilty of using; for example : "The lungs purify the blood"; "Digestion prepares the food to nourish the body"; "The veins carry impure blood"; "The kidneys remove the waste." These are not uncommon statements which are apt to be misleading — at any rate, they are scientifically inaccurate. In my opinion, the terms "purify," "pure," and "impure" should not be used even in elementary physiology. There can be no such thing as "pure" blood in the sense in which it is applied to blood returning from the lungs, for the "purification" in external respiration is at best only a change in the relative proportions of carbon dioxide and oxygen. According to recent treatises venous blood contains forty-six volumes of carbon dioxide in one hundred of blood, and arterial blood contains forty — only six lost in the circulation through the lungs. Similarly, arterial blood contains about twenty of oxygen, and venous blood from eight to twelve. Clearly the terms " pure," " impure," and " purify " are very misleading as applied to the gaseous contents of the blood. Moreover, blood which is relatively " pure " with reference to oxygen and carbon dioxide may be very " impure " with reference to nitrogenous wastes. It is evident that such terms would better be avoided altogether. Animal physiology in the high school should be expressed in accurate terms, as has long been the practice in elementary morphology.

And now with regard to beginning at the basis of physiology, I would refer the teacher to the chapters on " Why we eat and breathe," " Nutrition," and " Foods " (Chapters VIII., IX., and X., revised edition, 1898) in Martin's *Human Body, Briefer Course*.[1] It has been my practice to introduce my secondary-school class in zoölogy to the essentials of animal physiology by applying to the first animal studied morphologically the logical development of physiological principles which in Martin's text-book refer specifically to the physiology of man. The outline of a course in zoölogy in Chapter VIII. of this volume suggests the introduction to general principles of physiology as illustrated by the crayfish or frog. The same topics developed in connection with the morphological study of any other animal would give the same conception of the fundamental physiological processes involved in the animal machine.

Introduction to Essentials of Physiology.

The first formal consideration of animal physiology necessarily comes after a general summary of the structure, as indicated in the outline of a course in zoölogy in Chapter VIII. However, the study of function and structure should be kept closely correlated, as suggested in the discussion of the value of physiology as a phase of zoölogy (in Chapter II.).

Study of Structure and Function Correlated.

---

[1] The contents of these chapters are essentially similar in the older editions.

3. Protozoa and Metazoa as Introductory Types.

One of the most fundamental questions concerning the beginning work in elementary zoölogy relates to the selection of the animal type for the introductory study, for A Fundamental Question. upon whether a protozoan or a metazoan be chosen depends the nature of the entire course. It will therefore be of interest in this connection to examine the evidence on both sides of this much discussed question regarding the value of unicellular versus multicellular animals as types for the introductory study of zoölogy. Shall a course in elementary zoölogy be synthetical, beginning with unicellular animals and then progressing towards the more and more complex forms, or shall the study be analytical, and beginning with a complex multicellular animal, lead down the scale of structural and functional complexity to the simplest forms? In a purely natural-history course this is a relatively unimportant problem, which may well be neglected altogether; but it has great significance in its relation to the teaching of the fundamental principles of morphology and physiology.

The arguments in favor of beginning with the Protozoa are based chiefly on the position of these animals in systematic and synthetic morphology and physiology. The Protozoa in Synthetic Zoölogy. development of the cell-theory has led both morphologists and physiologists to centre their work in the cell as the synthetic basis, and we find in all recent treatises that the cell is regarded as the starting-point for all discussions of morphological and physiological problems. This applies not only to considerations of structure, functions, or development of higher forms, but the one-celled animals have come to hold a prominent place as the foundation for synthetic studies of animals in general; and from studies of these simple forms we pass to the more and more complex types.

It has been frequently stated that the order from simple to complex in the development of structural complexity in the animal series — the so-called "logical order" — should be followed in teaching elementary zoölogy, for the reason that "it Logical Order is best for teaching evolution" and "gives the and Evolution. principal data for the classification of animals." This, in the opinion of the writer, is a decidedly fallacious assumption. The stages in increasing complexity from the protozoans to the vertebrates do not necessarily teach relationship between the animals in that series. In the case of the usual series of types with isolated representatives of the great groups, the advance of structural complexity in Amœba, Hydra, earthworm, crayfish, etc., gives no criterion of relationships or line of derivation in this series, for their differences are so great that to a beginner in zoölogy they necessarily stand as *absolutely independent* types of animal forms. This has been exactly the experience of naturalists in the development of the evolution idea. Cuvier and many other early zoölogists were certainly familiar with types of all the great groups and must have recognized the ascending series in structural complexity, and yet the facts were not interpreted by them as meaning relationship and evolution. Likewise, Darwin was doubtless familiar with the structure of the phyletic types from Amœba to man long before studies of limited groups of closely related higher forms gave him the first suggestions of his evolution theories.[1] Again, all the great books which deal with the question of the truth of organic evolution, as distinguished from the factors, place little weight upon the supposed relationships of the various phyla, for the reason that the affinities in most cases are still more or less debatable and obscure. But within any given phylum the similarities of structure and therefore the suggestion of relationship are abundant and convincing, and these are the facts with which evolutionists support the theory. Comparative anatomy, the great support of the evolution theory, does not derive its most convincing

---

[1] See accounts of Darwin's observations on animals (chiefly vertebrates) of Galapagos Islands in his *Origin of Species*, *Journal of Researches*, and biographical works cited in chapter on "Zoölogical Books."

facts from comparisons of isolated types of different phyla. Who can point out to a young beginner in zoölogy convincing evidences of relationship between Amœba and Hydra, or Hydra and earthworm, or even earthworm and crayfish, not to mention the great chasm of structural difference which separates the existing vertebrates from all known types of invertebrates? On the other hand, the study of the comparative anatomy of a half-dozen selected arthropods or vertebrates leads one irresistibly to the idea of relationships and evolution. Clearly, the logical and synthetic order is not the best, or even a good one, for teaching the evolution idea. Comparison of a half-dozen insects, or decapods, or skeletons of vertebrates, will convey more and better evolutionary ideas than any study of a series of types of phyla can possibly do. We must, therefore, reject the view that the " logical order " of study from Protozoa to vertebrates is necessary, or even very useful, for teaching the principles of evolution.

A serious objection to a protozoan as an introductory type upon which the fundamental principles of morphology and physiology are to be based arises from the great difficulties which confront the beginner with the **Difficulty with Microscope.** compound microscope. By the use of the microscope I refer not merely to the mechanical manipulations in which very many pupils do not soon become expert enough for satisfactory work, but especially to accurate interpretation — a far more difficult thing for almost all beginners. As a direct result of the difficulties arising from the use of the microscope at the outset, it usually happens that very few pupils in a large class get any adequate conception of the first animals studied if they are exclusively microscopic. The writer has seen a class of forty pupils reciting about an Amœba which, owing to the difficulties of the beginning microscopic work, very few members of the class had been able to study as long as thirty minutes in a preceding two-hour session in the laboratory. Yet upon such unsatisfactory practical work it was attempted to base a discussion of the cell, protoplasm, processes of nutrition, and similar fundamental principles. Every college teacher knows that this is not an uncommon case, for dozens of pupils come to college with certificates of having completed high-school courses in zoölogy in which the Amœba remained unseen except in pictures and prepared slides. The absurdity of the situation is evident to every one who values careful and *thorough laboratory study as a basis for all general considerations.* Contrast the results in training in scientific method and in the information value of such introductory work on a protozoan with those from work on any larger animal which does not require the constant use of the microscope and from which any pupil in a large class may, with proper directions from the teacher, get definite and accurate results upon which considerations of general principles are later to be based.

But in defence of beginning with the microscope, it is often urged that " the pupil must learn to use the instrument some time and this might as well be done at the beginning." This sounds reasonable in theory, but the writer ventures to think that the elusive Amœba or an agile Paramœcium are not the best objects for practice. On the contrary, both the mechanical manipulation and the more difficult interpretations of the microscopic image are facilitated by learning to use the instrument through occasional practice while studying the gross structure of a multicellular animal of considerable size. Moreover, as already suggested, such an introduction to zoölogical principles and methods obviates the waste of time, discouragement, and bad training in methods of scientific study which a large percentage of pupils inevitably receive when the beginning depends entirely upon work with the compound microscope.

The advantages of beginning the study of structure with an animal about which the pupil knows something, or at least can Huxley's Experience. learn with the aid of no more uncommon apparatus than the eyes, were well stated by Huxley many years ago, after he had learned by experience the great disadvantages connected with beginning zoölogical study with a microscopic animal. In the first edition of the *Practical Biology* by Huxley and Martin the first lesson was on a one-celled animal and the last on the frog. The revised edition published many years later reversed this order, and in the preface Huxley stated that experience had taught him that the higher animals are really less difficult for beginners in zoölogy. Many teachers in colleges have since expressed agreement with this opinion of Huxley, and there appears to be a marked tendency towards widespread adoption of this order of study. Among elementary guides for college work Huxley and Martin's *Practical Biology* (revised edition), Sedgwick and Wilson's *General Biology* (1886, 1895), Parker and Parker's *Practical Zoölogy* (1900), Pratt's *Invertebrate Zoölogy* (1901) are examples of those which introduce the zoölogical study by means of higher animals.

With reference to elementary zoölogy in the secondary school where the pupils are undeveloped, the arguments advanced by Huxley and his followers are of greater weight than when applied to college work. Pupils encounter few serious difficulties in an introductory study of the important points of structure in a complex animal. The general relations and the essential structure of organs are in the very beginning readily determined and comprehended by very young pupils. The supposed difficulties arise largely when detailed study is attempted. The same arguments hold good from the physiological point of view. Every pupil knows something about the functions of his own body, and it is easy to grasp the fundamental principles of physiology when directly applied to organs of an animal in which there is considerable physiological division of labor. It is evident that this must be a decided gain compared with beginning physiology with an unicellular animal where all functions must be thought of abstractly in connection with a single cell. Beginning with the physiology of a multicellular animal, and considering a series of simpler forms which lead

Beginning with a Complex Animal in High School.

down the scale in the division of labor, the pupil can understand every step of the way, and in the end will have a clearer idea of the functions of both one- and many-celled forms in their relation to the great principles of physiological division of labor.

Both the morphological and the physiological arguments in favor of the multicellular animal are often based upon the **Pupils'** pupils' supposed knowledge of at least the human **Familiarity** body as a familiar type of higher animal. Against **with Higher** this it has often been urged that ordinary pupils **Forms.** are not in reality familiar in a scientific sense with any higher form; but this is far from true in these days when the vast majority of children in the elementary schools are taught "human physiology" and an increasingly large number are working at nature-study. Even some authors who have stated that high-school pupils are unfamiliar with higher forms have allowed inconsistency in their practice to support the opposing view, for in introductory lessons on Protozoa we find these questions: " Has the Amœba a stomach? " and " Is there evidence that Paramœcium can breathe? " Obviously such questions are of significance only on the assumption that pupils are more than ordinarily familiar with higher forms, for only some knowledge of the essentials of the physiological processes of respiration would give the pupil light on the question of breathing in the Paramœcium.

Again, another author has defended the " logical sequence " of his book by the statement[1] that " every one is more familiar — by sight, at least — with the frog than with the Amœba. The structure of the former resembles that of the human body far more than does that of the latter. But how many students have even the most general knowledge of human anatomy? They know, to be sure, that the body contains a heart, lungs, stomach, etc., but in the great majority of cases would fail to locate or, if shown them, even to recognize these organs.

---

[1] Preface to Dodge's *Practical Biology.*

Again, how many students, if called upon to do so, could tell more about the frog than that it usually lives in water, is greenish in color, has four legs, a mouth, etc., and can jump and swim? Whether or not the frog has a tail is usually a question for discussion. As a matter of fact, beginning students have no more real knowledge of the higher than of the lower forms." But in the light of this statement of the author's viewpoint we find difficulty in understanding the questions in the *first* lesson, which is on some Protozoa. Here are typical examples: "Can you find any organ corresponding to a heart? Stomach? Lungs or gills? Brain? Are nerves visible? How do they digest their food? Breathe?" We may comment by asking, How can any of the above questions be of significance to a beginner if pupils "fail to locate, or, if shown them, to recognize these organs" in a frog or other higher form? What can any such questions mean to one who has "no real knowledge of higher forms"? Obviously such inconsistency in practice offers no support for the contention that young pupils are unfamiliar with the higher animals.

The conclusion of our inquiry must be that so far as the work of secondary schools is concerned there is very little in favor of introducing the course in elementary zoölogy by the study of a unicellular animal, while there is much in favor of beginning with the study of the multicellular form. The simplest animals appear to be, after all, both morphologically and physiologically the most complex from the young beginner's standpoint. More than this, almost everything which is supposed to argue for a logical and synthetical order of study depends upon generalizations which are not appreciated by the average high-school pupil.

The More Complex Animals Simplest for Beginners.

The experience of large numbers of teachers seems to support strongly such conclusions, and recent books for secondary schools are decidedly in favor of this position. Thus Kingsley's *Comparative Zoölogy*, Harvey's *Introduction to Zoölogy*, French's *Animal Activities* and Colton's new *Zoölogy* all begin with the study of arthropods or

Recent Text-books.

vertebrates. The only exceptions since the publication of Needham's *Elements of Zoölogy* in 1895 is that of the laboratory manual *Studies of Animal Life* by Walter, Whitney, and Lucas (1900) and that by Weed and Crossman (1902) both of which follow the so-called logical series from Amœba to mammals.

4. Introduction to Zoölogical Principles.

The final proposition which I wish to discuss with reference to the beginning work is that the principles of all the various phases of zoölogy should be introduced early in the course with the study of some animal type from the point of view of general zoölogy. This is the method which Huxley so successfully employed in his now classical *The Crayfish as an Introduction to the Study of Zoölogy* (1879), in the preface of which occurs this statement of the aim of the book : —

Huxley's Method.

" I have desired, in fact, to show how the careful study of one of the commonest and most insignificant of animals, leads us, step by step, from every-day knowledge to the widest generalizations and the most difficult problems of zoölogy ; and, indeed, of biological science in general."

The success of this method of Huxley is sufficient defence of its value. Sedgwick and Wilson in their *General Biology* have followed the same plan applied to the earthworm as an introduction to zoölogical principles and methods of study ; and recently T. Jeffrey Parker and W. N. Parker, pupils of Huxley, have done the same in their *Elementary Course of Practical Zoölogy,* using the frog as their introductory type. These books have been favorably received in college work ; but they are far too advanced and technical for elementary pupils in a secondary school.

Other Applications of the Method.

Directly applying the method of Huxley,[1] the central idea of

---

[1] I follow here almost the exact words which I used in explaining the point of view of the Outline of the Course in Zoölogy in Horace Mann

the course in elementary zoölogy which is outlined in this book (Chapter VIII.), is that of an introductory study of a complex animal examined from the several viewpoints of zoölogy. Such a study includes important facts of anatomy, histology, embryology, classification in connection with the near allies of the introductory type, distribution, general fundamental principles of physiology and ecology touching upon habits of life and life-history. It may be necessary to remind the reader that *this is not to be misunderstood as meaning that any one of these phases of study should go far into details.* The question, What is essential for liberal education? should be strictly applied in eliminating all that has no good reason for inclusion in the course. The writer's interpretation of what may be considered valuable in this connection will be best represented by the detailed outline of such an introductory study of one animal which is given in Chapter VIII.

Such introductory study as has been suggested can be completed within the first five or six weeks of a half-year course, leaving ten or eleven weeks in which to examine types of various groups of the animal kingdom. This will be criticised on the ground that it gives too much attention to a single animal; but it will appear in the outline in Chapter VIII. that most of this time is devoted to zoölogical principles capable of wide application, and which are illustrated by the careful study of a single animal. After pupils once grasp these principles, application to any animals which are studied later is easily and quickly made. In other words, this method of introducing the study is designed to give pupils general ideas of the structure and activities of one animal which will aid in appreciating and interpreting any other animal. It is also intended to give intensive study of the fundamental principles of anatomy and physiology, and training in the methods of biological

Relation of Introduction to Later Study.

High School, in *Teachers College Record*, Vol. II. January, 1901. Pp. 14, 15.

23

study, and thus lay a foundation for later study of other animals representing important groups.   In short, the general aim is to lay a foundation which will make later study of animals, from whatever standpoint, more interesting and more intelligible, because there is included in the foundation work those great principles of animal structure and function which are of wide interest and application.

The writer is convinced that the broad view of a single animal and of some of the principles of zoölogy, gained from **Influence on Viewpoint of Pupils.** the introductory study along the lines suggested above, exerts a marked influence on all subsequent study of animals.   Pupils with such preliminary training may be required later to study some animals from a limited point of view, for example, ecology or morphology, but their general ideas of one animal from the various points of view lead them to think of all animals as presenting illustrations of the various aspects of zoölogy.   They will have that wide outlook upon animal life which has been called "zoölogical perspective."   Experience has demonstrated that interest is not lost by such extended introductory work.   On the contrary, the pupils, as a rule, are eager to study every animal brought into the course as thoroughly as the introductory type was studied — that is, from the various aspects of zoölogy.   Although time will obviously not allow such extensive study of more than one form, there is certainly great value in such an attitude of mind with its broad outlook and interest in the various phases of animal life.

In conclusion, it is claimed that upon a broad introductory study of one multicellular animal it is possible to base a course **Conclusion.** which combines the most valuable features of the various courses usually presented in secondary schools, and that it is possible at the same time to give as good training in scientific observing and thinking as can be done with any other plan.   Moreover, such a course gives a view of animals and animal life which is broader and more valuable from the standpoint of liberal education than that given by the ordinary courses which are limited to the view-points of either natural history or morphology, for it includes the fundamental principles of physiology in the natural relations with morphology and ecology, the importance of which relation has been discussed elsewhere.

It is not to be claimed that pupils who follow such a course will know much about the details of comparative anatomy in a series of animals, or understand the intricacies of physiological processes, or that they store up a mass of facts from natural history; but from the standpoint of liberal secondary education stores of zoölogical facts are not needed so much as broad general ideas, and an acquaintance with and interest in animals and their life.

General Ideas, not the Details.

CHAPTER VII

THE SELECTION OF ANIMAL TYPES FOR A LABORA-TORY COURSE IN ZOÖLOGY

THERE seems to be no question that an elementary course in zoölogy in a secondary school should be based upon and con-

Value of Types.

sist largely of the study of a series of types or examples representing the most important groups of animals.[1] No other plan is adaptable to the modern labora-tory method of teaching the principles of the science; and concentration of attention upon a limited number of forms un-doubtedly results in the most satisfactory training in the method of scientific study. Even from the standpoint of the acquisi-tion of information the type method has great advantages over the alternative plan of dealing in generalized comparative terms with characteristics of a group of animals with most of which the students must be entirely unfamiliar.

1. Types for the Introductory Work.

The problems relating to the selection of types upon which to base the course in zoölogy are closely involved with ques-tions concerning the order in which the examples are to be presented; hence it will be most convenient to give some at-tention first to the order of study.

In recent years there has been among teachers of zoölogy much discussion concerning the order of study of the animal

Order of the Animal Phyla.

types representing the great phyla. It was but natural that there should have been until recently an almost universal tendency to follow the order — Protozoa, Cœlenterata, worms, Arthropoda, Molluska, Ver-tebrata, for that is the one given in the modern systematic

---

[1] Special references: Huxley, essay On the Study of Biology, *Science and Education Essays*, p. 285; Harvey, *High School Bulletin*, No. 17, Uni-

treatises on zoölogy. But experience in teaching has called attention to various pedagogical and practical considerations which are now leading to wide departure from the systematic order from simplest to most complex. Accepting the conclusion in the preceding chapter that multicellular animals have advantages as types for introductory study, it remains to select the multicellular types which will best serve for the introduction to the general principles of the various phases of zoölogy according to the method of Huxley, as advocated in the last section of the preceding chapter.

It is not easy to decide between representatives of a half-dozen metazoan phyla. If we reject the protozoan as an introductory type, there is no good zoölogical reason for passing to the opposite extreme to a complex vertebrate and then passing backward along the series followed by the zoölogical treatises. A student will appreciate the relative complexity, the similarities and differences of an earthworm, a crayfish, or a frog without regard to the order of first study. Moreover, the order of study has no necessary significance in relation to developing ideas of the evolution of the metazoan phyla for the reason that to a beginning student the differences are so great that the phyla seem to stand isolated. Even granting that affinities between phyla can be demonstrated to the young beginner, then the worm, the arthropod, the mollusk, and the vertebrate are to be treated as diverging branches of the same tree, not as steps in a ladder; and until all four types are known, relationships cannot be clearly understood. What matters, then, whether the order of study be worm, arthropod, vertebrate; or vertebrate, arthropod, worm; or even arthropod, worm, vertebrate? Clearly it is not possible upon the basis of zoölogical facts alone to reach any decision as to the order of study of metazoan animals. Practical and pedagogical rather than zoölogical considerations must influence the selection of an introductory

Selection of Introductory Type.

---

versity of State of New York; Parker and Haswell, *Text-book of Zoölogy*, Preface to Vol. I.

type, and from this point of view we shall examine several animals which have claims to favor.

The Crayfish. — In the outline of a course in zoölogy which is presented in the following chapter the crayfish is treated as an introductory type. This selection was made after a consideration of the merits of six animals, — namely, mammal, frog, fish, crayfish, grasshopper, and earthworm, — which appear available and desirable for introducing a course which is to include the general principles of zoölogy. After starting secondary-school classes with four of these forms, the writer has come to believe that the crayfish has some decided advantages as a type with which to begin the practical study of animals and upon which to base many important general principles.

First, beginning pupils have less aversion to handling the crayfish than in the case of any of the other forms, except Its Favorable Points. the insect. Teachers will recognize that this is an important point, for the first impressions often influence the pupil's attitude toward a subject. Second, the external structure of the crayfish and its allies is very favorable for teaching principles of homology, classification, and adaptation to functions. In these respects it is not possible to begin with a better animal. There is still another great advantage in that the crayfish can be readily obtained in most places outside of New England, and is found in the markets of the cities. Moreover, the lobster may be substituted without modification of the outline. Finally, with regard to internal structure, the crayfish is easier to dissect than any of the other forms mentioned above, and the general plan of the organs is easily understood even by very young pupils. The internal organs are comparatively simple, and yet there is well-developed physiological division of labor. On this point the complexity of the crustacean not being so great as in the case of any vertebrate, it is easier for the pupil to gain a clear idea of the essential nature of the workings of organs as related to the life of the body as a whole ; and hence the crayfish is especially favorable as affording a basis for introduction to the essential principles of animal physiology.

The Mammal. — There is a small minority of teachers who advocate some common mammal — such as rat, rabbit, or cat — as an introductory type, for the reason that in structure and function it so closely resembles the human body. But there are weighty reasons against this.

Similar to Human Body.

So far as some classes of boys are concerned, the pupils have little or no aversion to dissection of mammals; but the teaching of zoölogy is not limited to the teaching of boys who take kindly to dissections of mammals, and the natural repulsion of the majority of beginning students makes it imperative that the dissection of a mammal be omitted in spite of its claims to favor because of its similarity to the human body. There are many professioual zoölogists who will sympathize with the position here taken, because in their own experience they have found mammalian dissection a disagreeable task.

Pupils' Aversion to Dissection.

Aside from the foregoing objections to a study of a mammal in the beginning work of the laboratory, the great complexity of its anatomy and correspondingly extreme physiological division of labor are certainly serious reasons which should militate against beginning the study of zoölogy with such a difficult type. Certainly from such an introduction the average beginner will not get a clear conception of the *essential* physiological processes.

Complexity of Structure and Functions.

With regard to the argument that the mammal admits of direct comparisons with the human body, it may be said that many teachers find a great gain in beginning study with some animal not very like the human body, and this for the reason that most pupils have derived many great misconceptions from the so-called " physiology " taught in the grammar school. It is far better to take a fresh start with such an animal as the crayfish which does not recall anything except essential general facts about the human body. For example, the respiration of the cray-

Comparison with Human Body.

fish will recall only the essentials of that process in the human body, and the relatively less important details of the mechanism of respiration being so dissimilar will not invite comparisons. Hence the attention will be concentrated upon essential facts.

The Frog. — The objections to the mammals do not in the experience of many teachers apply to the frog, which resem-

Frog more Favorable than Mammal. bles the mammalian body closely enough for the illustration of the general principles of structure and function which should be involved in high-school work. Beginning pupils under the control of a tactful teacher will not be averse to a study of the frog, provided that the material is in good condition. Availability of material, or the possibility of closer comparisons with the human body, may lead many teachers to prefer the frog to the crayfish as an introductory type, and provision has been made for this in the outline following this chapter. While I prefer the crayfish for the beginning study, and the frog for the last laboratory work of the course, experience has convinced me that quite as good general results have been obtained in classes which began with the frog. In case it is decided not to study the internal structure of more than one animal, then it is beyond question that the frog is the most favorable type.

The Earthworm. — This animal has been made the basis of the introduction to zoölogy in Sedgwick and Wilson's

Not a Favorable Type. *General Biology,* and well serves this purpose in college work. But experience has taught that it is not well adapted to high-school zoölogy. Beginners are not uncommonly averse to working with a " worm," and it is not easy to dissect so as to bring out clearly the chief organs. Except in favorable localities, there is difficulty in getting specimens large enough for satisfactory dissection, and unlike the frog and crayfish it is not to be obtained from provision markets. All these are objections to its selection for introductory work upon which a course is to be based, and in the absence of any important points of merit we must reject the earthworm as not well adapted to our purposes in the beginning work in zoölogy.

The Insect. — For introductory work which is to illustrate the general principles of zoölogy the insects are unsatisfactory for the reason that they are extremely specialized. Also, their small size makes a satisfactory study of the internal anatomy impossible for young beginners.

But the insects are especially valuable for introductory studies in natural history, which, as suggested in the chapter on the " Beginning Work," should at times precede the study of general principles of zoölogy. When- Place of Insects in the Course. ever it is desirable to begin the high-school zoölogy with natural history of some common animals, the wealth and variety of insect life at the beginning of the school year in September makes these animals the most desirable for such study. Two or three weeks of natural history, including field work, will prepare for the introduction to the general principles of zoölogy as illustrated by a careful study of some more favorable type, such as the crayfish (or frog).

It is clear from the foregoing considerations that the crayfish (or as a second choice the frog) appears best adapted to purposes of beginning work in the principles of zoölogy, as outlined in preceding chapters. The Summary. Crayfish or Frog Best Introductory Types. one feature of the outline (Chapter VIII.) for introductory work which I wish to emphasize as important is that whatever multicellular animal be chosen as the first type it should be studied in such a way as to make the work an introduction both to the general methods of zoölogical study and to the essential principles of animal structure, function, and relations. It is admitted that by efficient teachers such results might be obtained from the study of any one of many common animals ; but, as has been indicated above, certain types are especially favorable for the beginning work of secondary-school classes.

We must now make a survey of the various phyla in order
Supplemental   to select representatives which are to be studied
Types.   after the introductory type, thus broadening the
pupils' acquaintance with animals and extending the application of principles learned from the first animals studied.

2. Other Animals available for Laboratory Study.

Improved methods for preservation of animals for study in
the laboratory and the establishment of numerous dealers in
Use of Pre-   zoölogical materials have rendered available for
served For-   class study many animals which are obtainable
eign Animals
instead of   only in limited localities. This method of obtain-
Local Living
Forms.   ing material has great advantages from the standpoint of college work in morphology, but it has great dangers
for secondary schools. In the first place, material from dealers
is usually preserved and therefore of value only for morphological work; and, as we have seen, such special one-sided
study is not to be recommended for the secondary school.
A second danger arises from the fact that the ease of purchasing materials tends towards the introduction of numerous
foreign forms to the exclusion of common local types with
which the secondary-school course should be primarily concerned. To a certain extent purchase of materials is necessary, for it is obviously impossible that the teacher should
even supervise the collection of all materials required for a
high school in a great city; and it is not against such use
of supply stations that a protest is here made, but rather
against the purchasing of preserved material when living and
fresh specimens of common forms are locally obtainable.
Particularly is this directed against excessive use of preserved
marine materials, the trade in which has become enormous,
largely because of the patronage of high schools. Marine
fishes in formaldehyde have been shipped to cities on the
lakes and rivers where minnows, perch, and other fishes are
abundant. The sandworm Nereis is commonly substituted
for the ubiquitous earthworm, marine clams for the common

fresh-water mussels, marine gastropods for pond-snails and land-snails, hydroids and sea-anemone for Hydra; and in addition starfishes, sea-urchins, sea-cucumbers, squids, and other marine forms are given time which would be more profitably spent on common land and fresh-water animals. The excessive use of marine materials tends to give pupils the impression that common animals are not worthy of zoölogical study; and such a result is greatly to be deplored. Certainly the best elementary course in zoölogy is that which makes the most efficient use of and arouses interest in common animals; and the use of foreign animal forms in an elementary course in a high school should be largely limited to that of exhibition merely for the sake of more extended acquaintance with animals. One can scarcely imagine any locality where a high school is located which is so zoölogically impoverished that abundant material for class study throughout a first course is not obtainable. It is with the selection of the common materials for a course in zoölogy that we are here concerned, and we may now make a general survey of the great groups in search of familiar types which will illustrate the fundamental principles of the science of zoölogy.

Protozoa. — The Amœba[1] and Paramœcium are beyond question the most important of the unicellular animals which are easily obtained in most localities. Upon these the laboratory work concerning protozoans should be based, and other available forms may be exhibited for the purpose of giving pupils a wider acquaintance with the world of microscopic animal life.

Cœlenterates. — If only one cœlenterate can be studied in the laboratory, Hydra should be selected as the type of the group. The sea-anemone is often substituted, **Hydra.** even in schools so far from the sea-shore that preserved specimens must be used exclusively; but the sea-

---

[1] The chapter on " Materials and Methods " contains notes on collecting and keeping animals mentioned in this chapter as types desirable for laboratory study.

anemone does not illustrate the fundamental plan of the cœlenterate body as well as does the simple Hydra. The teacher who carefully examines the chapter in Parker's *Elementary Biology* will be convinced that this animal is an excellent type of a cœlenterate, and that it also illustrates many important principles of animal morphology and physiology. The fact that it is common in fresh water and may be studied living is a great advantage, for as a living animal it always arouses interest and enthusiasm in high-school students. An objection often urged is that it is not always easily obtainable when wanted for class study, but this difficulty may usually be overcome by attention to directions for collecting and keeping the animals (see chapter on " Materials and Methods ") ; at any rate, when preserved and permanently mounted entire and in sections they are superior to preserved sea-anemones. Another objection is that the Hydra is very small ; but this is not serious, for high powers of the microscope are not necessary.

Among marine cœlenterates with which the pupils should have some acquaintance, the following are certainly the most

Marine Forms. important : sea-anemone, coral polyp, hydroid colonies, hydromedusa, a scyphomedusa, and a ctenophore. Even for schools near the sea-shore most of these are not obtainable living during the regular school-year, and materials in formaldehyde must be used for demonstrations of their structure sufficient to give pupils acquaintance with these animals.

" *Worms.*" — Adequate representation of this heterogeneous assemblage would require at least a half-dozen types, but ex-

Some Common Forms. amples of the three or four most common phyla are sufficient for the most extensive high-school course. The common earthworm will always be selected as a type of segmented worms, and acquaintance should be made also with the leech and perhaps the sandworm (Nereis). Among the flat worms, the common planarians found under stones in brooks are important. The tape-worm and the liver-fluke, which well illustrate the complex life-histories of parasitic flat worms, are unfortunately rarely available in high schools, even for demonstrations. As examples of the round worms, the common vinegar eel is always obtainable in living condition, and parasitic species are usually to be found in lungs and bladder of frogs.

Echinoderms. — There has long been a widespread delusion that a proper course in elementary zoölogy in a secondary school should include a detailed study of at least a starfish as an example of echinoderms. But aside from giving a general acquaintance with these **Their Place in High-School Zoölogy.** animals, for which very brief study is sufficient, the echinoderms must be regarded as the least important animals from the standpoint of elementary zoölogy which is to present the most essential facts and principles of the science.[1] In support of this statement we may call attention to the fact that it is not possible in elementary work to study them comparatively along the lines usually followed in the case of animals of many other phyla. Aside from the apparent radiality, there are only a few minor points in which a high-school pupil can make comparisons between the starfish and sea-urchin, and a profitable comparison between these animals and a holothurian cannot be made on the basis of the pupil's own observations. It is clear that as a training in general morphological principles, laboratory study of echinoderms must be distinctively inferior to such study as that of representatives of arthropods and vertebrates in which many comparisons leading to general principles are easily made out by the pupils. It follows that studies of the external structure of echinoderms becomes largely a study of details for their own sake. The writer has seen a large class in a high school in a great city

---

[1] This is the position of most teachers in colleges, in which echinoderms are rarely included in a beginning course in general zoölogy. An echinoderm type is not planned for in any of the following well-known introductory courses for colleges: Marshall and Hurst's *Practical Zoölogy*, Parker and Parker's *Practical Zoology*, and Huxley and Martin's *Practical Biology*.

spend a two-hour period in examining and drawing with great care the aboral surfaces of dried and distorted specimens of star-fish. The only points of the exercise which were really of general importance should have been seen in two minutes. Such detailed anatomical study of echinoderms must be regarded as relatively unimportant in high-school work, and only a very superficial study of representative echinoderms is justifiable in a secondary school when an abundance of common animals of other groups is at hand to illustrate better the great principles of zoölogy.

In accordance with the views stated above, the brief outline on page 386 is designed (1) to call attention to the fact that the echinoderms are animals; (2) to give ac-quaintance with the general form, habitat, and chief types; and (3) to give them place in the general scheme of animal classification. The examination of structural features is designed to be limited to the broad characteristics underlying the classification within the group. Of course, the possible relations of this to other phyla must remain entirely in the dark in high-school work, for the embryological evidence of such affinities is certainly out of place in an elementary course.

Suggested Work on Echinoderms.

Mollusks. — The snails and clam are for the high-school work the most useful representatives of this phylum. Pond-snails of several genera and land-snails of the genus Helix are easily obtained in most localities. These native species should not be neglected. In addition, the European edible snail (Helix pomatia) is valuable because of its large size. Then there are the common garden-slugs of the genus Limax. These types will be sufficient for the study of gastropods; and there is no excuse for purchasing marine gastropods, such as the whelks, preserved in formalin.

Common Gastropods.

As representatives of the lamellibranchs, the river mussels of the genera Unio and Anodonta are obtainable from almost any stream in the Mississippi system, and are very common elsewhere. The common marine bivalves, such as the soft-shelled clam (Mya), the quahog (Venus), and

Bivalves.

the oyster, are easily obtainable in the sea-coast cities, and may be substituted for the fresh-water forms. The little fresh-water Cyclas is another common bivalve of interest to pupils who are getting acquainted with local forms.

Finally, with regard to the cephalopods, it is not possible in secondary-school work to demonstrate clearly the molluscan characteristics of these extremely specialized forms. Practically the pupil must accept these animals as mollusks on the authority of books and the teacher. I doubt whether in a secondary school these forms deserve more attention than is necessary in order that the pupils may gain an acquaintance with them. Certainly an attempt at the dissection of the squid, as suggested in certain elementary laboratory guides, is difficult to justify. Especially is it necessary to deprecate the presentation of theoretical modifications of other mollusks which might be supposed to convert them into the cephalopod plan of structure. As an example, one outline of a high-school course advises: " One day's morphological study of the squid, to show what can be done with the molluscan plan if the shell is discarded, supplements the clam study." Such speculation is more than misleading for beginners in zoölogy; and especially so in this case, for the comparison suggests a close relationship and definite line of derivation, whereas the origin of the cephalopods is still a mystery.

Place of Cephalopods.

Vertebrates. — As a preliminary to discussing the selection of vertebrate types for study in the laboratory, it is necessary to consider the general nature of the study to be made on representatives of this group.

First, I wish to urge that the general natural history of higher vertebrates deserves more attention than is now commonly given in courses of elementary zoölogy. Time was in the days of the old natural history when text-books, following the example of Cuvier's *Animal Kingdom*, first presented mammals, and then in turn birds, lower vertebrates, and finally invertebrates; and, ex-

Value of Natural History of Vertebrates.

cepting the ever-popular insects, the backboned animals then received more attention than those of all other phyla together. But all this was changed with the substitution of zoölogy as a science for the natural history which prevailed in schools before 1875. The study of vertebrates became narrowed down to that of a few or even a single type, such as fish or frog; and high-school zoölogy became primarily invertebrate zoölogy. This change in the selection of the animals to be studied was directly the result of the change from the text-book to the laboratory method of teaching, associated with which were necessary changes in the nature of the subject-matter. The former books on natural history placed the emphasis upon external characteristics, habits of life, life-histories, classification, and economic relations — all of which aspects of zoölogy of vertebrates are certainly very important in general education; and there was practically nothing of the anatomy of internal organs. In contrast with this, the elementary teaching concerning vertebrates tended later to become almost exclusively morphological because this phase is so well adapted to the laboratory method as applied in secondary schools. As a result, general information regarding vertebrate animals came to be rarely presented to pupils. Instead they learned the general classification of the inverte-brate groups, to classify and describe even the details of structure of gastropods, rhizopods, and echinoderms; but not to distinguish between whales and fishes, bats and birds, sala-manders and lizards. They learned to recognize at sight such names as Balanoglossus, Paramœcium, and Lumbricus; but with such names as rodents, carnivora, ungulates, and marsupials there was little acquaintance. And as an extreme case, students with a fair knowledge of invertebrate types have failed in college-entrance examinations to · distinguish between the terms mammalia and amphibia. All these results are not surprising in the light of the fact that an elementary course in zoölogy which omitted even the simple classification of vertebrates has not been a rarity in our high schools.

The recent return to natural history has been working against this lack of general knowledge of the vertebrates. Current books for secondary schools, for example, those by Davenport, Kellogg, Kingsley, Jordan and Heath, and Colton, aim to give much of the desirable information. But the use of these books must be carefully considered, for their subject-matter in the lines under discussion is essentially similar to that of the old natural histories which were displaced by the adoption of the practical method of teaching. The objection which is often urged against natural-history study of vertebrates is the undoubted fact that it is not easily managed as practical work; and consequently it is usually studied, if at all, as mere reading lessons which are supplemental to the actual examination of only one or two vertebrates and these chiefly from the morphological point of view.

Present Tendencies towards Natural History.

It must be admitted that there are great difficulties in the way of placing the teaching of natural history of vertebrates upon a laboratory basis, even when numerous and large collections of living animals are accessible. However, if we turn aside to name vertebrates which are everywhere common, or specimens of which are easily kept alive in aquaria or vivaria, it will be evident that practical study of the natural history of representative vertebrates is possible without zoölogical gardens or museums. For example, we may name many different species of fishes, several species of frogs, the common toads, newts, salamanders, snakes, the lizards, several species of turtles, alligators, birds, rat or mouse, horse, dog, cat, and man. A comparative survey of the general external characteristics and life-histories of even this limited list would certainly give the students a good view of the great group of the vertebrates; and for supplementary material illustrating the less common forms preserved museum specimens and even good pictures are not to be overlooked as unimportant and unscientific.

Difficulties of Practical Work.

So far we have considered vertebrates simply for the sake

24

of general acquaintance with the general natural history of the
group. But in a well-regulated course in general
zoölogy we must present the fundamental principles
of vertebrate morphology and physiology. Rarely
in a high-school course could more than one
vertebrate type be studied as a basis for this and the type
par excellence is the common frog. A few teachers would
prefer a mammal or fish, but in considering introductory types
we have seen that the frog has so much in its favor that
evidently a study of the structure and functions and general
development of this animal forms an excellent foundation for
a general survey of the natural history of vertebrates advocated
above.

The Frog as Basis of Vertebrate Morphology and Physiology.

CHAPTER VIII

AN OUTLINE FOR AN ELEMENTARY COURSE IN ZOÖLOGY

Introduction

THE outline here presented is in spirit and general form essentially similar to that which was published in *Teachers College Record*, Vol. II., No. 1, January, 1901. From it can be selected a series of lessons adapted to varying combinations of local school conditions. Suggestions regarding such selection and combination into courses for various time-limits are given at the end of the outline (see p. 390).

The principles which were the guiding factors in the development of this outline have been discussed in the preceding chapters. In essentials they may be here summarized as follows: The aim is to give pupils the best possible scientific training along with information regarding the essential facts and ideas of zoölogy. Accordingly, the materials are chosen to illustrate the leading principles of the various phases of the science. The introduction (Division A) aims directly at some important general principles, both of fundamental facts and of the scientific method of studying animals; in short, it aims to give a viewpoint and acquaintance with methods of study which will lay a foundation for all later zoölogical study by the pupil. Then following the introduction with its emphasis upon general principles, a study of animal types (Division B) serves to extend the illustration and application of the general principles, at the same time giving acquaintance with different forms of animal life.

The outline is intended simply to be suggestive to teachers, and obviously is not in suitable form for pupils' use. It is not intended to stand for a stereotyped course of study — such would be undesirable in any science, and absolute uniformity is intolerable in that it stifles the originality of the teacher. Far from attempting to dictate a plan which is to be followed literally and constantly, this outline, on the contrary, looks towards great flexibility at the option of the teacher. ˙In short, the outline is intended simply to suggest *one* mode of presentation of the most important zoölogical topics, at the same time indicating those which seem to the writer most important for secondary education; and the chief reason for its insertion in this volume is that it illustrates concretely many points which have been discussed in the preceding chapters dealing with the general principles of zoölogical teaching. Those discussions are all essentially prefatory to this outline and explanatory of its point of view.

In the introductory study (Division A) a multicellular animal with well-marked physiological division of labor is studied from various viewpoints, such as external structure, internal structure, classification, principles of physiology, etc. In elaborating these subjects it has been the aim, not so much to include those points which are of significance only as regards animals closely allied to the one being studied, but rather to bring to the attention of the pupils those facts and principles which are widely applicable throughout the animal kingdom. The minor points cannot be left out entirely, but it rests with the teacher to *emphasize those which are of primary importance.*

DIVISION A.

General Principles of Zoölogy.

I. A Study of the Crayfish as an Introduction to the Study of Animals.[1]

I. General External Structure of the Crayfish. — (All topics preceded by an asterisk * are suitable for supplementary lec-

------

[1] As suggested under the heading "The Insect as an Introductory Type" in the preceding chapter, this study of the crayfish from the standpoint of the general principles of zoölogy may be preceded by two

tures, readings, and recitations, which should be held in close correlation with the corresponding laboratory work.)

1. General form of animal, head-thorax, abdomen, appendages. Definitions and identification of anterior, posterior, dorsal, ventral, longitudinal, and transverse. Bilateral symmetry of this and other familiar animals, such as domesticated animals and man. Segments of the abdomen. Skeleton. *Moulting. Outline drawings[1] (natural size) from dorsal, ventral, and lateral views, labelling the chief structures represented.

2. Examination of the gills. Structure of a lobster gill. Diagram showing position of gills. Currents of water through gill-chamber of living animal as shown by the movement of powdered carmine or gamboge placed near the posterior end of gill-chamber.

3. Examination of appendages and comparisons of appendages VI. to XIII. and the abdominal appendages (drawings). Arrangement of appendages with reference to the segments of the abdomen — a pair of appendages represents each segment. How many segments in the abdomen? How many in the head-thorax? *The principle of homology.[2] *Automatic amputation of appendages and regeneration. Illustrate, if possible, by specimens found regenerating.

4. Examine and compare in a general way lobster, prawn, crab, and crayfish. In tabular form and with sketches record resemblances and differences in general form of body, number and form of appendages, and number of segments. Summarize the general characteristics of decapod crustacea as seen in

---

or three weeks of natural-history studies of the insects, following suggestions for such work as given in Division B of this outline. This order of study is recommended whenever a majority of the pupils have not had the benefit of nature-study in the elementary school. The study of the crayfish is planned for twenty-five hours in recitation and laboratory work. The reasons for selecting the crayfish are given in the discussions of some animals as introductory types in the preceding chapter.

[1] For suggestions regarding outline drawings and laboratory notes, see the preceding chapter.

[2] The homologies of the first five pairs of appendages are meaningless to the young beginner.

types examined.   *Principles of classification as illustrated by crayfish and its allies.   *Scientific names of animals — nomenclature.   *Species, genera, orders, illustrated by decapod crustacea.   (Last three topics are well discussed in Huxley's *Crayfish*.)

5. Study of the living crayfish in aquarium — movements, feeding, habits of life, senses,[1] uses of the appendages, adaptations.

6. *Natural history.   Economic importance.   Distribution shown by colored map.[2]   Fossil crayfishes.

References on External Structure and Natural History:

[NOTE.] Full bibliographical references to books mentioned in connection with this outline will be found in Chapter X. The references below and on later pages may be supplemented from Chapter X., especially in the line of supplementary reading from books on natural history and those designed primarily for school use. The school-books by Davenport, Kellogg, Jordan and Kellogg, Jordan and Heath, Colton, Kingsley, Needham, Morse, and Tenney, are excellent for such supplementary materials, and should be examined by the teacher in selecting readings for the pupils in connection with the study of each group of animals. For this reason I shall, as a rule, not mention them in the following lists of books, but simply refer to other important books.

---

[1] Within the limits of this outline it is impossible to specify in detail concerning the studies of the living crayfish and other animals.   It should be mentioned that those experiments which give uncertain results are avoided, or at least great care is taken to guard against wrong conclusions.   Illustration will make this clear ; for example, in the common experiment to test for a sense of hearing in the crayfish the possibility of the reaction being produced by ordinary vibrations aside from sound waves should be explained to the pupils.   (See paper by Prentiss in the *Bulletin Museum of Comparative Zoölogy*, Harvard College, 1901.) Similarly in experiments on taste and smell it is necessary to criticise severely results obtained by the use of irritants, such as ammonia, clove oil, and other like substances, which authors of certain laboratory guides recommend.

[2] The blank outline maps of the continents and of the world which are used by teachers of geography are extremely useful for teaching geographical distribution of animals.   The areas where a particular animal is said to occur should be shaded with a colored crayon, and by using several colors the distribution of several forms, *e. g.*, lobster and crayfish, can be compared.   See map in Huxley's *The Crayfish*.

For Pupils' Reading :

Morgan's *Animal Sketches*, Chapter XX.; Huxley's *Crayfish*, first chapters.

For Teachers :

Huxley's *Crayfish*, Marshall and Hurst's *Practical Zoölogy*, Parker and Parker's *Practical Zoölogy*, Kingsley's *Comparative Zoölogy*, Pratt's *Invertebrate Zoölogy*, Herrick's *The American Lobster* (Report of the United States Fish Commission), Thomson's *Outlines of Zoology*, Parker and Haswell's *Text-book of Zoölogy*.

II. General Internal Structure of Crayfish. — 7. Study of a series of stages[1] in dissections by pupils, and of preparations showing general arrangement of the internal organs — digestive, circulatory, respiratory, excretory, muscular, nervous, and reproductive.

III. Introductory Microscopic Work and Elementary Histology.

[NOTE.] In this connection the pupils are introduced to the compound microscope. (See discussion of microscope and multicellular animals in Chapter VI.) The instrument itself is studied during one hour, the pupils being guided by oral, printed, or typewritten directions involving a description of the microscope, accompanied with a diagram on which the parts are all labelled. Pictures cut from catalogues of dealers in compound microscopes and pasted on cardboard are useful for this purpose. Printed letters pasted on glass slides, cotton fibres and hairs mounted in water under a cover-slip are useful objects for practice with the instrument.

Most of the preparations mentioned below, which require high powers, are arranged by the instructor ; and, after explanation by diagrams, the preparations are examined by the pupils, and drawings are made.

8. Examination of preparations from various organs — liver, gill, intestine, muscle. (The aim here is to give some general ideas of tissues and cells in the structure of the animal body; nothing in line of formal histology is intended. It is therefore not absolutely necessary that preparations of the

---

[1] The series of most important stages and drawings suggested in *Teachers College Record*, Vol. II., No. 1, p. 17.

crayfish should be used to illustrate the facts of cellular structure, and preparations from frog or other animals may be
substituted in this connection.)

References for Teachers :

Parker's *Biology*, Lesson 6. Parker and Parker's *Practical Zoölogy*,
Chapter VII.

IV. Elementary Embryological Study. — 9. Demonstrations of preparations of the ovary and spermary of crayfish or
other animal, illustrating the cellular nature of the germ-cells
(egg-cells and sperm-cells). Demonstration of preparations
showing male and female pronuclei approaching and uniting
in fertilization.[1] Preparations showing phases of mitosis in
first and second cleavages in any favorable egg. *Cell-division. *Cells in development and growth of animals. *All
life from life and spontaneous generation. (See Parker's
Biology, Lesson 9.)

10. Examine a crayfish, lobster, or prawn, with eggs attached to the appendages. Examine stages in the development of the crayfish or lobster.

References for Teachers :

Huxley's *Crayfish*.

*V. *General Principles of Animal Physiology as Illustrated
by the Crayfish.* — 11. Movements and the muscular work of
the body. Source of the energy thus manifested. Statement
of the law of conservation of energy, and familiar applications.
Oxidation in liberation of energy and illustrations. Foods as
sources of energy. The need of oxygen. Waste, repair, and
growth of the body.

---

[1] Fertilization and cell-division are better illustrated by preparations
from animals other than the crayfish. At various times such material as
the starfish, sea-urchin, barnacle, and mollusk eggs have been used in
this connection and found satisfactory.

In the descriptions of cytological structures and processes all details
involving the intricacies of centrosomes and chromosomes should be
avoided.

12. The stages of nutrition and the *essential* processes involved in each — digestion, absorption, circulation, assimilation, respiration, dissimilation, excretion. Special attention should be given to the idea that physiological processes are ultimately referable to the component cells of the organs; and also emphasis should be placed on the consideration of each process as related to the life of the body as a whole, that is, to general nutrition. Finally, the nervous system should be considered as a regulating and coördinating mechanism, and as a medium of communication with the world external to the body.

13. Physiological division of labor in the crayfish. Illustrations of the principle as shown by specialization in human social organizations.

Relation of crayfish to its environment — Ecology.

Animals in their relation to plants in the ultimate food supply.

Reading for Pupils:

Kellogg's *Zoölogy*, Chapter III. Martin's *Human Body, Briefer Course*, Chapters II., VII., VIII., IX.

References for Teachers:

The general trend of the elaboration of the topics in physiology is planned to follow that of Chapters VIII., IX., and X. in Martin's *The Human Body, Briefer Course* (1898 edition). In earlier editions the chapters are numbered differently, but bear the same headings: "Why We Eat and Breathe," "Nutrition," and "Foods." These chapters are so general that they can easily be adapted to apply to any animal.

Many suggestions concerning the presentation of the general principles of physiology in connection with the study of the lower animals are to be found in *The Crayfish as an Introduction to the Study of Zoölogy*, by Huxley, and in the account of the earthworm in Sedgwick and Wilson's *General Biology*.

VI. Summary of the Introductory Study. — The teacher should call attention to the study of the crayfish as illustrating the various standpoints from which any animal may be studied, namely, external structures with homologies and adaptations, internal structure and functions, gross and minute anatomy, classification based upon resemblance of structures, distribution in space and time, development of the individual, relation to environmental conditions, life-histories, and habits — these phases of zoölogy are all illustrated by the study of the crayfish.[1]

Definitions of biology, zoölogy, botany, morphology, physiology, anatomy, histology, embryology, and ecology. All of these phases of zoölogical science are involved in the study of the crayfish, and reference should be made to exercises in which work in anatomy, physiology, etc., was introduced.

A Study of the Frog as an Introduction to the Study of Animals.

For reasons already stated (p. 360), the frog may be taken as the introductory type instead of the crayfish. If the frog is selected, it is urged that the study should follow the general lines of the preceding outlines for the study of the crayfish, including external and internal structures, introductory microscopic work and elementary histology, elementary embryology, and general principles of animal physiology — in all of these respects the frog should be treated as illustrating and introducing the general principles of zoölogy.

Other suggestions for elaborating such lesson plans for the study of the frog are given in the final part of this outline of a course. Parker and Parker's *Practical Zoölogy* will be indispensable for the teacher who adopts the plan of beginning with the frog, for the book well presents the animal from the combined standpoints of its structure, functions, and relations, as an introduction to the essentials of morphology, physiology, and other phases of zoölogical study.

If the teacher wishes to contrast a vertebrate and an invertebrate, an excellent plan is to study both frog and crayfish as introductory types; as suggested in Kellogg's *Elementary Zoölogy*. However, I prefer to leave the vertebrates until the end of the course and then make the study lead directly into application to the morphology and physiology of the human body.

---

[1] Throughout the course it should be continually impressed upon the pupils that no part of the present study is exhaustive, and suggestions for work beyond this course should be frequently made in order to stimulate the pupils to a wider interest. Pupils should never be allowed to get the impressions that they have really *finished* any topic.

II. *A Study of a One-Celled Animal.*

The crayfish (or frog) having served for introduction to some general principles of zoölogy and general methods of laboratory work, a protozoan should now be examined in order that in its structure and function it may be compared with the multicellular animal. Such comparisons will help to an understanding of many of the most important general principles of zoölogy which have been presented in the introductory study. After four or five weeks' work with the crayfish (or frog) the pupils are in a position to understand the study of a one-celled animal, for the study of a higher animal will have prepared them against many difficulties which always arise when a protozoan is used as the introductory type. (See discussion in chapter on "The Beginning Work.") The average pupil will probably grasp the meaning of a òne-celled animal as well now as later in the course, for at this stage the pupils will have in mind the general structure and function of at least one higher animal. It is not to be expected that at any stage of an elementary course the average pupil will grasp the full significance of the unicellular type in its synthetic relations to the cellular structure and functions of multicellular animals ; but many of the important points will be understood by all except the dullest pupils and interest in zoölogical study will be stimulated.

a. Paramœcium. Laboratory study : movements, form of body, apparatus for securing food, mechanism of locomotion — cilia, general appearance of body-substance, nucleus in stained preparations, food in body, contractile vacuoles, division in living and stained specimens.

[Note.] In elementary work it is best not to confuse by calling attention to the micro-, and mega-nuclei. Calling attention to the simple fact that there is a specially differentiated nuclear substance is sufficient for establishing general ideas of the cellular nature of a protozoan, a mass of protoplasm with a nucleus.

b. Amœba. Habitat of Amœba, form of body, method of

locomotion, appearance of body-substance (protoplasm), food, nucleus, and contractile vacuole.

[NOTE.] Unless material is very abundant, this animal will need to be demonstrated by the instructor. Some of the structures mentioned below are difficult to demonstrate, and many pupils will fail to see them. It is not probable that amœbas will often be found favorable for the observation of all such processes as division and reception of food, which most laboratory manuals direct pupils to "observe."

c. *Physiology of a one-celled animal: movement and energy, application of the law of conservation of energy as in case of crayfish, food as source of energy, intra-cellular digestion, assimilation, dissimilation (oxidation), and demand for oxygen, respiration, removal of products of dissimilation — excretion of CO_2 and nitrogenous waste. No need of special system of circulation for communication between exterior and innermost part of body. Irritability and nervous functions of Paramœcium. Growth as result of repair by assimilation exceeding waste by dissimilation. Division as a simple method of reproduction. Compare functions of Paramœcium with those of crayfish, and the physiological division of labor in the two animals. Differentiation of cells in the many-celled animals.

d. Various forms of Protozoa may be demonstrated in order that the pupils may gain some idea of the great variety of unicellular animal life. Stentor, Stylonichia, Vorticella, Spirostomum, and Euglena, are common forms which are easily demonstrated with low power of the compound microscope.

References for Teachers :

Parker's *Elementary Biology*, or Parker and Parker's *Practical Zoölogy*, chapters on Amœba, Paramœcium, and other protozoa ; Calkins's *The Protozoa.*

DIVISION B.

Studies of Animal Types.

The crayfish (or frog) and a protozoan having served as a basis for the introduction to some of the most important general principles of animal structure, functions, and relations, less extensive studies of representatives of the important groups of invertebrate animals may follow. This in turn may be followed by a study of common vertebrates at the close of the course.

In these studies of invertebrate animal types the aim is to give acquaintance with common animals and to extend the application of the principles of morphology and physiology which are first introduced by the study of the crayfish (or frog). Unless otherwise specified, the laboratory study is planned from the standpoint of external structure, especial attention being given to those characteristics which underlie general classification and adaptation to environment. It is urged that, with the exception of a few instances indicated in the outline, classification should not be carried below the orders. Pupils should always see the forms classified and understand the resemblances of structure upon which the grouping is based. In short, the study of classification should give pupils that training already discussed under this topic in Chapter II. The uses of parts should be determined by experiment whenever possible, and stress placed upon the study of habits, life-histories, and ecological relations.

Cœlenterates.[1]

a. Hydra. General structure as illustrated by a living animal and transverse and longitudinal sections, form of body, tentacles, mouth, base, two cellular layers of body-wall, digestive cavity, stinging organs. Reproduction by budding (asexual) and by eggs and sperms (sexual). Movements, responses to stimuli, feeding. * Life-history. * Radial symmetry. * Physiology of the hydra as compared with that of the crayfish. Regeneration of hydra (demonstrations).

References :

Parker's *Elementary Biology*, Parker and Parker's *Practical Zoölogy*.

---

[1] As a preface to this outline the reader should consult the notes on " Cœlenterates " in the preceding chapter.

b. Hydroid colony (Pennaria, Obelia, Campanularia). Structure of a colony and of the individual zoöids. Compare a zoöid with a hydra. Formation of medusæ. General structure of a hydromedusa (Gonionemus). * Life-history and alternation of generations in hydroids.

c. Corals.

Sea-anemone (Metridum or Sagartia). External structure and transverse and longitudinal sections. Skeletons of corals with and without zoöids in position. * Corals — life-history, distribution, formation of skeletons, island formation.

References:

Dana's *Corals and Coral Islands*, Parker and Haswell's *Text-Book of Zoölogy.*

Sponges.

Structure of Grantia. Fresh-water sponges[1] (Spongilla). Commercial sponges. Glass sponges. Life-history, and formation of the skeletons.

Worms.

[NOTE.] For the purpose of this outline it seems best not to use the modern subdivisions of this heterogeneous group. The various phyla into which the old sub-kingdom Vermes is now divided are not distinguished by characteristics which can be appreciated by a beginner, and for the purposes of a limited elementary course in a secondary school we must continue to follow the old classification, recognizing Vermes as one of the primary subdivisions of the animal kingdom. "The term 'worm' is little more than a name for a shape"; but coupled with the adjectives round, flat, and segmented, it gives in the very name about as complete and definite a characterization of the three important phyla, — Platyhelminthes, Nemathelminthes, and Annulata, — as it is possible for a beginner to understand.

a. Earthworm.

External structure — form of body, number of segments in large and small worms, setæ. Drawings: anterior end with

---

[1] These common sponges are too complex for elementary study, but specimens (preferably living) should be examined merely for the sake of gaining acquaintance with the type.

segments 1–35 ; posterior end, diagrams showing arrangement
of setæ. Movements and reactions of living worm. Field
observations. Examination of the general internal anatomy.[1]

* Life-history of the earthworm. * Economic importance.

Structure and function of earthworm and crayfish compared.

b. Nereis. (Supplementary work.)

External structure. Compare with earthworm. Specialized
head and appendages. Drawings — head-end with proboscis
extended and retracted, dorsal views : tail-end in dorsal view ;
ten adjacent segments in transverse section of a middle segment, showing appendages. If living worms are obtainable,
study movements and blood circulation as seen through the
transparent skin.

c. Leeches. (Supplementary work.)

External structure. Observe living leech in a glass of water.

d. Flat worms.

[NOTE.] It is not reasonable to suppose that pupils in the high
school can satisfactorily study the internal anatomy of the flat worms
and round worms. In a living planarian the alimentary canal will
attract attention, but otherwise external study alone is practicable.

Planarians (living) and tapeworm (preserved). * Life-histories. * Parasitism.

e. Round worms. (Supplementary.)

Vinegar-eel, trichina, and "horsehair snake" (Gordius).
* Life-histories.

f. Rotifers. (Supplementary.)

[NOTE.] Demonstrations merely for sake of giving acquaintance
with these common animals. It is not to be expected that high-school
pupils can see any relation between these and other "worms."

Reading for Pupils :

Kellogg's *Zoölogy*, Chapter XX. Davenport's *Zoölogy*, Chapters IX.
and X. Jordan and Heath's *Animal Forms*, Chapter VI., and Darwin's
Earthworm and Vegetable Mould.

---

[1] The earthworm is not easily dissected by a beginner, and preparations may be used to illustrate the internal structures. The worms are
dissected in the ordinary way, are pinned on strips of cork-carpet as suggested on p. 403.

References for Teachers:
    Sedgwick and Wilson's *General Biology.* Darwin's *Earthworm and Vegetable Mould.*

Insects.

a. The locust (grasshopper) or cricket.[1] Examination of external structure. Study of habits. Stages in life-history. Compare adults of two or more species. In tabular form compare the grasshopper with the crayfish.

b. Butterfly or moth.   Examination of adult caterpillar and chrysalis of some butterfly or moth, *e. g.,* the milkweed (Danais or Anosia), or the mourning cloak (Vanessa), or the Cecropia moth.   * Metamorphosis.

c. Determination of the distinguishing features of the important orders of insects by comparing the external structures of common representatives, *e. g.,* fly, beetle, dragon-fly, cicada, bee, locust, and butterfly.   Collection of insects with at least two representatives of each common order; only some very familiar forms to be identified as to genus and species.

d.   Life-histories of cricket, beetle, bee, ant, fly, May-fly, and cicada.   Examination of adults and larval stages.

* Protective resemblance, mimicry, parasitism, commensalism, social life, and economic relations.

Field study of insects.   This interesting and profitable study should be made as extensive as time and local conditions will permit.   Comstock's *Insect Life,* Needham's *Zoölogy* and Kellogg's *Zoölogies,* are full of suggestions for such work. Some natural-history studies of arachnids and myriapods may be added.

Summary of the phylum Arthropoda — general characteristics as illustrated by the types studied, general classification.   The wealth of numbers of species and individuals, and the variety of form in the phylum.   References on insects and arachnids are given under " Animal Natural History " in Chapter X.

---

[1] Good directions for the study of these orthopterans are found in many of the elementary laboratory manuals named in Chapter X.

Mollusks.

a. Snail.[1] Study of living animal, external structure and habits. Shell — apex, aperture, umbilicus, lines of growth, columella, direction of twist. Structure of shell — three layers. Test with dilute acid, and burn a piece in Bunsen flame. Examine shells of various marine gasteropods and also shells and living specimens of our common native snails of genera Helix, Physa, Limnæa, and Planorbis. Examine set of Helix nemorosa showing individual color variation. * Individual variation of animals.

Animal removed from shell by breaking away that structure. Location of the organs which are visible without dissection.

b. Slug (Limax). Examine living slug, and compare with snail. Observe movements and habits.

c. Mussels and clams, marine and fresh-water species. Examine shell, right and left valves, inside and outside, dorsal and ventral margin, anterior and posterior ends, hinge, lines of growth, hinge-teeth, muscle scars, pallial line, mouth, digestive gland, pericardial chamber. Structure of shell — three layers. *Pearl formation. Animal with one valve of shell removed — location of superficial organs without dissection — mantle, muscles, siphons, foot, gills, palps. Living clams in aquaria. Currents indicated by powdered carmine or India ink placed near the siphons (diagrams showing directions of current). Locomotion. Feeding. * Life-history of fresh-water clams.

d. Oyster. Examine several shells and compare forms. Effect of sedentary life upon the shell ; compare with the free-moving clams. Locate structures mentioned for clam-shell. Compare right and left valves. Currents in living oyster and relation to respiration and food-supply. Microscopic examination of moving cilia on oyster gill.[2] Cause of currents. Examine oyster with right valve removed. Locate principal organs without

---

[1] See note on European edible snail in the next chapter.

[2] A small piece of a living gill is cut off and mounted on a microscopic slide in a drop of the fluid found in the mantle chamber.

dissection. Examine young oysters ("spat"). *Growing oyster for markets.

Examine shells of other bivalves, comparing all points with shell of clam.

References on Oyster:

Morgan's *Animal Sketches*, Chapter XXI.

e. Cephalopods. (Supplementary work.)

If materials are available, the following points may be demonstrated in connection with a talk or reading on the natural history of cephalopods: External structure of squid and octopus. Nautilus shell sectioned to show chambers. Shell of paper nautilus. See discussion of cephalopods in the preceding chapter.

Echinoderms.

(Supplementary work.)

As explaining the point of view of this outline, see notes on echinoderms in the preceding chapter.

a. Starfish. General external structure. Demonstrate on preparations the principal internal organs. *Method of feeding and locomotion. *Power of regeneration. *Economic relations to the oyster industry. *Habitat and geographical distribution.

b. Exhibition of specimens of sea-urchins, sand-dollars, brittle stars, sea-cucumber, fossil and alcoholic specimens of crinoids; and demonstrations by the teacher of the chief characteristics which show relationships to starfish. Point out the general characteristics of the phylum as seen in these forms. *Habits of life and distribution.

Vertebrates.

I. The Frog as a Vertebrate Type.

Anatomy: Chief external characters. Bilateral symmetry; anterior, posterior, dorsal, and ventral; compare with dog and man.

General internal structure :[1] mouth-cavity; body-cavity; general plans of digestive, circulatory, respiratory, excretory, reproductive and nervous systems; identification of heart, liver, gall-bladder, lungs, digestive canal, pancreas, mesentery, peritoneum, urinary bladder, ovaries, oviducts, spermaries, sperm-ducts, kidneys, ureters, large blood-vessels, brain, spinal cord, and chief nerves. (Illustrate with diagrams of systems of organs.)

Histology: The simple tissues of the frog. Examine in a frog preserved in formalin the following tissues, and note their distinguishing features as seen by the unaided eye : epithelium of skin and lining of alimentary canal; muscle from leg; bone; cartilage from sternum ; connective tissue from beneath skin; nervous tissue, fatty tissue, and blood. It will be evident that these simple tissues make up the body. Make a table showing what tissues enter into various parts of the body. Microscopic study of the simple tissues.[2]

Physiology: It is suggested that the physiology of the frog be developed along the lines of the topics suggested for the introductory type (see p. 378). Parker and Parker's *Practical Zoology* gives a good general account of the subject and many experiments which the teacher can easily adapt to secondary-school pupils.

Embryology: Development of the amphibian egg.[3] Structure of the reproductive organs in the female frog. Escape of

---

[1] Dissections in part by the pupil. Preparations by the instructor should be kept at hand for reference and demonstration. It is recommended that the general plan of Chapter II. in Parker and Parker's *Practical Zoology* be followed.

[2] Fresh material is used for most of this work and is supplemented by prepared slides. Directions for preparing fresh tissues are given in Parker and Parker's *Practical Zoölogy*.

[3] If this work comes at a season when developing eggs cannot be obtained, preserved material (see page 408) may be used. When living eggs are obtainable they should be taken home by the pupils and the general development observed, and sketches made from day to day as long as it is possible to keep the tadpoles alive, by feeding on small pieces of meat, corn meal, and green water-plants.

eggs from ovaries to the water. *The essential histological nature of the fertilization process. Division of the egg (one cell) into many cells. General development of chief organs. General structure of tadpole and its metamorphosis.

* Oviparous and viviparous development — advantages and relative numbers of young individuals.[1]

Classification : To be taken up later after other amphibians are known.

Reading for Pupils :

Needham's *Lessons in Zoölogy,* pp. 196, 197. Morgan's *Animal Sketches,* Chapter XV. Jordan and Heath's *Animal Forms.* Kellogg's *Elementary Zoölogy.*

II. Studies of other Vertebrates.

a. The fishes.[2] Examination of a teleost and dogfish : general external characteristics. Living fishes : movements, habits, food, respiratory movements. *Development illustrated by a series of trout embryos. *Artificial propagation and its economic importance. *General characteristics of the class. *Economic value. *Geographical distribution.

b. The Amphibia. Examination of external characteristics and habits of the urodele amphibians (salamander, newt, mudpuppy). *The amphibia : characteristics of the orders. Com-

---

[1] This may be well illustrated by comparing ordinary fish or salamander with an Alpine salamander in which the eggs stop in lower part of the oviduct, and there develop, the young being born alive. In one species only two young are produced, whereas in ordinary salamanders with oviparous development the young are numerous. This offers a good opportunity for teaching the essentials of internal development suggesting that of mammals.

Toad tadpoles will complete their metamorphosis before the close of school in June and the transformation may be observed in all its stages.

Ziegler's wax models representing the development of the frog are very useful. The series of twenty-five models costs about $28 when imported duty free by dealers, for example, the Kny-Scheerer Co., New York.

[2] For the point of view in this and the following suggestions for study of types of vertebrates, see the notes on " Vertebrates " in the preceding chapter.

pare various species of frogs, toads, salamanders, newts, and other available amphibians with reference to their points of general similarity.

c. The reptiles. *Important orders and their characteristics; limited examination of lizard, snake, alligator, and turtle. *General characteristics of the class. *Geographical distribution. *Useful members of the class. *General aspects of the embryonic development; demonstrations of embryos.

d. The birds. General external structure of a bird. *Important orders and their chief characteristics. *Useful birds. *Suggestions for field study. Demonstration: series of chick embryos. *General sketch of the development.

e. The mammals. *Principal orders: their characteristics as seen in familiar representatives.

After completing examination of the common types of the vertebrate classes, a practical exercise dealing with the leading characteristics of the groups should be introduced, and pupils should review their notes and construct tables showing characteristics of the five classes of vertebrates with reference to the following points: nature of skin and its covering; method of locomotion; breathing organs; development — oviparous or viviparous; paired appendages; habitat — air, water, land; structures common to all vertebrates.

*Life-processes in vertebrates (Needham's *Zoölogy*, pp. 260–263).

*Examination of skeletons of frog, turtle, bird, cat, monkey, and man. Special attention should be directed to the homologies of the limbs.

*Homologies among vertebrates. *Analogies. (Illustrated by preparations and lantern slides.[1])

*Review of the distinguishing features of the five classes of vertebrates. *Evidences of relationships.

*Characteristics of the, phylum Chordata. *Primitive Chordates.

---

[1] Useful lantern slides for this purpose may be made by photographing illustrations in various books on evolution named in Chapter X.

*Fossil vertebrates and their relation to living types (demonstrations at museums).

General References on Vertebrates :—
  See list of books on animal natural history in Chapter X. The books marked with an asterisk, and the school-books of zoölogy by Davenport, Kellogg, Jordan and Heath, and Kingsley, contain excellent material for reading in connection with study of common vertebrates, especially their natural history.

*Review of the general classification of animals. Practical tests of pupils' ability to recognize representatives of important groups.

*The evidences of common descent of animals — evolution. See discussion of this topic in Chapter II.

Application of the general principles of morphology and physiology, which the course has introduced, to the structures

The Human Body. and activities of the human body. In the writer's opinion, human structure and functions should be carefully discussed from the standpoint of the work on the frog. During the last twenty lessons it is profitable to require supplementary study of the chapters dealing with general nutrition in such a book as Martin's *Human Body, Briefer Course*. Likewise, when studying skeletons of frog or other vertebrates is the proper time to examine the human skeleton. Such comparative study is the proper human physiology for the high school, and is far more useful than the usual study of a special text-book. For discussion of this and allied topics see the chapter on "Teaching Human Physiology."

Suggested Modifications of the Outline.

The outline as it stands represents a course requiring about five hours per week for a year of thirty-six weeks. In Chapter V. it is pointed out that there is a demand for a half-year of zoölogical study in correlation with a similar amount of botany. For such a short course in zoölogy the following should be selected for presentation along the lines indicated in the preceding outline. First, all of Division A, which presents the most important general principles, is essential.

This would leave about ten weeks to be devoted to brief study of a few representative types, such as Hydra, earthworm, snail and clam, and vertebrates. I would urge that six or seven of these weeks should be given to the general zoölogy of the frog, supplemented with a general survey of vertebrates, and special application to the essentials of human physiology.

With regard to the suggestion made elsewhere (Chapter V.) that a general biological course in the first year of the high school may be supplemented in the fourth year by elective courses in botany and zoölogy, each extending throughout the year, it is recommended that about one-third of the first-year course be devoted to plant study with special reference to life-activities, and the other two-thirds of the time used for the study of zoölogy, emphasizing general morphological and physiological principles with direct application to the structure and function of the human body. The botanical part of such a course demands materials which are obtainable in autumn as well as in spring; and in my opinion there is an important advantage in beginning such a course with plant study. However, whether the plant precedes or follows the animal study, correlation of the studies of the two aspects of organic life is the work of the teacher and not of the order of study; and comparisons regarding the fundamental similarity of life-processes in animals and plants may be satisfactorily reviewed and summarized in the final weeks of the course.

CHAPTER IX

ZOÖLOGICAL MATERIALS, METHODS, AND SPECIAL EQUIPMENT

ANYTHING approaching complete treatment of materials for laboratory work in zoölogy and the appropriate special technique would require a volume, and this attempt to deal with the subject in a single chapter is justified only in that some notes on materials constitute an important part of an outline such as is given in Chapter VIII. For most ordinary methods of dealing with materials — dissecting, injecting, preserving — there are good directions in text and appendices of many of the recent books for high schools, particularly those by Needham, Kellogg, Colton, French, Jordan and Price, and Harvey. All these the teacher should have for general reference. There are also numerous suggestions in all the laboratory manuals named in the chapter on "Zoölogical Books," especially in the *Practical Zoölogy* by the Parkers and in that by Marshall and Hurst. The following notes do not attempt to review such well-known directions for dealing with zoölogical materials, and it is possible here to give attention only to some points about which teachers frequently make inquiries.

1. Special Literature on Laboratory Technique.

The beginner with the microscope will find Bausch's little handbook (published by Bausch and Lomb, Rochester, N. Y.) an excellent guide to the use and care of the instrument. The

Books on Microscope. same firm also issues a smaller pamphlet on "The Use of the Microscope"; and other makers of microscopes supply their patrons with similar pamphlets. Larger works by Carpenter, Beal, and others are to be found in many public libraries.

Directions for making microscopical preparations are indispensable. For such work Clark's *Practical Methods in Micro-scopy* (Boston, Heath, $1.60) gives very simple directions, and it contains much other useful in-formation about the use of the microscope. It is especially valuable for "amateur microscopists." Another and one of the very best books in this line for the beginning teacher of zoölogy is Gage's *The Microscope and Microscopical Methods* (ninth edition, Comstock Pub. Co., Ithaca, N. Y., $1.50). This is good on general methods of manipulating the micro-scope and on making microscopic preparations of animal tissues. It also gives hints for photo-microscopy and use of projection microscope. Still another similar book is Mell's *Biological Laboratory Methods* (Macmillan). One who has already mastered the elementary technique of making microscopic preparations as presented in these books and who wishes to practise special methods will need Lee's *Microtomist's Vade Mecum* (fifth edition, Blakiston, Philadelphia, $4). There are numerous other works valuable for special methods, but the above are best for the general worker.

> **Books on Microscopical Preparations.**

In addition to these special books there are brief direc-tions for making preparations in many general text-books deal-ing with histology. Stirling's *Practical Histology* (Blakiston) is the best I have used. Parker and Parker's *Practical Zoölogy* has many very simple directions for study and preparation of tissues. Nearly all the laboratory guides mentioned in the chapter on "Zoölogical Books" give notes in this line.

> **Brief Direc-tions for Preparing Tissues.**

The following special references on management of aquaria and vivaria are useful to teachers: Bateman's *The Vivarium* (London, Gill, $2.40) ; Samuel's *Amateur Aquar-ist* (New York, Baker and Taylor) ; special chapters in Furneaux's *Life in Ponds and Streams* (Longmans) ; Bate-man's *Freshwater Aquaria* (Gill), and a more extensive work, *The Book of Aquaria*, by Bateman and Bennett (same pub-lishers) ; Murbach on fresh-water aquaria in *American Natu-ralist*, Vol. XXXIV., p. 203 ; and Wilder in *Journal of*

> **Books on Aquaria.**

Applied Microscopy, Vol. II., July, 1899.   Personally, I prefer the books by Bateman.

The following journals are sources of notes on methods, and the first two are quite indispensable. *Journal of Applied Microscopy and Laboratory Methods* (six volumes published; discontinued in December, 1903); *School Science*, Chicago, $2 per year; and the more expensive *Journal of Royal Microscopical Society*, London, which is on file in most college laboratories.

Journals dealing with Materials and Methods.

2. Materials for a Course in General Zoölogy.

Protozoa.

The amœba causes zoölogy teachers more trouble than any other animal which is commonly used. Numerous " sure " methods of obtaining cultures are recommended, but failure is common. Masses of green-felt (Oscillaria) growing on bottom of quiet pools are likely to contain amœbas. Carefully collect and place in shallow dishes, such as soup plates or crystallizing dishes, several weeks before needed. The slime on water-plants is another source of the material, and I have frequently found them abundant on the roots of duckweed growing in aquaria. Practically all the successful methods of cultivating amœbas in the laboratory depend upon the development of bacteria on which they feed. Some Paramœcium cultures (see below), with hay decaying in the water, should be kept until one year old, for amœbas often appear in vast numbers many months after Paramœcium disappears. Decaying water-plants, such as lily leaves or duckweed, or animals, such as fresh-water mussels, favor the development of bacteria. Such cultures should be started in the early spring or summer for use in the autumn. Simply fill several battery-jars with water and add chopped hay and some decaying water-plants from aquaria and ponds. It is only necessary to add water occasionally in order to make up for evaporation, and this may be largely prevented by covering the jars with plates of glass.

Amœba.

For ciliated protozoa, such as Paramœcium, Stylonichia, Vorticella, and Stentor, the most convenient artificial culture-medium is an infusion of hay in which bacteria develop. In preparing the infusion, pour warm water over a small mass of chopped hay, and after twenty-four hours transfer both hay and infusion into a glass battery-jar and add some water and decaying sticks and leaves taken from various ponds in which Protozoa are commonly found. It is well to distribute the infusion into several small vessels, such as ordinary glass tumblers, and to place in them sticks and leaves from different ponds. Within three or four weeks the infusion will probably develop infusoria, especially Paramœcium, in great numbers, and they will collect in the bacterial scum on the surface or around the periphery of the dish from which they are easily collected by a pipette.

Cultures of Ciliates.

When a culture is once obtained, it is advisable to start a new culture fortnightly by transferring some of the surface scum to hay infusion which is a day old.

New Cultures.

Another method is to collect decaying sticks and leaves and add water from ponds, place in battery-jars, and allow to stand for some weeks, when infusoria of various kinds will doubtless be abundant. If a quantity of pond water, together with an abundance of leaves and water-plants, be placed in a glass dish, it will often be found just as putrefaction sets in that vorticellas are present in great numbers in the surface scum. They may also appear after Paramœcium in the hay infusion. Some aquaria in which infusoria appear should be kept until the following year, for in this way some excellent cultures of amœbas, stentors, and other forms are often obtained in the second year.

Another Method.

In some parts of this country the specific gravity of Paramœcium is such that they will quickly rise to the surface of a body of water, and advantage may be taken of this tendency in order to concentrate the animals. A glass tube one-fourth inch in diameter and ten inches long, sealed at one end and supported vertically, is

Method of Concentrating Paramœcium.

filled with fluid taken from the surface of a culture dish and after a short time most of the animals will have risen to the surface. In this way the animals in many cubic centimetres of fluid can be concentrated into a single drop. I have had success with this method at Chicago, but at Boston the specific gravity of the Paramœcium is apparently so nearly that of water that they do not collect at the surface. The method is well worth the trial in other localities. .

In order to restrain the movements of active infusoria, such as Paramœcium, a thick solution of gelatine is commonly used.

Restraining Movements. A sheet of gelatine should be soaked for several hours in water, then removed and melted in a glass beaker or evaporating dish. When cooled to the temperature of the laboratory, it should have the consistency of thick mucilage. If too solid when cooled, add water and remelt. The correct proportions are about three grams of gelatine to one hundred cubic centimetres of water. A ring of this semi-fluid gelatine is made on the microscopic slide, a small drop of the fluid containing the infusoria is then placed inside the ring and the cover-glass gently lowered into position. If the gelatine is of the proper consistency, the movements of the animals will soon be retarded sufficiently for study even with the high-power objective. The animals do not live long in the gelatine and new preparations must be made several times hourly.

The method of ingesting food in ciliated forms may be demonstrated by placing the animals in water in which some **Ingestion of Food.** finely powdered carmine is suspended. Murbach (*School Science*, Vol. I., p. 36) uses water-color carmine such as artists use, rubbing a small piece in a drop of water and then adding the animals.

Intra-vitam staining often gives very interesting results with Paramœcium. Place the animals in a drop of aqueous solution **Intra-vitam Staining.** of methylene-blue so dilute that little of the blue color appears; 1 : 10000 is the best proportion of water and dry dye. The color will be slowly taken up by the nucleus. Dahlia, malachite green, and other anilines may be used in the same way.

For staining infusoria certain aniline dyes are combined with a killing reagent. For general purposes dissolve methylene green to one per cent acetic acid in water. Draw **Stain for** this under the cover-glass with a bit of absorbing **Infusoria.** paper.

Cœlenterates.

Specimens of marine forms, such as corals, sea-anemones, medusæ, and ctenophores may be purchased from **Marine** dealers (see list on page 414). **Forms.**

Hydra, which is by far the most important cœlenterate for high-school work, is regarded by most teachers as rather difficult to manage, and for this reason a rather full **Hydra Col-** account of methods follows. Two species are **lecting.** common, the brown hydra (H. fusca) and the green hydra (H. viridis); but the latter is the most widely distributed. The brown hydra is usually found only in permanent streams and ponds, but the green species is also common in temporary pools which are dry during the midsummer season of drought. Unless hydras are to be used early in the school-year, it is usually best to collect them for stocking aquaria late in the autumn after the summer heat is over and the water in shallow pools has become quite cold. At such a time the animals appear in great abundance in many ponds where they are rare in midsummer, and also in temporary pools which are dry during the summer season. They are usually found attached to submerged objects, such as stones, sticks, living and dead water-plants, and decaying leaves of deciduous trees. In examining such objects in search for the animals, a hand-lens is useful for certain identification of any organism which to the unaided eye may resemble a hydra; or these objects may be placed in a small jar of clear water in which hydras will quickly expand so as to be seen easily. If hydras are found, a quantity of the materials to which they are attached should be collected, carried in water to the laboratory, and placed in a glass vessel (battery-jar or fruit-jar). Under the influence of diffused light the hydras will migrate to the sides of the vessel.

The hardy green hydras may often be collected even in midwinter by cutting holes in the ice and collecting some of **Collecting in** the submerged objects, such as dead leaves and **Winter.** filamentous algæ. The writer has found as many as a hundred hydras on a single oak leaf taken from beneath six inches of ice. In the case of green hydras on algæ, the animals are not easily seen until they have migrated to the wall of a glass aquarium.

Another method of obtaining an abundance of green hydras consists in taking advantage of the fact that in the midsummer **Encysted** season of drought numerous encysted eggs lie **Eggs.** embedded in the dry soil on the bottom of temporary pools. Soil collected from such places where hydras are known or supposed to exist when water is present, may be stored in the dry condition for months; and when placed in water in a glass or earthen vessel and covered with a glass plate the eggs will develop, the animals appearing first on the surface of mud and thence migrating to the sides of the vessel. If hydras do appear, the aquarium should be supplied with green plants and small entomostracan crustaceans.

A glass battery-jar (four by five or six by eight inches), or a common fruit-jar, are convenient vessels in which to keep **Aquarium for** hydras. It is better to use several small jars in- **Hydras.** stead of one large one, since the danger of a complete failure is thus lessened by the possibility of variable conditions. The jars should be kept loosely covered with plates of glass, which not only prevents rapid evaporation, but also largely checks the development of bacterial scums, which are so unfavorable to the hydras that success with the aquarium largely depends upon preventing extensive growth of bacteria. Substances, such as grasses from temporary pools, which are likely to undergo decay should be excluded from the aquarium. Hydras collected on green aquatic plants are easily kept so long as the plants are in good condition. After the animals have migrated to the sides of the aquarium fresh plants may be supplied from time to time. The writer has also had success with green hydras found adhering to dead leaves of oak, elm, and maple. These leaves are favorable for small entomostraĉan crustacea which serve as food for the hydras, but do not favor the extensive development of bacteria, and a dozen placed in two or three litres of water in a covered vessel will be sufficient for hundreds of hydras. The presence of a few green plants will do no harm, but in the case of the green hydras are unnecessary since symbiotic algæ maintain the physiological balance. Usually some of the lower algæ will develop on the sides of the aquarium and assist in maintaining the balance.

Snails, which are so useful in the aquarium for larger animals, must be excluded from those in which hydras are to be kept, since they feed upon the animals. **Snails.**

Running water is not necessary, but the water should be changed by means of a syphon whenever there is any turbidity or development of bacterial scum. Rain water or that taken from the ponds where the animals are **Changing Water.** collected is best, but the animals may be accustomed to the hydrant water in most cities by gradually adding it to the water in which the animals lived originally. This precaution in changing water is more necessary in case of the brown species; the green ones may usually be directly transferred to hydrant water.

The writer has made some observations which suggest that brown hydras and undoubtedly green ones would live well in an aquarium if the temperature could be kept **Low Temperature.** between 40° and 50° F., which is not favorable to excessive bacterial growth. Near a window in a basement with temperature slightly above freezing would be best.

Owing to great contractility, hydras must be killed with rapid fixing agents, such as solutions containing corrosive sublimate.

Water containing one per cent of acetic acid and saturated with corrosive sublimate is very successful for general work.

Killing and Preserving Hydras. A few hydras should be placed in a small watch-crystal half full of water and allowed to expand. Then quickly pour into the crystal enough of the sublimate solution to fill it completely and allow it to stand five minutes. Then, with a wide-mouthed pipette (in transferring these delicate animals from one fluid to another they must not at any time be lifted out of the fluid, because they will very likely collapse) remove the hydra to fifty per cent alcohol and then in ten minutes to seventy per cent alcohol. The sublimate should then be washed out by changing the alcohol several times. Preserve in ninety per cent alcohol until animals are wanted for further preparation, either in sections or entire.

Mounting hydras entire may be accomplished as follows: Transfer through successive grades of alcohol to water and **Mounting Entire.** stain for one hour in Delafield's hæmatoxylin diluted ten times, or for twelve hours in alum carmine diluted ten times. Then dehydrate, clear in cedar oil or turpentine, and mount in xylol balsam.

If it is desired to make sections of hydra, they should be dehydrated, cleared in turpentine, embedded in paraffin, **Sections.** sectioned, sections mounted, paraffin removed, and stained on the slide with dilute Delafield's hæmatoxylin or iron-hæmotoxylin. They may be stained in borax-carmine before sectioning.

Earthworm.[1]

Large specimens of Lumbricus terrestris are often found in the soil of gardens, lawns, etc., but they are not everywhere as **Common Species.** common as the smaller Allolobophora mucosa, which is not so favorable for laboratory work in the line of anatomical study, but it may serve for study of the

---

[1] References — Sedgwick and Wilson's *General Biology*, appendix. Darwin's *Earthworm*.

living animal. The striped earthworm (L. fœtidus or Allolobophora fœtidus) lives in and near heaps of manure.

The worms may be collected by digging the soil in places where "castings" from the earthworm's intestine are to be found on the surface, especially under stones and timbers which have lain for a long time in the Collecting. same place. The worms are abundant on well-manured lawns, where digging is impossible; but they may be taken by quietly searching with a lantern at night, when they frequently lie out of their burrows. Most satisfactory of all methods is to collect during or just after heavy rains in spring and summer, and keep the worms in vivaria until wanted.

A rich soil containing much decaying organic matter is most suitable in vivaria for these animals. If obtained from localities where large earthworms abound, success with the vivarium is certain. The soil should be Vivarium. placed in a wooden box and covered with a layer of grassy sod which is to be kept damp (not wet) by occasional sprinkling with water. Some sort of a cover for preventing evaporation is important if the box is to be kept in the dry atmosphere of the laboratory. It is much better to keep the earthworms in a cool, damp place in the cellar or basement, removing the vivarium to the laboratory when observations are to be made by the class. Bits of potato or apple or leaves should be left on the surface of the soil to serve as food for the worms. It is interesting to have one vivarium in which the sod covers not more than one-half the surface, the remainder being composed of fine soil carefully levelled. Under these conditions the burrows and the "castings" can be easily seen.

Living worms intended for preservation should first be washed and then placed in a shallow vessel containing enough water to cover them. Alcohol (commercial ninety- five per cent, or diluted) is then added so gradu- Preserving. ally that the worms are not stimulated into violent contractions, but are slowly stupefied. The alcohol may from time to time be sprayed over the surface of the water; but a more convenient way is to place a sponge or wad of cotton in the centre of the dish and pour upon it the alcohol, which will gradually diffuse through the surrounding water. The vessel should be kept covered. The worms are often found stupefied after two to four hours; a few worms may be tested by removing them to fifty per cent alcohol, and if violent contractions do not ensue, all the worms may be removed to alcohol of this strength. As soon as movements cease, the worms should be carefully straightened out and placed side by side in a shallow dish with enough fifty per cent alcohol to cover them. A shallow rectangular dish is preferable for this purpose. The animals may be kept from one to four hours in fifty per cent alcohol, and then this should be drained off, seventy per cent alcohol should be added and changed after a few hours. After ten to twenty hours in this alcohol the animals may be placed for permanent preservation in a liberal quantity of ninety per cent alcohol, or, preferably, in a solution of commercial formalin four parts and water ninety-six parts. The worms should be kept straight, either by lying horizontally in wide jars, or glass cylinders which stand vertically may be used, the worms being inserted while the cylinder lies almost horizontally and packed so closely with cotton that bending is prevented when the jar is placed upright and filled with preserving liquid.

Worms preserved in alcohol as described in above paragraph may be used for microscopic preparations as well as for dis-
Sections.   sections; but if sections are to be cut through the alimentary canal, it is necessary to free that structure from soil before killing the animals. The worms should be washed and placed in a wide jar with a quantity of shreds of moistened filter-paper, which should be removed and washed daily. The moist paper is eaten by the worms and passing through the intestine it removes the particles of soil. Some of the paper remaining in the alimentary canal often renders sectioning very difficult. Sometimes the worms will eat apples, potato, and lettuce, and these may be used in place of filter-paper. Some zoölogists state that the intestine may be very

satisfactorily cleaned by inserting a slender pipette into the mouth or anus and gently forcing a stream of water through the intestine. It has also been recommended that the intestine of the earthworm be cleaned by placing the animals in a box filled with cleaned sphagnum moss upon which the animals will feed. The box must be kept covered and the moss moist. After a few weeks, the intestine will be free from soil, and the animals ready for preservation.

The best histological preservation is obtained by suddenly plunging the animals into some strong killing fluid, but this usually results in more or less distortion of the general form of the body. To avoid such distortion it is best to stupefy with alcohol before plunging into the fixing fluid. Kleinenberg's strong picro-sulphuric and solutions with corrosive sublimate are recommended. After the worms have been in the fluid ten minutes it is well to cut them into pieces one-half inch long and leave one hour longer before washing with seventy per cent alcohol.

The following are the most useful preparations for micro-scopic examination : transverse section through intestinal region, sagittal section through first ten to twenty segments, ovary mounted entire, cuticle. (See Sedgwick & Wilson's *General Biology.*)

It is customary to pin worms to the wax in the bottom of a dissecting pan ; but for convenience in preserving dissections which cannot be completed in one laboratory period, the worms may be pinned to strips of **Dissection.** cork, soft wood, or cork-carpet. These strips can be placed in a pan while dissection is in progress, and during intervals removed to jars of preserving fluid — commercial formalin two parts in water one hundred parts will answer this purpose. Pieces of sheet lead may be used to keep the cork from float-ing in the water which fills the dissecting pan, or the strips may be pinned to the wax or pinning board of the pan. A convenient size for cork strips is about one and one-half by seven inches and one-fourth inch in thickness. They will cost very little when cut from " remnants " of cork-carpet obtainable from carpet stores.

Crustacea.

Lower entomostracea, such as Daphnia and Cyclops, are usually abundant in ponds and may be kept in aquaria without **Lower** special attention. In very early spring, pond water **Crustacea.** usually teems with cladocerans, copepods, and ostracods. This is also the time to look for the fairy shrimp, Branchipus. A dip-net made of cheese-cloth is best for catching all these lower crustaceans.

Many amphipods are common in fresh-water ponds and may be kept in aquaria with green plants. Among isopods, **Amphipods** the common sow-bug (Oniscus) and the pill-bug **and Isopods.** (Armadillidum) are common under stones and rotten logs which have lain for a long time in one place. They are easily kept in any jar from which light is excluded (*e. g.,* a battery-jar covered with dark paper). It is only necessary to put in some pieces of decaying wood, keep these moist (not wet) and occasionally pieces of bread and meat for food. Our common myriapods found in the same places may be kept in the same vivarium. The Asellus, an isopod living in ponds, is frequently abundant in masses of water-plants collected for the aquaria.

Among the decapods, the crayfishes are most important because they are so easily kept alive in the schoolroom. **Crayfish** These crustaceans which are common in the prin- **Collecting.** cipal North American river systems, with the exception of New England, are frequently to be found under stones in shallow clear water where they are easily captured with a strong dip-net. Sometimes they may be taken in minnow seines which are heavily weighted so as to drag on the bottom. They are also often captured in traps made of wire netting arranged so that the animals may be led by bait into a cage through a cone-shaped entrance whose inner opening is not over two inches in diameter and as far as possible above the floor of the cage. Any meat or fish serves as bait.

Crayfish may be purchased in the markets of large cities during September and sometimes even later. In New York they usually cost $3 or $4 per hundred, but in Chicago they frequently sell for $1 per hundred at **Dealers.** the market of Booth & Co., State and Lake Streets. Dealers in zoölogical supplies named on page 414 furnish them both living and preserved at all seasons; but of course prices must be higher than those above.

A good cheap aquarium for crayfish is any shallow pan made of galvanized iron, such as the common metal wash-tubs; or a wooden water-tight box will answer the **Crayfish in** purpose. The bottom may be covered with sand **Aquaria.** or gravel; and flat stones or broken pottery placed so as to form retreats for the animals. Unless running water can be had, it is important that the water be shallow — not deeper than enough to cover the animals. Keep in a cool place (*e. g.*, in cellar) except when wanted for study. Twenty-five of the animals can be kept in a pan sixteen by eighteen inches, which should be divided by at least one movable partition. The water need not be changed more than three times a week, unless some of the animals die and foul the water. The cray-fishes rarely eat during the winter months, but occasionally they may eat green water-plants, carrots, small pieces of meat, and earthworm. Rejected food must not be allowed to decay in the aquarium. The animals can easily be kept alive from September until June, thus obviating the necessity of using preserved material, which in the case of all large crustacea is at best very unsatisfactory.

The animals may be anæsthetized by means of chloroform. Preserve in ninety per cent alcohol. With a **Preserving** syringe or rubber-bulbed pipette alcohol should **Crayfish.** be injected into mouth and anus, and also into an opening made in the carapace. It is also advisable to insert the needle of a hypodermic syringe and inject alcohol beneath the posterior edge of the carapace and also through the soft abdominal sterna into the ventral blood-sinus. Formaldehyde does not preserve well unless the organs are well exposed by cutting away parts of the exoskeleton. It also has the disadvantage of decalcifying the calcareous structures. It is recommended that crayfish be kept alive until wanted for study when they may be chloroformed and the dissection begun on the fresh material. One per cent commercial formaldehyde in water will preserve the partially dissected animals for several weeks if they are immersed in the solution during the intervals between laboratory periods.

The European Edible Snail.

The European edible snails (Helix pomatia) are now regularly imported from France and Germany, and may be found in the provision markets of the large cities during the cooler months, *i. e.*, from about October 15 to April 1. In New York they may be ordered from C. Perceval, dealer in table delicacies and fine provisions, 100 Sixth Avenue. They usually cost about $1.50 per hundred. The Brooklyn Biological Supply Co., 333 Halsey Street, Brooklyn, supplies them in small quantities. Less than two dozen in a package may be sent by mail.

These snails are brought from Europe in the dormant or winter condition, the aperture of the shell being sealed by the temporary plate (epiphragm) of calcified mucus. In this condition they may be packed, shipped, and stored for months in dry sawdust or " excelsior." The snails may be purchased in autumn and the stock kept in some *cool, dry* place until they are wanted for class study, perhaps in late spring. When active snails are needed, it is only necessary to put them in a warm, wet place on grassy sod, moss, sand, or sawdust; under the influence of the moisture the epiphragm soon softens and the head and foot emerge from the shell. The emergence may be hastened by first removing the epiphragm.

The active snails may be kept so for months in a simple

vivarium, which consists of a shallow box or bucket covered with coarse wire netting and having the bottom covered with grassy sod or coarse sand. I prefer the sand, because it may be washed in running water occasionally, which is desirable in case the vivarium is kept in the schoolroom. The snails may be fed with lettuce, cabbage, and other vegetables.

Perhaps the most convenient way to handle the living snail in the class room is to allow it to crawl on a plate of glass to which the foot soon firmly adheres. All external parts and movements are then easily seen from any desired point of view. Lettuce leaves may be placed near the mouth and the process of feeding observed through the glass; and in the same way the remarkable muscular movements of the foot may be seen. If the snails are sluggish when wanted for class study, stimulate them by repeated dipping into lukewarm water. (From note in *School Science*, January, 1903.)

Insects.

There are so many good directions for collecting and rearing insects that I shall simply refer to some of the best sources of information. Needham's *Elements of Zoölogy*, Comstock's *Insect Life*, Colton's *Zoölogy* (new **References.** edition), all give good directions for insect work. In fact, almost every book dealing with insects (see list in Chapter X.) gives notes on collecting, preserving, mounting, and rearing larvæ. In addition a bulletin of the National Museum by Riley is very valuable (Part F, Bull. 39, U. S. Nat. Mus.)

Some insects may be preserved in commercial formalin two parts and water ninety-eight parts. Grain or ethyl alcohol is best for others. Grasshoppers preserve well in **Preserving** wood or methyl alcohol. Various mixtures are **Fluids.** recommended by Riley in the bulletin cited above. In general, the formalin is best for museum specimens such as are wanted in high schools. In some cases the addition of a small quantity of baking soda to the formalin tends to better preservation of colors.

Vertebrates.

In general, all vertebrates intended for museum purposes or dissection are best preserved in a solution of commercial

Preservation. formalin four or five parts in one hundred parts of water. The body-cavity should be opened to allow rapid penetration of the preservative. This should also be injected into mouth and anus (using a large rubber-bulbed pipette). Formalin causes swelling in some cases (*e.g.*, oviducts of frog), and then alcohol may be more desirable.

All vertebrate tissue require special methods for microscopi-

Tissues. cal work (see books named on the first pages of this chapter).

The preparation of dry museum specimens of vertebrates is   .

Museum well treated in Rowley's *Art of Taxidermy* (Ap-
Specimens. pletons, $2), and in the practical part of Colton's new *Zoölogy.*

Formaldehyde is an excellent permanent preservative for eggs and embryos which are to be used for study without

Amphibian sectioning. The segmenting eggs or early embryos
Eggs. surrounded by the jelly should be placed directly in a mixture of commercial formalin four or five parts in one hundred parts of water, and require no further attention. It is well not to attempt preservation of large masses of eggs, such as those of the frog and the spotted amblystoma, for the preservative does not readily penetrate through the jelly to the innermost eggs. In such cases, small pieces of the jelly containing not more than ten eggs insures good preservation. The eggs of the common toad are well preserved by simply dropping the egg-strings into the diluted formaldehyde.

Eggs and embryos preserved as directed above may be examined with low powers (a dissecting microscope with lenses magnifying twelve to twenty times) without preparation other than isolating the eggs from the mass of jelly (using needles). A thin coat of the jelly usually adheres to the egg, but it is so transparent that the surface of the egg is clearly visible.

3. Some Special Laboratory Equipment for Zoölogical Work.

Various forms of fancy glass aquaria are to be found described in the catalogues of dealers, but most of these are not valuable for school purposes. For aquaria holding less than five gallons of water, plain glass cylin- **Aquaria.** drical vessels are best. The solid glass aquaria which have square corners are extremely liable to crack, and this serious defect overbalances the favor accorded to their neat appearance. For most purposes the cylindrical aquaria of sizes smaller than eight by nine inches are recommended, because it is best not to attempt to keep too many kinds of material in one large aquarium in which the entire stock of specimens may be destroyed by one accident. Instead of the regular aquarium of the smaller sizes, white glass battery-jars may be used with great economy. Jars six by eight inches, "shop furniture" style, cost (Whitall, Tatum & Co., New York) about $4.25 per dozen; and four by four inches cost about $1.40. The six by eight inch size in the "iron mould" style cost $2.15 per dozen. The "iron mould" jars are more liable to crack, particularly if wet jars be allowed to dry by evaporation, but if care be taken to wipe them dry immediately after washing few such breakages will occur. Various forms of cheap glass vessels, such as fruit-jars, tumblers, etc., are convenient for small aquaria. An excellent plan for aquaria made of plates of glass cemented together in a metal frame is given in Hodge's *Nature Study and Life.* Others are described in special books on aquaria named in the first part of this chapter.

If many jars are used as aquaria it may be desirable to have in the laboratory a set of shelves for holding them. The best form consists of a frame made of right-angled iron **Aquaria** about one-fourth inch thick and two inches wide **Racks.** riveted together so as to form supports for shelves made of wood or thick glass plates such as are used for skylights. If an iron frame is used it should be enamelled.

Cheap aquaria or vivaria for animals, such as frogs, salamanders, and crayfish, may be made of galvanized sheet-iron,
Metal Aquaria which for the sake of appearance may be painted
and Vivaria. or enamelled on the outside. Convenient sizes
are sixteen by twenty-four by six inches, and twelve by sixteen
by six inches. The edges should be rolled over a one-fourth
inch iron frame in order to stiffen the pan. To prevent crowd-
ing, or to separate different kinds of animals, it is sometimes
necessary to divide the space of the pan temporarily into sections, and for this purpose a movable partition can be made
of the galvanized sheet-iron. A sheet five inches wide and
four inches longer than the width of the pan is bent at right
angles two inches from each end. By slightly bending the
strip in the middle while adjusting it may be set· in to any
desired position, and will hold itself in place. Of course, a
less permanent partition could be made of any convenient
wood. Shallow pans should have movable covers of galvanized netting of about one-half inch mesh. This should be
soldered to a frame made of L-shaped galvanized iron, or
ordinary iron which may be painted or enamelled. This
frame should be slightly larger than the outside dimensions
of the pan in order that the downwardly projecting edge of
the L-shaped frame may serve to hold the cover in place. The
pans may have drain cocks soldered into one side near the
bottom, or a metal tube with plug on the inside may be used,
as in an ordinary wash-basin. Various forms of enamelled and
galvanized iron pans, small wash-tubs, etc., are now on the
market, and these when fitted with covers are excellent for
aquaria and vivaria. Being regular market commodities they
are less expensive than any made to order. (In New York
City the fourteen by eighteen by six inch size with cover described above costs about $2.50.) Water-tight wooden boxes
are easily constructed and in some laboratories serve as cheap
substitutes for galvanized iron pans; but if the labor must be
paid for at the usual prices the metal vessels will be cheaper
in the end.

A convenient size of pan for general dissection is about six by nine inches at the top, five and one-half by eight and one-half inches at the bottom and two and one-half inches deep. Such pans can be purchased from **Dissecting Pans.** dealers in general laboratory supplies, but it is usually cheaper to get them from a dealer in tinware. Pans of approximately this size made of tin and enamelled ware are now a regular market commodity at prices ranging from a dollar and a half to three dollars per dozen, depending upon quality. Pans made of zinc are the most durable, but the first cost is somewhat greater. They are not regularly on the market, but may be made by any tinsmith.

In order that pins may be used in fastening specimens, the bottom is usually lined with paraffin, colored with lampblack and held in place by metal projections soldered into the corners of the pan, or the wax is weighted with pieces of lead which are placed in the pan while the wax is in a molten condition. Sometimes instead of wax a thin board of soft wood is fitted to the bottom. The ordinary cork-carpet is excellent for this purpose. Wood or cork pinning boards should be kept from floating when the pans are filled with water either by means of metal projections soldered in the corners, by weighting with pieces of lead, or by small wedges of wood inserted at the corners of the pan.

Another dissecting dish is made from an enamelled baking-pan, six by eight by two inches, corners rounded, with wide rim, white inside and outside ; costs about twenty-five cents each in department stores. This may be fitted with cork-carpet or wooden bottom, held in place by wire clips which clamp under the wide rim on the outside, and thus equipped it may be used as a dissecting pan, or after removal of pinning board it is useful for table use in the study of living animals, such as water insects, tadpoles, fishes, frogs' eggs, snails, slugs, earthworms, etc.

The Riker mount, a cardboard box filled with sheet cotton

on which specimens are placed and then held in place with a
Specimen   glass cover. The five by six inch size costs $2.50
Cases.   per dozen ; eight by twelve inch costs $6.00 per
dozen. Kny-Scheerer Co., New York, and other dealers.

A new patent mount for insects, by Denton Brothers,
Wellesley, Mass., allows unobstructed view of both sides of
the specimens and requires no pin. Price from five to
twenty-three cents each. The smallest size is about one by
one and one-half inches.

A plaster tablet mount is made by the Denton Brothers.

Large boxes suitable for life-histories of insects are made by
American Entomological Co., Brooklyn ; and by Kny-Scheerer
Co., New York.

For systematic collections of insects the Comstock cases
described in the Cornell Nature Study Leaflets and in appendix to Comstock's *Insect Life* are most convenient.

I have used for four years a case, seven by nine inches with
glass on each side, specimens pinned to corks or placed in glass
tubes which are glued to one glass. The frame of this case
is made of whitewood, one-half inch thick by one inch wide.
This frame is grooved on either side to receive the glass which is
held in place by small brads and a strip of lantern-slide or
passe-partout paper which is glued over the edges of glass and
frame, thus keeping out dust and insect pests. An expensive
improvement consists in the addition of a tongue and groove
uniting the top and bottom halves of the frame so that it can
be easily opened for changing specimens. This case in several
sizes is now being made by the "Home Made" Scientific
Apparatus Co., Mechanicsburg, O.

Simple cages made of mosquito netting and wooden boxes
Insect Breed- are described in Comstock's *Insect Life*, by Riley,
ing Cages.   in Part F, Bulletin 39, U. S. Nat. Mus., 1892, and
in many popular books on insects.

A simple cage which I consider most useful consists of a
cylinder of ordinary wire-screen such as is used for doors,
closed at one end with a disk of the same netting. The net-

ting is easily fastened together by riveting with staples of copper wire made in the shape of two pointed carpet tacks, or by sewing with fine wire. This cage may be set over plants in pots, boxes containing soil, etc. A convenient size is eight inches in diameter by fourteen inches long.

Folding cages made of galvanized netting are made by the Kny-Scheerer Co., New York. One twelve by twelve by fourteen inches costs about $2.50. Other styles are made by American Entomological Co., Brooklyn, N. Y.

Cheapest of all are, of course, the various forms of fruit-jars, best of which are the patented jars with glass covers. The Mason jars and others with metal covers are useless with formalin. But for choice specimens neater jars are **Museum Jars.** wanted. "Salt mouth" bottles used by druggists are the cheapest glass-stopped bottles which are useful for the school museum. Whitall, Tatum & Co., New York, make many styles smaller than "twenty ounce," which are as useful as much more expensive museum jars made by the same firm. Rectangular jars of various sizes are imported by the Kny-Scheerer Co., New York.

The method of mounting on glass plates set in museum jars is well known to preparateurs, but deserves review here. Cut the glass — transparent, opalescent, or black — so **Mounting** that it fits inside of a jar when cover is on. Clean **Specimens in** it thoroughly. Specimens previously hardened in **Museum Jars.** alcohol or formalin should be soaked for an hour in water. Ordinary gelatine soaked in water and then melted should be dropped on the glass where the specimens are to be fixed. Then put specimens in position, and if they are heavy, support by a thread around the glass. When the gelatine has hardened, gently flood the glass plate with formalin (five parts of commercial formalin to one hundred parts of water) and after a few minutes the plate may be lowered into the jar filled with formalin of the same strength. This method is especially useful for life-histories of insects and for series of embryos of vertebrates, such as the chick.

The preceding pages have been limited chiefly to special equipment which deserves to be better known by teachers of zoölogy. For general equipment, useful also for botany, see the catalogues of dealers named in following list. The completed (December, 1903) volumes of the *Journal of Applied Microscopy and Laboratory Methods* are especially valuable for suggestions on planning and equipping biological laboratories. See also Mell's *Biological Laboratory Methods* (Macmillan, New York).

Other Laboratory Equipment.

Dealers in Zoölogical Materials and Museum Specimens.

AMERICAN ENTOMOLOGICAL CO., 1040 DeKalb Ave., Brooklyn, N. Y. (Mounted insects, type collections, living pupæ of lepidoptera, mimicry sets, insects identified at two cents each, breeding boxes, cabinets, nets. Catalogue for sale.)

BIOLOGICAL LABORATORY, Cold Spring Harbor, Long Island, N. Y. (Preserved materials, chiefly marine. Price-list issued.)

BOOTH & CO., State and Lake Streets, Chicago, Ill. (Fish market. Crayfish in September.)

BRIMLEY, H. H., AND C. S., Raleigh, N. C. (Land, fresh-water, and marine animals, living and preserved. Catalogue issued.)

BROOKLYN BIOLOGICAL SUPPLY CO. (Land, fresh-water, and marine animals, living and preserved; also microscopical preparations. Catalogue.)

DENTON BROS., Wellesley, Mass. (Insects, mimicry sets, mounting cases. Circulars.)

FICKLIN, W. H., 2640 E. 8th St., Kansas City, Mo. (Materials for laboratory study.)

HOPKINS SEASIDE LABORATORY, Stanford University, Cal. (Preserved marine animals. Circular.)

KNOLL & SON, Washington Market, New York City. (Living crayfish, prawns, crabs, lobsters, marine clams.)

KNY-SCHEERER CO., New York. (Great variety of zoölogical materials for museum specimens. Catalogues.)

MARINE BIOLOGICAL LABORATORY, Supply Department, Woods Hole, Mass. (Living and preserved materials, chiefly marine. Catalogue.)

MAYNARD, C. J., Newton, Mass. (A great variety of preserved and living animals. Circular)

McCURDY & CO., 618 E. 71 St., Chicago, Ill. (Living frogs, turtles, clams, and crayfish.)

NIELSON, ALEX, Venice, Erie Co., Ohio. (Necturus, turtles.)

PERCEVAL, C., dealer in delicatessen, 100 Sixth Ave., New York.

(Importer of European edible snail [Helix pomatia], September to March. About $1.50 per 100.)

SPHUNG, A. A. North Judson, Ind. (Living frogs, turtles, snakes, fresh-water clams, and crayfish.)

TUFTS COLLEGE BIOLOGICAL LABORATORY, South Harpswell, Me. Address in college year is Tùfts College, Mass. (Preserved marine material. Circular.)

WARD'S NATURAL SCIENCE ESTABLISHMENT, Rochester, N. Y. (Skeletons, taxidermic materials, and museum specimens in great variety. Catalogues for sale.)

C. H. WARD, Rochester, N. Y. (Anatomical preparations.)

WEBSTER CO., Hyde Park, Mass. (Birds' skins and taxidermists' supplies.)

Dealers in General Laboratory Apparatus and Supplies.

BAUSCH & LOMB OPTICAL CO., Rochester, N. Y., New York City, Chicago, and Boston.

CAMBRIDGE BOTANICAL SUPPLY CO., Cambridge, Mass.

CENTRAL SCHOOL SUPPLY CO., Chicago, Ill.

C. H. STOELTING CO., Successors to Chicago Scale and Laboratory Supply Co., Chicago, Ill.

EBERBACH & SON, Ann Arbor, Mich.

EIMER & AMEND, New York.

EMIL GREINER, New York.

"HOME-MADE" SCIENTIFIC APPARATUS CO., Mechanicsburg, O. (Makers of specimen cases and simple apparatus.)

KNOTT SCIENTIFIC APPARATUS CO., Boston.

KNY-SCHEERER CO., 17 Park Pl., New York.

LEITZ & CO., of Wetzlar, Germany. American agency at 411 W. 59th St., New York. W. Krafft, Mgr.

LENTZ & SONS, Philadelphia, Penn.

PENNOCK, EDWARD, 3609 Woodland Ave., Philadelphia, Penn.

QUEEN & CO., Philadelphia and New York.

SARGENT & CO., Chicago, Ill.

SPENCER LENS CO., Buffalo, N. Y.

WHITALL, TATUM & CO., Philadelphia, New York, and Boston. (Makers of glassware.)

WILLIAMS, BROWN & EARLE, Philadelphia.

MICROSCOPES are made or imported direct by Bausch & Lomb, Eimer & Amend, Kny-Scheerer Co., Leitz & Co., Spencer Lens Co., Williams, Brown & Earle, and Queen & Co.

LANTERN SLIDES on zoölogical subjects are made by R. P. Woodford, Pullman, Ill.; A. T. Thompson & Co., Boston; Kny-Scheerer Co., New York; N. F. Davis, Bucknell College, Lewiston, Pa.

CHARTS. Leuckart's zoölogical charts, a series of 100, mounted on cloth and rolled, about $1.70 each when imported duty free. Less than one-third of these charts are useful for high-school work. Descriptive catalogues and the charts may be obtained from the Kny-Scheerer Co., and other firms dealing in laboratory supplies. Jung's zoölogical charts, series of 30, 30 by 39 inches, cloth, $1.50 each are published by J. L. Hammett & Co., New York and Boston.

PORTRAITS OF BIOLOGISTS.   Excellent platinotypes of Darwin and Huxley, from Collier's paintings, are sold by A. D. Batson, Allston, Mass., at $3.50 each. A number of biologists are represented in Macmillan's series of Nature Portraits. India proofs at $1.50 each. The Open Court Co., Chicago, publishes photogravures, 11 by 14, of Herbert Spencer, Lloyd Morgan, Romanes, Darwin, and Haeckel.

MODELS. Ziegler's wax models of frog development are most useful. Imported by Kny-Scheerer Co. Set of twenty-five cost, duty free, about $28. Various anatomical models in papier-mache, plaster, and wax are imported by the same firm.

HOELEMANN'S anatomical plates of the human body are sold by Rand, McNally & Co., Chicago. Series of five plates, 26 by 37, $4.00 each. These and other charts are obtainable through the Kny-Scheerer Co., New York.

CHAPTER X

ZOÖLOGICAL BOOKS

THE books of the following lists have been selected with special reference to their usefulness to teachers and students of zoölogy in schools below the grade of college. Aims guiding The list for the teacher includes not only books the Selecting. for use in direct connection with teaching, but also many zoölogical masterpieces with which every beginner in zoölogical teaching should aim to become acquainted as soon as possible. It has seemed best to select books of a general nature rather than to compile an extensive bibliography including many special works which would be rarely, if ever, used in connection with the work or study of the average teacher in a secondary school. In justification of many omissions of great works familiar to working zoölogists it may be said that teachers in secondary schools who would obtain and make efficient use of these works are generally those who are specially trained by years of graduate study in zoölogy and these may be supposed to be familiar with the existence and general contents of the important zoölogical literature. But the great majority of teachers of zoölogy in high schools are those who have had the advantages of only a limited undergraduate training in the science, and these therefore need references to some of the most useful general works rather than to the special treatises, memoirs, and monographs, which have special interest for the professional zoölogist. Obviously, to extend the list by adding many special works would be to introduce confusion, instead of aiding in the selection of books.

27

Teachers who need more books or special works more technical than those here listed will find many additional **References to Special Literature.** references in Parker and Haswell's *Text-book of Zoölogy*, Vol. II., pp. 628–655; and in appendices to Thompson's *Outlines of Zoölogy* and to his *Study of Animal Life*. References to important special literature is given in many of the general text-books; for example, in McMurrich's *Invertebrate Morphology*, Wilson's *Cell*, and Schafer's *Physiology*. An appendix to Davenport's *Introduction to Zoölogy* includes many special works relating to ecological and systematic zoölogy of American animals.

To the teacher and student of zoology whose unfamiliarity with the general literature of the science leads them to seek **An Important Guide to Books on Zoölogy.** suggestions regarding the selection of books I would recommend especially the reading of the appendix in Thomson's *Study of Animal Life*.

The question of obtaining even the absolutely necessary general reference books is often a serious problem for the **School Libraries.** teacher in some localities, but the rapid growth of public and school libraries is solving this problem. Most of the reference books named on the following pages while directly valuable to the teacher are also useful to the pupils in that selected pages, and especially the illustrations, often make interesting additions to the elementary books. A good selection of such books should be a part of the equipment of the biological laboratory of the school. It is a reasonable expenditure of school funds.

1. General Reference Books for Teachers of Zoölogy.

1. *General Zoölogy, Advanced Text-books and Reference Works.*

The most useful work for general reference by advanced student or teacher is Parker and Haswell's *Text-book of Zoölogy*. Claus and Sedgwick's *Text-book of Zoölogy* has long had such distinction, but the last edition bears the date 1884, and some parts of it are now out of line with later investigations. However, it is still very useful. Probably the most popular single volume covering the general field of zoölogy is Thomson's *Outlines*, but the text-books by Shipley and Mac-Bride, Hertwig, Packard, and the abridgment of Parker and Haswell's *Text-book* have many good points in their favor. As text-books aiming to present the elements of the general principles of zoology rather than a systematic account of the animal kingdom, there are at least five which are excellent : Huxley's *Study of Zoölogy* (*Crayfish*), Parker's *Elementary Biology*, Sedgwick and Wilson's *General Biology*, Parker and Parker's *Practical Zoölogy*, and Morgan's *Animal Biology*. All of these are limited to descriptions of comparatively few animals, but for elementary presentation of general principles of zoölogy they are unquestionably the best. More advanced than these, and valuable for the special student and teacher is Hertwig's *General Principles*.

Parker, T. J., and Haswell. Text-book of Zoölogy. London, Macmillan.[1] 1897. 2 vols., pp. 779, 683; figs, 663, 509. Vol. I., Invertebrates; Vol. II., Chordates (not sold separately). $9.00.

Claus, C. Text-book of Zoölogy. Translated by A. Sedgwick. London, Macmillan. 1884, 1885. 2 vols., pp. 615, 352, figs., 491, 215. Vol. I., Protozoa to Insects; Vol. II., Mollusks to Mammals.

Thomson, J. A. Outlines of Zoölogy. London, Pentland. New York, Appleton. Third edition, 1899. Pp. 819, figs. 332. $3.50.

Hertwig, R. Manual of Zoölogy. Translated by J. S. Kingsley. New York, Holt. London, Bell. 1902. Pp. 704, figs. 672. $3.00.

---

[1] In the following list the names of well-known publishing houses have been abbreviated by using the leading part of the name. Thus Macmillan stands for Macmillan & Co., of London, and The Macmillan Co., of New York; Longmans for Longmans, Green & Co., of London and New York; Doubleday for Doubleday, Page & Co., of New York.

In regard to place of publication and publisher, it is intended to give the place of original publication first, followed by name and address of the foreign agents or reprinters. In case of such well-known houses as those of Longmans and Macmillan, with branches both here and abroad, simply the place of original publication is given, usually London for English authors and New York for American.

In several cases, at least, the publishers of certain books named have remaining in their possession few copies, but copies may usually be obtained from general dealers.

Parker and Haswell. Manual of Zoölogy. New York, Macmillan. American edition, 1900. Pp. 563, figs. 327. $1.60. (An abridgment of the text-book by the same authors.)

Packard, A. S. Zoölogy (advanced). New York, Holt. Seventh edition, 1886. Pp. 721, ill. 545. $2.40.

Shipley, A. E., and MacBride, E. W. Zoölogy — An Elementary Text-book. New York, Macmillan. 1901. Pp. 632, ill. 349. $3.00.

Huxley, T. H. An Introduction to the Study of Zoology, illustrated by the Crayfish. London, Kegan Paul. New York, Appleton. 1879. Pp. 371, figs. 82. $1.75. (A zoölogical classic. Deals with crayfish from the viewpoints of all phases of zoölogical study.)

Morgan, C. L. Animal Biology. London and New York, Longmans. 1889. Pp. 388. (Part I. deals with internal anatomy and embryology as illustrated by frog, bird, rabbit. Part II. presents some invertebrate types.)

Parker, T. J. Elementary Biology. London, Macmillan. Third edition, 1897. Pp. 503, figs. 127. $2.60. (The chief animal types considered are Amœba, Paramœcium, Vorticella, Hydra, Polygordius, starfish, crayfish, mussel, dogfish. Beyond question this is the best introduction to general biology of animals and plants.)

Parker, T. J., and Parker, W. N. An Elementary Course of Practical Zoölogy. London, Macmillan. 1900. Pp. 608, figs. 156. $2.60. (Part I. is an introduction to general principles of zoölogy. It treats of anatomy, histology, embryology, and physiology of frog. Part II. deals with the animals included in Parker's Elementary Biology and in addition several vertebrates.)

Sedgwick, W. T., and Wilson, E. B. General Biology. New York, Holt. Revised edition, 1895. Pp. 231, figs. 105. $1.75. (The zoölogical part is based upon a study of morphology and physiology of earthworm.)

Hertwig, R. General principles of Zoölogy. Translated by G. W. Field. New York, Holt. London, Bell. 1896. Pp. 226, figs. 110. $1.60. (This is part I. of the Manual of Zoölogy by the same author, see above.)

2. *Special Morphology.*

The books named below are more or less special works limited to certain groups of animals or to certain aspects of the science. In all of them the morphological predominates, strictly physiological literature being reserved for a later section.

Calkins, G. N. The Protozoa. New York, Macmillan. 1901. Pp. 347, figs. 152. $3.00. (Important for the general student of zoölogy.)

Dean, B. Fishes, Living and Fossil. New York, Macmillan. 1895. Pp. 300, figs. 344. $2.50. (A concise account for general students. Covers anatomy, embryology, and palæontology.)

Foster, M., and Balfour, F. M. Elements of Embryology. New edition by A. Sedgwick and W. Heape. London, Macmillan. 1883. Pp. 486, illus. 141. $2.60. (General account of embryology of chick and rabbit, with directions for practical study.)

Huxley, T. H. Anatomy of Vertebrated Animals. Anatomy of Invertebrated Animals. 1877. New York, Appleton. (These famous text-books are still useful for reference.)

Kingsley, J. S. Text-book of Vertebrate Zoölogy. New York, Holt. 1899. Pp. 439, figs. 378. $3.00.

Lang, A. Comparative Anatomy. Translated by H. M. and M. Bernard. London, Macmillan. 1891, 1895. 2 vols. $5.50. (Excellent for reference.)

Marshall, A. M. Vertebrate Embryology. London, Smith, Elder. New York, Putnam. 1893. Pp. 640, figs. 240. $6.00. (Excellent. Deals with development of Amphioxus, frog, chick, rabbit, and human.)

McMurrich, J. P. Invertebrate Morphology. New York, Holt 1894. Pp. 661, figs. 291. $3.00.

Wiedersheim, R. Elements of Comparative Anatomy of Vertebrates. Translated by W. N. Parker. London, Macmillan. Revised edition, 1897. Pp. 345, figs. 270. $3.25.

Wilson, E. B. The Cell in Development and in Inheritance. New York, Macmillan. Revised edition, 1901. Pp. 371, figs. 142. $3.00. (For the cellular side of zoölogy, indeed of biology in general, this is indispensable.)

Zoölogical Articles in Encyclopedia Britannica by Lankester and others.

3. *Animal Physiology.*

Verworn's *General Physiology* gives the broadest analysis of general vital activities. There are several excellent text-books dealing with vertebrate physiology with special reference to the human body. Those by Huxley, Martin, and Halliburton (Kirkes) are more general than those which follow them in the list below; in addition to physiology, these present the essentials of anatomy and histology. Stewart's *Manual* has been recommended by some prominent physiologists as the best recent volume devoted strictly to physiological problems for the general student. The last two, by Howell and Shafer, are more extensive treatises primarily of interest to those who have been specially trained in physiology, but also valuable reference works for the teacher of general zoölogy and physiology.

Verworn, M.   General Physiology.   Translated by F. S. Lee.   New York, Macmillan.   1898.   Pp. 599, figs. 285. $4.00.

Huxley, T. H.   Lessons in Elementary Physiology.   New York, Macmillan.   American revised edition by F. S. Lee.   1900.   Pp. 577 figs. 179. $1.10.

Martin, H. N.   The Human Body, Advanced Course.   New York, Holt.   London, Bell.   Fifth edition, 1898.   Pp. 408, figs. 152. $2.50.

Halliburton, W. D.   Kirkes' Handbook of Physiology.   Seventeenth edition, 1901.   London, Murray.   Philadelphia, Blakiston.   Pp, 888, illus. 681. $3.00.   (An unauthorized reprint of an earlier edition is on the market, and it is necessary to name the above publishers in orders for the book.)

Stewart, G. N.)   Manual of Physiology.   Philadelphia and London, Saunders.   Fourth edition, revised, 1900.   Pp. 894, figs. 336. $3.75.

Howell, W. H.   Editor.   American Text-Book of Physiology. Philadelphia, Saunders.   Second edition, revised, 1901.   2 volumes, 1,200 pages. $6.00.

Schafer, E. A.   Editor.   Text-Book of Physiology.   London, Macmillan.   1898.   2 volumes, pp. 1036, 1365.   Vol. I., $8.00; Vol. II., $10.00.   (Contributed by prominent physiologists.   Full and precise information and references to original authorities.)

4. *Bacteriology and Hygiene.*

Books on these subjects are closely associated with human physiology, and hence properly belong in a list of zoölogical books. The books by Conn, Mrs. Frankland, and Prudden are excellent brief introductions to the bacteria. As more extensive general accounts, the larger volumes by Newman and Frankland are excellent. With special reference to the pathogenic bacteria Muir and Ritchie's *Manual* is well recommended as one of the latest books on the subject. Teachers who wish to introduce study of bacteria into their courses will find excellent practical directions for beginners in the handbooks by Gorham and Moore. The general field of sanitary science is well presented by Sedgwick's *Principles ;* and as a general survey of personal hygiene, Pyle's book has the advantage of having been written by a number of workers in special lines of this subject which is usually treated more or less arbitrarily.

Conn, H. W. Story of Germ Life. New York, Appleton. 1897. Pp. 197. 35 cents.

Prudden, T. M. Story of the Bacteria. Dust and its Dangers. Water and Ice. New York, Putnam. Each, 75 cents.

Newman, G. The Bacteria. London, Murray. New York, Putnam. 1899. Pp. 348. $2.00. (A non-technical account of the general relations of bacteria.)

Franklin, P. Our Secret Friends and Foes. London, Society for Promoting Christian Knowledge. Third edition, 1897. (Excellent for general readers.)

Frankland, P., Mrs. Bacteria in Daily Life. London, Longmans. 1903. Pp. 206.

Muir, R., and Ritchie, J. Manual of Bacteriology. Edinburg and London, Pentland. New York, Macmillan. Second edition, 1899. Pp. 550, figs. 126. There is also a larger American edition. New York, Macmillan. 1903. $3.75. (Good on methods. Deals only with pathogenic bacteria affecting man.)

Gorham, F. P. Laboratory Course in Bacteriology. Philadelphia and London, Saunders. 1901. Pp. 192, figs. 97. $1.25.

Moore, V. A. Laboratory Directions for Beginners in Bacteriology. Boston, Ginn. Second edition, 1900. Pp. 141. $1.00.

Sedgwick, W. T. Principles of Sanitary Science and the Public Health. New York, Macmillan. 1902. Pp. 388. $3.00.

Pyle, W. L. Editor. Personal Hygiene. Philadelphia and London, Saunders. 1900. Pp. 344. $1.50.

5. *Laboratory Manuals, chiefly Morphological.*

A set of the best guides for laboratory work is almost indispensable for the teacher's reference while planning laboratory work for classes, and for direction and suggestion in personal studies. Those named below are all too technical for use as laboratory guides by pupils in the high school. Guides adapted for school use are mentioned in this chapter on page 442. The first five books named below are most generally useful.

Marshall, A. M., and Hurst, C. H. Practical Zoölogy. London, Smith, Elder. New York, Putnam. Fifth edition, 1898. Pp. 486, figs. 73. $3.50. (The fourth edition (1895) is still useful. Laboratory directions for Amœba, Vorticella, Paramœcium, Hydra, liver-fluke, leech, earthworm, crayfish, cockroach, mussel, snail, Amphioxus, dogfish, pigeon, rabbit.)

Huxley, T. H., and Martin, H. N. Course of Practical Instruction in Elementary Biology. London, Macmillan. Revised edition by

G. B. Howes and D. H. Scott. 1888. Pp. 279. $2.60. The zoölogical part has descriptions and laboratory directions for Amœba, Vorticella, Paramœcium, Opalina, Hydra, earthworm, crayfish, mussel, snail, frog.

Parker and Parker. Practical Zoölogy. (See under "general zoölogy.") This combines laboratory directions and descriptions of frog, Amœba, Hæmatococcus, Euglena, Paramœcium and Vorticella, Hydra and hydroids, earthworm, crayfish, mussel, amphioxus, dogfish, rabbit.

Pratt, H. S. Invertebrate Zoölogy. Boston, Ginn. 1902. Pp. 210. $1.25. (A laboratory guide dealing with about thirty common representatives of invertebrate groups.)

Brooks, W. K. Handbook of Invertebrate Zoölogy. Boston. 1882. Pp. 392, figs. 202. For sale by Knight & Millet, Boston. (Revision is needed in some parts.)

Bumpus, H. C. Invertebrate Zoölogy. New York, Holt. Second edition, 1892. Pp. 157. $1.00.

Parker, T. J. Zoötomy. London, Macmillan. Second edition, 1884. Pp. 397, figs. 74. $1.25. (Dissection of lamprey, skate, cod, lizard, pigeon, rabbit.)

Marshall, A. M. The Frog — An Introduction to Anatomy, Histology, and Embryology. London, Macmillan. Sixth edition, 1896. Pp. 163, figs. 35. $1.10.

Howes, G. B. Atlas of Practical Elementary Biology. London, Macmillan. Second edition, 1902. $3.50. (Excellent illustrations to accompany Huxley and Martin's Practical Biology. Now out of print, but zoölogical part is issued with title "Atlas of Practical Elementary Zoötomy." $3.50.

6. *Laboratory Guides, Physiology and Histology.*

Hall, W. S. A Laboratory Guide in Physiology. Chicago, Chicago Medical Book Co. 1897. Pp. 359, illus. 60.

Stirling, W. Outlines of Practical Physiology. London, Lewis. Philadelphia, Blakiston. Third edition, 1895. $2.00.

Stirling, W. Outlines of Practical Histology. London, Lewis. Philadelphia, Blakiston. Revised edition, 1898. Pp. 419, illus. 368. $2.00. (Indispensable for those who need practical directions for preparing tissues for microscopic study.)

7. *Systematic Work.*

General text-books of zoölogy, especially those by Claus and Sedgwick, Parker and Haswell, and Thomson, often suffice for finding the approximate zoölogical position of an unknown animal, but for the determination of genera and species other literature is frequently necessary. For the identification of common American animals the works named below will in general prove most useful. More special literature primarily of interest to the taxonomist is mentioned in an appendix to Davenport's *Zoölogy*. This is the most useful small volume for general identification, containing keys and descriptions of the most common forms, both vertebrate and invertebrate. Jordan's *Manual* is the only single volume covering the group of the vertebrates. This and Chapman's *Birds of Eastern North America*, or in Western States, Bailey's *Handbook*, are sufficient for the general student. In fact, such popular books as Chapman's *Bird Life*, Jordan and Evermann's *Food and Game Fishes*, Stone and Cram's *American Animals*, and others which are mentioned in the list of books on natural history (p. 438), will identify the most common forms with sufficient accuracy for general purposes. Likewise in the case of insects and spiders the popular books will often be sufficient; but, if possible, Comstock's *Manual* should be at hand for reference. The *American Naturalist* has, since 1899, published from time to time synopses by well-known specialists on certain North American groups of animals. Finally, the *Riverside Natural History*, edited by Kingsley, should be mentioned as excellent for general classification of American animals.

Davenport, C. B., and G. C. Introduction to Zoölogy. New York, Macmillan. 1899.

Jordan, D. S. Manual of Vertebrate Animals of Northern United States. Chicago, McClurg. Fifth edition, 1888. Pp. 375. $2.50.

Chapman, F. M. Handbook of Birds of Eastern North America. New York, Appleton. 1895. Pp. 430, figs. 150. $3.00.

Bailey, F. Merriam. Handbook of Birds of Western United States. New York, Houghton. 1902. $3.50.

Comstock, J. H., and A. B. Manual for the Study of Insects. Ithaca, N. Y., Comstock Pub. Co. Second edition, 1895. Pp. 701, illus. 797.

American Naturalist. A monthly journal published by Ginn & Co., Boston. $4.00 per year.

Kingsley, J. S., Editor. Riverside (formerly Standard) Natural History. Boston, Houghton. 6 volumes.

8. *Animal Ecology.*

Animal ecology as the phase of zoölogy dealing with relations of animals to environment constitutes a prominent part of most works on " natural history " named under that heading (p. 435). But there are some works which are limited more closely to ecological considerations, and the leading ones of these are named below. The first two are admirable elementary accounts, treating broadly the relations of animals to environments from the standpoint of adaptations in structure and habit.

Thomson, J. A. The Study of Animal Life. London, Murray. New York, Scribner. Third edition, 1896. $1.50.

Jordan, D. S., and Kellogg, V. L. Animal Life. New York, Appleton. 1900. Pp. 329, figs. 180. $1.20.

Semper, K. Animal Life as affected by the natural conditions of existence. London, Kegan Paul. New York, Appleton. 1880. Pp. 472, figs. 106. $2.00.

Beddard, F. E. Animal Coloration. London, Sonnenschein. New York, Macmillan. Second edition, 1895. Pp. 288, figs. 36, 4 colored plates.

Poulton, E. B. The Colors of Animals. London, Kegan Paul. New York, Appleton. 1889. Pp. 360, figs. 67. $1.75. (Special attention to insects.)

Darwin, C. Fertilization of Orchids. Insectivorous Plants. Vegetable Mould and Earthworms. New York, Appleton.

9. *Zoögeography (Distribution).*

For the general student of zoölogy any one of the first three books will be satisfactory after reading the chapters on this subject in general text-books, — for example, in Parker and Haswell's Zoölogy. Those more specially interested will also read Wallace's great works on this subject.

Beddard, F. E. Text-Book of Zoögeography. Cambridge, University Press. New York, Macmillan. 1894. Pp. 246. $1.50.

Heilprin, A. Geographical and Geological Distribution of Animals. New York, Appleton. 1886. Pp. 435. $2.00.

Lyddeker, R. Geographical History of Mammals. Cambridge, University Press. New York, Macmillan. 1896. Pp. 400, figs. 82.

Wallace, A. R. Geographical Distribution. New York, Harpers. 1876. 2 volumes.

Wallace, A. R. Island Life. London, Macmillan. First edition, 1880; second, 1895. Pp. 563. $1.75.

10. *Animal Psychology.*

The most important books along the lines of general psychology of animals are those by Lloyd Morgan and Romanes.

Morgan, C. L. Animal Behavior. London, Arnold. 1900. New York, Longmans. Pp. 344. $3.50. (This should be read before the author's Animal Life and Intelligence, and as an introduction to the subject.)

Morgan, C. L. Animal Life and Intelligence. Boston, Ginn. 1891. Pp. 512. (In addition to mental processes there is much interesting discussion of problems of general zoölogy, such as evolution, heredity, etc.)

Morgan, C. L. Introduction to Comparative Psychology. London, Walter Scott. 1894. Pp. 378.

Morgan, C. L. Habit and Instinct. London, Arnold. New York, Longmans. 1896. Pp. 351. $5.50.

Romanes, G. J. Animal Intelligence. New York, Appleton. 1882. Pp. 520. $1.75.

Romanes, G. J. Mental Evolution in Animals. New York, Appleton. 1883. $2.00.

Groos, K. The Play of Animals. Translated by E. L. Baldwin. New York, Appleton. 1898. Pp. 341. $1.75.

Lubbock, John. Ants, Bees, and Wasps. London, Kegan Paul. New York, Appleton. $2.00. (Deals with mental conditions and powers of sense in these insects.)

11. *Economic Zoölogy.*

There is no concise work which adequately treats the economic side of animals in general. Incidental references to economic importance may usually be found in books on general "natural history" of animals. In addition to the books named below, it should be stated that some of the best literature in the field of economic zoölogy has been published by the United States Department of Agriculture, and by the United States Fish Commission. Besides the annual reports of these two departments, there are many separate bulletins issued, especially in agricultural lines. Those interested should write to the Division of Publications, United States Department of Agriculture, Washington, D. C., for the latest " List of Publications Available for Distribution," and also make application for the "Monthly List of Publications," to be sent regularly (free). Also apply to Superintendent of Public Documents for " List of Publications for Sale." These lists will give full information regarding many good bulletins, some of which may be obtained free upon application, and others at small cost. Some of the most useful which were available in 1902 are named below. Others which are now out of print may be reprinted, and in that event will be noted in future monthly lists.

The complete bibliographical references to the first six books are given on pages 437 and 438.

Miall, L. C.　Injurious and Useful Insects.
Smith, J. B.　Economic Entomology.
Sanderson, E. D.　Insects Injurious to Staple Crops.
Shaler, N. S.　Domesticated Animals.
Wood, J. G.　The Dominion of Man.
Simmonds, P. L.　Animal Products, their Preparation, Commercial Uses and Values.　London, Chapman & Hall.　1877.　Pp. 477.

Bulletins of Division of Entomology.　Principal household insects of United States (*Bulletin*, No. 4, n. s., 10c.); Insects affecting domestic animals (No. 5, n. s., 20c.); Some insects injurious to garden and orchard crops (No. 19, n. s., 10c.); Some insects injurious to garden crops (No. 23, n. s., 10c.); Some insects injurious to vegetable crops (No. 33, n. s., 10c.); Hessian fly in United States (No. 16, n. s., 10c.); Honey bee (No. 1, n. s., 15c.); Destructive locusts (No. 25, 15c.); Periodical cicada (No. 14, n. s., 15c.); and the following circulars which are free: Hessian fly (No. 12); Mosquitoes and fleas (No. 13); House ants (No. 34); House flies (No. 35); Clothes moth (No. 36); Bedbug (No. 47); House centipede (No. 48); Cockroaches (No. 51).

Bulletins of Division of Biological Survey.　Common crow (No. 6, 10c.); Jack rabbits (No. 8, 10c.); Cuckoos and shrikes (No. 9, 5c.); Food of bobolink, blackbirds, and grackles (No. 13, 5c.); Relation of sparrows to agriculture (No. 15, 10c.).

Farmers' Bulletins (Free).　Insects injurious to stored grain (No. 45); Standard varieties of chickens (No. 51); Some common birds in their relation to agriculture (No. 54); Bee-keeping (No. 59); Ducks and geese (No. 64); Insect enemies of the grape (No. 70); Three insect enemies of shade trees (No. 99); Breeds of dairy cattle (No. 106); How insects affect health in rural districts (No. 155).

Extracts from Year-Books (Free).　Hawks and owls from the standpoint of the farmer (No. 10, 1894); Danger of introducing noxious animals (No. 132, 1898); Review of economic entomology in United

States (No. 177, 1899); The food of nestling birds (No. 194, 1900); How birds affect the orchard (No. 197, 1900); The prairie dog (No. 227, 1901); Insects as carriers and spreaders of disease (No. 235, 1901).

Bureau of Animal Industry. American breeds of fowls: I. The Plymouth Rock (No. 29, 15c.); II. The Wyandotte (No. 31, 15c.).

12. *Philosophical Zoölogy and Evolution.*

An intimate knowledge of the special literature of this phase of biology (for here it is practically impossible to draw a sharp line between plants and animals), dealing as it does with abstract generalizations deduced from the known facts, is not as necessary for the actual work of the teacher in the high school as is familiarity with the leading facts of morphology, physiology, and ecology, which are essential for elementary work in the science of zoölogy. Nevertheless, the philosophical phase is important for the intellectual growth of the teacher, for study along this line tends to deepen vastly the interest in the great problems involved in the science of life.

Philosophical zoölogy has its broadest outlook in such works as Spencer's *Principles of Biology*, Brooks's *Foundations of Zoölogy*, and stated largely in terms of general science in Pearson's *Grammar of Science*. But these will have more significance for the reader after study of those more limited phases of philosophical zoölogy which centre directly around the theory of evolution.

Spencer, Herbert. Principles of Biology. London, Williams & Norgate. New York, Appleton. 1864–1867. Revised edition, 1899. 2 volumes. $4.00.

Brooks, W. K. Foundations of Zoölogy. New York, Macmillan, 1899. Pp. 339. $2.50. (A philosophical discussion of fundamental problems.)

Pearson, Karl. Grammar of Science. London, Black. New York, Macmillan. 1892. Second revised and enlarged edition, 1900. Pp. 548. $2.50. (Chapters IX., X., and XI. are biological; but the entire work is of interest to workers in any science.)

The place of honor in a list of books on evolution must be assigned to Darwin's great biological classic, the *Origin of Species*. However, this epoch-making work will be better understŏod and appreciated if read after some introduction to the lines of evidence for evolution. As such an introduction, the first volume of *Darwin and after Darwin*, by Romanes, and also his *Scientific Evidences of Organic Evolution*, hold very high rank. Other important and well-written elementary accounts are Clodd's *Story of Creation* and his *Primer of Evolution*, Bergen's *Primer of Darwinism*, Thomson's *Study of Animal Life*, Part IV., and also his *Outlines of Zoölogy*, Chapter XXIX. The first part of LeConte's *Evolution* is a clear exposition of the general theory and the lines of evidence favoring it.

Darwin, C. R. Origin of Species by means of Natural Selection. London, first edition, 1859; sixth, 1872. London, Murray. Many reprints of the sixth edition are on the market. The American authorized edition is by Appleton, New York, in one and two volume editions. ($2.00 and $4.00.)

Romanes, G. J. Darwin and After Darwin. London, Longmans. Chicago, Open Court Co. 1892. Vol. I., The Darwinian Theory, pp. 460, figs. 125. $2.00. (Volumes II. and III. deal with the debatable questions relating to factors of evolution and appeal only to special readers.)

Romanes, G. J. Scientific Evidences of Organic Evolution. London, Macmillan. 50c.

Clodd, E. Primer of Evolution. London, Longmans. 1895. Pp. 186, figs. 3. 75c.

Clodd, E. Story of Creation. Longmans. $1.25.

Bergen, J. Y., and **F. D.** A Primer of Darwinism and Organic Evolution. Boston, Lee & Shepard. New edition, 1890. $1.25.

Thomson, J. A. Study of Animal Life. London, Murray. New York, Scribner. Third edition, 1896. $1.50.

Thomson, J. A. Outlines of Zoölogy. London, Pentland. New York, Appleton. Third edition, 1899.

LeConte, J. Evolution and its Relation to Religious Thought. New York, Appleton. Second edition, 1891. Pp. 382, figs. 70. $1.50.

After some of the above books as introductions, followed by the *Origin of Species*, the reader will be interested in Wallace's *Darwinism*, Huxley's *Darwiniana*, and *Man's Place in Nature*, and his article, "Evolution," in the *Encyclopedia Britannica*, *Animals and Plants under Domestication* and the

Descent of Man, by Darwin, and the part on evolution in Herbert Spencer's masterful *Principles of Biology*. These are the great pioneer works which supported the *Origin of Species* so convincingly that the evidences of organic evolution have come to be generally accepted even beyond the limits of the scientific world. But there was one dissenter even among the great naturalists, and to understand Agassiz's point of view in opposition to organic evolution one should read his *Methods of Study in Natural History*.

Wallace, A. R. Darwinism. London, Macmillan. 1890. Pp. 494.

Huxley, T. H. Darwiniana. Collection of essays on evolution (1859–1888). New York, Appleton. 1895. Pp. 475. $1.25.

Huxley, T. H. Man's Place in Nature. New York, Appleton. 1863. Pp. 328, figs. 32. $1.25.

Huxley, T. H. Article, "Evolution," in Encyclopedia Britannica.

Darwin, C. R. Animals and Plants under Domestication. London, Murray. New York, Appleton. Second edition, 1875. 2 volumes. Pp. 473, 495. $5.00.

Darwin, C. R. Descent of Man. Second edition, London, 1874. Many reprints are on the market; the authorized one is by Appleton, New York, in one and two volume editions. Cheap reprint by Burt, New York.

Agassiz, Louis. Methods of Study in Natural History. Boston, Houghton. 1863. Eighteenth edition, 1887. Pp. 319. $1.50. (Agassiz's famous protest against the evolution theory.)

Interest in the factors or methods of evolution naturally comes after study of the evidences for the truth of the theory. Some of the works already mentioned, notably Darwin's *Origin of Species*, Spencer's *Principles* and Wallace's *Darwinism* deal with both fact and factors. In addition, there has been developed a mass of special literature on the still uncertain questions involved in the factors — heredity, variation, natural selection, etc. It is difficult to select one volume as best for the beginning study of the factors or for a general view of the whole field. Thomson in his *Science of Life* (see under History of Zoölogy, p. 432) succinctly summarizes the points at issue, and in his *Study of Animal Life* there is a good literature list to which those specially interested can refer.

Those who have interest in the ethical, religious, or sociological bearings of evolution will find the great questions well discussed in LeConte's *Evolution and Religious Thought,* Fiske's *Cosmic Philosophy* and his *Destiny of Man* with its companion volumes, Huxley's *Evolution and Ethics,* Calderwood's *Evolution and Man's Place in Nature,* and Drummond's *Ascent of Man.*

Fiske, John. Outlines of Cosmic Philosophy. Boston, Houghton. 4 volumes. $8.00.

Fiske, John. Destiny of Man, Idea of God, and other small volumes in the same series. Same publishers. $1.00 each.

Huxley, T. H. Evolution and Ethics. In collected essays in volume with same title, New York, Appleton. Also in POPULAR SCIENCE MONTHLY, Vol. XLIV., November and December, 1893.

Calderwood, H. Evolution and Man's Place in Nature. London, Macmillan. 1893.

Drummond, H. Ascent of Man. New York, Pott. 1894. (Although not always as rigidly scientific as is demanded by specialists this book has proved valuable for reading by those not specially educated in sciences.)

13. *History of Zoölogy.*

The only extensive special history of the science of zoölogy is Carus's *Geschichte der Zoölogie* (1872), but this is valuable to the specialist rather than to the general student of the science. The leading facts may be found in the works named below. The first is especially interesting, and should be read by all teachers of biology. It contains an excellent list of references to historical literature; and other references are given in the *Outlines of Zoölogy* by the same author.

Thomson, J. A. The Science of Life, An Outline History of Biology and its Recent Advances. London, Blackie. Chicago, Stone. 1899. Pp. 246. $1.25.

Buckley, A. B. A Short History of Natural Science. New York, Appleton. 1888. Pp. 467. $2.00.

Parker and Haswell. Text-Book of Zoölogy. Historical section, Vol. II., pp. 628–650.

Hertwig, R. General Principles of Zoölogy. Translated by Field. New York, Holt. 1896. Chapter II., on history of zoölogy.

Lankester, E. R. Article "Zoölogy," in Encyclopædia Britannica.

Closely associated with the history of zoölogy is the history of evolution theories. This is the subject-matter of Clodd's *Pioneers of Evolution* and Osborn's *From the Greeks to Darwin*. Excellent short accounts may be found in chapters on "Evolution of Evolution-Theories" in Thomson's *Science of Life* and in his *Study of Animal Life* ; and also the historical side is treated in the chapter on "Philosophical Zoölogy" in Parker and Haswell's *Text-book of Zoölogy*.

Clodd, E. Pioneers of Evolution (from Thales to Huxley). New York, Appleton. 1897. Pp. 274. $1.50. (Contains good pictures of Darwin, Huxley, Spencer, and Wallace.)

Osborn, H. F. From the Greeks to Darwin. An Outline of the Development of the Evolution Idea. New York, Macmillan. 1894. Pp. 259. $2.00.

Thomson, J. A. Study of Animal Life. London, Murray. New York, Scribner. Third edition, 1896. $1.50.

14. *Biography.*

Closely associated with the history of biology are the biographies of the leaders in the development of the science. Especially interesting in connection with the history of zoölogy in the nineteenth century are the lives of such prominent naturalists as Darwin, Huxley, Agassiz, and Pasteur. These have been honored with extensive biographies. For sketches of many of the less prominent biologists one must consult articles in magazines and in the proceedings of learned societies. The files of *Nature* and *Popular Science Monthly*, and the *Proceedings of the Royal Society of London* are especially rich in biographical notes on scientific men who have lived within the last half-century.

Darwin, F. Life and Letters of Charles Darwin. New York, Appleton. 1887. 2 volumes, pp. 558, 562. $4.50.

Darwin, F. Charles Darwin's Life. N. Y., Appleton. $1.50.

Allen, Grant. Darwin. London, Longmans. 1888. Pp. 206. (Probably the best short biography of Darwin.)

Bettany, G. T. Darwin. London, W. Scott. 1887. Pp. 175 + 31. (Contains a list of Darwin's works, and a selected bibliography of books and magazine articles on the naturalist and his work.)

Wallace, A. R.   Debt of Science to Darwin.   CENTURY MAGAZINE, January, 1883.

Huxley, L.   Life and Letters of T. H. Huxley.   New York, Appleton.   1900.   2 volumes, pp. 539, 541.

Agassiz, E. C.   Louis Agassiz, his Life and Correspondence.   Boston, Houghton.   1885.   Pp. 794. $2.50.   (After this eulogy the next work should be read.)

Marcou, J.   Life, Letters, and Work of L. Agassiz.   New York, Macmillan.   1895.   2 volumes, pp. 302, 318.

Jordan, D. S.   Agassiz at Penikese.   Chapter in volume known as Science Sketches.   Chicago, McClurg.   New edition, 1896.   Also in POPULAR SCIENCE MONTHLY, Vol. XL., pp. 721, 1892.

Radot, V.   Louis Pasteur, his Life and Labors.   Translated from the French by Lady Hamilton.   Introduction by John Tyndall.   New York, Appleton.   1886.   (Written under Pasteur's supervision by his son-in-law, Radot.)

Frankland, P.   Life of Pasteur.   London, Macmillan.

Nicholson, H. A.   Lives and Labors of Leading Naturalists.   Edinburg, Chambers.   1890.

Wright, H. A.   Children's Stories of the Great Scientists.   New York, Scribner.   1888.

15. Periodicals.

SCHOOL SCIENCE.   Chicago.   Monthly. $2.00 per year.   Important for all science teachers of secondary schools.   Contains pedagogical discussions, reviews of new books, practical notes, reports of meetings of teachers' associations, and notes on advances of scientific knowledge.

JOURNAL OF APPLIED MICROSCOPY AND LABORATORY METHODS.   Rochester, N. Y.   Six volumes published; discontinued in December, 1903.   Valuable for suggestions on laboratory practice and teaching, and descriptions of new apparatus.

SCIENCE.   New York, Macmillan.   Weekly. $5.00 per year.   Sent free of charge to members of the American Association for the Advancement of Science.   (Concerning application for membership write to Dr. L. O. Howard, Permanent Secretary, Washington, D. C.   All science teachers are eligible.   Entrance fee is $5.00 and annual dues $3.00.)   Interesting to all American workers in science because it gives reports of meetings of the important scientific societies, scientific addresses, reviews of recent books and numerous notes on science progress in general.

AMERICAN NATURALIST.   Boston, Ginn & Co.   Monthly. $4.00 per year.   Publishes many original articles of general interest to zoölogists, and also abstracts of many recent articles.

POPULAR SCIENCE MONTHLY.   New York, The Science Press.   Monthly. $5.00 per year.   Devoted to non-technical summaries of scientific advances. Many biological articles of general interest are published.

JOURNAL OF THE ROYAL MICROSCOPICAL SOCIETY. London. Bimonthly. Gives special attention to abstracts of leading original papers in zoölogy, botany, and microscopy. Valuable for the teacher who wishes to keep in touch with the progress of investigation. Too expensive for individual subscription, but found in many public and college libraries.

16. *Animal Natural History.*

In presenting facts which are of general or popular interest, as well as in a less rigidly technical style, the books of this list stand in contrast to those of the preceding pages, most of which appeal chiefly to special students of the science of zoölogy. Practically all the books here named are of interest to the adult general reader. The books marked with an asterisk (*) are especially suitable for supplementary reading by high-school pupils. In fact, many of these books have been reported as interesting to children of the seventh and eighth grades in the elementary school. Selected parts of many other books intended by their authors to appeal primarily to adult readers might be used by high-school pupils; and special references to many of these are given in the outline of a course in Chapter VIII. Some of the school books of zoölogy named on page 444 are such excellent introductions to animal natural history that they deserve a place also in this list of books for reading and reference.

General Works.

Hodge, C. F. Nature Study and Life. Boston, Ginn. 1902. Pp. 514, figs. 196. $1.50. (Excellent guide to nature-study.)

Ingersoll, E. Nature's Calendar. A guide and record for outdoor observations. New York, Harpers. 1900. Pp. 270. $1.50. (Suggestions for field work in nature-study.)

Johnson's Universal Cyclopedia. Zoölogical articles edited by D. S. Jordan are excellent for scientific and popular names and notes on American animals.

International Encyclopedia. New York, Dodd, Mead. 1902. Zoölogical articles under the supervision of well-known American zoölogists.

Jordan, D. S., and Kellogg, V. L. *Animal Life. New York, Apple-ton. 1900. Pp. 329, figs. 180. $1.20. (An introduction to animal ecology).

Jordan, D. S., and Heath, H. *Animal Forms. New York, Apple-ton. 1902. Pp. 258, figs. 140. $1.10. This book and the preceding are also bound in one volume with the title " Animals." Excellent.

Kingsley, J. S., Editor. *Riverside Natural History (formerly known as the Standard). Boston, Houghton. 6 volumes, $30.00. (The best extensive work giving attention to American animals.)

Margesson, Lady. Editor. *Handbook of Natural History for Use of Beginners. London, G. Philip. 1894. (Some well-known contrib-utors.)

Morgan, C. L. *Animal Sketches. London, Arnold. 1891. New York, Longmans. Pp. 312. (A series of interesting sketches of some twenty commonly known animals, vertebrates and invertebrates.)

Thomson, J. A. *The Study of Animal Life. London, Murray. New York, Scribner. Third edition, 1896. Pp. 375. (Part I. is an ex-cellent introduction to natural history.)

Wood, J. G. *All the books on general natural history by this author are interesting. Longmans, New York.

Books on Lower Animals, Chiefly Insects.

Badenoch, L. N. Romance of the Insect World. London, Mac-millan. 1893. Pp. 341, figs. 60.

Ballard, J. P. *Moths and Butterflies. New York, Putnams. $1.50.

Buckley, A. B. *Life and Her Children, Glimpses of Animal Life from Amœba to Insects. London, Stanford. New York, Appleton. $1.50.

Comstock, J. H. Insect Life. New York, Appleton. 1897. Pp. 349, illus. 296. $1.50. Edition in colors. $1.75.

Cragin, B. S. *Our Insect Friends and Foes. New York, Putnams. 1899. Pp. 374, figs. 235. $1.75.

Darwin, C. Vegetable Mould and Earthworms. New York, Apple-ton. Also in Humboldt Library of Science. $1.50.

Emerton, J. H. *The Structure and Habits of Spiders. Boston. 1878. Pp. 118, illus. 67. (For sale by Knight & Millet, Boston.)

Emerton, J. H. Common Spiders of the United States. Boston, Ginn. 1902. Pp. 225.

Emerton, J. H. Life on the Seashore. Salem, 1880. A convenient popular guide to animals of the New England coast. (For sale by Knight & Millet, Boston, $1.50.)

Gibson, W. H. *Eye Spy, *Sharp Eyes, and other books. New York, Harper.

Hyatt, A., and others. Guides for Science Teaching. Boston, Heath. III. Commercial and Other Sponges. 1886. 20c. V. Corals and Echinoderms. 1889. 20c. VI. Molluska (oyster, clam). 1888. 25c. VII. Worms and Crustacea. 1888. 25c.

Heilprin, A. *Animal Life of our Seashore. Philadelphia, Lippincott. 1888. Pp. 130, many illustrations. $1.25. (Animals of coast of New Jersey and southern Long Island.)

Holland, W. J. *The Butterfly Book. New York, Doubleday. 1898. Pp. 382. 48 plates in color photography. $3.00. (Butterflies of North America.)

Holland, W. J. * The Moth Book. 1903. Pp. 400, 48 plates. $4.00.

Howard, L. O. *The Insect Book. New York, Doubleday. 1901. Pp. 429, plates 48. (North American insects exclusive of butterflies moths, and beetles.) $3.co.

Lubbock (now Lord Avebury). Ants, Bees, and Wasps. London, Kegan Paul. New York, Appleton. $2.00.

Miall, L. C. Natural History of Aquatic Insects. London, Macmillan. 1895. Pp. 395. $1.75.

Miall, L. C. *Injurious and Useful Insects, An Introduction to the Study of Economic Entomology. London, Macmillan. 1902. Pp. 256. $1.00.

Needham, J. G. *Outdoor Studies. American Book Co. 1898. Pp. 90, figs. 88. 40c. (Deals chiefly with insects.)

Sanderson, E. D. Insects Injurious to Staple Crops. New York, Wiley. 1902. Pp. 295, figs. 162. $1.50.

Scudder, S. H. *Everyday Butterflies. Boston, Houghton. 1899. Pp. 391, 71 illustrations. $2.00.

Smith, J. B. Economic Entomology. Philadelphia, Lippincott. 1896. Pp. 480, figs. 483. $2.50.

Van Beneden, P. J. Animal Parasites and Messmates. London, Kegan Paul. New York, Appleton. Pp. 274, illus, 83. $1.50.

Weed, C. M. *Life Histories of American Insects. New York, Macmillan. 1897. Pp. 272, 21 full-page plates and 94 figures in text. (About twenty-five interesting common insects.) $1.50.

Weed, C. M. *The Insect World. New York, Appleton. 1899. 60c.

Weed, C. M. *Stories of Insect Life. First series. Boston, Ginn. 1897. Pp. 54, figs. 51. 25c.

Weed, C. M. *Nature Biographies. New York, Doubleday. 1901. Pp. 164, 150 photographic illustrations. (Lives of some every-day insects.)

Murtfeldt, M. E., and Weed, C. M. *Stories of Insect Life. Second series. Boston, Ginn. 1899. Pp. 72, figs. 34. 30c.

Wood, J. G. Insects Abroad. New York, Longmans.

Books on Backboned Animals.

Buckley, A. B. *Winners in Life's Race, or the Great Backboned Family. London, Stanford. New York, Appleton. $1.50.

Darwin, C. Animals and Plants under Domestication. New York, Appleton. $5.00. (Contains much interesting natural history of domesticated animals, especially birds and mammals.)

Ingersoll, E. *Wild Life of Orchard and Field. New York, Harper. 1902. Pp. 346, 25 illustrations from photographs. $1.40.

Jordan, D. S., and **Evermann, B. W.** *American Food and Game Fishes. New York, Doubleday. 1902. Pp. 573. Many colored plates and half-tones from excellent photographs by Dugmore. $4.00.

Lucas, F. A. *Animals of the Past. New York, McClure, Phillips. 1902. $2.00. (Good popular account of palæontology.)

Mathews, S. *Familiar Life in Field and Forest. New York, Appleton. 1898. Pp. 284, many illustrations. $1.75. (Mammals, birds, frogs, and salamanders.)

Mivart, St. G. The Common Frog. London, Macmillan. 1881. Pp. 158. (Now out of print and obtainable only from dealers in old books.)

Mivart, St. G. *American Types of Animal Life. Boston, Little, Brown. 1891. Pp. 374, illus. 102. (Deals with animals peculiar to America — opossum, turkey, bison, raccoon, sea-lion, bullfrog, rattlesnake, sloth, and many others.)

Shaler, N. S. *Domesticated Animals, their Relation to Man and to his Advancement in Civilization. New York, Scribners. 1895. Pp. 267. $2.50. (Mammals, birds, bee, silkworm.)

Sharp, D. L. *Wild Life near Home. New York, Century Co. 1901. Pp. 357, many illustrations. $2.00. (Birds and mammals, fish, frogs.) *A Watcher in the Woods is an abridged edition for schools.

Wood, J. G. *The Dominion of Man. London, Bentley. 1889. Pp. 400. (Domesticated and tamed animals useful to man.)

Birds.

" **Bird Lore.** A bi-monthly magazine. New York, Macmillan. $1.00 per year.

Blanchan, Neltje (Mrs. F. N. Doubleday). *Bird Neighbors. New York, Doubleday. 1898. Pp. 234, 52 colored plates. $2.00. (150 common birds.)

Blanchan, Neltje. *Birds that Hunt and are Hunted. New York, Doubleday. 1899. Pp. 359, 48 colored plates. $2.00. (170 birds of prey, game birds, and waterfowl.)

Blanchan, N. How to Attract the Birds. New York, Doubleday. $1.35.

Chapman, F. M. *Bird-Life. A guide to study of our common birds. New York, Appleton. 1897. Pp. 270, 75 full-page plates from drawings by Thompson-Seton. Popular edition, 1901, has plates in colors and appendix for teachers. $2.00. (An excellent introduction to birds.)

Chapman, F. M. *Bird Studies with a Camera. New York, Appleton. 1900. Pp. 218, 100 photographs from nature. $1.75.

Herrick, F. H. *Home Life of Wild Birds. New York, Putnam. $2.50. (Numerous photographs. Suggestions for study of the birds.)

Merriam, F. A. (Mrs. Bailey). Birds of Village and Field. Boston, Houghton. 1898. Pp. 398, figs. 228, and 28 plates. $2.00. (Contains excellent outlines for field observations and a list of books on birds.)

Parkhurst, H. E. Song Birds and Waterfowl. New York, Scribners. 1877. Pp. 285. Illustrated by L. A. Fuertes. $1.50.

Weed, C. M., and Dearborn, N. Birds in their Relation to Man. Philadelphia, Lippincott. 1903. Pp. 378. Illustrated. $2.50.

Wright, M. O., and Coues, E. *Citizen Bird. New York, Macmillan. 1897. Pp. 428, figs. 111, by L. A. Fuertes. $1.50. (Plain English for beginners.)

Wright, M. O. *Birdcraft. A field book of 200 birds. New York, Macmillan. 1895. Pp. 306, 30 full-page plates in color. $2.50.

Mammals.

In addition to the more general books by Buckley, Matthews, Ingersoll, Mivart, and others, which are named above, the following deal particularly with the mammals.

Baker, S. W. *Wild Beasts and Their Ways. London, Macmillan. 1890, 1898. Pp. 455.

Burroughs, J. *Squirrels and other Fur-bearers. Boston, Houghton. 1900. $1.00.

Flower, W. H. The Horse. New York, Appleton. (Out of print.)

Ingersoll, E. *Wild Neighbors, Outdoor Studies in the United States. New York, Macmillan. 1897. Pp. 301. $1.50. (Squirrels, puma, coyote, badger, porcupine, skunk, woodchuck, raccoon.)

Long. *Ways of Wood Folk. *School of the Woods. *Wilderness Ways, and similar books. Boston, Ginn. (Interesting stories of wild animals interpreted from the human viewpoint. See criticism by John Burroughs in ATLANTIC MONTHLY, March, 1903, and reply by Long in NORTH AMERICAN REVIEW, May, 1903.)

Stone, W., and Cram, W. E. *American Animals. New York, Doubleday. 1902. Pp. 318. $3.00. (Mammals of North America, north of Mexico with sketches of the more familiar species. Splendidly illustrated from photographs and drawings.)

Wallihan, A. S. *Camera Shots at Big Game. New York, Doubleday. 1901. Pp. 77. (Recommended for its beautiful illustrations.) $10.00.

Wright, M. O. *Four-Footed Americans. New York, Macmillan. 1898. Pp. 413. Many illustrations by Thompson-Seton. $1.50. (Well adapted to young readers. Simple key to North American Mammals.)

17. *General Natural History.*

The books named above represent only the animal side of natural history. But the real student of nature will feel the need of books with a greater outlook upon all living and life-

less things. Such may be found in many books which have
an established place in English literature. The titles of many
of them are generally familiar; but in these days when new
books are demanded there is danger that the contents of many
of these classics may remain unknown to the younger generation of readers. Perhaps the most interesting books are
those which reflect the personal environment of their authors.
"One's own landscape," says John Burroughs, "comes in time
to be a sort of outlying part of himself. . . . This is one source
of Gilbert White's charm, and of the charm of Thoreau's
Walden," — and we may add that this is the charm of the
best of the books by Burroughs himself. The most famous
book of this class is Gilbert White's *Natural History of
Selborne*, first published in 1789, and now available in many
modern editions. Thoreau's *Walden* (Houghton, Mifflin) gives
the best view of the writings of this naturalist. The best introduction to the books of John Burroughs is a book of selections
entitled *A Year in the Fields* (Houghton, Mifflin). After this
the reader will want his *Wake Robin* (1871); *Locusts and Wild
Honey* (1879); *Signs and Seasons* (1886); *Riverby* (1894); and
others published by Houghton, Mifflin & Co., at $1.25 per
volume. The same publishers issue some of Burroughs's essays
in pamphlet form for use in schools, price fifteen cents each.

Among the numerous books by traveller-naturalists the following contain much of interest to the student of biology: Bates's
The Naturalist on the River Amazon (1863), (good edition
by Appleton, a cheap one in Humboldt Library of Science); ·
Darwin's *Voyage of the Beagle* (Appleton); Belt's *Naturalist in
Nicaraugua*; Hudson's *Naturalist in La Plata* and *Idle Days
in Patagonia* (Appleton); Drummond's *Tropical Africa* (Scribner); Agassiz's *A Journey in Brazil*.

2. Special Lists of Selected Books.

a. Limited Selection of Books for a School Library.

The limited list of books given below includes those which
appeal to the writer as most important in a library for the use

of pupils. The following lists of books for teachers should be added, because they too are valuable to students. They should be at hand so that the teacher can cite paragraphs and especially illustrations for reference. With the growth of the school library, it will be desirable to add many others from the list on natural history.

Blanchan. Bird Neighbors.
Chapman. Bird Life.
Comstock. Insect Life.
Conn. Story of Germ Life.
Davenport. Introduction to Zoölogy.
French. Animal Activities.
Hodge. Nature Study and Life.
Holland. Butterfly Book.
Harvey. Introduction to Study of Zoölogy.
Jordan and Evermann. American Fishes.
Jordan and Kellogg. Animal Life.
Jordan and Heath. Animal Forms.
Kellogg. Elementary Zoölogy.
Kingsley. Comparative Zoölogy.
Martin. Human Body, Briefer Course.
Miall. Injurious and Useful Insects.
Morse. First Book in Zoölogy.
Needham. Lessons in Zoölogy. Outdoor Studies.
Prudden. Story of Bacteria. Dust and its Dangers. Water and Ice.
Romanes. Darwin and After Darwin. Vol. I.
Scudder. Everyday Butterflies.
Shaler. Domesticated Animals.
Sharp. Wild Life Near Home. A Watcher in the Woods.
Stone and Cram. American Animals.
Thomson. Study of Animal Life.
Weed. Life Histories of American Insects. Stories of Insect Life.
Wright. Four-Footed Americans.

b. Limited Selection of Books on Animals for the Teacher of Nature-Study.

All the books on natural history named on earlier pages are useful to teachers of nature study in the elementary school; but those of the following list are, in the opinion of the writer, of exceptional value. The list below gives a general survey of the field, and additions from the larger list on natural history must depend upon the reader's interest. This list aims to include only books giving information about animals; for special literature on the teaching of nature study, see Chapter IV.

> **Hodge.** Nature Study and Life.
> **Thomson.** Study of Animal Life.
> **Jordan, Kellogg, and Heath.** Animals.
> **Chapman.** Bird Life.
> **Comstock.** Insect Life.
> **Needham.** Outdoor Studies.
> **Wright.** Four-Footed Americans.

c. Limited Selection of Books for the Teacher of Zoölogy.

This is a selected list of the most indispensable books, such as a beginning teacher or student of general zoölogy will wish to purchase for the foundation of a private library. I would preface the list with the preceding one on nature-study.

> **Parker and Haswell.** Text-Book of Zoölogy.
> **Thomson.** Outlines of Zoölogy.
> **Parker.** Elementary Biology.
> **Parker and Parker.** Practical Zoölogy.
> **Sedgwick and Wilson.** General Biology.
> **Hertwig.** General Principles of Zoölogy.
> **Marshall.** Vertebrate Embryology.
> **Huxley.** Lessons in Physiology.
> **Huxley.** The Crayfish (The Study of Zoölogy).
> **Stewart.** Manual of Physiology.
> **Newman.** The Bacteria.
> **Pyle.** Personal Hygiene.
> **Morgan.** Animal Behavior.
> **Romanes.** Darwin and After Darwin. Vol. I.
> **Darwin.** Origin of Species.
> **Thomson.** Science of Life.
> **Huxley.** Science and Education Essays (Appleton).

3. **Text-books and Guides for Zoölogy and Physiology in Secondary Schools.**

a. Books on Zoölogy.

This list names most of the books in zoology for secondary schools which have been published within thirty years. Most of the older ones of these are still common in the school

libraries, and, in fact, with few exceptions, all are in the market
to-day. · The list is arranged in the chronological order of
publication of the books.

Hooker, W. Natural History. New York, Harper. 1860. Pp.
382, figs. 278. (A text-book, a type of the old-time text-books on
animals.)

Tenney, S. and A. A. Natural History of Animals. New York,
American Book Co. 1866. Pp. 260, 520 woodcuts. (An interesting
account of common animals. Still useful for reading.)

Morse, E. S. First Book of Zoölogy. New York, American Book
Co. 1875. Pp. 190, 168 excellent illustrations. 87c. (A reading book
arranged so as to lead pupils to observe. Excellent.)

Packard, A. S. Zoölogy, Briefer Course. New York, Holt. First
edition, 1883; seventh, 1897. Pp. 364, figs. 338. $1.12. (A text-book.)

Holder, C. F. and J. B. Elements of Zoölogy. New York, Appleton. 1884. Pp. 391, figs. 383. (A text-book.)

Colton, B. P. Practical Zoölogy. Boston, Heath. 1886. Pp. 185.
60c. New edition (1903) referred to below. This was the pioneer
laboratory guide for high schools. Chiefly anatomical.)

Packard, A. S. First Lessons in Zoölogy. New York, Holt. 1886.
Pp. 290, figs. 266. (An excellent text-book in its day.)

Steele, J. D., and Jenks, J. W. P. Popular Zoölogy. New York,
American Book Co. 1887. Pp. 319, figs. 480. (A text-book.)

Montmahon and Beauregard. A Course in Zoölogy for Secondary
Education. Translated from French by W. H. Green. Philadelphia,
Lippincott. 1892. Pp. 358, figs. 319. (A type of the text-book which
has been used in France for more than seventy years. The general plan
appears to have remained unchanged since the time of Cuvier.)

Pillsbury, J. H. A Laboratory Guide in General Biology. Boston.
1894.

Dodge, C. W. Elementary Practical Biology. New York, American Book Co. 1894. (A laboratory guide for animals and plants intended for high school and college.)

Boyer, E. R. Elementary Biology. Boston, Heath. 1894. Pp.
235. 80c. Part I. deals with animals. (A laboratory guide. Almost
entirely anatomical.)

Needham, J. G. Elementary Lessons in Zoölogy. New York,
American Book Co. 1895. Pp. 302. 90c. (A text-book and laboratory
guide. The text presents a good general view of the field of zoölogy.
Laboratory work is chiefly anatomical. Excellent on field work, especially on insects.)

Chapin, H. E., and Rettger, M. A. Elementary Zoölogy and
Laboratory Guide. Chicago, Engelhard. 1896. Pp. 212, figs. 144.

Kingsley, J. S. Elements of Comparative Zoölogy. New York,
Holt. 1897. Pp. 355, figs. 148. $1.20. (Text-book and laboratory

guide. Text excellent for general accounts of animals. Laboratory work is entirely anatomical.)

Beddard, F. E. Elementary Zoölogy. London and New York, Longmans. 1898. Pp. 208, figs. 93. (Review in SCIENCE, March, 1899. A text-book.)

Davenport, C. B. and G. C. Introduction to Zoölogy. New York, Macmillan. 1900. Pp. 412, figs. 311. $1.10. (Review in SCIENCE, n. s., Vol. XII., p. 442. September, 1900. A text-book with appendix on practical work. Exclusively devoted to natural history.)

Walter, Whitney, and Lucas. Studies of Animal Life. Boston, Heath. 1900. Pp. 106. 50c. (Review in AMERICAN NATURALIST, May, 1901. A laboratory guide, chiefly on external structure and ecology of living animals.)

Kellogg, V. L. Elementary Zoölogy. New York, Holt. 1901. Pp. 492, figs. 172. $1.20. (A text-book and guide. Text gives a general view of the field of zoölogy. Laboratory work is anatomical and ecological.)

Harvey, N. A. Introduction to the Study of Zoölogy. New York, American Book Co. 1901. Pp. 208, figs. 35. 80c. (A guide to practical study, with additional notes. Chiefly anatomical. Contains many useful pedagogical suggestions.)

French, N. S. Animal Activities. New York, Longmans, Green. 1901. Pp. 262, figs. 196. $1.20. (Review in SCHOOL SCIENCE, January, 1903. A text-book and guide in natural history.)

Jordan, D. S., and Kellogg, V. L. Animal Life. New York, Appleton. 1900. Pp. 329, figs. 180. $1.20. (A text-book on animal ecology.)

Jordan, D. S., and Heath, H. Animal Forms. New York, Appleton. 1902. Pp. 258, figs. 140. $1.10. (Review in AMERICAN NATURALIST, October, 1902. A text-book dealing with animal structure, with some reference to functions, habits, and life-history.)

Jordan, Kellogg, and Heath. Animals ($1.80), and Animal Studies ($1.25). The first book, Animals, consists of Animal Life and Animal Forms, bound together, and the second is composed of selections from these with some modifications.

Jordan and Price. Animal Structures. New York, Appleton. 1903. Pp. 100. 75c. (A laboratory guide for studies of structure of Amœba, Paramœcium, starfish, Hydra, earthworm, crayfish, grasshopper, mussel, toad. Too much detailed anatomy for high-school work. It, however, contains useful suggestions for teachers in secondary schools.)

Merrill, J. A. Studies in Zoölogy. New York, American Book Co. 1902. (A laboratory guide. Emphasizes anatomy and classification.)

Weed, C. M., and Crossman, R. W. A Laboratory Guide for Beginners in Zoölogy. Boston, Heath. 1902. Pp. 105. (Special attention given to structure and classification.)

Dodge, C. W. General Zoölogy. New York, American Book Co. 1903. (This text-book is based on Orton's Zoölogy (1876), and the remains of the old book are so prominent that the change of author's name is, to say the least, unjustifiable.)

Colton, B. P. Zoology, Descriptive and Practical. Boston, Heath. 1903. Part I., Descriptive. Pp. 375, figs. 200. $1.00. Part II., Practical. 60c. The two parts are also bound together. $1.50. (This revision of the earlier edition of the practical part is improved by adding directions for study of living animals in field and laboratory. It is still largely anatomical. The text gives a general view of the field of zoölogy.)

Kellogg, V. L. First Lessons in Zoölogy. New York, Holt. 1903. Pp. 363, figs. 257. $1.12. (A text-book and guide for study of natural history of common animals.)

The books by Needham, Colton, Kingsley, Davenport, Kellogg, and Jordan, Kellogg, and Heath, are in the writer's opinion the best of the available books for use in secondary schools. Copies of all these should be on the reference shelf. A comparative study of these books will prove invaluable to teachers. Needham's *Zoölogy*, Colton's new *Zoölogy*, and Kellogg's *Elementary Zoölogy* are the most useful books combining text and practical work in general zoölogy for pupils' use. *Animal Life* and *Animal Forms* are beyond question the best existing books for pupil's supplementary reading. Davenport's *Introduction*, Kellogg's *Lessons*, and French's *Animal Activities* are the best guides for a course in natural history. Special booklets of suggestions to teachers accompany *Animal Life*, Walter, Whitney, and Lucas's *Studies*, and Colton's new *Zoölogy*. Jordan and Price's *Animal Structures*, Kellogg's books, and French's *Animal Activities* have similar materials in appendices.

b. *Text-books of Elementary Human Physiology.*

[NOTE.] This list includes the most important current text-books which are much used in schools. No attempt is made to compile a complete bibliography of American text-books on this subject. It would be a thankless task to catalogue the large number of "physiologies" for schools which have been published since 1880, most of which are on the market to-day. One publishing house alone had over thirty text-books of "physiology" for public schools in print last year; and probably more than one hundred for all grades between primary and high school are now in the American market. Many of these are simply compilations of no special merit by authors who have had rather limited experience both as students and teachers of physiology.

Books for High School:

Blaisdell, A. F.   Practical Physiology.   Boston, Ginn.   1897.   Pp. 448, illus. 170. $1.10.

Brinckley, W. J.   Physiology by the Laboratory Method.   For Secondary Schools.   Chicago, Ainsworth.   1903.   Pp. 536, figs. 181. $1.25.   (Contains some good suggestions for teachers; but, on the whole, the book is not well adapted for use by high-school pupils, because there is too much which is technical and non-essential.)

Brown, B. M.   Physiology for the Laboratory.   Boston, Ginn. 1900.   Pp. 167, figs. 19.   75c.   (Suggestive for teachers of physiology.)

Colton, B. P.   Physiology, Experimental and Descriptive.   Boston, Heath.   1897.   Pp. 399, illus. 103. $1.12.   (Contains numerous practical suggestions.   Pedagogically it is one of the best books in this line.)

Cutter, J. C.   Comprehensive Anatomy, Physiology, and Hygiene. Philadelphia, Lippincott.   1884, 1888.   Pp. 375, illus. 142. $1.00.

Foster, M., and Shore.   Physiology for Beginners.   New York, Macmillan.   1894.   Pp. 247, illus. 111.   75c.   (An excellent book on the essentials of physiology.   Distinguished by its brief presentation of the facts about alcohol.)

Furneaux, W. S.   Animal Physiology.   New York, Longmans. 1888.   80c.   Pp. 243, illus. 218.

Hewes, H. F.   Anatomy, Physiology, and Hygiene for High Schools. American Book Co.   1900.   Pp. 320, illus. 88. $1.00.

Martin, H. N.   The Human Body, Briefer Course.   New York, Holt.   1883.   Fifth edition, revised by G. W. Fitz, 1898.   Pp. 408, illus. 157. $1.20.   (The most important text-book for high schools.)

Macy, M. L., and Norris, H. W.   Physiology for High Schools. American Book Co.   1900.   Pp. 408, illus. 143. $1.10.   (This book differs from others of its class chiefly in emphasis upon the nervous system, around which the whole book is centred.)

Overton, F.   Applied Physiology.   American Book Co.   1897.   Pp. 432.   80c.   (Mentioned here in order to call the attention of teachers to the fact that it contains numerous erroneous and misleading statements.)

Peabody, J. E.   Laboratory Exercises in Anatomy and Physiology. New York, Holt.   1898.   Revised, 1902.   Pp. 79.   60c.   (An excellent guide for practical work with classes.)

Peabody, J. E.   Studies in Physiology, Anatomy, and Hygiene. New York, Macmillan.   1903.   Pp. 332, figs. 147. $1.20.   (An excellent guide to teaching physiology on a practical basis.)

Walker, J.   Anatomy, Physiology, and Hygiene.   Boston, Allyn & Bacon.   Second edition, 1900.   Pp. 490, illus. 121.   (Especially excellent on hygienic topics.   Treatment of alcohol scientific.   See review in OUTLOOK, Vol. LXVI, 706–709, November 17, 1900.)

For a Short Course in a High School the Following Books are Recommended:

Colton, B. P. Physiology (Briefer Course). Boston, Heath. 1899. Pp. 386. 90c. (The Elementary Course by same author and publisher is somewhat simpler.)

Blaisdell, A. F. Life and Health. Boston, Ginn. 1902. Pp. 345. 90c.

Hall, W. S. Elementary Physiology. American Book Co. 75c.

CHAPTER XI

THE RELATION OF ZOÖLOGY IN SECONDARY SCHOOL AND COLLEGE

BIBLIOGRAPHY

Davenport, C. B. Zoölogy as a Condition for Admission to College. Sixth (1898) Report High School Department, University of State of New York. Pp. 459–476. (H. S. Bulletin, No. 2, November, 1899.)

Ganong, W. F. Suggestions for an Attempt to Secure a Standard College Entrance Option in Botany. SCIENCE, N. S., Vol. XIII., pp. 611–616. April, 1901.

Osborn, H. L. The Differentiation of Zoölogy for the High-School and College Curriculum. SCHOOL REVIEW, Vol. IX., 1901, p. 567.

Report of Committee on Secondary School Studies (Committee of Ten), National Educational Association. United States Bureau of Education. 1893.

Report of Sub-committee on Zoölogy, National Educational Association. Proceedings N. E. A., 1899, pp. 805–809.

1. Differentiation of Work for School and College.

No aspect of zoölogical teaching in secondary schools has been the subject of so much discussion as has that of its relation to the first college course in zoölogy. To some extent this interest may have been associated with the general attention given to college-admission credit for all subjects of the secondary curriculum; but certainly it was stimulated largely by the extensive overlapping of college and secondary work in zoölogy.

The duplication of work resulting from the introduction of the Huxleyan morphological course of the colleges into the

Duplication of Work in School and College. secondary schools began to attract the general attention of zoölogists in the early years of the last decade when high-school graduates first applied for advance credit in college zoölogy on the ground that the work done in the high school was closely similar to that of the first course of the college. This condition of affairs suggested that at least from the college standpoint there was need of differentiation between the zoölogical work of the school and college. But with the exception of casual references at meetings of local educational and scientific societies the subject received little attention; and no definite and organized protest against the overlapping and duplication of college and secondary courses in zoölogy appears to have been made before 1898. Previous to that time those colleges which made provision for admission credit in zoölogy made no requirement looking towards differentiation of college and secondary courses in zoölogy.

In 1898 Harvard University published an " Outline of Requirements intended for use in preparing students for the Lawrence Scientific School." [1] This appears to have been the first clear suggestion of differentiation between college and secondary-school courses in zoölogy. The Harvard Outline. The course outlined was "an attempt to restore the old-time instruction in natural history" in secondary schools, leaving the general principles of the science for the first college course in the science. The influence of this Harvard pamphlet was widespread, and it has led to very general advocacy, especially from the college standpoint, of natural history as the proper work for high schools and for college-entrance credit.

It is to be noted that considerations along three lines have entered into the supporting arguments : First, natural history is a phase of animal study which is valuable in preparation for college work in zoölogy; second, Arguments for Natural History. its adoption in high schools would quite differentiate the secondary work from the common first course of the colleges; and third, the line of work proposed for the attainment of the above ends is the most valuable for general

---

[1] This outline, which was later developed into Davenport's *Introduction to Zoölogy*, has already been referred to in Chapter II. in connection with the discussion of the value of natural history.

liberal education in the secondary school. Let us now examine more closely the arguments along these three lines.

With regard to the first, there can be no doubt that knowledge of the natural history of common animals is a most valu-

Natural History in Preparation for College. able preparation for college courses in zoölogy which are largely composed of those phases of the science (especially morphology, physiology, and embryology) which have little direct concern with natural history.

With regard to the supposed demand for differentiation, there is reason for thinking that the arguments from the

Is Differentiation needed? college standpoint have been based upon an over-estimation of the existing conditions. In considering the merits of this question we must not lose sight of the fact that probably not one high-school pupil in a hundred studies zoölogy in the school and later in college. It follows, then, that the overlapping of courses of zoölogy in schools and colleges, while theoretically a source of confusion for students entering college, is practically a very minor problem affecting relatively few individuals. Therefore, if differentiation of courses is to be made it must have some basis other than preparation for college courses and the avoidance of occasional duplication by the rare students who may take zoölogy in both school and college. The oft-quoted story of the student who found the same course in zoölogy "*a la Huxley*" in high school, college, and university is interesting, but such a case is so rare that it is without significance so far as it has been taken to indicate that the secondary school should avoid teaching that which belongs primarily to the college. In short, it appears upon critical examination that the question of differentiation offers a very unimportant line of argument in favor of natural history as the exclusive zoölogical work of secondary schools.

Finally, with regard to the third argument, that natural history alone constitutes the proper work for the high school, we have been led in an earlier chapter (p. 271) to the conclusion that strict limitation of high-school work to natural history is not satisfactory from the viewpoint of liberal secondary education. It is evident, then, that the plan proposed for complete differentiation between college and school courses cannot be accepted as a final arrangement; for however satisfactory strict limitation of high-school zoölogy to natural history may seem from the college standpoint, such a course is only a part of the zoölogy which is needed in secondary education. Natural History Inadequate for the High School.

Now, although it appears to be undesirable from the viewpoint of the high school to differentiate the subject-matter of zoölogy sharply from that of some parts of college courses in the science, it is nevertheless important that, just as far as possible without interfering with the fulfilment of the aims governing high-school zoölogy, the work of the school should not come into serious conflict with that of the colleges; and, furthermore, that the zoölogical work of the school should be recognized for credit on college-admission requirements. For these reasons I wish now to indicate how a general course in zoölogy in the high school, for example, a course along the lines advocated in Chapter VIII., would stand in relation to the first college course in which there is the most similiarity.

In the first place, there could be no such confusion for the student taking the college course in general zoölogy as there might have been formerly when the morphological courses in school and college were almost identical. In point of view, in order of study, in less attention to details and minute structure, in avoidance of all highly theoretical and problematical questions, in emphasis upon physiology and some natural history — in these and other minor respects a general course in zoölogy adapted to the high-school conditions would be decidedly different from the first course of the leading colleges. It is true that many of the general principles of zoölogy would be touched upon in the high-school course in anticipation of the college work; but owing to the differences above noted, there is no Relation of General Zoölogy in School and College.

reason why even the same animal types might not with greater profit be repeated in the college by the occasional pupil who elects zoölogy in college after studying it in the high school. The advanced viewpoint of the college work, the greater maturity of students and increased facilities for critical scientific study — these ought to work to the end that the general view of the science and its methods obtained in the high school should fit the student for more rigid accuracy in work of the detailed type demanded in college laboratories. In short, I regard it as no serious matter if the high school does touch upon some principles and even illustrate them by the same animal types which are used in college; for it rests with the college instructor to demand of the student with previous training more detailed and more supplementary work than may be required of most members of the class who will have had no high-school work in the science.

It will be objected that many pupils who have studied high-school zoölogy will have the impression that they have mas-

Danger in "finishing" Zoology in High School. tered the science. This is too true. Fortunately very few of these will trouble the college department by electing zoölogy. But it is the duty of the high-school teacher to work against the development of such an attitude on the part of pupils. Not only should great care be taken to avoid giving the impression that any topic or type has been studied exhaustively (" finished"); but no opportunity should be lost for emphasizing the fact that, owing to limitations of time and other conditions, only the more superficial facts can be learned in the high-school course, leaving most of the finer points for the more advanced work of those who have time and opportunity to pursue the subject farther in college. Finally, as a means of emphasizing the superiority of the college work, let it be clearly understood that work done in the high school is not equivalent and may not be substituted for advance credit in a college course, but let the high-school work be given its proper credit as such on entrance to college.

Working along the lines indicated in the foregoing discussion it seems possible to bring the high-school and the college course in zoölogy, each with its own peculiar aims, into a harmonious relation, with the result that the work best adapted for the general high school will also give an advantageous, although not required, preparation for advanced college work in the same science. This must be the basis of any generally satisfactory scheme of college-entrance credits in zoölogy.

Finally, we may profitably look at the question of the relation of college and secondary zoölogy from a point of view entirely different from that of regarding the lower work as leading to the higher. Colleges now offer so many elective courses in science that many students have opportunity to pursue those which they did not study in the secondary school, and we may doubt whether it is advisable to encourage the mass of students to continue in college the sciences to which they gave most attention in the high school. Rather it seems wise to advise in general that new sciences be first undertaken to the end that a wider view of general science may be obtained. Personally, I have no sympathy with the too-common departmental selfishness which encourages three or four years of specializing in one science while the student remains almost absolutely ignorant of the essentials of other sciences. Such specialization is the proper work of the university. Undergraduate college work in science should primarily consist of a general view of the field of each of the three great phases of natural science, viz., physical (physics and chemistry), earth science (geography and geology), and biology. Scientific discipline is gained by each of these as taught by modern methods ; and with regard to information, either as a foundation for later specializing in any science or for the purpose of liberal culture, a view of natural science in general is surely more valuable than a special knowledge of detailed facts in any limited field, however interesting they may be to the student.

2. Zoölogy for College-Entrance Credit.

It may be taken for granted that no teacher of zoölogy in school or college seriously advocates placing zoölogy on the list of subjects required for entrance. Among many reasons why it should not be so, we may note that it is not necessary as a preparation for the zoölogical study in college, since elementary courses in the science are now given in all leading colleges; second, that very many good high schools and academies are not prepared to conform with such a requirement; and third, it is the opinion of very many, perhaps a majority, of professors of zoölogy in leading colleges that, with the exception of studies in general natural history, the elements of the science can be presented so much better in colleges that it seems best not to encourage the study of zoölogy in the schools by the pupils who are aiming directly at preparation for college.

Zoölogy should not be required.

Obviously, general acceptance of the last expressed opinion would not militate against the desirability of offering zoölogy in schools for the benefit of the vast majority who are not preparing for college. As we have seen, zoölogy has facts and principles wherein it is valuable as a part of a liberal education; and for the sake of the great majority of pupils who can never go to college the science deserves to be taught in secondary schools, excepting, perhaps, the special academies which aim directly at preparation for college entrance and may well advise their pupils to leave zoölogy for college study.

Zoölogy Primary for those not preparing for College.

But evidently it is impossible to draw a distinct line between those pupils who are likely to go to college and those who are not. Many pupils cannot decide about college before graduation from the high school. Hence, it becomes important that at least all pupils who do not look forward with considerable certainty to college work may be able to study zoölogy with assurance that in the event of change of their plan the work done in the schools may be credited for

An Option in Zoölogy desirable.

college entrance. We see, then, that whereas a uniform requirement in zoölogy is highly undesirable, an option for credit on admission to college is a great desideratum. Recognizing this, the American Society of Zoölogists has appointed (1903) a committee of five, with instructions to consider the question of a college-entrance option in zoölogy as viewed from the standpoint of secondary education. The final reports of this committee will probably be published in *Science* and *School Science*, early in 1905.

CHAPTER XII

THE TEACHING OF HUMAN PHYSIOLOGY IN SECONDARY SCHOOLS

"Such a course of physiology as is needful for the comprehension of its general truths and their bearings on daily conduct, is an all-essential part of a rational education." — HERBERT SPENCER, in *Education*.

BIBLIOGRAPHY

Gage, S. H. Physiology in the Schools. SCIENCE, n. s., Vol. IV., 1896, pp. 29–33. Also in Regents' Bulletin, No. 36, University of State of New York, pp. 66–72.

Hall, W. S. The Presentation of Physiology to High-School Classes. SCHOOL SCIENCE, Vol. I., 1901, pp. 58–61.

Hall, W. S. The Teaching of Physiology in the Common Schools. SCHOOL SCIENCE, Vol. III., 425–431. February, 1904.

Foster, M. On the Teaching of Physiology in Schools. NATURE, Vol. LI., p. 487. 1895.

Huxley, T. H. On Elementary Instruction in Physiology (1877). In Essays on Science and Education. New York, Appleton. Also in NATURE, Vol. XVI., p. 223; and in POPULAR SCIENCE MONTHLY, Vol. XI., p. 668.

Lee, F. S. Teaching Physiology in Secondary Schools. Paper before New York State Science Teachers' Association. University of State of New York, High School Bulletin, No. 13, pp. 807–832. (This bulletin is obtainable from Secretary of University of State of New York, Albany. Price, 35 cents.)

Peabody, J. E. Physiology in the High School. NEW YORK TEACHERS' MAGAZINE, Vol. I., No. 2, 1899, pp. 163–170.

Peabody, J. E. Study of Bacteria in the Public Schools. SCHOOL SCIENCE, Vol. I. November and December, 1901.

Peabody, J. E. Physiology in the Peter Cooper High School, New York City. JOURNAL OF APPLIED MICROSCOPY, Vol. III., pp. 917–932. July, 1900.

Report of Committee of Ten on Secondary School Studies, National Educational Association, 1893. Physiology in Primary and Secondary Schools, pp. 158–161. Washington, United States Bureau of Education.

Sedgwick, W. T. What Training in Physiology and Hygiene may we Reasonably Expect of the Public Schools? SCIENCE, n. s., Vol. XVIII. Also in SCHOOL SCIENCE, Vol. III. February, 1904. SCIENCE, Vol. XVIII., pp. 353–360. September 18, 1903.

Bigelow, M. A. The Study of the Human Body. W. VA. SCHOOL JOURNAL, Vol. XIX. January, February, and April, 1900.

Bigelow, M. A. Elementary Study of the Nervous System. NEW YORK TEACHERS' MONOGRAPHS, Vol. IV., No. 1, pp. 102–105. 1902.

A Teacher. Teaching Physiology in the Public Schools. POPULAR SCIENCE MONTHLY, Vol. XXXIII., pp. 509–620. 1888.

Elementary Text-books of Human Physiology are Listed in the Chapter on " Zoölogical Books."

THE term "physiology" as commonly used to designate a special course of instruction in elementary and secondary schools refers to study of the human body from the combined standpoints of anatomy (structure), pure physiology (functions of organs), and hygiene (laws and conditions of health) ; and hence the term "physiology" is used inexactly. However, this has some justification from the fact that the study of functions and activities — that is, physiology in the strict sense — is the central point in the elementary work, the facts of structure (anatomy) being a necessary basis for study of functions, and hygienic rules a logical application of the physiological principles. For the purposes of discussion it is necessary to accept the common usage, but to avoid possible confusion the quotation marks will serve to distinguish "human physiology," the combination of elementary studies of anatomy, physiology, and hygiene, from pure physiology, the science of functional activity.

Scope of Elementary Physiology.

1. The Relation of "Human Physiology" to Other Biological Sciences in the High School.

The nature of the common courses in high-school "physiology" is so familiar to those who have examined the text-books by Martin, Blaisdell, Colton, and others (see p. 446) that description is unnecessary as a basis for our discussions. Suffice it to say that the most striking features of this course as presented in the text-books are : first, that there is little important difference between this work for high-school pupils and that presented in other books for the last year of the elementary school ; and second, that

The Separate Course in Physiology.

although human physiology is a phase of biology it is commonly presented quite independently of the biological courses. On the basis of these two points it will be maintained that the separate course in physiology should be omitted from the high-school curriculum.[1]

With regard to the similarity between the high-school and elementary-school physiology, careful comparisons of subject-matter in text-books and of results in certain schools has convinced the writer that there is no good reason why the peculiar line of study represented by the courses with direct reference to the human body should not stop with the end of the elementary-school work, for the high-school course adds nothing but details, except as it enters upon the field of other high-school sciences, thus producing a wasteful duplication of work. One argument for the high-school course is that this may be taught by the laboratory method. But I must answer that this laboratory work so far as it is individual work, is almost entirely the kind of duplication referred to above. Moreover, many elementary schools have successfully taught in the eighth grade the essentials of physiology by means of demonstrations which require no special laboratory — in fact, the very same demonstrations which are available in high schools where the physiology does not largely duplicate work of other science courses.

Similarity of the Work in High and Elementary School.

These serious objections to the separate course in high school leads us directly to our main proposition that the study of "human physiology" should in the very nature of its subject-matter be closely connected with the study of biological sciences, and it is desirable that high-school "physiology" should be an integral part of the first course in biology in which it will naturally be closely associated with the animal phase. The importance of direct continuity with biology which furnishes important illus-

Physiology closely related to Biology.

---

[1] Excepting the few schools with five-year courses in which the first year corresponds to the eighth grade of the grammar school.

trative and comparative materials, especially in the line of practical work; the difficulty of adjusting a separate course to the high-school curriculum; and the difficulty of teaching a separate course so as to differentiate between the elementary-school work on the one hand and the high-school course on the other — these and other reasons appeal to teachers who have had experience with the present arrangement, and lead to the conclusion that to continue the separation of "physiology" from the high-school course in zoölogy is a serious mistake.

This is no new opinion, but one which has been gaining favor for several years. Several prominent teachers have suggested a close correlation between "human physiology" and zoölogy, and also between these studies in the high school and the nature-study and elementary "physiology" of the lower schools. No one has expressed this idea more suggestively than Professor W. S. Hall of Northwestern University:

"In the high school the pupil receives for the first time instruction in nature sufficiently systematic to be dignified by the name of *Biology*. In the first year he should have a thorough course in elementary botany. It should be a **Professor Hall's View.** laboratory course supplemented by recitations. The plants studied should be few in number and the technicalities of a detailed morphology should not be attempted. What the student at this age needs is a knowledge of the life histories of plants and animals. How do they live? How do they reproduce their kind? What becomes of them when they die? Why do two plants of the same species differ, one from the other? How do these living forms come to be? Are they changing? If so, why? In the high-school course in botany, physiology should be made more prominent than morphology.

"In the second year of the high school there should be a course in zoölogy planned, like the botany, to emphasize the life histories, and to answer for animals, questions similar to those raised in the study of plants. All of this in preparation for the study of high-school physiology.

"With a preparation for physiology so thorough as that outlined above, I should make this branch rather the *biology of man* than simple human physiology. Let the class study the animal — *Homo;* his species, varieties, and races; the geographical distribution of the races and their characteristics. Let them review the morphology of man in its general features, and institute comparisons between man and his nearest associates among the vertebrates. . . .

"Questions of life history, reproduction, whence, how, and whither would better not be discussed. The courses in botany and zoölogy have sharpened the senses and incited the thoughtful questioning of the pupil. When he comes to the study of man, leave him alone with his thoughts on these deeper and more delicate questions, and he will arrive at the Truth."[1]

In the above paragraphs there is expressed the essentials of an idea which has long been developing in the minds of many teachers. It is the inevitable outgrowth of the introduction into secondary schools of the modern courses in botany and zoölogy taught by the laboratory method. The study of the structures and activities of the human body apart from its relation to other animals is a loss both to "human physiology" and to zoölogy, for each subject may contribute much of importance to the other.

Accepting the view that it is desirable to combine or correlate the teaching of "human physiology" and other biological work in the secondary school, what is
How unite Physiology and Biology ? the best method of accomplishing this union of the two subjects which are commonly presented independently?

The arrangement which may first be discussed is that suggested in the above quotation from Professor Hall's paper.
Professor Hall's Suggestion. It is that a course in botany in the first high-school year and zoölogy in the second should prepare for a biological study of the human body in a later year. This is excellent in ideal; but the practical objection is that "human physiology" is usually required and should be studied by all high-school pupils; and therefore it would be

---

[1] *School Science,* Vol. I. April, 1901. Pp. 60, 61.

impracticable, and certainly undesirable, to compel all pupils to take courses in botany and zoölogy as a preparation for the study of the structure and functions of the human body. Elsewhere it has been pointed out (Chapter V) that from the standpoint of the general curriculum it is desirable that the general field of the biological sciences be presented in a single year's course in the high school. Certainly it is not advisable to make a uniform requirement, or even recommendation of more than one year of biology for the high school; and, even if wholly or in part elective, the biological sciences cannot without undue emphasis be extended beyond two years. It follows that if the work in "human physiology" is to be articulated with the biological sciences the combination must be adjusted to either a one-year or, at most, a two-year scheme.

Now these are the possible arrangements: first, one year may be required and given to a course which aims to present the most important facts of botany and zoölogy and Possible "human physiology"; or, second, zoölogy and Arrangements. "human physiology" being most closely allied may be presented in one required year and botany offered either elective or required, as a second course in biological science.

It may be objected that in either case the year including the "physiology" would include an impossible amount of work. In answer to this it may be stated that the study Impossible of "physiology" in the elementary school may be Amount of assumed to have given the general view of the Work? study of the human body. With this foundation the proper work of the high school would be, not study of the usual type of special text-book which is slightly different from that studied in the elementary school, but rather a comparative study based on the animals studied in zoölogy and on physiological principles growing out of both the animal and plant phases of biological study. Viewing high-school "physiology" in this light, it is not impracticable to include the important principles of human anatomy, physiology, and hygiene in a year's course in biology; or, if one prefers the second suggestion given above, it would be a perfectly simple matter to unite " physiology " with zoölogy in a course of one year, leaving the botany as an independent course.

In some high schools the demand for concentration of the biological sciences into a single course has been met by divid-
Three-Term ing the year into three terms, for botany, zoölogy,
Plan. and " physiology " respectively. But in most cases this plan of uniting the required " human physiology " with other biological courses seems to have resulted simply in a combination of three courses and not in a true correlation of subject-matter so as to make one unified course in biology. Very commonly in such combined courses the presentation of the zoölogy and botany part is on the basis of the laboratory method and the study of " human physiology " consists merely of recitations from an ordinary text-book — a method of conducting the course which is sure to break up the continuity. In another place (p. 340) I have argued for a unified course in biology as opposed to the usual combination of half-years in botany and zoölogy in which there is a sudden transition at the mid-year period, and it has been noted that there are serious objections to such a break in the continuity of a year's course. The addition of " physiology " without correlation and unification of the whole course would give two such sudden transitions in subject-matter, and it is clear that we cannot justify the inclusion of " physiology " in a course in either zoölogy or biology unless the material can be so arranged as to make a continuous development throughout the year.

Another possible plan for the concentration of the biological sciences consists in making " human physiology " the central
Another idea of a year's course in biology which includes
Plan. studies of plants and animals so far as by comparison of structure and functions they throw light upon the study of the human body. Such a course would be primarily " human physiology " for which illustrative materials would be

drawn both from zoölogy and botany.[1] The advantages of such a high-school biological course on the basis of "human physiology" would be that it provides for the "physiology" which the laws require, and which is needed in general education, because of the practical importance of its subject-matter. Also it would present the subject from the biological viewpoint and methods, and would introduce the pupil to the general field of biological science by including in the course of "physiology" many of the principles of general biology which are so important as to merit a place in a required part of the secondary curriculum.

But there is at least one serious objection to such a high-school course in biology based upon "human physiology." Pupils are wearied by the continuous study of the latter subject in the elementary school; and for the sake of an *entirely new approach* in the high school it seems desirable to present the principles of biology apart from direct reference to the human body to which they may later be applied. There would also be an advantage in that erroneous impressions gained from the elementary work are more likely to be corrected when the facts of human structure and function are approached from the animal standpoint instead of from the familiar human aspect of elementary-school "physiology." The study of animals and plants would give the proper perspective for the biological study of man, making this vastly more interesting and intelligible. With the preliminary work in the elementary school, it will not be necessary to spend much time in the high school upon the special conditions of human structure and function. These are largely matters of detail of little general importance. In the high school the broader comparative view should prevail. Emphasis should be placed upon the resemblance in structure and function between man and other animals; then in the next step the

A New Method of Approach Desirable.

---

[1] The recent *Studies in Physiology*, by Peabody (New York, Macmillan, 1903) is essentially such a course.

resemblance to all living things; next the similarities to all vertebrates; and finally the chief resemblances and differences of man as compared with other mammals. The greater part of this work will naturally be directly connected with the work in zoölogy, but this in turn should be closely correlated with the work in botany so as to place emphasis upon the great biological features, especially the physiological, in which plants and animals are essentially similar. Incidental references to human structure and functions may come up in connection with any lessons, but the formal comparative study will best be taken up by way of summary at the end of the course in zoölogy, which will then have prepared for an intelligent appreciation of the biological study of man.

The outline of a course in zoölogy which is given in Chapter VIII. involves the essentials of general morphology and physiology of animals which are directly applicable to the human body; and it may be referred to for further explanation of the suggestions in the above paragraphs.

Finally, it should be noted that in some States it is scarcely possible at the present time to involve " human physiology " in **Laws opposed to Proper Correlation.** close correlation with a course in zoölogy, as has been suggested above, for the reason that laws require that " physiology " be taught as a separate study *from a text-book* for a specified number of lessons. Furthermore, the book must include peculiar subject-matter, especially " temperance instruction," most of which could not be correlated with a good biological course. Under such conditions the absurd laws must be obeyed and a period of weeks set aside from which to teach " from text-books in the hands of the pupils." If this must be so, let the subject of " physiology " continue to stand alone in the secondary curriculum until possible changes or repeal of existing laws leave science teachers free to correlate, as they may think best, " physiology " with the other courses of biology in the high school.

Summarizing the above considerations of the relation of high-school "physiology" to other biological courses, it has been pointed out: (1) That much is to be gained by close correlation with botany and zoölogy, especially the latter. (2) Simply assigning " physiology" to a term of ten weeks in a year devoted to biology is not sufficient; there must be complete correlation. (3) One plan for this consists in making "human physiology" the centre of a year's course into which animal and plants are brought as illustrating the structure and functions of man. The objection to this is that the line of approach is too much like that in the elementary school. (4) The plan which obviates this objection consists in making all references to " human physiology" grow out of studies of zoölogy.

Summary.

2. Teaching the Essentials of " Human Physiology."

No matter whether " human physiology" is to be presented in the high school as a separate course or as an integral part of a course in zoölogy or biology, the emphasis of the instruction should be placed upon the essentials of the subject, and needless details neglected altogether.

The Essentials needed.

The general criticism on the text-books of " physiology" which are commonly in use in our public schools is that almost without exception they give prominence to many topics and especially details which are of exceedingly doubtful value in either elementary or secondary education. Moreover, the great foundation ideas of the science are usually so intermingled in the text with minor points that beginners must fail to distinguish between essentials and comparatively insignificant facts. There is need of selection of the important subject-matter whose place in public-school education can be justified on the ground of its applicability to every-day life. With this aim in mind, we shall discuss the teaching of some aspects of "physiology" which are commonly over-emphasized in the public schools, and later consider some whose general importance demands for them more at-

General Criticism of Text-books.

tention than is commonly given in the elementary courses of "physiology."

After " temperance instruction," which we shall discuss later, the topic which first appeals to us as being treated in elementary books more extensively than its practical or disciplinary importance justifies is that of anatomy. Bones and muscles, minor blood-vessels and nerves, and the details of minute structure have for years received emphasis in most of our text-books. As taught by the book method this anatomical study is simply memorizing of useless names and descriptions. In most cases only the general facts of structure are needed for the study of functions, and detailed facts of anatomy which have no relation to general functions are useless in public schools. To illustrate : The important physiological point concerning the heart is that it is a pump, and the essential facts of its structure can be demonstrated in five or ten minutes with a heart obtained from the market. Such details as those regarding bicuspid and tricuspid valves with their papillary muscles and chordæ tendineæ are no more essential for high-school physiology than are these names themselves. The only essential thing is that pupils see that there are valves so arranged that blood must pass in one direction only.

Excessive Attention to Anatomy.

Applying to the study of structure in general this idea of what is essential in the anatomical line would greatly reduce the amount of material to be taught in " physiology" as a separate course ; and if presented with a course in zoölogy as the basis, the study of several types of animals along the lines discussed in Chapter II. would make it unnecessary to give much special attention to anatomy in direct connection with " human physiology."

Zoölogy as a Basis for Study of Structure.

The incidental remarks which have been made above with reference to the technical terminology in certain cases should also be applied to that of all the other systems of the body. Our common elementary text-books include a large number of scientific terms which have no legiti-

Technical Terminology.

mate place in public-school education, and especially is the emphasis placed upon mere names, probably an inheritance from the old-time natural history, still too prominent in the teaching of elementary " physiology." Some technical names are in such common use in every-day life that they have lost their strangeness, and it is certainly profitable for the pupil to learn them [1] in association with the thing designated. I have in mind here names such as : mesentery, pancreas, æsophagus, trachea, pharynx, and larynx. These are needed ; but quite different is the case with uncommon special terms like valvulæ conniventes, chordæ tendineæ, alveoli, duodenum, and many other similar terms found in elementary text-books. Especially is the technical nomenclature carried to an extreme as applied to nerves and blood-vessels. In the case of the cranial nerves four should be associated with their names — namely, olfactory, optic, facial, and auditory ; but I see no good reason for a special attempt at memorizing the names and numbers and distribution of the others. A diagram and a dissection of a frog will teach the general facts concerning the distribution of nerves without recourse to special terminology and complicated descriptions in words. The same is true of the blood system ; the primary vessels connected with the heart and the main branches — such as, carotid, hepatic, renal, iliac — may be considered well worth knowing by name ; but there is no justification for naming in public schools such minor branches as popliteal, azygos, peroneal, and tibial.

In this connection may be mentioned the common use of chemical terms which are meaningless to elementary pupils. It is absurd to suppose that pupils in the public schools may understand better the action of pancreatic juice after being enlightened by the statement that "the fluid contains the ferments trypsin, amylopsin,

Useless Chemical Names in Physiology.

---

[1] It is interesting to note that less than fifty years ago authors of certain elementary text-books felt constrained to defend in their prefaces the use of lungs for " lights," abdomen for " stomach," intestine for " bowel." These terms do not now appeal to us as technical scientific terms.

and steapsin." Likewise there can be no definite meaning in elementary work for these statements: "Bile contains glycocholic and taurocholic acids"; "The chief fats are margarin, olein, palmatin, and stearin"; "Coffee contains caffein and tea theobromin," and "Muscle contains myosin and syntonin." Elementary chemistry has some important applications in connection with the study of "physiology," but the above examples from elementary books represent special chemistry which is utterly useless in public-school education and should be omitted altogether.

Turning now to discuss certain topics which are not adequately treated in most of the usual elementary courses in this subject, the most important of these is that of the fundamental processes of general nutrition. Usually the processes of digestion, circulation, respiration, assimilation, dissimilation, and excretion are defined and discussed in separate chapters, and elementary pupils are led to think of so many isolated processes which have little or no relation or interdependence. The great principle of co-ordination between these processes is more often than otherwise not clearly set forth and emphasized, and the reason for the existence of each process is not as a rule clearly presented to elementary pupils. For example, a chapter in the text-book deals with food in nutrition without reference to the necessity for food as shown by a logical application of the law of conservation of energy. If pupils are asked to give an answer to the question, "Why does the body need food?" a very common reply is, "To keep the body alive." But such an indefinite statement is no more scientific than the common knowledge which any one with common sense possesses. If more definite ideas are to be given, the principle of conservation of energy must be explained and its logical application to the human body made clear to the pupils at the very beginning of the discussion of nutritive functions. Unless the essentials are thus made clear at the outset, the pupils are likely to become bewildered by the mass of details concerning the

Inadequate Treatment of Fundamental Processes of Nutrition.

structure of the organs, minor processes, varieties of foods, effects of alcohol and hygiene of digestion — all of which in many text-books are given just as promi- Essentials should be nent a setting as that given to the fundamental distinguished from Minor nature and purpose of food. Likewise in the Facts. study of blood and its circulation pupils learn much about hæmoglobin, corpuscles, fibrinogen, etc., but often fail to grasp the *fundamental* idea that the blood is essen- Essential tially a transporting medium between the tissues and Facts in Study of the outside world, and made necessary by the Blood. demands of the tissues for supply of food and oxygen, for removal of waste matters, and for distribution of heat. Ask average pupils the question, "Why does the body need blood and its circulation?" and again comes the all-explanatory answer to all general physiological questions, "To keep the body alive." Of course, this is quite true, but we have no justification for science study which stops with such facts of common observation.

And such is the story of the usual presentation of the whole series of functions involved in general nutrition. Essentials and facts of secondary importance are massed indiscriminately, and to the average pupil all are of equal importance. This is certainly a very undesirable result. To guard against it, the most important aim should be that the pupils come The Aim in to understand the essential nature, the interdepend- teaching Physiology ence and the part which each process of internal of Internal organs plays as a step in general nutrition. It is Organs. essential that the body be considered a working whole composed of interdependent and co-ordinated organs, and around this central idea should be arranged all other minor facts of function and of structure considered as the working machine. These are the *essentials* which should first of all be clearly presented in a general way, and secondarily there may be added as much of the minor details of the general processes as the time and age of pupils will allow. Space here will not allow more than these general remarks, but it may be suggested that

this idea is well developed in the eighth and ninth chapters of
Martin's *Human Body, Briefer Course.* In these
Martin's "Human Body." chapters the fundamental processes are clearly defined and emphasized apart from the secondary
facts which follow in later chapters. The plan is an excellent
one, which no other author seems to have developed so well.
It can be applied by teachers who use other text-books with
their classes.

The subject-matter dealing with hygiene is usually well presented by the text-books, except, as has been incidentally
suggested in the preceding paragraphs, that the
Hygiene. ordinary arrangement often tends to a confusion of
essential physiological principles. This is avoided if, as recommended above, a general survey of physiological essentials apart
from hygiene be made first, for then the later detailed study
of the various functions will lead to a logical presentation of
hygiene facts and principles. With sound understanding of
physiological fundamentals much of the hygiene will be better
understood and appreciated ; in fact, many of its rules become
applied common sense.

As to the method of teaching hygiene, one general suggestion
deserves emphasis, namely, that an attempt should be made
to develop the practical method, for memorizing
Practical Method in teaching Hygiene. from the book without immediate practice is of
doubtful value, as in all other science work. The
teacher can accomplish much in the line of practical teaching
by leading the pupils to begin at once in their home life the
practice of some of the hygienic principles which they learn.
Moreover, in many cases, particularly in connection with the
notes on emergencies, it is possible to give demonstrations
which teach more and better than would volumes of printed
matter. For examples, artificial respiration, aseptic treatment
of wounds, simple bandaging, and applying tourniquet to
arteries are some of the important topics which should be
taught carefully by direct illustration.

The very important topic of the relation of bacteria to health

and disease has in the past received little attention in connection with elementary hygiene, but the best recent Study of
text-books give short accounts of the subject. It Bacteria.
is of the greatest importance that there be widely diffused
knowledge of the general principles of bacteriology.   Even a
superficial knowledge will convince the public that sanitary
principles and laws are well founded, and the simple practical
prophylactic measures against such diseases as typhoid, malaria,
cholera, tuberculosis, etc., are more often applied when the
relation of the causative germs to air and water are understood.
The nature of infectious diseases, isolation in contagious
diseases, the principles and methods of disinfection, the principles of inoculation and vaccination, the importance of general
sanitary cleanliness in cities as well as in homes, pure food,
water, and air — these are examples of topics in which every
citizen should have an interest, and no part of the course in
elementary hygiene is of so great importance from the practical
standpoint. These should be well taught. The teacher will
find useful reading for pupils in *The Story of the Bacteria*
and *Dust and its Dangers*, by Prudden ; in the *Story of Germ
Life*, by Conn; and in Mrs. Frankland's *Bacteria in Daily
Life*. Other books of interest to the teacher are named under
" Bacteriology" in Chapter X. The importance and ease of
teaching by practical work in this line should be emphasized.
Many recent text-books (see p. 446) have some suggestions,
but worthy of special mention is Peabody's recent *Studies in
Physiology* (Macmillan, 1903).[1]

In conclusion, I have attempted to present some general
suggestions for improving our teaching of high-school " physiology " by limiting its subject-matter to those facts
and ideas which have a possible value as applied Summary.
knowledge. To select for emphasis the essentials of " physiol-

---

[1] See also a paper by same author in *Journal of Applied Microscopy*,
Vol. IV., No. 2, p. 1164; also his *Laboratory Exercises* (Holt, New
York) ; and papers by Frost and Hastings in *Journal of Applied*

ogy " is a problem to which experts in science teaching will surely give more attention before many years pass. We need concise text-books which concentrate in their one hundred pages all and more than is now given in three and four hundred pages. But at present in the absence of such guides to the essentials, teachers will, I think, find that their own experience teaches the relative values of many minor parts of the subject-matter of which it has been possible here to suggest only the most general outlines.

3. "Scientific Temperance " or " Temperance Instruction."

BIBLIOGRAPHY

Atwater, W. O. Alcohol Physiology and Superintendence. EDU-CATIONAL REVIEW, Vol. XX., pp. 1–29. June, 1900. Also in Proc. N. E. A., 1900, pp. 229–266.

Atwater, W. O. Alcohol Physiology and Temperance Reform. HARPER'S MAGAZINE, Vol. CI., pp. 850–858. November, 1900.

Atwater, W. O. Nutritive Value of Alcohol. *Ibid.*, pp. 675–684. October, 1900.

Atwater, W. O. Alcohol Physiology in Public Schools. Printed with report of committee of New York State Science Teachers' Association, which see below.

Dutton, S. T. Scientific Temperance Legislation. SCHOOL JOURNAL, Vol. LX., pp. 268, 269. 1900.

Eliot, C. W. Educational Reform. Pp. 190–191. New York. Century Co. 1898.

Ferguson, W. B. Temperance Teaching and Recent Legislation in Connecticut. EDUCATIONAL REVIEW, Vol. XXIII., pp. 233–249. March, 1902.

Hunt, Mary H. A History of the First Decade of the Department of Scientific Instruction in Schools and Colleges of the Woman's Christian Temperance Union. Boston, second edition, 1891.

Hunt, Mary H. An Epoch of the Nineteenth Century. An Outline for the Work for Scientific Temperance Education in the Public Schools of the United States. Boston, 1897.

Jordan, D. S. Scientific Temperance. POPULAR SCIENCE MONTHLY, Vol. XLVIII., pp. 343–354. January, 1895.

Microscopy, Vol. VI., series of papers beginning in March, 1903. These latter have many good suggestions, but are not, on the whole, as practicable for the average high school as are the books and papers by Peabody.

Sabin, H. Education. May, 1900. (Answer to Atwater's paper on Alcohol and Superintendence.)

Sedgwick, W. T. The Modern Subjection of Science and Education to Propaganda. SCIENCE, n. s., Vol. XV., pp. 44–54. January 10, 1902. Presidential Address before American Society of Naturalists.

Articles on "temperance text-books" and Atwater's experiments in OUTLOOK. Vol. LXII., 703–706, 700–702, July 29, 1899. Vol. LXII., 882, 883, 908–911, August 19, 1899. Vol. LXIII., 483–485, 493–497, October 28, 1899. Vol. LXIV., 390, February 17, 1900. Vol. LXVI., 706–709, November 17, 1900. Vol. LXVI., 974, 996–999, December 22, 1900.

Report of Committee on Alcohol and Narcotics, New York State Science Teachers' Association. Sixth conference, 1901. University of the State of New York, High School Bulletin, No. 17, pp. 745–762.

Discussion of report and paper by Atwater (see above), pp. 763–815. (Bulletin No. 17 may be obtained from Secretary of University of State of New York, Albany. Price, 40 cents.)

Reply to above report. A circular by New York State Central Committee on Scientific Temperance Instruction in Public Schools. Obtainable from A. L. Manierre, Secretary of Committee, 31 Nassau St., New York City.

School Instruction in the Effects of Alcohol and Narcotics. From the report of a committee of the New York State Science Teachers' Association (see above). EDUCATIONAL REVIEW, Vol. XXIV., pp. 31–47. June, 1902.

Protest against bill to increase instruction in physiology, with special reference to alcohol and narcotics. Signed by many leaders of science and education in the State of New York. Department of Public Instruction, State of New York, Albany, 1895.

Report to the Committee of Fifty. Physiological Aspects of the Liquor Problem. Based on investigations by and under direction of Atwater, Billings, Bowditch, Chittenden, and Welch. 2 volumes, pp. 396, 379. Boston, Houghton, Mifflin. 1903. $4.50.

Reply to above report. Senate Document, No. 171, 58th Congress, Second Session. Also obtainable from A. L. Manierre, 31 Nassau St., New York.

The most characteristic feature of the present teaching of "physiology" in public schools of the United States is the so-called "temperance instruction," or "scientific temperance" which deals with the nature and effects of alcohol and narcotics. So prominent

Prominence of Temperance Instruction.

is this in the subject-matter of most elementary text-books that in almost every case the topic is mentioned on the title-page; and even that most excellent among elementary books, Martin's

Human Body, Briefer Course, bore on the cover of the last edition prepared by the author the strange title, *The Human Body and the Effects of Narcotics.* Viewed from the standpoint of advanced study of pure physiology, such prominence for alcohol and narcotics is surprising; for, except in special investigations, little attention is paid to them in college and university courses. But in fact, as will be shown later, the "temperance instruction" included in elementary books is only in part physiological. For this reason and also because the introduction of this material has had a very peculiar influence upon the teaching of "physiology" in public schools, it has seemed best to discuss the subject apart from the preceding section on the essentials of a course in "physiology."

It is not my purpose to review here the history of the development of this phase of instruction in connection with "physiology." Suffice it to say that its general introduction into our public schools has been in conformity with laws which have been enacted in many States; and these enactments were the direct result of a well-organized movement on the part of certain "temperance" societies which have aimed to make "physiology" a basis for instruction with special reference to the effects of alcohol and narcotics.[1]

Special Legislation.

It is now generally agreed by at least a large majority of the most prominent educators and scientific men that the "temperance instruction" movement has had a very harmful influence upon the teaching of "physiology" in public schools in the United States. I am aware that this statement might be challenged on the basis

Harmful Influence upon Teaching of Physiology.

[1] The history of the movement to secure legislation has been written by Mary H. Hunt, a leader of the movement (see two books cited in the bibliography of this section).

The address by Professor W. T. Sedgwick of the Massachusetts Institute of Technology concisely reviews the important points in the history of the movement. His critical remarks met with the general approval of the national scientific society before which they were made, and hence may be taken as expressing the consensus of opinion of very many of the leading scientific men of the United States. Every teacher of "physiology" should read the address.

of the claim of "temperance" leaders that to the movement for special instruction concerning alcohol and narcotics is due the introduction of "physiology" into the schools. It is true that laws have made the study required in schools, but we must not overlook the fact that long before the beginning of the "scientific temperance" crusade there was a strong movement in favor of "physiology" in general education. In support of this it is only necessary to call attention to the papers by Huxley, Horace Mann, and others. Moreover, the earlier school reports prove that "physiology" was not uncommon in many States long before it was required by laws framed in the interests of "temperance instruction." We admit that the movement for "scientific temperance" may in some cases have hastened the introduction of physiology, but in the very importance of its subject-matter we see good reason for believing that the subject would be taught to-day in all schools fitted to teach it, even if there had been no laws requiring the teaching.

Physiology before Temperance Instruction.

In general the injurious influence which "temperance instruction" has had upon the teaching of "physiology" has come from the laws[1] which, framed to meet the demands of the "temperance" leaders, have specified in detail concerning the nature, amount, and arrangement of instruction on the subject of alcohol and narcotics. It is true that only in certain States have such

Nature and Effect of Laws.

---

[1] Some form of "temperance instruction" laws now (1902) exist in nearly every State and Territory. In over thirty States and Territories the study of "scientific temperance" is required in all public schools, and all pupils who pass through the schools must pursue the study. In about twenty of these not only is such teaching required but penalties are provided for non-compliance with the laws. At least fifteen of these require the study from "text-books in the hands of all pupils able to read." About ten States require that text-books for elementary schools must have one-fourth or one-fifth of their space devoted to "temperance," and in the case of high-school books not less than twenty pages. And in at least thirty-two States teachers must pass examinations on the subject of "scientific temperance." The laws of New York and Illinois are the most extreme. In New York all pupils below the second year of

limitations been placed upon the teaching of "physiology";
but even where the laws have not thus specified the influence
has been essentially the same, for the text-books of the most
prominent publishers have been made to conform with the most
extreme laws.

We may now inquire more specifically concerning the nature
of "temperance instruction," considering first the methods of
teaching the subject, and second the subject-matter itself.

The "approved" method of giving "temperance instruction" is that of reading and recitation from text-books. Upon

The "Ap- this point the leaders of the movement have been
proved"
Method of insistent, and through their agitation it has been
Temperance
Instruction. required by law in many States that the effects of
alcohol and narcotics must be studied from "graded text-books
in the hands of all pupils able to read." It has, therefore,
come about that the "scientific temperance" laws of some
States and the resulting text-books have worked together in
producing and maintaining the widespread use of the recitation
method in the teaching of "physiology," which is decidedly out

Opposed to of line with all modern science teaching. To these
Scientific criticisms it may be answered that teachers are
Method.
free, even in New York and Illinois, to introduce
as much practical work as they wish, and that the "approved"
text-books have appendices directing such practical study; but
the fact is that the nature and arrangement of required book
work is such as to interfere seriously with a logical develop-

---

high school and above the third grade shall be taught this subject every
year with suitable text-books in the hands of all pupils, and not less than
thirty lessons per year. Text-books for the elementary schools are
"suitable" and "approved" only when one-fifth of their space is devoted
to alcohol and narcotics, and high-school books must have not less than
twenty pages. It is further provided that the material on alcohol and
narcotics must be distributed throughout the book. The revised Connecticut law is a slight advance. It provides for "temperance instruction" in all grades above the third and excepting high school. Text-
books must be used above the fifth grade. But it does not specify concerning the nature and amount of "temperance instruction."

ment of " physiology " on a practical basis. Moreover, owing to the requirement for the book work, the practical work becomes optional supplementary work. In short, the whole arrangement of books on " physiology " is in conformity with the idea that they are to be used primarily as text-books, and this is opposed so completely to the practical method that only highly trained teachers are able to make the proper rearrangement of the materials. In all other sciences practical work is made the basis, and the leading books in botany, zoölogy, physics, and chemistry are arranged on a foundation of laboratory work which practically precludes their exclusive use for recitation.

Method in Books of Physiology and other Sciences.

The order of study now approved by the leaders of " temperance instruction," and required by laws in some States, is regarded as pedagogically absurd by many leading educators and scientific men. In the earlier " temperance physiologies " alcohol and narcotics were treated in special chapters, often in appendices; but to avoid any possibility that the pages on alcohol might escape the eyes of pupils, and in order to gain in emphasis, it is now required in some States that this subject-matter must be distributed throughout the book, showing the effects of alcohol and narcotics on each system of organs — even the bones ! Only books with this distribution of subject-matter are now approved by the self-appointed censors in the ranks of the temperance leaders. The result of this arrangement is a wearying reiteration for pupils, for the " temperance " matter consists largely of repeated application of general statements to each system of organs. Add to all this the fact that in very similar books this must be gone over year after year from the early grades to the high school and in books with at least one-fifth of their space devoted to teaching "temperance," and we have the explanation why children commonly think that the most important topics in " human physiology " are those of alcohol and tobacco. Such over-emphasis is certainly scientifically and pedagogically unsound.

Order of Study as " approved."

Reiteration results.

Elsewhere (p. 469) it is pointed out that the "sandwiching" of relatively unimportant topics, such as that of alcohol,

Continuity broken. breaks up the continuity of the scientific study of physiology. On this ground alone we may urge that if "temperance instruction" must be given, it should be confined to a separate chapter where it will not interfere with the scientific teachings of the principles of physiology. To this

A Temperance, not a Physiological Movement. a statement [1] made by a temperance leader answers that "temperance" and not "physiology" is the more important subject-matter for which the arrangement of lessons should be adapted. But with this we cannot agree after reading the dissertations by Horace Mann, Huxley, Herbert Spencer, and others who have written in defence of the study of "human physiology," but have made no reference to the effects of alcohol and narcotics.

Another pedagogical feature of "temperance instruction" in which it is unique among subjects commonly taught in elementary schools is that of citations from original sources.

Citation from Original Sources. We are all familiar with the common form: "Professor —— or Dr. —— states it as his opinion that alcohol," etc. On page after page of some "approved" text-books there are such citations, many of which are merely personal opinions which are absolutely worthless in science. In no other subject taught in elementary schools are original authorities thus mentioned; and all other text-books are compiled from the common fund of established and accepted knowledge. Citation of original authorities in "temperance instruction" suggests the suspicion that there is no such common fund from which to draw materials on this subject.

The nature of the subject-matter relating to the effects of

---

[1] "This is not a physiological, but a temperance movement. In all grades below the high school this instruction should contain only physiology enough to make the hygiene of temperance and other laws of health intelligible. Temperance should be the chief and not the subordinate topic and should occupy at least one-fourth the space in text-books for these grades."— Mary H. Hunt, *loc. cit.*, 1897, p. 47.

alcohol and narcotics in "approved" text-books has been much discussed in recent years. Within the limits of this chapter it is impossible to do more than indicate the lines of the discussions.[1] Most prominent in these have been the questions, Is alcohol a food? or, Is it a poison? Atwater's experiments demonstrating, what had long been supposed true, that to a slight extent alcohol may be a source of energy, led to the charge of inaccuracy in many "approved" text-books which teach that alcohol is always a poison. We cannot here discuss the technical side of this question, but by way of summary it may be stated that physiologists now agree that in minute quantities alcohol is a food in the sense that it is a source of energy. *But it does not follow that alcohol should be recommended as a regular part of human diet.* The important question, which physiologists clearly appreciate is not, Is alcohol a food? but, What are its effects as a stimulant? This is shown by the following quotations :

Discussion of Subject-Matter of Temperance Instruction.

Is Alcohol a Food?

Alcohol a Stimulant.

"Man has recourse to alcohol, not for the minute quantity of energy which is supplied by itself, but for its powerful influence on the distribution of energy furnished by other things." [2]

"Wine, beer, tea, coffee, etc., belong to the important class of stimulants. Some of them contain small quantities of food substance, but these are of secondary interest." [3]

"In a preceding article I have hinted at the fallacy of attempting to measure the real effects of alcohol by experiments in which small quantities are taken for a short time, and only its nutritive action is tested. . . . That alcohol serves as a nutriment, there is no reasonable doubt. But its nutritive effect may be, often is, counterbalanced by its ulterior action." [4]

---

[1] The teacher should read the editorial articles in the *Outlook,* and the papers by President Jordan, Professor Atwater, and others named in the bibliography.

[2] Foster — *Text-book of Physiology.* Fifth edition, 1889. Book II., p. 837.

[3] Stewart — *Manual of Physiology.* Fourth edition, 1900, p. 481.

[4] Atwater — *Harper's Magazine,* Vol. CI., p. 850.

But admitting that the food value of alcohol is small, and its effect as a stimulant great, are these influences absolutely and constantly harmful or beneficial? The answer to this question may be found in the following summary which expresses the demonstrated facts about the physiological effect of alcohol, as it is commonly accepted by leaders in physiology.

Are its Stimulating Effects harmful?

1. In small quantities alcohol is oxidized in the body, but the energy derived is insignificant. No one takes alcohol as a source of energy, but rather as a stimulant.

Summary of Physiological Effects of Alcohol.

2. Its stimulating influences are injurious or harmless, depending upon many conditions. While undoubtedly injurious in certain quantities and conditions, it may in smaller quantities be harmless or even beneficial, *e. g.*, as a drug in certain diseases. More specifically, alcohol especially affects the nervous and vascular systems, dilating blood-vessels, accelerating heart-beat, and stimulating nervous organs. All these effects may be injurious, harmless, or even beneficial, depending upon highly variable conditions, such as, quantity of alcohol, presence of other food, and various physiological conditions of the individual.

3. The limit of possible beneficial effect of alcohol is soon reached, and beyond that harm is likely to result. The limit is, however, variable with individuals; a so-called strictly moderate quantity being harmless to one man and decidedly injurious to another.

4. Undoubtedly habitual excessive use tends to induce diseases of many organs.

5. No individual can absolutely estimate the limit between harmless moderate use and injurious excessive use. Hence, habitual use of even limited quantities may have its dangers.

6. The dangers of developing habitual excessive use are so well known as to require no scientific demonstration.

7. While alcohol *may be harmless* under certain conditions, there is *no evidence that it is useful to healthy men.*

8. It is frequently overlooked that many common liquors do not have the same effect as pure alcohol, for the reason that they contain substances far more powerful than alcohol itself.

It is clear that in the light of present-day knowledge of the physiological effects of alcoholic liquors we cannot state without qualification that they are injurious. This may or may not be true, depending upon highly variable conditions ; and any general statement is at once inaccurate and misleading. We see the impossibility of firmly basing *total abstinence* from the use of alcohol upon physiological facts, for this could be done only by scientifically demonstrating that inevitable and invariable results follow the use of any alcoholic liquors even in limited quantities. To teach this was the original purpose of the promoters of the movement, and many of the present text-books tend, through over-emphasis, to give pupils such an impression. But although present-day physiology is unable to afford support for such absolute temperance principles, its well-established facts, as summarized above, show clearly that alcohol is not demonstrably useful to the normal healthy man. This and the undisputed danger of developing uncontrollable habits offers important support to appeals from considerations other than physiological. Here is safe material for "scientific temperance instruction," but to teach total abstinence from alcohol as an established law of personal hygiene is educationally wrong because it is so obviously false. Nothing of permanent value is to be gained by over-estimating the physiological facts regarding the effects of alcohol, for while the young children may be misled for a time, they are sure to discover the truth which will lower their respect for teachers and text-books, and especially for a school system which encourages the teaching of things which are very doubtful or untrue.

It is to be noted that in the various physiological papers written within the past five years the chief discussion of the effects of alcohol are centred around the question of its limited use. This is so because the injurious effects of large doses are so well known as to require no scientific demonstration. Any person with ordinary intelligence is well enough aware of the **Instruction** physical, mental, and moral ruin wrought by exces- **concerning** sive use of alcohol, without having studied in the **Chronic** **Alcoholism.** public schools the horrible descriptions of chronic alcoholism illustrated by awful pictures of drunkards' stomachs and hobnailed livers. Such teaching has no justification, for detailed knowledge of such extreme pathological conditions is likely to have little influence in comparison with that exerted by the well-known facts which every one gains from every-day life. If horrible facts in this line will have any influence, absolute temperance reform ought to be possible on the basis of common knowledge without any appeal to the science of pathology.

The summary above includes all the important well-estab- lished principles regarding the physiological effects of alcohol, **Few Facts** and little could be added except in details or **to be taught.** along the line of scientific hypotheses. Certainly the latter do not belong in elementary text-books, for no sane educator would approve teaching in elementary schools that which is subject to change with advancing knowledge; and especially should uncertain physiological theories be avoided in a subject like "temperance instruction," which finds its one justification in that it is made the basis for moral instruction. If the leading physiological facts about alcohol, as stated above, are to be presented to young pupils, they would, of course, **Less Space in** require some expansion into simple elementary **Text-books.** form, but at most half a dozen pages would suffice to state all the important general truths. In the excellent little text-book, *Physiology for Beginners*, by Foster and Shore, two pages (instead of fifty) include all important demonstrated physiological facts about alcohol, but the book is quite free from the unimportant details, the platitudes, the reiterations, the wild guesses, and the hypotheses which enter so prominently into the "temperance instruction" in most "approved" text- books. Comparing this book with the advanced treatises and with the "approved" elementary books, we are forced to conclude that the important demonstrated facts on the strictly physiological side of "temperance instruction" should be presented in a text-book in at most one-tenth of the space required by law and demanded by the leaders of the movement. Moreover, our limited knowledge of the physiological effects of alcohol does not justify repetition of the study of physiology for the sake of giving temperance instruction in from five to seven years of the school course. At most the strictly physiological facts deserve not more than six or eight pages to be studied in some one year, preferably the seventh or eighth grade, for such instruction must be meaningless to younger children.

We must now consider "temperance" teaching in another aspect, for in many text-books a larger part of the subject-matter relating to alcohol is not physiology, but more properly belongs to economics, ethics, and sociology. **Subject-Matter not all Physiological.**

With regard to the economical aspect of "scientific temperance," we believe with Professor Atwater that "statistics of the nation's liquor bill do not appeal very strongly to the ordinary man, still less does the average boy care for them." The only economical considerations which will make much impression upon a modern boy is the fact that chances of employment for responsible positions are vastly increased for total abstainers. But why should such teaching be coupled with physiology? **Economics in Temperance Instruction.**

With regard to the matter of ethical import, there is a growing belief among educators and men of science that the greatest value of "temperance instruction" lies along this line; but this is no more physiological than is the teaching of manners, honesty, and the like. **Ethical Teaching as such.**
Many teachers and men of science urge that "temperance instruction" take primarily the form of ethical appeal; but this should be made as such and not under the guise of physiology. Let all "temperance instruction," except a few pages in the text-book devoted to strictly physiological facts, be given, if it

is to be given in the schools, as part of the general instruction in morals ; and, we believe, a more lasting impression for good will be made upon the pupil than can be obtained from any attempt to warp the physiological facts into a material basis for moral instruction. In short, let the study of "human physiology" be freed from all non-physiological phases of "temperance instruction." There is no sufficient reason why this subject should continue to be the scapegoat, for literature and history might with much less juggling of subject-matter, be made to teach temperance as regards the use of alcohol.

In conclusion, we have seen in our examination of "temperance instruction" that the extremely unsatisfactory conditions, especially those arising from the absurd and intolerable laws, not only interfere seriously with the teaching of "physiology" in our public schools, but also degrade it in the estimation of many prominent educators and scientific men. This should not be so. The study of the human body is a great and important subject which deserves to be freed from the influence of propagandism, and the teaching developed to the efficiency becoming a study which is an "all-essential part of a rational education." To this end all educators and men of science Need of should make a united effort for decided changes in United Effort. the present conditions which prohibit advances in the teaching of "physiology" in the public schools. At present teachers in many States are so hampered by the absurd laws that little improvement is possible. In some States the laws are not stringent or else are not enforced, and hence the teachers are more or less free to choose regarding the subject-matter. But Changes great and decided improvement in the teaching of Necessary. physiology throughout the United States can be secured only by beginning with the following changes : —

1. Repeal of all existing laws and the defeat of all proposed ones which place any limitations upon the teaching of "physiology."

2. Selection of text-books which give only concise state-

ments of the essential *physiological* facts relating to alcohol, and these confined to *one chapter* to be studied in one of the last two years of the elementary-school course.

3. The teaching of non-physiological facts of ethics and economics which relate to temperance as such and not as part of "physiology."

We agree with President Jordan that the only adequate remedy for present conditions "lies in allowing that science shall be free to teach its own lessons, and that the public schools shall not be used by advocates of any kind of social or political reform, no matter how meritorious the cause may be in itself." **Freedom in Science Teaching.**

"The whole 'scientific temperance' movement is opposed to the movement for good schools through the choice of good teachers. It has been judged by its motives, which are good. It will come to be judged by its results, and these are bad." [1]

---

[1] *Popular Science Monthly*, Vol. XLVIII., p. 354. January, 1896.

Index

Lightning Source UK Ltd.
Milton Keynes UK
UKHW021347051118
331796UK00014B/1074/P

9 781330 692172